"The US Review of Books"
By Donna Ford

"What I do know is...a Shaman would state that witnessing and being aware of synchronicities is a sign you are on the right path."

The author begins with the retelling of a late-nineties Target commercial. He claims that this spiritually aware advertisement is full of symbolism to encode a warning regarding mankind's future. **Were the writers and the singer, Petula Clark, aware of what they created?** He promises clues hidden in plain sight, such as those in numerology, will reveal ancient truths.

Like an *Ancient Aliens* **TV theorist, Beringer weaves in pre-civilization artifacts...Biblical events... revelations,** such as the wedding at Cana likely being that of Mary Magdalene to Jesus... **Gnostic theories mix with a dash of Freemasonry, Kabbalah, and Illuminati mentions.**

Beringer knows his target audience. They are other conspiracy buffs, like some readers of the Dan Brown books. Although this book lacks the dramatic pacing of a **Dan Brown mystery, it is likewise filled with religious and symbolic explanations.** Personal experiences shared in this **memoir/exposé answer the question of who benefits** from our civilization's current delusion. **Does the author bombard his readers with so much hidden information** in order to separate those who are "near the top of the collective pyramid' from those casually curious? **If Beringer wants to sound an alarm, this book is a strong contender.** Four appendices expound basic truths that underpin his insights and wisdom.

Scott's Synopsis

The sixties saw massive shifts in consciousness as a higher authority was setting the stage for "The Coming." Camelot was meant to fall, with the 5th Dimension singing background, as Petula sings curious lyrics to a "distant love" while Target, in preparation, changed its logo of 6 elements to that of 3. The equation promptly balanced itself out as its polar opposite was forming in the hills of OZark, and egos shopped as if nothing was approaching. The "Inconvenient Truth" of climate change is however, an allegory of Earth's rising frequency as we align at the galactic plane on our Equinox, bringing our 3-D winter to an end. The smoke in the shape of a galaxy on its cover speak to the aware, confirming Global Warming to be an Alagôrē, along with Al's assertion that he took the initiative in creating the Internet (the dark side of Internal Unity), as it too was an allegory for the developing Aquarian Awareness. "The weather, very peculiar, Don't you think?" Like a Bronze Phoenix, the organic 5D NWO will "Spring" from the wintry rubble of rust, that was the dark polarities artificial nwo. This mystical setting is for my fellow Prodigals, "to whom it is given," who are "Coming to their senses", realizing their true identities amid the emptiness of the 3D Las Vegash folly within the 7-11 School of Duality.

As the new millennium began, the ultimate paradox was played out. Understated symbolism with an ironic twist, as a president tells his countrymen to shop after 9-11 with wars planned, while Target, in contradiction, airs a television commercial that has nothing to do with shopping, but everything to do with our spiritual advancement beyond this 3D setting. A divine message, seen by billions and "not seen". If You have not retreated, then perhaps it is Your time to take this information and prepare yourself. It is the most Sirius, choice you will ever make to finally understand why, there will be a cleansing viral "Reckoning", and a cosmological "Final Judgement", which Springs from a very precise program that develops new Stars and their Darker polar partners, within the expanding Cosmos. Learn the real meaning of 9-11 and 7-11, and why "The Fall" of Man, the Angels, and Lucifer was preordained and had to occur for this "Polar" expansion. When you Know Yourself, you will understand your own "Arc" frequency and how to adjust it, making you the Master of your game! This was the "Ark" Noah was "building" to adjust and align His, with the "higher frequency" of the next Age, discovering the Narrow Gate! Time has come to pay attention to the "invisible" Man behind the curtain and the "visible" Lucifer. Know the truth of the "Light-Bearer" and the "Tree of Life", that was hidden from the children until the Prodigals were ready for adult understanding of the very real Path to The Fountain of Youth. Discover the esoteric meaning of the George Floyd incident and you'll know "You've always had the power", and no evil can steal your "sole, Dorothy". The Signs of the Times point to the multitude of clue filled counterfeit current "events" displaying the erosion of the old paradigm. Oh thank heaven for 7-11, as the old play concludes, to then illuminate your new role as the Star of the Divine remake of, "A Star is Born". ~Scott Beringer

Target Aquarius

Scott Beringer

Library of Congress Control Number: 2014908025
ISBN: Hardcover   978-1-6485-8512-8
        Softcover   978-1-6485-8514-2
        eBook   978-1-6485-8513-5

To order additional copies of this book, contact:
Matchstick Literary
1-888-306-8885
www.matchliterary.com

Contents

Introduction

If you want to hide something, "hide" it in plain sight.

You see them every day. Images that have entirely different meanings than what you have been led to believe; if you even think they mean anything at all. The **two** primary characteristics of the atomic universe are hidden and yet they're everywhere you look. Virtually everything you experience results from frequency and duality, and they dictate how you live your life. In the never-ending clues of duality, for instance, one retail giant points to God, while the *other* – in keeping with most of the world – point to man.

These *apparent positive and negative* anomalies and a prominent Target commercial that aired at the beginning of the new millennium, confirm my view that life is an Oz-like chess game. We all play the game whether we realize it or not. And when the latter is the case (because most of us don't realize), then we are played. Our creator has filled the board with virtually endless clues and films with monumental messages, that only those becoming **Self**-aware begin to see, and you will not believe how *blue sky* obvious most of them are. They point back to the creator and tell us who we really are, what this place is and why we are here. *"The whole world is in chess. Any move can be the death of you. Do anything except remain where you started, and you can't be sure of your end."* ~Kingdom of Heaven

While your body is an amazing machine, it is still a temporary vehicle designed to convince the young and innocent of its tangibility, while the *Dark* program bombards you with, messages enticing you to *buy* into its seductive reality with never-ending *distractions* to keep you always looking *out*. A president telling you to "go shop" is an example of this, along with an endless supply of anxiety-riddled news, much of it completely fabricated, from a mainstream media, owned and controlled by a select few who censor and dictate, down to the soundbites, what is fed to the masses. It caters to a puerile audience conditioned to consume folly masquerading as "news". The never-ending tabloid news, completely devoid of substantive content, to keep you in a never-ending state of lowest common denominator fear and pointless distraction.

They are also benevolent enough to provide us with free pornography from dozens of providers, along with cooking shows, shopping, gambling and video-gaming sites on television and the Internet designed to keep your desires always within sight, and just an oh-so-tempting click away to satisfy any impulse and urge towards the endless pursuit of 5 sense sensations. When you finish this book, you will know why the Internet, television, and advertising are loaded with images of sex, violence, food, fashion, and every imaginable material desire, with endless predictable wars, pandemics and *drama*, all directed at us for a very precise reason, and certainly not one you could even guess, at this point.

The body's self-aware property, the ego, with its insatiable desires, does not want the game to stop as it continually attempts to fulfill, satisfy, and validate itself with sensations and dualistic conflicts, as we are given the choice away from our ultimate identity – God. The game is programmed to more than accommodate all the young sons and daughters with intoxicating indulgence, the path away, and the spiritually young give in and revel in the sensory stimulating events and perceived freedom and autonomy supplied by the game. But as they eventually find out, it always leaves you wanting, and it takes all that you have leaving you in a cell you can't see, and all things come and go in the game, most notably, the people.

The body has built-in warning systems (which the young tend to ignore) that are designed to thwart overindulgence. Most are obvious, but there is one that almost no one is aware of. It's beyond five-sense perception and subtly alerts you that indulging is not in your best interest. Our bodies are machines that are powered by electricity, and indulging exacts a power drain, lowering your frequency, which is felt only by the aware, and fewer still, understand *why*. I will tell you how this drain on your frequency correlates to "the coming" and what it means to you personally and to all of us collectively.

Make no mistake, the evil we experience in this life is truly a necessary evil, and I am *really* speaking to the prodigals now. Just as Glinda allowed the evil to envelop Dorothy, the evil that leads the *children* astray speaks directly to the hearts of the *prodigals* who *discover* **it** within themselves, and the ones who are ready to go *home* know immediately where the velvet-gloved evil originates having acquiesced to what they now know was a Divine lesson. Without evil, **there is no canvas to paint your story**, and in the movie Bedazzled, *the devil may just be your best friend.* We are all conduits of the divine plan, as there is literally nothing, that is not divine. It is only a matter of time until you find your Glinda, who will lovingly guide and say or withhold just the right comment to make you look in the right direction. To allow *you* to discover it so that you can appreciate it and take ownership of it, as nothing worthwhile gets handed to you on a silver platter!

The network of the Illuminati knowingly and unknowingly does the work of God in this great classroom. *That which is meant to lead the unaware astray to more of the duality game can provide the aware with powerful insights to expose the programmed weaknesses within that need to be dealt with.* To this point in my life, the most powerful moment was the moment one of those messages spoke directly to me, meaning it was there for my benefit to see it. This was even more powerful than the matter fluctuating around me (just as in The Matrix) at the moment I realized sexual and satanic messages are encoded in all Disney animated films. What I had initially thought to be veiled evil trying to influence me to jump into decadent behavior, was an even more profound message speaking directly to **my** issue that I struggled with. All of a sudden, *the entire good and evil* clear *dichotomy became blurred.* My world is now *white sun,* crystal clear. I see why I was led to act, and how Hollywood points us in directions, both to and away from the Light.

The Disney-created Lion King spoke to me as the leaves and grass that spelled *sex* in the air as he fell to the ground spoke to the issue he had to control, as it was for me, before he could go home. This rocked me when I realized this was not an ordinary satanic message as I had originally thought when I first saw it but a loving clue to my mission here in the grander scheme of spiritual development. The Disney-owned Marvel movie Thor, spoke to me. Right after the government seizes the equipment and data of the scientists, look at their address as they very deliberately show the 1001 of the building they used in New Mexico, as I had lived in New Mexico and my address in Boulder City, Nevada, was **1001 New Mexico Street.** My *awakening* occurred at this address, and I have been ripped from ego since.

The building in Thor, with *Smith* on top of it, my mother's maiden name, and sits at the top of a T intersection just as my house did in Boulder City, and when you looked out of my living room window, it looked down **F** Street to the Masonic Temple. Interestingly, the condo in PC, where I realized all of this, that fitted my needs perfectly and the only one available, was unit 11F and the sign next to my door seen at the street is A-F 11, which is 7-11. There is much more and all will be explained in detail and in the Disney-created town of Puente Antiguo, the first thing they show you after the town sign is a 7-Eleven, as the chapter of the same name will mystically reveal.

Look at the hand sign of those in power, like my hands on the cover of the book in the box that looks like 11 because it is! I will once and for all, in unambiguous language, dispel all myth and legend surrounding the ancient "Satanic" Devil horns hand-sign and it's hotly debated, thumb extended, "I love you" variation near the end because that's when you'll be ready for it. No more accepting the misleads or "guessing" what they mean! Seven and nine with eleven are everywhere in movies and life, and it's time to know. Our Sun is no longer orange-yellow because it was never what they told us it was, and this is NASA's grandest lie. *I am a fallen prodigal, looking to go home*, and if you are compelled to read on, you may be too and will find clues about your life encoded in films, commercials, songs, among many others, as our parents speak to us through them.

The more awake you become, the more clues appear, and synchronicity sets appointments with you to administer just the right therapy. Clue after clue, dot after dot connecting lines and you begin to see a picture and realize, very suddenly, you are the amnesia-stricken Jason Bourne. You're the beast trapped in the body in Beauty and the Beast and the lost Lion King who has lived a dreamlike Matrix reality with temporary surrogates, programmed with weaknesses to conquer before you can assume your rightful place. **She** cries over the Beast and Thor, as they die to *this*. Thor and the Beast had to learn humility, love, **unity** and empathy, and so do we. And if not you, I sure as hell had to. **You** are always the star in your own perfectly choreographed play as you journey step-by-step to achieve that which symbolically exceeds the perfect set of 10.

You and I are 7 on our journey of 11, oh, thank heaven, striving *to go beyond the dualistic 11*, that internal fight within, the rebellion of the Ego. Those towers (9+1+1=11) had to crumble at the hands of 11, that represents someone who comes out victorious of the temptations, disciplined and battle tested, with the acquired knowledge that transcends the bait of polar dualism. I write this on my avatar's birthday as I just turned 56 (5+6=11) on the twenty-first in this twenty-first century (2+1=3), 9-21-1957=7, as I now finish this in 2014=7.

The coming years will be incredible even as the witch sends the flying monkeys (as she must) for where would we be without her? Why, we would still be in ego, in the illusion of Camelot, but Camelot must always fall and could not be saved by his brother or son. The dark never stops, and the black-robed warlock will make sure ego is crushed in the prodigals. If you are a prodigal, you have your Glinda, and we have our collective witch and our personal witch, and I certainly know mine. I am Simba, and the witch had me, as the leaves and grass that spelled the word had me chained, but that was then, and this is *Now*.

Hollywood is sending the prodigals another clue that The Big Bang Theory is an Iron Age lie not to be taken seriously. CBS, with their eye of God logo, has named one of their comedy sitcoms The Big Bang Theory. They are telling you the Vatican's theory is laughable! Yes, that is its origin, but then again, all stem from the one! It was in 1927 that a Belgian Catholic priest, Georges Lemaitre, proposed what he called, "The Hypothesis of the Primeval Atom," which later became known as The Big Bang Theory. You will want to read Appendix One and Two before you continue.

Boeing is front and center and numerically equals 7, and of course, their planes are all 7 series, as they *fly*. Their legendary flagship, the 707 that equals 14, which equals 5, set the standard. The 707's first flight was in '57, wouldn't you know, and the full date of 12/20/1957 equals 9, the vibration that proves intelligent design. It is no coincidence that the towers look like an 11 and their architects used a fully loaded 707 as the standard for the amount of kinetic energy the towers could with-stand (and remain standing) which was more energy than the BOEING jets that hit them – if they were ever in fact, hit. And of course the smok-ing gun, the building *never hit by a plane* yet mysteriously and perfectly collapses into its own foundation is number 7 in NY 57. Then there is the 727, which equals 16, which equals 7 and the first time I flew in one, I was five, going from Baltimore to Houston to a family reunion with my Smith grandparents. The 747, their mainstay for so many years, is nine, and now the 777, which is 21, 3, and me, as with LV-7-232. In the movie "Unstoppable", they end up stopping the train, but what "they" are tell-ing you, is that the coming of 777, Helel, is unstoppable! I completely expose the *real Helel* by the end!

Like two golden birds perched on the selfsame tree,
Intimate friends, the ego and the Self
Dwell in the same body. The former eats
The sweet and sour fruits of the tree of life
While the other looks on in detachment.
As long as we think we are the ego,
We feel detached and fall into sorrow.

But realize that you are the Self, the Lord
Of life, and you will be freed from sorrow.
When you realize that you are the Self,
Supreme source of light, supreme source of love,
You transcend the duality of life
And enter into the unitive state.
The Lord of Love shines in the hearts of all.
Seeing him in all creatures, the wise
Forget themselves in the service of all.
The Lord is their joy, the Lord is their rest;
Such as they are the lovers of the Lord.

~ Mundaka Upanishad

The evil younger brother is a frequent Disney theme in movies like The Lion King, Thor, and Prince of Persia – who knows and is quite agitated with the fact that he will never be the king. The younger brothers symbolize the adversarial ego, as does Agent Smith in The Matrix. Later in the book, I will show you that these are examples of a developmental "Smith" equation for Prodigals. Ego, by itself, is like the Tinman. It has no heart, the real you, and that is the meaning of the quote "It will never be you. You will never be king. You don't have the heart. You will die in the shadow of a great man" from Disney's Prince of Persia. The great man is the Self who is King, and by the end, you will understand the identity of 'He who is King', and those who masquerade, who must "step aside", to serve the *True, **Master of the House!***

*You belong to your father, the devil [Satan/ego], and you want to carry out your father's desires. He was a murderer from the beginning, not holding to the truth, for there is no truth in him. When he lies, he speaks his **native language**, for he is a liar and the father of lies.*

-John 8:44

You're a talented liar, brother. Always have been.

-Thor 2011

How many men did Danny Ocean need? My *first* credited speaking part in a feature film is in Ocean's 11. When we start college, all the introductory classes are 101 until we become indoctrinated – wearing the black square on our head that represents, **so** much more than you think. All American public schools provide an Apple for the children. Here is the real meaning of their logo. It symbolizes a dark parallel forbidden fruit, and to eat of it, technology, you will be as God, as AI (artificial intelligence) is looking you in the eye! I will show you the complete identity of the forbidden fruit, both trees, and the Garden He planted in "the east", along with the hidden identities of the 4 Cardinal directions. And **so** much more. Don't skip to them though, because it builds and fills dots and connects lines to allow you to "see" the picture that 7 through 14 paints, so that in the later chapters showing you, the Solar layout and true identity of America, the identity of the Na'vi and Pandora in Avatar (2009=11), the identity of gravity and time, and why our Sun is now white, will be more easily understood and will take you **where *no other* will**. It's **time** to know *who* you are, and what it **IS**, that you perceive as *out-there*.

We haven't even scratched the surface, so please be seated during chapter 1, as you may faint when you fully understand and actually hear (but don't hear it until I explain it) Target's "Sign of the Times" television commercial. **This is the red pill**, and you can wash it *down* with your **7 UP!**

When the superior man hears of the Way, he investigates it with diligence to it's length.
When the mediocre man hears of the Way, he picks it up, looks at it and then puts it down.
When the lesser man hears of the Way, he laughs and ridicules it greatly.
For if he did not laugh, it would not be the Way.

Lao-Tzu

1. A Sign of the Times

I know it sounds dubious and improbable, but read what I am about to show you with an open mind because Target, appears to be concerned with your spiritual awareness. The hidden in-plain-view clues are all around us, and the more aware you are, the more you will see. One of the world's largest retail giants has a logo, theme, and thirty-second television commercial that defy any explanation in terms of ordinary marketing strategies. Here is what I can only describe as a divine message, delivered to us at the beginning of the new millennium of the 21st century, and it has nothing to do with shopping. Let's start with what is seen by the unaware as a target, but their logo is not a target, it is a circumpunct. It's comprised of three elements (the Trinity) and is one of the oldest symbols representing the eye of God, our place or position within God, and it is the symbol of the Sun. It's red and white (redwhite=11)* and the white represents the white-light purity of God, and red represents base flesh-and-blood creation. While it may look similar to a target, why not just choose a target, which prior to 1968, they did! Why the change? No one can be...told, you have to see it for yourself. Time to take off the glasses.

This target is similar to Target's Logo from 1962 to 1968

I will now lay out the sequence of frames and images from the Target television commercial, with Petula Clark singing two verses of her 60's hit "A Sign of the Times" (11). Numerically, Petula adds up to 21, which equals 3, and even when you include her last name, they add up to 39, which adds to 12, which equals 3.

Look at the title and keep in mind the monumental times we find ourselves in as the precession of the equinoxes closes out the age of Pisces within the greater Iron Age and ushers in the dawning of the Age of Aquarius within the greater Bronze Age. Earth is changing from 3-D Iron Age and moving to 5-D Bronze Age. Another in-plain-view clue, "The Age of Aquarius," sung by the 5th Dimension, released in 1969=25=7. There's that 5 and 7 again! Now go online and pull up, the Target "Sign of the Times" television commercial on Youtube and follow along with me, frame by frame, but make sure you turn off the sound as we break it down and I explain the video. When you really understand what you are seeing, watch it again with the audio and expect some goosebumps, as 3 speaks to you!

It starts with a lava lamp in a completely white room in an Astral Realm, which is not *"here"*. The all white representing the all-encompassing light of God, where there is no separation. The only color in the room is the red lava (lv 34=7 and aa 11, showing 7-11 which equal 9) at the bottom of the lamp. Then it begins to swell at the top of the red substance that rests at the bottom, and you see the Target circumpunct expelled or born like an egg coming out of the female ovum. This has two symbolic meanings, as above, so below, our God is born from its God **and** *our physical birth*. As this is occurring, a man dressed in all white, showing you that this is not a physical man but an Astral **Self**-aspect of God, is walking by the opening to the room. The activity within the lamp grabs his attention, and he is fixated on it and then walks to the lamp with a large open-mouthed smile as he enters the room. He is the Divine Masculine of Soul.

Look to the left of the opening, you see five lines above the Target name and logo, which is the number of the divine message, and while you can't make out what is producing those five lines, you will at the end of the commercial, and it is very relevant. He is wearing large dark-colored glasses altering his vision, meaning he is now prepared to go to school and be incarnated on earth. The glasses symbolizes he will be viewing life through his projected *separate* body and its egoistic frame of reference. He knows this is what he needs to do to develop and is very happy.

He views his birth, and the *reflection is not his* astral-smiling reflection but that of his physical reflection in this life; unaware, looking through ego at an uncertain world and, because of it, not smiling. We are a holographic projection of the real us, the spirit, and this scene tells you this. The fact that the reflection is not his, at that moment, should tell you, if you are skeptical, that this commercial is more than it appears to be, and they are trying to tell you something hidden from most! Next to his projected image is a cube, a symbol of our dark lord of the rings, Saturn and our current class of 6. I will be explaining this in far more detail.

The next scene is the birth and you see a woman spring from the third circumpunct, as we are the third and final aspect of the Trinity, the Holy Spirit. They make sure you know it is the third by putting 4 up there because we read from left to right. Just displaying 3 would not ensure you know it is the third as you *could* think it was the first. The 4 also represent the 4 Cardinal directions of North, South, West, and East (they mean far more than just directions), and the woman springing from the 3rd one is West. This won't make much sense now, but by the end of the book, you will understand why it is a woman that pops out of that half ball (egg) representing the body of Astral Soul who just viewed His birth.

In the next scene, you have a woman representing a human from God, as she is clothed in the proper circumpunct symbols. She is using man's technology with an inverse color scheme to clean that which is of God, implying *we* can make it better. The floor, or earth, is of God, and the rear wall is man made with inverse color schemes showing it is not of God but man-made. The **left** wall displays the inverse circumpunct, while the **right** wall has the normal God circumpunct color scheme. The inverse circumpunct on the left wall represents ego. Look at the frame around it, which adds a fourth element. Four represents this earth's masculine Iron Age reality. The left side or *"masculine"* side of the brain sees in the "separation" and 4 is its number. That which is of God on the right wall represents the spiritual or feminine holistic *right* brain function.

In the next scene, you see a background of God and, in contrast, a silhouette of a female human ego torso that turns into a woman just for a split second and then turns into two of the same woman. This means we are seeing in duality or left brain, and it signifies that we have a projected body (a projection of the spirit). It then shifts to a different woman with the clothing of God on a different woman who has her back to us (out of sight) but then turns to us with a knowing grin. This means right brain thought has not been in use and God has been ignored or unknown. She turns around to us, signifying that this is changing, a *Sign* of the changing times! Then the man in the glasses is ecstatic because he now gets it and knows his true identity, which is why he is dressed in God symbols against the God-symbol wall.

In the next image, this woman symbolizes our Divine Feminine, who we have been separated from during the Iron Age. She was also the one in the last frame showing us that She will again be known, as our awareness rises. Our union with Her and our move to our Right Brain perceiving in Unity, means our development will be greatly accelerated and this is symbolized by Her driving of the God golf ball (her children) to new heights, and she shows her bliss. The man – now SELF-aware – with eyes to see, no longer identifies with ego (him now taking off the glasses), with its illusory, distorted view, and he is turning to point to the heavens. This means he is now seeing beyond just five-sense reality. He now knows the totality of who he is.

The next scene begins with a lady showing us a gelatin mold of the circumpunct at an angle so that it more closely resembles an eye. The screen then goes to solid white, meaning it is referring you back to the all-white Astral Realm. As she walks away, she keeps looking back at us with the knowing laugh or huge smile, and her eyes are telling you she knows something, that you don't. She, Like the Astral Soul male, is not of this world. She Is his Spirit in red and white with no symbols. Her bringing the *Eye of God* means she is there, but she cannot be seen, *according to our 5 senses.*

The God circumpunct also being the table and the seats mean this *meeting* is internal and there is absolutely nothing that is not of God. The blonde woman represents Spirit, He represents Soul, and the **dark**-haired woman represents their body. He now knows who and what He is and that He creates. He will now direct his thoughts and choices in life to the Light, increasing His/Their frequency. Along with representing his body, she also represents his AI mind. She is receiving his new awareness like new software (there are only a few ego symbols), acknowledging that HE is in control of their Sacred Marriage, and she will take them **Up** as a result. Her act of looking up tells us that her frequency is increasing and she will take him up, to find the "Narrow Gate" out of the Iron Age. It then goes to her Spirit on opposite sides of the table, and they mirror each other, as they walk around the table, because Spirit inhabits the body. The body is the atomic manifestation of the Spirit. **All** of this will be crystal clear by the end of the book. A person looking at the table would only see one person sitting there.

The now Self-aware man *knows* his Spirit is there, even though she can't be seen symbolized by him reaching out to her and then reaches out to his body, with the other arm. The child of God, with the 11 symbols on his pant leg, on the Trinity tricycle who was being developed by them is now ready to take the next step as the *traffic lights* are now allowing him to proceed, as the three lights, diagonal up and to the Right, represent the two coming together to form The One. A path opened, that was not previously there. This means the Prodigal Son, is no longer following, the away from God, Satanic dark of pure ego identification and is now *found* on the path of Christ consciousness, going toward the light of God. He now sees in Unity! As the last 3 huge scenes unfold, keep this in mind.

Be aware that you have spiritual business to attend to, and the development of your soul is paramount. This IS school, and addressing your "issues" that we are all faced with, must be addressed if you want to move on. Don Juan says as much with this advice, "To have such clarity you must lead a disciplined life." Yes, you cannot be a slave to your body's passions. A balance must be struck. Siddhartha heard the teacher say "if you wind the string too tight it will break and if you have the string too loose, there will be no music." On hearing these words, Siddhartha came to the realization of the middle way of life—it must be neither too strict nor undisciplined. You must take control and not allow the passions or desires of the ego/body to dictate to your actions. Our astral Soul is always guiding us to a higher state of being, because we are, growing Up.

The man at the ironing board is not the man; it is his astral **Self,** and there are 12 (3) circumpuncts behind him. Notice he is dressed only in white, and notice what he is working on—his ego/body, symbolized by the shirt. The shirt represents the man inside the program of the Iron Age represented by the shirt being on the **ironing** board. As stated above, our astral soul is the real us going to school, so to speak, inside the computer-programmed school of 11 that we call life. Our Astral Selves are always guiding us to achieve our spiritual goals, as symbolized by him ironing the shirt. And *now* that his physical projection is aware of him, he can now communicate with him much more effectively, as symbolized by the man's astral Self on the **red** phone.

He lifts the iron, representing the Iron Age, and the God symbols on the perimeter (1) of the iron **point** to the way out, to the Bronze Age. This is fully symbolized by the fact that his projected physical body and mind is now fully SELF-aware as they now openly knowingly communicate. And *the fact that the shirt is perfectly pressed means the physical man has worked out or conquered all his issues and pro-*

grammed weaknesses. He is mature, humble, at peace and no longer bites at the first temptation, **and** he is now aware of his true Astral Self. His **temple** (Her, and more on that at the end) is no longer defiled and he has now "let go" of his egoistic plans, and raised his frequency completing His spiritual agenda here. He is now ready to move to the Bronze Age and there will be far more on the internal and external "locations" of this next level or class.

Remember the five lines to the left of the opening above the Target name at the beginning of the commercial? We couldn't quite make out what it was, but you can see it better now. It is a heating radiator (5) that is still at the left of the opening, but the room is now on the other side with red in it, (it is radiating or transmitting this false reality) symbolizing this life is a mirror reflection, but they are now living within True Reality. The SELF-aware couple symbolizes the union of the Divine Masculine with the Feminine Feminine coming together again. She, with the inverted physical body symbols, symbolizing Spirit, and He, with the God symbols, symbolizing Soul. They are now in union working together toward the light, and her discarding the pillow means she is no longer asleep. The Prince (Soul), has kissed his, **Sleeping Beauty.** He has fully embraced his Dark and regained his Divine Feminine.

When playing chess, *they both* move their pieces to a white square, and by them playing, they are telling you that they have taken control and now knowingly make *their* own moves, having now transcended lower dualism. She then moves her piece to his white square, taking his, (isn't this always the case guys, haha) as he now sees in Unity and knows who "He" is really married to, as they are the One Flesh. They are all now **One** with the symbol on the bottom of the piece. By the end, you'll understand why the woman moves the last piece and emerges from the "Trinity". The game of chess is an ancient game and a symbol of this life of duality, with its eternal struggle of good versus evil, the material versus spirit, and the decisions we make every day that takes us to (as symbolized by the white squares) or away from (the black squares) the loving light of God.

The chess pieces are the various body-vessel cosmic archetypes as they move in life, taking loving or fearful steps in relation to their perceived separate opponent's moves. The chessboard symbolizes the esoteric life, and that is why the floors of many old cathedrals (thanks to the Masons), like Notre Dame, look like a chessboard. We all play chess whether you realize it or not. The unaware are played, while the aware make their own moves and that is why they are showing them make their own moves! *"A king may move a man, a father may claim a son, but that man can also move himself, and only then does that man truly begin his own game."* ~ *"Kingdom of Heaven"*

Then the chessboard disappears, just as this dream, we live in will, and there is just the God symbol against an all-white background, meaning everything is of the one mind. The Eye of God symbol morphs into the same symbol painted on the face of a *white* dog (which is God spelled backward) that smiles — showing God is pleased. Look how the circumpunct is positioned on its face so that the eye is perfectly in the center of the dot that represents the all-seeing eye of God within us. It ends with the dog walking away, moving up and to the right side of the screen, getting smaller (meaning away from this frequency), inside a white dot surrounded by red. It means God consciousness (within all creation and specifically here on earth) moving to the right brain. The dog they use is a bull terrier, which numerically equals 59 = 14 = 5, the messenger of divine information.

And through it all, Petula is singing the two verses: *"It's a sign of the times, when your love for ME is growing so much stronger. It's a sign of the times, and I know that I won't have to wait much longer."* The Father of his prodigal children is happy with his children's progress. So many of us are becoming aware and are now seeking out our parent, and realizing who we REALLY are! Notice also that all three major racial groups are used in this, further indicating this message is for all humanity, as we are all the expression of the one. It is amazing they fit all this into a thirty-second commercial, and I am sure there are messages I missed.

Let me expand on the woman driving the golf ball, but by the end of the book, this will be fully understood. You see, the evolution of the soul goes slowly, while the token, with its self-aware ego, only identifies with itself and the game of life as the only reality. Once it recognizes the game for what it is and knows it houses an aspect of God, then the evolution accelerates dramatically. "Do you not know that you are a temple of God and that the Spirit of God dwells in you?" (1 Corinthians 3:16). Now that she is aware of her true identity, the body now works with the soul, and they not only cease to be at odds with one another, the body now actively helps the soul achieve its goals. I will reinforce this when I talk about other huge clues in The Matrix and Terminator movies (among others) and how something that begins as your adversary, with enlightenment, becomes your ally.

I have always liked Petula Clark, and this song was my favorite, but like most, I never *really* understood it! Even when I began putting the pieces of the above puzzle together, and I knew the title referred to the shifting of our consciousness because of the arrival of the new age, I had already seen the Target "Sign of the Times" thirty-second television commercial many times but never completely listened to the song's lyrics. It wasn't until I was going to send it to someone that I really listened to it, being now stunned at the words (and all of a sudden understanding the symbolism of the commercial too). This is not a woman speaking to her boyfriend in any way, shape, or form! The entire song has telling lines, along with "Don't Sleep in the Subway," with its message saying that no matter what ego tells you, you are what you are; fight though you may, there IS nowhere else to go. We are what we are, so stop pretending you have somewhere else to go.

It alludes to the fact that this is just a big classroom, as you worry about corrupt governments and comets. We are Chicken Little, scurrying about, doing, what we do, very self-important within the matrix. Stop sleeping in the subway, love, and stop standing in the rain. The night will be long, so just forget your childish pride. All is right when you are beside me again. The real lyrics are so much better than that, and I suggest you look them all up online as I was not given permission to show them to you here from the company that owns the rights to the songs. Maybe someone's lucky star, at last, decided to shine. Indeed! I get the feeling Mr. Hatch would have allowed me, but it matters not, as the lyrics and this commercial speak for themselves! Only in the context of one's relationship with God does any of this make ANY sense!

I was asked, "Why would Target do this?" First off, this is hardly isolated to only Target, as there are countless movies, television shows, commercials, corporate logos, natural landmasses, events separated by centuries and yet linked, etc., that point to massive changes and clues that this *"life" is not what you think it is.* All have similar themes that communicate this new level of awareness that is clearly above and beyond the scope of face value advertising, marketing, entertainment or random "natural occurrences". This commercial though stunned me with the level and scope of its message and it was certainly not "accidental". This isn't just deciding to go with a different logo because you think it looks cleaner or better, not knowing it to be an ancient symbol of God, unconsciously being guided by a higher power. This is not the case with this commercial. Whoever created this commercial knew exactly what they were doing, and it has nothing to do with shopping at Target, and everything to do with your spiritual identity and development.

Now, when I first wrote this book, I must say that I really didn't have the "Why would Target do this?", completely figured out. If you ask the question, you really don't know what this place is or who you are and an in-depth explanation would simply not be understood. Just read on and by the end of the book, you will, because if you don't have the "eyes to see and ears to hear", you simply won't make it to the end of the book!

Now that we are on the doorsteps of a new age, the stakes are now higher, and the in-plain-view clues and messages are hitting new heights. Revelations 12:12, "Therefore, rejoice, O heavens and you who dwell in them! But woe to you, O earth and sea, for *the devil* has come down to you in great wrath because he knows that his time is short!" With the light of spring on the horizon, the *devil* is pulling out all the stops, and I can't wait to show you who *he, she, they, it* **is,** and I will reveal it when you least expect it, so be attentive. If you are not far enough along the path, then what you see, it will not be seen.

We are lovingly monitored by people who are further along the path than you or me, who know we are one and what we are here for. My hat is off to *someone* at Target for creating this or at least approving it and to Tony Hatch and Jackie Trent, as they had to have known what they were writing. It is not just them though, as those who love us are all around us, attempting to show us this game and what we need to do so that you can know yourself—but it is all up to YOU. The light and the dark will both show you their way, and you only have two choices. It is all YOU.

This is obviously not a retail sales commercial, and "someone" spent a great deal of money to produce a clue pointing to our spiritual agenda here, and in fact tell us that **all of this**, is a spiritual exercise, a class level in a school of spirit. Our Christ-conscious ascended parents are speaking to us through this retail giant's commercial and logo, while the polar Satanic programs speak to us through many others. Let's take a closer look at this program we call life and what is expected of us while we attend the 7-11 School of Duality. Oh thank heaven for 7-11! I love saying that, as you, no doubt have noticed. Alright, who took my Slurpee?

*See appendix 3 for Bill Donahue's "Journey to the Promised Land" for a special take on our internal journey to that which so many believe is an external journey to a physical place.

2. The All That IS

We are *fortunate* to be at our position along the path to live in a period of amazingly easy, at-your-fingertips access to information. The creator wants us to thrive and succeed, but graduation out of this Iron Age loop is very difficult. The program *never* stops tempting you, displaying evil, spreading fear, and throwing roadblocks at you, for very specific developmental reasons. If you are *trapped* in dualism, it is mind-bogglingly real and seemingly impossible to overcome. Those firmly entrenched will not escape as they allow the good versus evil conflicts with associated judgments, passions, weaknesses, and challenges programmed within to set themselves at the rim of the Grand Canyon at a sheer drop, with a raging Colorado River bisecting it. You simply will not reach the other side and will *continue* here, in the karmic chess game, for as long as it takes you to see the game for what it is, to then make the *right* choices. It's not that the *other* choices are "wrong", but they (left choices, as you will learn) are simply those that keep you at this level of development.

When life finally *makes* you look in the *right* direction, away from the illusion, drama, and dualism of the game, you will see (now having the "Eyes to See") the path that takes you to the other rim and onto new horizons and heights that we cannot imagine. Knowing your world though is part in parcel to knowing yourself, and *is* a necessary first step to passing this class, and identifying the evil element at its core is necessary *before* you can step beyond it. Just as you must know the rules in order to intelligently bend or break them, you must first see the box you have been born into in order to escape its confines. Being born into the box was neither an accident nor some unfair twist of fate. There are many stages of awareness! More on this later, but if you believe we are free and our *rulers* are not puppets, then none of this will resonate with you, as you have not yet looked behind the facade, which is necessary for this level, and all you saw was a Target commercial, but love to you!

The "Light" Bearer?

We are at the doorstep of the Bronze Age. I am happy to tell you that the universe and God are perfect, and there is no eternal cancer in or out of God. The black pope's god could not be more misunderstood as the conduit to the dark is necessary even though most can't *see* it and is at the same time the creative force of God within all of us. The lines between "good and bad" become blurred as awareness rises. All information comes to us as light, and *evil* information is no exception, as we are here to experience the *full* spectrum.

"Lucifer, the *Light-bearer!* Strange and mysterious name to give to the Spirit of Darkness! Lucifer, the Son of the Morning! Is it *he* who bears the Light, and with its splendors intolerable, blinds feeble, sensual, or selfish souls? Doubt it not!" -*Albert Pike, Morals and Dogma of the Ancient and Accepted Scottish Rite of Freemasonry, p. 321, 19th Degree of Grand Pontiff*

Everyone is entirely free to reject and dissent from whatsoever herein may seem to him to be untrue or unsound. -Albert Pike, from the preface of Morals and Dogma

From one of the, if not the most, *informative* works of literature, explaining, if you can decipher it, the philosophy of Freemasonry first published in 1872, was not meant to be understood by the multitude. I have come to discover that nothing is as it seems, and there are three basic levels of awareness on this journey, and of course, the third level is the most esoteric. Lucifer, the light bearer AND the *spirit* of darkness, is not what has been disseminated to the masses. If you are unworthy of the genie as determined by your choices in life, then it will remain trapped within the lamp, and as he points out, then blinded you shall be, and remain confined by the serpent that has the power to hold or set you free.

What the Ego desires is almost always in conflict with what the spirit needs. In time you will see that the incredible creative force of the serpent within, will keep you in darkness and on the karmic wheel, as long as you remain "feeble, sensual, or selfish", as Pike tells us. When you are ready, *disciplined and worthy*, the same serpent, now directed from the other polarity perspective, will set you free. This dynamic is biblically communicated by the staff of Moses turning into a serpent that consumes the weaker serpent of Pharaoh.

This book will introduce you to polarity and fully explain it, from the very easy to grasp positive and negative aspects of atoms, to the far deeper polar perspectives that dictate our lives. The enemy and the liberator are *one and the same*, who gives you all the rope you need, to either hang yourself or climb to new heights of awareness. And if that wasn't mysterious enough, you will spend the better part of your life confusing the two. As the enemy, and that "word" may not be the most accurate description, the dark never stops tempting and brings forth the seven-headed dragon of fear/anger, greed, lust, pride, envy, laziness, and gluttony. Aren't we the lucky ones?

Adam and Eve (and more later on their true identities) fell so they could learn and experience the full spectrum of who and what they were, by being exposed to what they were not, and yes, it was *very much meant to happen*. They are symbolic of the two *serpents* that wind up either side of the thirty-three (highest Masonic degree) ver-tebrae of the spinal cord (the staff), and while they are known by many names, in esoteric Christianity they are known as Adam and Eve. Think of the in-plain-view clue of the symbol that represents the medical profession. Our material manipulative creative powers, outside of creating bodies through procreation, are only accessible in higher frequencies which can only be attained through discipline and the willpower to turn from selfish indulgence.

Not only are you not able to exercise your power, but indulging keeps you within the third-dimensional Iron Age realm of shortened, lim-ited lifetimes programmed to dispense evil, fear, suffering, and mis-ery *proportional* to your greed, indulgence, cruelty and indifference that you radiate. It is the perfect system to send you into the class that teaches what you what you need to learn. This is why God said, after the man ate of the fruit, "Behold, the man is become as one of us, to know good AND [now] evil", which are necessary developmental lessons. As soon as you have developed your willpower to control your *carnal desires* and addictions, and how to control your thoughts, you will set yourself on the road to regaining it. And *it*, will make *it*self known, as you read.

Information comes to us as light and we pay homage to our two polarity extremes, Sun*day* and Saturn*day*, every cyclical **7** day week. That leaves 5 *work* days between them, as 5 is the number of man, here working on himself. As our work week starts on Monday, first and foremost, we must strive and provide for ourselves and our children. As the week progresses, life demands that we pay attention to **it**, in all of its 5-sense glory. We must pay bills, have appointments to keep, business empires to build, dragons to slay, frontiers to explore and conquer, so that by Friday, you are once again hopelessly lost in the world of your 5 senses and absolutely convinced of its realness, not to mention **tired.** Lost in the senses and frazzled from the workweek, it is time to unwind and have some well-earned fun, as "thank God it's Friday" rolls around. It's time to TGIF the night away in our laurel wreaths and goat leggings (sorry, I got carried away there) until that 6th-day tribute to our God of time and ego on Saturday. The other week *end,* Sunday, is our day to rest and *reflect* on *beyond 5 sense* concepts, although these introspective spiritual reflections seldom exceed the flock cheering for the Saints or the Angels.

Saturn is a brown dwarf star and emits light, just not in the *visible* spectrum. It looks like a radio dish for a good reason. I could do another chapter on the real dark prince, the lord of the rings that transmits the messages of our Dark Lord to our little corner of the solar system, but it is already out there and only a click away. David Icke puts out some of the best Saturn-Moon matrix information out there to be sure and I **must** give the man his due, because he was one of the men to open my eyes at the beginning of my awakening, and I am **forever indebted.*** I want to keep my information to you as original as possible without regurgitating that which is already out there, and I will expand on the *hidden* identities of Saturn and Lucifer during the book that few, if any, share. I will tell you **real** identities of those two luminous heavenly bodies in our sky that **No** one else shares, including Icke.

Look into black cubes as you will be amazed where you see them along with Bells and Rings, and they represent our God of time, Saturn. From the Kaaba to the square they put on your head once you are "inDoctorateinated", in "Universe-ites", they speak of Saturn in our Iron Age 3D "box" we were born into with it's altered projected reality. The big cube-shaped ship of the Borg from Star Trek, and when you watch TNG's opening credits, on their continuing mission, guess which one is the only showcased *"planet"* looking more starlike than *normal*? And on a side note, Saturn has at least one moon that is *positively* not *natural*, if anything **is** or **not**, *"Natural" or normal!*

Here are the two areas I *very* respectfully disagree with David Icke. He tells us that near the beginning of his awakening, a *female* voice spoke to him for "about 5 hours about the nature of reality". Among the shared insights, she told him, "If it vibrates, it's illusion", but he never addresses why the *number* is 5, or why the voice is *feminine*, or **who** was speaking to him. After initially telling us he was spoken to by a female voice, all future references to this *other feminine entity speaking to him,* is just "it", like, *"**It** was just laying out what bloody illusion we live in and how funny it is that we take it seriously."* By the end of the book, I'll show you how *massive* these unacknowledged clues are.

Now, do we find ourselves in a *vibrating* waveform realm? Yes, and on the face of it, its illusory nature is true, but he never addresses *why we experience it* and implies it's some joke by saying how funny it is that we take the illusion seriously like it's some cosmic mistake or random occurrence that we find ourselves in this *dream*. The "taking it seriously illusion" is you living in the totality of the five senses and *firmly buying the be all end all illusion of all things being solid and sep-*

arate, with a waveform self-aware property called an Ego, that is itself
part of the dream that identifies itself individually, as **You**.

Here too, by the end of the book, you'll know precisely why we are
here, what cosmically divine purpose it serves, and how, "taking it
seriously", before we figure out how to create our own reality, **is** a
necessary learning level. Like Elementary School is to High School,
there is a progression that you go through, and that you simply **can't**
get to "**Creating your Own**", without the superficial *"taking it seri-*
ously" level. And really, describing just that level with "taking it seriously" is a bit vague, as once you recognise what you are engaged in,
you still take it seriously, because you still must deal in it, but now,
you know how to make your own moves to "manipulate your reality",
by making some of your own moves rather than simply being played
by forces outside of yourself.

The hide-in-plain-sight program puts a truth out there but couples it
with either lies, misleads, or gaping holes to lead you in a Dark direction so that when someone gets a glimpse at the truth, the planted
mislead or intentional omission of another key truth, will send his
mind back to the a path that keeps his identity hidden. This again is
no mistake as the alternate paths are simply extended lessons needed
within the School. It will all be revealed and by the end, David's missing gaps will be filled in, along with so much more, but you'll be the
judge of that.

The universe **is** electromagnetic waveform energy, and electricity
permeates the universe, which gives *shape* to our galaxies and powers everything. Brush it off as an *inconsequential* illusion all you want
but you **must** *still deal in it* and it is a distinct aspect of the *manifest*
waveform God. The other aspect being the still, unmanifest, silent-lov-
ing aspect that weaves the tapestry of the waveform universe, is only
hinted at by David, but again never **identified**. God **is** light, and there
is *nothing* that is, *something else.* I'll show you that what everyone
perceives as **Something else** is simply "less of", the only reality that
you and I are an integral part of.

God is light, and in him is no darkness at all, but there is a veiled dark aspect of "form" that is also God, and there is **no evolving or growth without it**. *Without that which vibrates, there is stagnation, and to dismiss or not acknowledge it, instills a loss of identity which creates a form of "Insanity", that mires you in fear, and he absolutely peddle's fear!* David and the rest of us were born into this condition that has been around for a few thousand years and I'll identify exactly *what* this *insanity* is. Here is his misleading dance around God, as Icke somewhat points to, but never identifies anything, other than "infinite love". *"Nothing"* cannot infinitely love, (or have a female voice) but you will never hear him speak of God, which infinitely loves and can actively communicate with him and this is the perfect segue to my next point of contention.

I believe the universe is perfect, and earth's polarity Iron Age classroom is as it should be. There are no reptilian humanoid forces controlling, *that are not meant to **control**.* Jesus answered, "You would have no power over me *if it were not given to you from above.*" That goes for any *other* intelligent life-form, as *everything* is an aspect of the greater mind. Ego has imagined control here, and rings are a symbol of that control and perceived autonomy. This *controlled* class is **meant** to engage and eventually subdue Ego, and it is Ego that condemns this *controlled situation* and demands you be angry about it.

If there are nonhuman vessels at work here, they are puzzle pieces in the perfect workings of God. God is expressing and experiencing through all the various vessels, and everything is as it should be. When you are ready to move on and fulfill your destiny, *you will.* The *pawns* of programmed evil, are following the alternative "away from the light" choice, and so **you** have a perceived *choice*, and since Icke always leads close to, but always around God, staying fearful, **know** that he is omitting (he may be following instructions) the most important *feminine* piece of the puzzle. (remember, I think he is amazing) It is all **You**, as they have no real power over you, as Dorothy found out, in this fractal holographic dreamworld most see as the be all end all and *so* totally invested in, but that is how it should be to *most*, but I am not speaking to them. I am speaking to **You.**

The spiritually young will always bite at the bait to stay in duality, and some are just destined for a life of misery as that is their lesson. It is heavy, to be sure. Life is an amazing apparatus. There are no accidents, no *luck*, as everyone or thing gets what it needs to spiritually advance. Even those who are killed don't just happen to have been "unlucky". It doesn't work that way! Few can accept this point I am making because they see in the separation and don't know what they don't know. Ego and this really goes to my Camelot references, always wants pleasure, comfort, victory, fun, **fairness**, immortality (in One waveform lifetime), and cannot comprehend that anything unpleasant or imperfect can be good for you.

What ego wants is usually contrary to what spirit needs. Trust me, anyone who is killed or murdered is meant to die, and this in no way justifies the murderer (watch out for the vase) as they will reap what they sow. I don't take lightly, matters this heavy of suffering and of life and death. I pull from my past experiences, of having my life flash before me at the age of fourteen, my years in law enforcement, my encounter with one who was not of this *world*, the messages from numerology, nature and having my Astral Self appear to a friend of mine and interact with him, only for him to be stunned and quite shaken up when he found out I was miles away and couldn't have been there. I now know why "I" appeared to him.

As the serial killer walks the path of darkness, he administers what is spiritually needed, but they, of course, don't realize it, and we, of course, do what we need to do to stop them. For those who die, it's the end of their class here, and those affected by their death is the sorrow they need to experience to know the heights of love. I have been fortunate that whenever I did something *negative* to someone, *it was returned to me in immediate fashion ("quick enough" so I knew what happened to me was programmed karma),* where I knew it was a universal law enforcing itself. This told me that what I did to them, was what they needed to experience as well.

While on set, my friend *Thomas,* advised me to see The Thirteenth Floor, and I did so. While I never bought this concept, I have had some good conversations with those who believe this world we live in is an imperfect copy of God's creation, as in Lucifer rebelling and creating his own universe to rule. Their slant being that the misery, wars, cruelty, and innately imperfect condition of our world proves a cruel and unjust god rules this world. The movie made me think it was another clue and that I may be wrong. There was also a point in the movie that an Apple logo was shown in an obvious way to make sure you saw it. Its face value tells you it's an advertisement, but it had more of an effect on me as I knew they are an important cog in the Luciferian world's organization. I got my answer that night as I had a crystal clear vision in a dream that again supports the overall God-controlled goodness of this Iron Age realm of a classroom we call life.

An XXX (666) appeared to me and then 1776 appeared over the three Xs. I clearly remembered it when I woke up. Here is my interpretation. I know the 666 mark of the beast to be the mark of a man, with its mind and ego, and I know that 1776 is the birth of the Illuminati. There is a reason the Masonic founding fathers chose 1776, but add them up and you get 21, which, added together, gives you 3, the number of God here. This school is a creation of God and perfect in every way, along with every aspect of the program that allows us to choose. Because underlying all, including the dark, is God, who are directed themselves. When the dark forces play us, and we do get played, it is for our own good, because when we get played, we are engaged in a lower frequency form of learning and when you no longer need it, you will no longer allow yourself to be played. In the grand scheme too, the dark forces that play us, are administering what is needed, and ultimately are themselves played. I get far too many clues that the cabal would not want displayed, pointing us in the right direction if this was, in fact, a creation of a lesser god, wanting to keep us permanently down. We are one mind, and no evil god is stealing people's souls. No one can **take** your slippers, Dorothy!

Far too many of us believe Satan is a *separate* entity, because that is what mainstream religion has told us for thousands of years, and it is an Iron Age lie. It was a necessary lie, like monsters eat bad children, to tell the Iron Age, spiritually young, children of God, but it is time to let this one go. They have fashioned a developmental box for us, and the most are in it because they are still young. Since you are reading this, you no longer want to be in the box, *so* let's investigate the identity of the beast and why 666, as identified in the Bible, is his number! Six is the earthly plane that God created in six. Light circumnavigates earth 6.66 times in one second, and until you get it, you are stuck here in this loop in a Groundhog Day-type situation. Our God of time provided us with a time grid that governs our entire lives. You cannot get through a day without checking the time, made up of 60 seconds, 60 minutes, and twenty-four hours (2+4=6), and it is on every business transaction. Our bodies are carbon-based, which has six protons, six neutrons, six electrons. The Torah identifies pregnancy as the mark of the beast, and the Kabbalah tells us Satan is our ego. When you don't know the totality of who you are, you will identify with only your ego, and you will exist in a somewhat satanic state.

Ego doesn't like the fact that it is temporary and dies, which is natural law (God's law), and so opposes it. Satan is the agent of our dark prince Saturn, our god of Time, and black is *his* color. Saturn just happens to have 6 letters and is the 6th planet with a 6 sided hexagon shape at its northern pole. Another of its symbols is the six-pointed star, the hexagram. Satan is definitely the body ego that fights with God because many of us are at that adolescent stage of development, like the teens who think they know everything. The "evil" simply "fights" this, like fighting fire with fire. You fight and struggle until you learn it is a dead end, and at that point, like the prodigal son, you choose God and stop choosing the lie. In the end, we are what we are, and you either run with it or run away from it.

The School never stops being in session! We live in an electromag-netic *light* hologram, and all information comes to us as light. That's why Lucifer is the light bearer, and Satan is always referred to as *his* agent! When Jesus refers to a synagogue of Satan, he means the *church of ego,* and he tells us Satan rules this world. We have two aspects within us, the Sun (the Self), and Saturn (Ego). Virtually no one knows what being Satanic really is, as 99% believe it is just being evil, and most think it is just another name for the guy with horns. You can be kind and concerned and still be *satanic because you still do not know your true identity.* "Blaspheming the Holy Spirit" **is,** not knowing who you are and seeing in separation, and by the end of the book, I think you'll know what I mean! When Jesus told Peter, "Away from me Satan", Peter was telling him, he would not allow them to take him, so he was being very concerned and protective, but seeing only through Ego as a "man" in separation. When Jesus was being tempted by Satan during his forty-day fast, it was his ego and body trying to pull him down and keep him *here*, just as we are tempted every day! Because there is no singular immortal Devil, the program needs an Antichrist. Why would the immortal prince of darkness, need a human Antichrist if this were not the case? God can't seem to get rid of him, so why the need to use the puny, little human sur-rogate? Well, now you know, and you'll know far more! The "Christ" means Christ consciousness, the path *up* to the light and "Antichrist" is simply the opposite end of the spectrum or the path to the dark.

Do you want to know who crucified Christ? It is a bit too simplistic to say the Jews or the Romans, as Ego crucified Christ, and if you think that was a one-time event, then like creation that never stops, maybe it's time for a new perspective. The one-time event you are thinking of is not what you thought because what you thought or are thinking is a Roman creation to keep you looking out there and waiting, which is the old perspective. The Luciferian program will never stop tempt-ing and misleading, telling you that you are a sinful unworthy nobody as these are necessary hurdles for young spirits to overcome. The ultimate survivor reality show. The man they crucified was known as the Christ. His name was Yeshua Ben Hur. Remember the hidden-in-plain-view clue movie Ben-Hur? In the movie, the main character was Juda Ben Hur, but Jesus was always on the periphery, and Judah is translated Yehudah. This was another classic half-truth, like The Big Bang Theory. He is our Lord in our upline and I will get into upline and pyramids and how they relate to the visual concept of God soon. He came to guide and direct the prodigals among us to keep us focused on the task at hand and not buy into the realness of the illusory, temporary, classroom of duality. Yeshua Ben Hur was known as the Christ and always made it clear he was not the Father, although He was much further along the path, and our God in our upline, as I will show you later, and was well aware of his status as a child of God within the all that is.

How can the All-Knowing be the All-Knowing without knowledge of the dark, and if you claim it, you must own all of it instead of pointing at a completely separate "devil" that manifests the dark? The All That IS, has been around every block! Every light is identified by the dark. God is light, and we are children of God, and as such, light beings who are required to learn the dark, to become the All That Is and so God grows. The Self is who we really are, but the Ego is that aspect that allows us, the young, to *identify* ourselves. Without it, we can't focus on a point to identify, experience and *improve*. Every star, regardless of size, has its dark counterpart and that is what Disney is trying to tell us in so many movies. In the "Prince of Persia," the King has his evil younger brother, Simba has Scar, Thor has Loki. The clay tablets of Sumer describe the same dynamic between their gods Enki and Enlil, for as above, so below, as a proton needs its electron to attain everlasting life!

* See appendix 4 on how all this began.

3. The Divine Pyramid Scheme

There is a parental clue as to the makeup of God through the name the Father, but an even more all-inclusive name comes from God. When asked for a name by Moses, God replied, "I AM THAT I AM", but the Bible is missing a crucial punctuation mark that has caused some misunderstanding concerning its meaning. It should rightly be displayed, "I AM THAT, I AM!" The comma makes all the difference, as God is telling Moses that everything he lays his eyes on, "I am that." No matter what it is, "I am that", or I AM the totality of everything. Here is what the name also shows us! Remember when I referred to *Jesus* in our upline? It's pyramid time. You can pick the second line down and choose a 3 as a representation of Yeshua/Jesus, and we would then be further down in his pyramid, so who better to judge who passes than the ascended parent, as the more successful his judging, the more it elevates him. You will see a bit later why I used 3s to represent the all-seeing eye, but you can replace the 3s with eyes because that's what they are, considering what I saw. Now you can see why *I and eye sound the same* and of course the number of I is 9, and every time you call yourself I, you proclaim it!

Now you see the structure of the one mind that is I AM THAT, I AM, and now you can see why the ancients, who were seeded here from the Pleiades, used the pyramid to symbolize the structural essence of God. The triangle, that a pyramid built from, is the base deterministic material structure that our "solid" world springs from. The pyramidal structure of God is like the structure of a multi-level marketing company. God is at the top and, hence, why the Masons display a pyramid, such as the one on the back of the USA **One**-dollar bill and why the Giza pyramids were capped at the top with gold pyramids. This symbolizes the identity of the one mind and the holographic nature that is God within all the aspects of God, and within all the aspects, we have the entirety of the whole. The gold pyramid caps had both a symbolic meaning and a practical application. Gold symbolizes wisdom, prosperity, health, triumph, and the gift given to kings. The gold caps also served a conductive purpose as the Giza pyramids were *electrical* power plants and all formed a resonating power grid, all powered by water, like us, and Giza's very location on the globe.

Now here is where I tie in Yeshua as our upline and how the Roman egos plan to fool you did, in fact, give us a clue to our ultimate destination. The circumpunct, because of the holographic nature of the universe, is a symbol of both God and man. Remember the birth of the circumpunct in the lava lamp of the Target commercial? Well, as above, so below, as it signified the birth of man and the birth of God. This is where it starts to get a bit complicated because you see a beginning to that, which has no beginning. Try to take in these next few sentences as pieces of the puzzle of God, and keep in mind everything is electromagnetic energy.

Our God, who is the God of Yeshua and everything in this universe, was at some point, in the universe of its God. Yeshua, who is our older sibling within our God, will at some point be God. It is eternal in both directions. Our God had a God and that God had a God and so on, and I will visually show you this growth near the end. When Yeshua becomes God, and if you followed the path of Christ consciousness, you will be doing that which Yeshua did with us and guiding the young souls under you. If you reach that level, you will most certainly become, at some point, God. Like the colors *of* the white light, we are all aspects of the one mind, and our God is by no means alone with its uniqueness within the greater one mind. The scope of what I am describing is mind-boggling as it is infinite in both directions, big and small.

The universe is God growing and expressing itself, and all life within the universe is God living through the vessel of spirit to experience, for then it is truly known once experienced. As the spirit evolves, it grows and increases in voltage, inhabiting more complex (higher voltage and more advanced geometrical structure) physical life-forms each time to accommodate its charge. At some point, its voltage, at about the time it reaches a level of self, sentient being awareness, its voltage has reached a level sufficient to receive a soul. This is an important event, for before the spirit receives a soul, it is just a vessel of expression for God within the universe. Once the spirit receives that metaphysical essence, that blank slate of God, which is the soul, is now on a mission of its own, and that mission, my friends, is to become God. You are now not just a vessel for expression; you are the source of God's growth! And your ultimate destiny, as a "child of God", is growing up, to be God.

From my Glinda: We have arrived at a time, and our souls choose to be here to be witnesses to the dawn of a new era. The light of Orion is returning and, with it, God consciousness. The weighing of the feather ceremony against the heart is upon us all, and none will escape. We always knew that getting out of here meant the shedding of the material skin we know as our body. This was a temporary skin. At the heart, we are light beings born from the heavens, and it's their our story that is told and will either continue or end. A world without ending, forever and ever. As you noted with a quote from scriptures (Mark 13:32) about the owner of the house returning, that no one knows the minute or the hour, not even the angels in heaven, but not to be asleep when the owner of the house returns. Well, you are not asleep, Scott. We've been awoken so that we can be prepared for the coming judgment or, as the Egyptians called it, the weighing of the feather against the heart, the harvest of souls. Do we evolve as loving souls and receive the gift of Zep Tepi, the gift of all knowledge and all-knowing, or do we return to galactic center to be erased completely from the book of life? To go back to Atum, where nothing is wasted, to be recycled again in the hopes that in another incarnation we get it right this time around. (Ever heard of Zep cleaning products? The clues abound.)

Who, for "specific" reasons, failed to learn or ignore what we learned about 100 years ago from men like Planck, Bohr and Einstein, that everything is electromagnetic energy, and that what appears "solid", is but an illusion, and that the "observer effect" confirms that the "illusion" is very much affected by what we believe as we observe, because we are co-creators? Who can't see that numbers are encoded into the fabric of the universe and that the Fibonacci sequence and Golden ratio, 1.6180... is found in virtually every system and organism, from plants and animals to breaking waves and the spiraling arms of the billions of Galaxies? The young of course. We are all connected. When one is strong, they pull everyone, especially those "close" up, and when you are weak, you pull others down as well. Now I'll say something that is a stretch for most, but there is now more evidence that recently identifies a numeric code in universal systems, similar to the binary code we use to program computers. The image you see on television screens are produced with a series of 0's and 1's. Now, the code of the universe is far more complex and uses, I believe 9 digits, 0 to 8. We have known for about 100 years that matter is energy, or better yet "condensed space" and that there is no true solid.

According to Dr. Stephen C. Meyer, an advocate of the principle of intelligent design, not only is our DNA digitally encoded, but that there are unmistakable design patterns and strategies that are genetically encoded and clearly at work in the information processing systems in the whole of the cellular gene expression system that parallel the operating systems of computers. He said, what we used to refer to as "Junk DNA" is, in fact, a functional operating system which is directing the timing and regulation of the data files of the DNA coding regions. There are "Automated Error Corrections" and "Files within Folders Hierarchical Filing System" at the cellular level. There are "Distributed Storage and Retrieval Informational Modules", for example, if the cell or cells need to build new proteins, on a needs basis, they can access these files for the information to do so. That the body uses "Nested Coding" of Information (dual coding or encryption). Computer programmers use all these same design patterns and strategies. He believes that Organic life, like computers, HAD to be designed and created by an intelligent mind.

Our God has its parent and has many siblings, and you are the head of an amazing family. The real you, your Astral Self, is intimately familiar with it, but as the Target commercial tells us, this life is a computer-programmed holographic projection for our development, and your knowledge of the big picture has been withheld in this projected life for a very good reason. If it were not withheld, you wouldn't see this as real, and there would be reduced urgency and motivation to work on yourself to get the wrinkles pressed. Besides, the you and I here is a fraction of the real you and I taking this class. I believe most of the people you come in contact with in life are the closest relatives within your astral family, and in loving them, helping them, and picking them up, you are doing the same to yourself. Likewise, showing hate, disdain, or indifference is in fact done to you. And when I say everyone, I'm including nonhuman vessels. Your astral child may come to you in a vessel of a different color or socioeconomic status, and how you treat and judge them will be the measure of how your parent will ultimately judge and treat you.

On the last day, Jesus will say to those on His right hand, "Come, enter the Kingdom. For I was hungry and you gave me food, I was thirsty and you gave me drink, I was sick and you visited me." Then Jesus will turn to those on His left hand and say, "Depart from me because I was hungry and you did not feed me, I was thirsty and you did not give me to drink, I was sick and you did not visit me." These will ask Him, "When did we see You hungry, or thirsty or sick and did not come to Your help?" And Jesus will answer them, "Whatever you neglected to do unto one of the least of these, you neglected to do unto Me!"

The Lion Heart

The head of the Sphinx was **originally** a lioness with features that were a bit more human and feminine as the Sphinx represents the goddess Tefnut. She is usually depicted either as a lioness-headed woman or in fully leonine form, as is the case here. The largest and oldest stone sculpture is Tefnut 5, and she looks to the constellation of Leo 5 and Regulus, the lion's heart, and heart is no small point. The animating force from God that creates you and your world around you springs forth from your heart. The heart, intuition, knows before the head, and the compassion and love you feel are centered there. The lion 5 represents heart 7, for the world you see around you is made manifest from the heart, and heart's number 7 points to the ethereal realm of our Astral Selves.

Regulus is also known as the ruler, the **lawgiver**, and as the brightest star in Leo, Regulus has been almost universally associated in ancient cultures with the concept of royal or kingly power. The name Regulus actually comes from the Latin rex, or king. Esoterically, Regulus acts as a lens for Sirius, the major star in our trinary star system that includes our Sun and Sirius B. Sirius is the star of Christ consciousness, and we associate the Christ with the heart center. As Sirius is known as the Dog Star (God star), then the star Regulus (the heart of the lion, the lawgiver), its lens, serves as the regulator of Sirian energy to earth, stimulating the response in humanity to express heart consciousness, the quality we call love.

The Soul is synonymous with love and Christ, the heart consciousness. Tefnut and the pyramids have been standing there for tens of thousands of years as a sentinel and a beacon of truth to show the aware who they are, where they come from, and where they are going. The official mainstream information concerning the age of the Sphinx and pyramid—at three to six thousand years—and the pyramids being tombs are just exoteric Iron Age misleads for the spiritually young to keep the unaware, unaware, believing in "linear time development", and playing in duality. It is incumbent on YOU to find the truth. You will not be shown the exits in the walled marts as you must find them, and that is part of this test we call life.

From my Glinda: "The numbers are very important, Scott, as you may or may not know, so I won't assume what you may know. The number 6 is the creation we are bound to, and seven is the ethereal plain our consciousness 'soul' comes from. The number 10 is the divine, and 3, as you know, is the Trinity, which you have isolated yourself from Petula's name. The number 3 divided into 10 gives a number that is infinity."

We defaced the lion's head and made it a human head, and then de*faced* it again by those not liking *the features,* of the face. Ego stole the top gold cap representing God because God is shunned by ego. The remainder of the pyramid represents us (the son, the universe), but the outer limestone covering is stripped to show our imperfect, broken-down state in this dark Iron Age. Each individual stone is each one of us. Those above us are in our upline, and those below us are in our downline. When it was new, it was a perfect representation of God and showed the holographic nature of the universe with the top golden pyramid 5 a perfectly proportioned image of the whole. This is a divine, sacred geometry shape that is a universal conduit of energy, and carrier of consciousness.

The Giza "star map" pyramids were perfect ecological electric power plants due to their shape, planetary chakra location and the abundant water aquifers below them, at that time. There is *no soot* evidence in their interiors to prove that fire did not provide their light source. The Great Pyramid was also a harmonic resonance chamber designed to act as a "gate", and I'll leave that to you, if you wish to investigate that further, along with the fact it IS the embodiment of mathematical and engineering perfection, encoded by our Masonic administrators to speak to a future "winter" class, showing the calendar to the few coming of age, to reveal the new class that Spring brings, and hint of their Golden future! The obelisk, with its pyramid at the top, symbolizes the pyramid expanding infinitely and is the electric masculine sundial that creates the shadowed cross from the sun's light, our symbol of Christ consciousness. The horizontal line of the cross represents the equinox, while the vertical line represents the solstices. The shorter line above the horizontal represents the summer solstice, and the long line below is winter. The cross also represents the intersection of the *masculine with the feminine energies* to produce the Christic fire, the creative force.

To my Glinda: "I went back and read what you wrote me again, and of course, I got something else out of it. '10 = the perfectly divine soul and 3 = Trinity, 10 divided by 3 = an infinite number that does not end. *Yes*, and it is why the first, and only one of the 3s (the only whole number), is to the left of the decimal point, and all to the right that never ends are a fraction of the whole and every 3 moving to the right is less divine than the ones to its left. The closer the fractional 3 is to the decimal point, the more divine it is, and the further away it is, the less divine, but no matter how far down the line it is, it will never *not have* some percentage of divinity, meaning there is nothing that is not from or of God."

3.333333333333333333333333333333333 . . .

A more accurate representation of the spiritual "Heart-Based" lineage of the growth of God, are the vertical 3's, as depicted in the display of the obelisk, with the 3.(only whole 3) being God at the top and all the 3's to the right of the decimal point below it in a straight line down. SO at some point, the .3 is born as 3., full God. Our universe is like a galaxy within an even greater universe, and this sequence never stops. Conversely, a galaxy has huge trinary star systems with stars so extraordinarily large that we can hardly imagine it, with massive super-solar systems made up of smaller systems. Our sun is part of a trinary system with Sirius A+B; and remember *"My Three Sons"*, so our solar system is part of a larger system. Within each solar system, each star has multiple planets with moons, like little solar systems within them. The planets are alive with life-forms *familiar* and unfamiliar to us, as they MUST be alive as nothing, absolutely nothing, is dead. The everything that is, is everything! The planets and all matter are made up of atoms from the various eighty-one (**9**) stable elements, and the **3** states of matter, solid, liquid, gas. The atomic (**3** atomic components) solar systems within the larger molecular systems within the body universe. There is no smallest unit just as there is no largest.

Speaking of our trinary star system, didn't the Son of man shine like the sun with two others? Don't we also know that God is light? Why, yes we do. And who better to judge man than his source of light. "No one goes to The Father, except through me," the Father Sirius through the "Sun" of Man. **God is light, as the spiritually young endlessly apply sunscreen.** No wonder I spent so much time in the Valley of the Sun. Sunscreen free of course!

"We are still on the threshold of fully understanding the complex relationship between light and life, but we can now say emphatically, that the function of our entire metabolism is dependent on light."

"We know today that man, essentially, is a being of light."

~ Dr. Fritz Albert Popp

4. Earth's Darth Sidious

The mystery schools have existed far longer than we have been told, and to *most,* serve the adversarial perspective. It is the main cog of the *evil* program on this plane that most of you know as the Illuminati. They are the very essence of the Satanic perspective, to *most* totally invested in the body/ego, with all its dualistic perspectives, and it is the adversarial aspect opposed to God and all that is "of God". Its main goal is to keep you mired in Ego by distracting, tempting, misleading, and generating fear to keep you away from the light and love of Christ consciousness, for very specific reasons that will be outlined. It is an amazingly effective, albeit predictable, program and is one and the same as the Nazi playbook, that we see played out and repeated throughout history. "For many are called, but few are chosen" because the test **must** be difficult. Evil is programmed in because you **must** have a choice. At least on the surface of it!

"The dark is generous, and it is patient. It is the dark that seeds cruelty into justice, that drips contempt into compassion, that poisons love with grains of doubt. The dark can be patient, because the slightest drop of rain will cause those seeds to sprout. The rain will come, and the seeds will sprout, for the dark is the soil in which they grow, and it is the clouds above them, and it waits behind the star that gives them light. The dark's patience is infinite. Eventually, even stars burn out.

The dark is generous and it is patient and it always wins—but in the heart of its strength lies its weakness: one lone candle is enough to hold it back. Love is more than a candle. Love can ignite the stars."
                    -Matthew Stover, Star Wars novelist

The dark Matthew Stover is referring to is the computer program that *never* stops doing what it is programmed to do, and that is to tempt you and lead you away from the Creator. It has no real power over you, and the little it has is granted by you and can be taken away at any time, again, by you. If your weakness is food, it will always place

43

your favorite *"candy bar"* in front of your mouth, and if your weakness is the sexual climax, it will always place your favorite ... *you get the picture!* Without the adversarial program, there is no growth, no discipline, and no ultimate knowledge of SELF, with all its different faces and facets.

Manifestations of the Dark

A grown man knows the world he lives in. For the moment, that world is Rome.

—PONTIUS PILATE from Ben-Hur

This magnificent quote rings true on so many levels. You cannot truly be grown if you are ignorant of the world you live in and as incredible as it may seem, the "moment" has lasted well over two thousand years, and the left brain reality of Rome is still firmly in control of humanity. Their symbol was, and is the eagle. Are there eagles representing your country? Here in duality, most things have two meanings! Virtually every symbol is one side of a negative/left and positive/right polarity coin and they do appear as eagles*, to those who only identify with this lower frequency level. To those of heightened awareness, the bird represents the internal Phoenix, the long-lived bird of mythology that is cyclically regenerated, and it represents our next 5-D stage of development rising in Aquarius. The Phoenix is associated with the sun, more light, more awareness, as Phoenix, Arizona, is located in the Valley of the Sun. Their NBA team is the Suns, and one of their team colors, as is the case with the Ravens (Odin the raven god, look at the years they win, the beginning of the new millennium, and the beginning of the new age), is purple, and the other is orange.

The Phoenix is a very important Masonic symbol passed on to them by the Sons of the Phoenix, the mysterious Phoenicians. Their origins, knowledge, symbols, and their royal color, Tyrian purple, have been shrouded in mystery, myth, and misleads to hide their identity, the divinity of the symbols, and the seeds they planted in Northern Italy (Venetians) along the Adriatic. It is why they use the obelisk, pyramid, and the capstone with God's eye in full view of all while hiding the true meaning for those who cannot yet handle the truth, but some of you are ready now. So you see, the Phoenicians became the Aryan race, with their symbol of the sun wheel and cross and their *other* descendants, the Britons, Scots, Celts, and Ashkenazim. Yes, you see the end correctly.

Their current capital is Rome, but that will change as they prepare Zion, and **he** of 4, the bridge between 3 and 5, who is a small child, will innocently take center stage and orchestrate the destruction of the 3D Iron Age world so that the 5D Phoenix can rise from its ashes. So many Disney and Marvel movies are giving us clues to this inevitability. The next stage of human development within the New World. In the trailer for Captain America: The Winter Soldier (so that spring may bring bronze), "Alexander Pierce: Captain, to build a better world, sometimes means tearing the old one down . . . And that makes enemies." Yes, the 3D egos (the ordinary humans in X-Men) will fight it! And did you see the Phoenix in the lobby of SHIELD? Monumental clues veiled within entertainment. Now back to reality.

"I AM the Senate" -Darth Sidious

Your presidents or prime ministers are puppets in a vast web of political, socio-economic, religious, and scientific manipulation that permeates every thread of Western civilization, down to dictating the misinformation in school textbooks from kindergarten to graduate universities. You are misinformed chattel slaves, unaware of your status and equally unaware of your ruler who sits in Rome and prepares your new capital in a conquered land, while you *live,* in *their* world, distracted, watching your TV with his programming and responding to its dictates with the predictable precision of Pavlov's dog. A precious few don't quite feel free, and for *good* reason, because you are anything but, in the duality playground of illusory walls. When you gain more awareness, you will have crystal clear knowledge of who the *"they"* are, in the above *"their* world" reference.

The Vatican is the great arcanum, loaded with symbols that few understand. The obelisk, God's structure, is also the phallic symbol, interestingly situated in the vagina of Vatican's St. Peter's *Square*. The obelisk, with the cross on top within the symbolic oval, IS the supreme Christian symbol, as I pointed out, and does transcend religion. "My kingdom is not of this world," but as you can see, in an opulent, materialistic setting, nothing is as it seems within the city of polarity contradictions. An anomaly full of Egyptian, Sumerian and Roman symbols—bees, hives, dragons, snakes, pinecones, sagging crosses displaying the most emaciated Jesus, in what is **now** the Dark city of the 7 kings. A varied assortment of Masonic and satanic symbols that speak only to the most aware as 99 percent of the Christians walking around them, having no clue what they represent. If I also seem to contradict myself, it is because many symbols have multiple meanings, just as light can exist as a particle and a wave. What it communicates to you depends on your level of awareness, so be aware of **this** as I tell you *that*.

The Vatican is the current seat of the world's dominant Luciferian program, orchestrating the Zionists, and yes, that's right, they are on the same side of the self-same coin. The Pope, like most world leaders that come and go and are puppets doing the bidding of this duality program. So I hear you asking, if not the Pope, then who runs the show? Alexandre Dumas knew, and in The Count of Monte Cristo, he symbolically tells you, but it is heard by only the most aware. One of our greatest presidents was on to them, and they killed him because of his resistance to their bankers. And according to the Catholic priest Father Charles Chiniquy, Lincoln had this to say about them.

"This war would never have been possible without the sinister influence of the Jesuits. We owe it to Popery that we now see our land reddened with the blood of her noblest sons. Though there were great differences of opinion between the South and North, on the question of slavery, neither Jeff Davis nor any one of the leading men of the Confederacy would

have dared to attack the North, had they not relied on the promise of the Jesuits, that, under the mask of Democracy, the money and the arms of the Roman Catholics, even the arms of France, were at their disposal if they would attack us . . . . The Jesuits have not yet killed me. But they would have surely done it when I passed through their most devoted city, Baltimore, had I not defeated their plans, by passing incognito a few hours before they expected me." (Charles Chiniquy, Fifty Years in the Church of Rome, The Wickliffe Press, Protestant Truth Society, Wickliffe Avenue, 104 Hendon Lane, Finchley, London, N3, 1885, p. 388)

The Jesuits, but more specifically their leader, who is the real leader of the Vatican in the shadows. The society is headed by a superior general, and whoever is in this position IS the conduit of the dark information and known by the aware as the black pope. He is the *head* of the Zion beast, but having said this, *the ultimate power that never rests, that speaks to him and those in the shadows, **will** **never** **be** **seen***. He and his select counsel of advisors are sorcerers who worship the Dark and through the dark Mass access the dictates of *our Dark Lord*. It is *he* that controls the G5 governments, the UN, Israel, the British monarchy, the world's banking families, Big Oil, and the list goes on and on! While this is the global source, we all have access to the adversarial satanic program on a personal level. Its control is virtually everywhere in the game of ego. And their main goal is to keep as many of you here in the Iron Age as they can while awakening (duality, remember?) as many of the prodigals, and those ready to move on, as they can. It has been prophesied and you can't deny the similarities between the end time descriptions as recorded by "Matthew" 24:1 to 51 "quoting" "Jesus" **and** Albert Pike, describing how the Masonically choreographed **three** World Wars, would bring about the end of this age! They are strikingly similar.

"The whole aim of practical politics is to keep the populace alarmed (and hence clamorous to be led to safety) by menacing it with an endless series of hobgoblins, all of them imaginary."

-H. L. Mencken

"Many a tear has to fall. But it's all, in the game. All in the wonderful game."

-"It's All in the Game" lyrics by Carl Sigman

A magnificently sophisticated game that teaches. Just as The Matrix shows us, many of the people we see are not soul-carrying vessels like we are, but just programmed vessels like Agent Smith in The Matrix. How else could the bloodlines, that have ruled us for thousands of years, have been able to hold on to their wealth and power? We all know crime doesn't pay for the vessels carrying souls, but the criminal banksters are no different from the mansions they live in. They are just programmed parts of the scenery, like the barking dog. It is so good you believe it to be completely real. Its lessons are absolute and ALWAYS perfect and precisely what **you** need!

There are distractions and evil everywhere, and when you respond to them from a dualistic good and evil perspective, which the 99 percent do, it means you need more time here, and you will most certainly get it. It, along with the temptations I outline in the next chapter, is a test of your awareness and willpower. When you finally see it as the lesson plan that it is and know its loving source, you can then step back from it, and assert your autonomy. From that point, when you see from a holistic point of view, you can then begin to radiate love and maintain it as a state of being as you walk the walk, meaning you see the distractions and material pleasures for the illusory bait that they are!

"The Matrix is a "system", Neo. That system is our enemy (opponent, and you are playing against, the computer). *But when you're inside* (born into a body), *what do you see? Businessmen, teachers, lawyers, carpenters* (all of the people "playing their parts"). *The very minds of the people we are trying to save* (liberate from the game). *But until we do, these people are a part of that system... and that makes them our enemy. You have to understand...most of these people are not ready to be unplugged* (too young and still

need the lessons the game dispenses, or they are going deeper into the dark). *And many of them are so inert...so hopelessly dependent on the system...that they will fight to protect it* (you don't know what you don't "know", and Caesar's game is all they know, and they will fight to preserve the only life "they know", and the few that "may" know, are now, as "Red" from "The Shawshank Redemption" points out, "Institutionalized", and are afraid to venture out beyond the walls of our "Walled" mart). *Were you listening to me or looking at the woman in the red dress?* (was your "attention" where it should be, to raise your frequency, or were you distracted by all the *desirable* bait designed to lower your frequency) *Look again."* (no matter how beautiful and desirable it looks, it still has a hook to keep you in the game, and soon loses its luster) ~Morpheus, "The Matrix", in bold

While enemy "works" for the movie, a better interpretation is *opponent,* and very very few beat the computer. And you know he had to include Lawyers up there, as no profession takes you further into the Satanic game, than those who are consumed with and administer "Man's Laws", and Satan "must" control. That's why those who "Govern" us are primarily Lawyers! The legal system, by its very nature, is in an adversarial position with respect to Natural law. I do understand the need for man made laws in a world of reduced awareness in a highly populated area, but that system is always ripe to be drug further down the rabbit hole of Satanic identification, and every new law makes any divine identification harder and harder to perceive. It starts, innocently enough, with a very basic "10 commandments", as an example, and before you know it you have libraries full of Codes of Federal Regulations (CFR's), Uniform Commercial Codes (UCC's), Executive Orders, Constitutional dictates and federal BAR codes and rules for the courts, along with the endless State, County and Municipal Statutes and Codes that regulate virtually every nuanced aspect of life with a goal of driving out the human condition or any thought of Divine Order. Endless laws telling you who you can or can't marry, what plant you can or can't grow, what you can or can't put in your own body, and the dark is supremely blind to the natural consequence of actions, and they just have to control *everything.* They believe in "Luck", and have "backup plans" to protect you from, as Bush (Bush-Jungle Lol) called it, the "Law of the Jungle", which deals in "Chaos" (to them), and makes you a *victim of Bad Luck.*

I have newfound respect for the highest levels of the Masons, knowing them now to be the keepers of the golden age knowledge. *Before enlightenment, you have no idea who you are or who or what they are. During enlightenment, you identify them, if you have done your homework, as the corrupting evil behind the world's governments, religions, corporations, and crime syndicates. After enlightenment, you see them as the divine administrators of the karmic wheel, set in place to break our collective Ego, because you have broken yours. You now know who you are, and what everything is. Your mountains are once again mountains.* **They administer that which is designed to keep those who are not ready, *here*, and the loving message to those who have discovered their true identity, who are ready to graduate.** It was an amazing revelation for me to finally see this. I now know why all of the "conspiratorial" events, like the JFK assassination and 9-11, **had** to happen, as we come to the unavoidable fork in the road, the "inconvenient" Truth. The illumined ones, who see all, are **just that**. (Remember this paragraph while you are reading the rest of the book, when it sounds a bit like conspiracy. I am not returning to conspiracy, I am just making a point.)

*Another huge clue is in NFL logos. If you look them up on nfl.com all at the top of the home page, you will see that all, are symmetrical or point to the right. . .but one! This is by no means an accident! It is the logo of the Eagles. If you "identify" with the "Eagle", Rome, Mars, as opposed to seeing the Phoenix, you will be headed to the Left, to the "wide gate"! Or now if you can perceive it as a Phoenix from its perspective, looking up at you, it is the only one looking to the Right, and they are from the city of Brotherly Love!

5. Building Treasures

In what is only meant to reflect?

Do not store up for yourselves treasures on earth, where moths and vermin destroy, where thieves break in and steal.

He tells us as much! This is an illusory classroom that is not meant to be perfect or permanent. It's Oz here, the 7-11 School of Duality, as the movie and Target commercial tell us, and Oz will *never* be permanent. It is *perfectly* programmed to be *flawed*, to take you out of your comfort zone and it's very temporary. It is all about the choices YOU make as you navigate through this imperfect training class put before you, designed to make you deal with situations that **demand** you make tough choices. There are no accidents or coincidences as you are constantly monitored, and synchronicity is a normal part of life, to the aware. A complaint I hear very often is "Why can't we just be left alone?" Were you left alone in elementary school? You know the answer to that question! We are not here to be left alone, and whether you like it or not, we are what we are. A lifetime of blaming the rain will just extend your stormy "tour of duty"!

What are earthly treasures? They are of course tied to *attachments,* and the pull to comfort and pleasure. They are any bait on the hook that causes you to bite and hold on, like monetary attachments, believing it to have value and power that you want to possess or pleasure that you want to feel and experience, like so many carnal addictions. We *all* have our favorite bait that we **so** desire, and they are here, to keep you here.

Not only is evil programmed into this experience, but we are programmed with *personality* challenges and your body is programmed with inherent weaknesses. You *know* what yours are, which you spend a lifetime dealing with them. The body has tools, sensations, and instincts that we need, to navigate through the game of life, the ultimate classroom, but some of these can and do overwhelm and cloud your good sense. Herein lies the genius of creation making you believe as that you must strive (eat, drink, protect yourself, and find shelter) to survive, and this appears to be carved in stone at first glance. This programmed condition makes Iron Age life tough, so we are programmed with what we have identified as instincts that compel us to, *"tough it out"*.

The strongest, most basic instinct in all organisms is that of simply surviving. The will and the need to continue to live makes us go through and overcome incredible adversities that, without it, we simply wouldn't. The survival instinct has another aspect that is just as important as wanting to stay alive, once born, and that is the instinctual desire to procreate and spread your genetic program. To ensure the steady availability of bodies, our creator attached another huge incentive to aid and enhance the instinct like the sexual orgasm, the "gift" from God as the religions tell us (as I laugh), one of the most pleasurable physical sensations we can experience every time we let loose and spread that seed. And it's the perfect bait to keep the less aware, who have more to learn from what only duality can teach, here in the Iron Age. How many rich and powerful, with much to lose, have been brought down by this urge? Sorry if all the seed talk is getting you worked up, as it's a compelling motivator, and the images immediately pop up in your internal monitor, and you're not thinking of almond butter unless of course, your weakness is food!

The orgasm is a drug unto itself and, with the exception of a very slim percentage of those who engage in the act from a base of pure love (where the pleasure is not the sole goal) who knowingly want to procreate using the energy to create new life, getting your fix, regardless of the means to achieve it, has the same frequency-depleting effect on your body. It doesn't matter if it happens in a vagina, a rectum, mouth or your hand, speaking from a man's perspective, of course, the depletion is the same. Heterosexuals can get smug and judgmental toward homosexuals, but as I stated above, the effects of the climax are the same when you are strictly getting your fix. The atomic energy life force that you spill has the power to create or destroy, symbolized by the Serpent. Keeping it harnesses its power for spiritual growth beyond this cell while spilling it for desire reduces your frequency and drains your creative energy to that which *desires* to keep you.

The Dark needs this material creating force to *continue doing what it is meant to do*, similar to how the Matrix needs us plugged in. When Delilah came to Samson, her "cutting his hair", was symbolic of Samson *squandering* his creative power within the seductive *Philistine* (like Eve) thus reducing his frequency (his fall) to become just an ordinary man with normal strength. Control the serpent and use its power, or *it controls* and consumes you, if you are not disciplined and worthy. You will never become God, so long as you give it away to the Dark by squandering it for you own personal pleasure. This is why we have free pornography all over the internet to keep the climax bait in front of you, with men's health journals telling us that daily orgasms keep the prostate healthy. I believe The *Serpent* wrote that article.

When you see the image of a red devil with his coiled tail going down with a pointing arrow at the tip, it symbolizes the serpent. It is your *creative energy essence* being spilled down lowering your frequency and keeping you *down*. If you are not spiritually ready for this, you simply won't get it and you literally *won't* **want** to *get it.* You'll examine this from the perspective of your conditioning, what you perceive you (because you are still Thomas Anderson) need, see it as a "natural" function, that like eating and eliminating, as just something you *must and certainly want,* to do here. I know, because when I was first introduced to this polarity dynamic being translated into what you *should,* and should *no longer,* practice, some years ago, I wasn't ready for this. And even when you are, it still requires every ounce of your willpower!

"This is the Age of knowing what you are made of!" An incredible clue cloaked in a Viagra Slogan, telling you that *biting* long after your teeth are gone, will confirm *that you don't!*

Now that God has ensured we will pump out enough bodies for his young spirits, we must keep them operating, and we must again be motivated with some extra sensations to keep us *wanting* to eat. This ensures our survival and provides more bait and tests that make this the ultimate school for young gods in training, as so many people live to eat. Now they tell us taste is nothing more than sweet, salt, sour, bitter sensations that when combined give us all the different flavors we taste during a fabulous four or five-course meal. I'm not buying it, as there are so many tastes, to me, that defy any of the four root tastes, like smoke flavor, among others! Anyway, flavor is a powerful motivator to get us to eat, and boy, don't we bite! FISH ON!

Another huge consideration is what you are eating and where it comes from. Once you identify the foods that originate from cruelty, like pork factories, if you continue to consume them the cycle will flow through you. After you know and continue to eat it, then you actively participate in the torture, and karma will do what karma does, it teaches. We were introduced to it by our ascended parents for that reason. Very young children only take or receive, and so cannot yet learn to give, so we are taught about Santa, to take a step at a time, and to teach them how their behavior affects how much they get. If we are good, we get more, and if we are bad, we get less. People who eat meat are still spiritually young. They are not to be hated or looked down on, but seen for what they are, children in that particular grade or those who will eventually expand to the dark. *Eating meat lowers vibration* and keeps them at a low-grade learning level. Once you get older, you are ready to ascend to new levels of learning and you move beyond ignorance and then beyond the childish, "taste trumps the suffering of others" state.

*"If you want to find the secrets of the universe, think in terms of energy, **frequency** and vibration."* ~Nikola Tesla

First, flesh is heavy and dense and consuming it *lowers your frequency*. Second, the meat industry is a Hell on Earth, abomination in every sense, and that the lifetime treatment and extreme torture that these animals endure is something you would no sooner put your dog through much less you or your child, and the vibrational signature of the suffering and torture the animal experiences then flows into you when you consume it. Now comes the choice of choices, because *now you know,* and you can't hide behind ignorance. **Every bite makes you complicit in their agony**, once you know. When you live in a society that allows slavery, no one is free, and when you take it to the next step to torture and then consume them...**all** participants will be consumed.

Of course, meat is delicious and the meat and dairy industry is *subsidized,* by the *same forces* that provide us all with free pornography on the web, to make it *seductively* cheaper than the non-meat alternatives. Of course, the vast majority of restaurants, don't cater to vegans and there are burger, steakhouse and pizza joints on every 7-11 street corner. An inconvenient truth and your *unavoidable* choice! Do I *ignore* the plight of the animals for **taste, convenience, and *price***, or do I turn from it and endure a more austere life that spirit needs and *ego always fights.* "Addictively indulging" in all *carnal* pleasures ensures continued *incarceration*, while turning from them raises your frequency.

They are giving you sign after sign and clue after clue, to turn away from them, with the endless pandemics *obviously* (okay, not obvious to most) pointed at every carnal pleasure aspect. STD's and AIDs (there is no "Aids virus") point to sex; Mad Cow to beef, Swine flu to pork, Bird flu to poultry, E coli to meat and dairy in general and oceanic radiation and mercury poisoning to fish. Also, the fear generated by the *news* of new illnesses lowers your frequency as well. *The unplugged SELF-aware crew in their austere little* **sub** *in The Matrix symbolized this dynamic, to turn away from, what you are submerged within.* It's not easy as your ego fights it and your body makes you uncomfortable while tempting you to indulge. "Ignorance is bliss," Cypher laments, as he no longer has the willpower to resist and bites, taking the *savory* carnal bait. The harp that immediately plays is the clue to you that he reduced his frequency, and his death is symbolic for his fall back into the 3D matrix of the Iron Age, as Hollywood keeps cranking out the clues.

Every choice, action, and thought leads you to or away from the light. To the light raises vibration, and to the dark lowers. Everything, minus the "Still Point" observing, is a vibration in the universe, and we "here" at this level operate within a particular spectrum. You are either at the higher end or the lower end that maintain your illusory "solid" reality you see as your body and the environment of your life. The, "No one knows the day or hour", means that your path to the light, increasing your frequency, **has to be a way of life**.

Matthew 24:38 "For as in the days that were before the flood they were *eating and drinking, marrying and giving in marriage,* until the day that Noah entered into the ark, And knew not until the flood came, and took them all away; so shall also the coming of the Son of man be. Then shall two be in the field; the one shall be taken, and the other left. Two women shall be grinding at the mill; the one shall be taken, and the other left. Watch therefore: for ye know not what hour your Lord doth come."

Noah was no longer of the world, living like the others lived. We are told by a credible, though attacked, authority, that the world loves its own, so as Noah spent his time *away from them,* to build his Ark, he was becoming less *popular* and more demonized and castigated by the day. What castigated Noah, is what crucified the *credible authority,* we are all submerged within. His now all-important daily work was to insulate himself by working on his Ark, but it wasn't a boat he was creating. Noah spent years increasing his frequency, working tirelessly on his **Arc**! Here are the **shocking** details!

An Arc in electricity is a highly luminous hot discharge between two electrodes, that *arches* between the two. *An electric Arc. . .hold that thought! (It also has a geometric identity). An Arch, along with supporting weight, is a curved structure spanning an opening, like a curved bridge between two points. A bridge between two points. . . hold that thought!* The 7-11 School of Duality is, as I have said, a polarity school, and everything in our "electric universe" runs on, well, electricity! If you have not read "Thunderbolts of the Gods" or "The Electric Universe" by David Talbott and Wallace Thornhill, or seen their videos, then I suggest you take a look, as their evidence and conclusions are fascinating and very compelling. *"Exploring feature after feature of the planet, he* *finds that only electric arcs could produce the observed patterns." -David Talbott, "Symbols of an Alien Sky"* In a positive and negative world of ever-flowing currents, you've heard me say "a few times" that every thought, action or choice takes you to or away from the light.

Do you really want to remain in a negative world? You will not move to the class of 8 if you hold on to the trappings of 6 that keep your frequency at the lower end of the spectrum. **"Cymatics"** shows that every vibration produces a corresponding geometric form. *Form* is the organization of energy at certain rates of vibration and that those forms are maintained within a particular spectrum. It also amazingly demonstrates that that change in form, from one spectrum to another is *virtually instantaneous.* As frequency increases, or decreases, to the limits that maintain the particular form, the form rapidly fluctuates *far more than normal*, and then right at that critical fraction of a moment, as frequency changes, even more, it has now moved beyond the spectrum and the form changes to reflect the *new form* of the *new spectrum*, and **that change happens in the blink of an eye**! It is nice to now know, what the "Harps and Trumpets" mean in SO many movies and stories!

"Enter through the narrow gate; for the gate is wide and the way is broad that leads to destruction, and there are many who enter through it. 14 "For the gate is small and the way is narrow that leads to life, and there are few who find it." -Matthew 7:13 - 14

*"In a moment, **faster** than an **eye can blink,** at the sound of the last trumpet. Indeed, that trumpet will sound, and then the dead will be raised never to decay, and we will be **changed.**"*

-1 Corinthians 15:52

In one of the more "hard to swallow" biblical accounts, we have a **man,** Noah, and more about his special identity later in 12, who found favor with the Lord. *"Noah was a righteous man, blameless among the people of his time, and he walked faithfully with God."* This from Genesis which leads you to believe that Noah's thoughts, choices, and actions, were taking him to the light. My fellow truth seekers, of all the stories that hint of an allegorical interpretation, the story of a man building a giant wooden boat, big enough to hold two of every kind of animal on earth, and all the necessary food, to ride out a world covering flood for 150 days, this one blows horns loud enough to destroy more than just the walls of Jericho. Let me offer this interpretation as this came to me at about the same time as the "Smith Equation".

Noah was preparing, as we are now, for the advent of a new spectrum, or better known as, a new age! Noah wasn't working on a wooden Ark all those years, but he was working on a vessel, his body, and the *"Ark"* he was working on was his own internal Arc, his frequency! He was, through his thoughts, choices, and lifestyle, as he was no longer "of the world", increasing his frequency to match the increased planetary frequency. He knew the "Inconvenient Truth", and knew what to do, to find the narrow gate to the new spectrum of higher vibrational resonance. As the Age made that "blink of an eye" change to the new, more complex geometric reality, his signature allowed his *Arch* to "bridge" the gap between the two realities. He and **his line** found the "Narrow Gate"!

Now, what do the animals in Noah's Ark really mean? Here is my take as I go out on another limb. I am reminded of something I heard on a fascinating video that my son brought to my attention in 2015, so I am adding this in the revision. Sometimes you need to see or hear something that you know, worded a bit differently, to make sense of something else that you couldn't previously put your finger on. Writing this revision made me look again at what the animals meant, within what I already knew was Noah's "Temple", because of something I remembered from "Kymatica". This is one of the ways my mind works, but as I'm writing about who the Apes, in "Planet of the Apes", really represent, I am on the part where "Caesar", the leader of his band of Apes, changes his perspective toward "The Colonel", and by shedding his hate, ultimately allowed him to save the Apes confined by the Colonel, who are under him. As I am writing, I am hearing Ben Stewart say these words, and I immediately connect it to this concept:

"Homosapien's gestation period of 9 months mimics the 3.8 billion years evolution of all life on Earth. The human embryo repeats the evolution of all species. When the sperm and egg unite, this new creation is a single-celled organism. Within hours, this single cell divides and multiplies more rapidly than any other species. Four weeks later, the embryo begins to develop gills mimicking aquatic life. A few weeks later it develops lungs and a tail with reptilian appearance. From there, a mammal is recognizable, and then on to a primate form. It then sheds its lacuna which is the embryonic fur. And at last, shows the characteristics of a human child." ~ *"Kymatica"*

And that, to me, crystallized the meaning of the animals he *saved.* Just as everything here is contained within and *under* God, in the hier**arch**ical progression here, the animals are below, and contained within **us**. They are the decimal 3's below us within our pyramid so to speak, so Noah being saved was saving the *world's* **animals** that He contained. His family represented his human spiritual children and the animals represented his non-human spiritual children below them. If he made to the next spectrum, he would pull them up as well. And this is another example of how eating meat is cancerous to humans, as they are literally consuming aspects of themselves. This is also why I put animals in bold, as polarity dictates two directions, and plants will always be an aspect of waveform creation, (this ties directly into what **Evita** adds at the end of this chapter), but animals take the step to begin the progression *back* (making the 2, polarity end perspectives) *to the light,* step by evolutionary step, as the quote from Kymatica, so eloquently demonstrates.

More *ARCtic antARCtic POLEarity* clues

Also look at all of the clues encoded in "Arc", and in what words we find these 3 letters. I've already covered its electrical meaning. In Geometry, an Arc is a closed segment of a differentiable curve. I've covered Arch, and when it is used as a prefix, it designates a *chief* or *principal* title, but it too begins to take on an obvious *electrical* polarity characteristic. Words like Archdiocese, Archenemy, Archnemesis (I know her!, sorry I digress) and the list goes on and on and you see the polar picture taking shape. And then there is the typical example of a certain person or also a thing, we call an Archetype. Carl Jung applied this concept of identifying the basic makeup of the human psyche into categories that represent fundamental human motifs, like Creator, Ruler, Explorer, Outlaw, to name a few. When arch is used as a suffix, it again designates leading, leader, ruler or principal, like Monarch. Archeology, the study of human history, has not been accurately portrayed. We have to discover it for ourselves, as we become the Chief Builders or Architects of our personal development. And remembering I've pointed out that the Divine Feminine is the waveform **core** of creation with curved lines being feminine, while straight lines and the angles produced by intersecting straight lines are masculine... Well, one of the most famous Arch prefix words incorporates these 2 principles to describe *who* the title identifies. It is none other than **Archangel** (the curved Arch + Angle = Arch-Angel) communicating the divine union of the 2 Royal polar dynamics. Back to "Treasures"!

Hearing can and does far exceed its base survival usefulness by addicting many of us to music, as I recall the introduction of *Apple's* iPod. Endlessly listening to music does not allow for "Stillness". Keeping young mind's distracted is key and the vast majority of the music is tuned away from love and into frequencies that stimulate aggression, which exacerbates the dynamic. And nothing distracts you from living like a cell phone that keeps you addicted to never-ending texting and internet *searches*. They don't call them *Cell* phones for nothing as they keep you in a dopamine addicted loop, of endless *searching*. Few interact physically anymore, as people out at the parks are looking at their phones. I actually saw a woman looking at her phone while skiing in PC.

Speaking of phones, we are the individual smartphones receiving the Internet signal and pictures our eyes see, which is, in fact, the decoded signal. So knowing the matter around you is a picture made in your mind, solid matter around you is an illusion, including your body! An important point here, when you give in to the body and take the bait, you are giving in to an illusion. The urge to bite and the fleeting pleasure sensations are illusions. When you spend your life consumed with chasing one illusory, fleeting pleasure after the other, you are playing a dead-end game and you are a slave. You are a child who spends his day eating candy. The moment after you swallow the food, that sensation is a distant memory, just the same as if you had swallowed it a year ago. You are all consumed with the next morsel you can put into your mouth, and the sensation only lasts as long as the food is in your mouth.

All body ego pleasures have the same urge to fulfill, and after you do so, it's gone, and you set out in the same cycle in drug addict-like fashion. The orgasm (and 99% of the time it matters *not* how you achieve it), the adrenaline rush of base jumpers, drugs, gambling, sugar, cigarettes, alcohol, you name the addiction, is the bait put on the hook. If you are addicted to one or any combination, then you are *punished* in several ways. Most only think the obvious consequence of obesity or ill health due to various addictions to be the only physical malady of excessive sensory overindulgence. It isn't, and until you recognize it as the illusory worm that it is, you will take the bait and suffer the consequences for getting hooked by the low-frequency bait.

Anytime you bite, just for the pleasure in an additive fashion, your frequency is lowered, and that is why you feel drained and used after you give in to the urge. You don't feel good about yourself, and reducing your electrical energy negatively manifests itself in three major ways: (1) The reduced power leads to system failures and an overall reduction in operating integrity. This is the real reason we contract illness and bring injury accidents onto our reality, as they are not out there, is due to this power and frequency reduction. There are no accidents. If you become ill or break your leg skiing, you brought it on yourself. (2) You are also setting the table or dialing in a new frequency, and your body will change channels for the new path you are choosing, as I will explain in the next chapter dealing with sleep. If you keep biting and staying undisciplined, you won't like the new frequency path you wake up to. (3) Leading an undisciplined life guarantees you stay in ego and continued blaspheming of the Holy Spirit.

Time is of the essence to **be** the change you want to see in this *Twilight World*, as there is no miraculous overnight transformation. It occurs one mind *and body* at a time and it is hard, NOT EASY!!! I was as tied to eating FLESH as anyone! I DESIRE the taste, like candy. I came from a very modest middle-class urban household bordering Baltimore, and my grandmother worked at a pork slaughter plant and she took much of her pay in meat. She was a good cook, and I ate meat daily. Before about 2010, I could never have imagined I would ever not eat meat. After I saw what went on in slaughter plants, I was devastated at the level of pain and suffering these animals endured and I simply HAD to give up pork, no matter how much I coveted the taste. When someone tells me that they could never give it up because they like the taste too much, I don't argue because that is where they are at, but that doesn't mean that I can't (or you) and move beyond consuming flesh even if others don't. I took it a step at a time and it started at end of the year of 11. First pork, and then very early in 2012, beef and all other "red" meats and then poultry in 2013. Cutting out eggs and dairy was the last to go, and tough as can be because dairy is in *so* many things. "It is done"! That line means dying to "this", the pursuit of the Material, and it *matters not if others don't* do this. Can you control what others choose or think? Of course not! All you can do is control You and You alone control what you choose to think and do! I didn't get permission or wait for the world to turn vegan to give up consuming flesh and dairy. It matters not that the slaughterhouses still operate and others still eat what they kill. All that matters is You! You will never *see* your "evolution" until you take the step to "evolve". The journey of a thousand miles begins with the first step! If you don't, *I couldn't care less,* because I can't control what you think or do...only *me*. The choice is yours!

Because we exist within a programmed equation, any desired pleasure you seek and then obtain, must at some point be accompanied by the *opposite of pleasure* as the equation balances itself out. I have seen this SO many times in Vampire movies, where the vampire goes through immediate extreme pain (flesh getting ripped off, or something) after he experiences extreme pleasure, and I always wondered why, up to now. It stands to reason that there must be universal laws in place to thwart excessive overindulgence or it would never stop. Parents know this all too well. There simply must be limits on the cookies the little monsters consume, and if you don't set limits, the universe will.

Someone brought up that "satisfied" feeling you get after consuming the "perfect" steak dinner, as justification to continue and that it "must" be good for you. Think of it as an extension of taste and an added pleasure that your body experiences to get you to continue to "bite" and feed that which can never be quenched. The beast in the east will do what it needs to do to survive and be fed. Consuming meat and dairy is literally a drug addiction, and your body reacts the same way after you get, *your fix, you feel great like they do.* I know it is hard to wrap your brain around, and few can. You will hear, "it's good for you", and from their body-centric perspective as most are in. They are giving you great advice from their lower frequency, separated level, for a healthy, "long" class stay, erh, I mean life! While fasting is good for you, it is something that shouldn't be "forced" on someone, especially a young developing child, and my polar, who would be the first one to sneak "animal proteins" would raise "Hell", if I made exceptions for our children.

A common *justification* argument for meat eaters is that something *must* die for life to continue and since *killing is killing,* we will continue eating both plants and animals because plants are no less sentient than animals. An arguable point, as everything seems to be these days, but even from a superficial evaluation, at least Vegans are cutting out the animal half of the equation or the *middleman* so to speak. The animals that they are eating still ate the plants they claim they want to save. And that's not even taking Light eating and higher frequency into consideration, and the goal is to need as little as possible to avoid death, which of course opposes "life", and they simply can't address frequency and polarity. I have become more of a "Frugivore", that only consumes the reproductive product of the plant, to nourish life. Fruits, seeds, nuts, and beans, are "naturally fabricated" reproductive aspect of plants to give, sustain or create more life. The bulk of my diet comes from these plant reproductive "sacrifices", that don't require killing the plant. And I eat a fraction of what I used to eat on top of that, because as I said, the higher your frequency, because you are more *Whole*, the less you need of anything, as opposed to Separation, that pulls you in, and like any addiction, always leaves you wanting more, never full, never quenched.

"13 Jesus said to her, "Everyone who drinks this water will be thirsty again. 14 But whoever drinks the water I give him will never thirst. Indeed, the water I give him will become in him a fount of water springing up to eternal life." 15 The woman said to Him, "Sir, give me this water so that I will not get thirsty and have to keep coming here to draw water." ~John 4

It is amazing how I now permanently "fast" from animal products that I had such a hard time with earlier in my life. I now know that my frequency was much lower and my body wanted to maintain that frequency and made fasting very uncomfortable for me causing me to attack it and turn from it. I bought into that mindset because I desired it and I did not yet have the knowledge of my true Self. Nothing is as it seems and belief, discipline, and faith can overcome what you have been conditioned to believe you need as much as the "oxygen" you breathe. Believe a "virus" causes your illness, and you will exist in that frequency to manifest this belief. That "satisfied" feeling, is generated to motivate you to reproduce it to keep you consuming dense lower vibrational flesh to keep your "flesh" at that frequency! What the spirit needs, and what the body wants, will almost always be at "odds".

She's like EF Hutton, when Evita Ochel speaks, I listen!

"In my 15 plus years of research and education in the field of human health and nutrition, it is safe to say that I have heard it all when it comes to the various justifications used against plant-based and vegan eating. And I empathize, for I was once there too. This is why I am not in the business of convincing anyone of anything, as I know that we each get to where we need to get to when the time is right. I focus on educating and helping those who are ready. And so whether from a health perspective

or a spiritual perspective, there is no other food more ideal for humans than plants — specifically real, whole plants as created by nature.

The reasoning used by some that we have to "kill something" in order to live goes completely against the basic biology of plants. This most specifically applies to their botanical parts known as fruits, but also to any other parts that they readily produce and release, namely seeds, which include most nuts, grains, and beans. However, it can even apply to leafy greens and other plant foods, depending on how they are harvested. For example, we can easily pluck leaves from a plant without destroying the organism itself. Regardless, whatever our individual perspectives may be about the various plant parts, the message is undeniably clear when it comes to fruits and their purpose as a deliberate and perfect food source for us. Everything about a fruit — its color, odor, and flavor makes itself appealing to us. Fruits are abundant in all areas of the Earth most suitable for human life, minimal effort is required to obtain them and they are perfect to eat in their raw form, where no cooking is required. When we consume a fruit, we are NOT killing it, rather we are integrating it with our body and honoring its life purpose. If we don't eat the fruit, it breaks down and decomposes on the ground. If you don't eat an animal, on the other hand, it continues running around and carrying on with its own activities and life purpose.

Unfortunately, much misinformation has been circulated about limiting our fruit intake in our modern-day society, with some people fearing it will lead to certain undesired consequences. However, fruits have never been, nor will they ever be the problem responsible for our health woes. Fruits are the most energizing, cleansing, detoxifying, healing and nourishing foods available to us and most easily digested by us. Fruits and other whole, plant foods rich in sugars or starches only become a problem when our bodies are already taxed by diets high in fat, from animal foods and oils. Fat, not carbohydrates, are at the root of insulin resistance, which leads to blood glucose regulation problems. Wholesome fruit sugars readily supply our body with its optimal and much needed fuel — glucose, which our human body is perfectly suited to deal with. Unfortunately, we've mistakenly equated the destructive man-made, iso-

lated and refined sugars with the natural sweetness of fruits. Fortunately, times are changing and we have increasing amounts of enlightened information, even backed by quality science, coming to the forefront.

There is a reason why ALL spiritual (not religious) traditions pointed to the exact thing **Scott Beringer** *is saying — non-violence / Ahimsa. Yes, all life is sacred and this means we respect plants and fungi and even bacteria too! But the biological clues plants give us and their very different nature and makeup allows them to feed animals (including us) and continue living and giving. Fruits aside, take even an Oak tree (or any similar seed or nut plant). Nature provides an abundance of acorns (seeds) to start new life, much more than is required for the continuity of that species, and the excess will either go to waste (decompose) or be eaten. The acorns are just laying there and no violence is involved in eating them; either we pick them up and use them or they go to waste. The same cannot be said about eating any animal parts, where some degree of violence is always involved in consuming their flesh or secretions."*

~**Evita Ochel**, Consciousness Expansion Teacher & Author

"Do not pray for an easy life, pray for the strength to endure a difficult one"

— *Bruce Lee*

6. Superhighway to Heaven

Sleepy? You Drowsy Driver, You!

"Each morning we are born again. What we do today is what matters most."
—Jack Kornfield's The Buddha's Little Instruction Book (page 79)

Dorothy discovered that Oz was a dream. We all know that when we dream, we just start dealing in it, and don't remember anything "before" it. No matter how ridiculous it is, we don't question the unbelievable nature of it. No matter how insane, we just live it and go with the flow. Your thoughts radiate 24/7, and create your world around you, within the *dream* of the collective.

"We are what we think. All that we are arises with our thoughts. With our thoughts, we make the world." ~Buddha

This 7-11 School of Duality in this electromagnetic universe we find ourselves in is the ultimate school of the divine, where its graduates get the ultimate divinity degree. The school we are enrolled in is an all-encompassing interactive video game, where every choice we make leads to a different outcome, reality and of course, consequence. All possibilities are built into the game so no matter what choice we make, the game has the appropriate reality or consequence based on what you choose. Every decision you make and the thoughts you radiate affect what path or reality will come your way. You can look at it as being rewarded or punished for your actions, and the beauty of it is that not only will you learn from both, but being *punished,* tends to transmit the greater, more impactful lesson with longer lasting retention. Try to think of it as the appropriate consequence for any choice you make to allow you to learn the most.

Let us now look at how our choices and thoughts program the appropriate paths we are set on to best teach us. The frequencies, we call our thoughts and actions, tell the program what we need, and what it gives us, even if we end up losing money (psych!), is the perfect response, no matter how much your ego tries to tell you differently. There are endless riches to rags stories of people who lost millions along with their reputations because of *poor* choices, and the multitude, seeing only this reality, lament their situations as horrible, but fail to realize that their "fall", is a lesson they must experience! Of course you empathize and of course, you will protect the weak, but know that no one or thing gets what it does not need to experience, whether you understand it or not!

Sleepy? Time to Change Lanes!

You start your day in harmonic resonance with your surroundings, whether you like it or not. Your frequency, produced by the choices you made the previous day, are now in harmony with the path you find yourself on as you awaken. As your day progresses, you will make choices based on your thoughts, beliefs, temptations that you give in to or resist, and new information that alters thoughts and, if profound enough, shifts your paradigm. At the end of the day, because of the changes to your frequency that your thoughts and choices have produced, you may now be at a different frequency to the path you woke up to. Sleeping is what brings the two back into balance and harmony. When you fall asleep with the new frequency you emit, the mechanism of sleep changes the channel to the proper path or, as I will explain below, changes lanes of like frequency so that upon awakening, you are once again in harmonic resonance with your path. As you sleep, the act of changing realities or frequencies manifests themselves as dreams. If your dream starts out somewhat unpleasant but ends pleasant, the good choices you made are taking you to a path of higher frequency (to the light) of more love, and you will no doubt like what the new day brings you. Conversely, the more fear-based, ego/body pleasure-driven choices you make, the more they will bring you unpleasant nightmares, and the path you awaken to will include the luck you don't want and may be laced with misery in all its different manifestations to some higher or lower degree.

Whether or not you consciously like the station (path) you wake up to, rest assured, you dialed it up. And it isn't necessarily the "you" here, as it may be the "real astral You", who has an agenda that you are, as yet, unaware of.

Instead of Path, Think Highway

Strap on your seatbelts, because once we change lanes to the next right lane and the highway *splits*, it's going to be a long ride! Think of life as the ultimate superhighway, and your path as a lane of travel. Your smart car, the one you look at every day in the mirror, is on cruise control, and all you have to do is change lanes to the left or right. You steer to the new lanes by the choices you make and the thoughts you radiate. You emit a frequency and you increase or decrease its frequency with every passing thought and action. Those you resonate with are in lanes closest to you, and those you do not are farther away. As you set off on your daily adventure, your travels take you to what you need to experience.

Most of your choices are trivial, as in drinking one more cup of tea. Others, though, take a bit more thought, and the weightier choices will no doubt affect which lane you wake up in. The cashier makes a mistake and gives you more change and you know the twenty extra you received will come out of their pocket. Give it back, a lane change to the right, keep it, go left. The coworker who thinks you're hot just happens to push all the right buttons in you, and you are married, but it's right there, and your body is screaming at you to dive in. Giving in to this is multiple left lane changes in one fell swoop. Step over the man on the sidewalk who *is in need*, and you have the means and time to help, so you just steered to the left. Dwell on the negative and fear all day, gets you a left change. Every action or thought turns your wheel to the right or to the left. The left lanes take you to the darkness of separation and ego identification, while the right lanes take you to the light and love of Unity.

There are a vast number of lanes, and those closest to you on either side don't seem to change, just as from one day to the next, you don't seem to age, but there is a difference. Every lane to your right is slightly less curved and slightly more elevated, and of course, those to the left are slightly more curved and slightly lower. The left descends into the dark depths of ego and materialism, with story after pleasure / misery-laced karmic story. The right ascends to the light of divine SELF-awareness within the unified whole. If you look at it from above, it looks like a huge circle with four lines that branch off. Within the outermost unbroken circle are circles inside the circle, all the way to the center bulls-eye. There's that target again! But this looks like a real target and you don't want to hit this bullseye, or I should say fall in! If you look at it from the side, it looks like a huge cone, like a funnel, with a handle, and what looks like a bullseye dot from above is a hole. Now a few of the extreme right lanes, let's say three, all the way to the outer edge and top, split away and take you from the Route 666 loop in Iron County. There really is an Iron County in the Masonic state of the golden plates.

Most of the people in your daily lives occupy lanes pretty close to you, and they come in and go out of your life. As you change or they do, you drift apart. Everything matters, and even being indifferent keeps you changing lanes to the left. Being openly rude, confrontational, or condescending will get you multiple lanes to the left, and as I said, you will come into contact more often with those in like lanes. Inflicting pain, with cruelty and humiliation, having no respect for life, and you will find yourself near the bottom of the funnel in the company of similar ilk. You can send love to your brothers and sisters with a simple look, and if I speak to someone, I try (I said try, haha) to always be respectful and try to leave them with a smile. When you speak from the heart, people know it, and most respond and you can feel it. Be of service and help with a smile, for as I said, not only are we one mind, but those in your life are usually your extended astral family that are oh so connected to you. And the travel lane you wake up in will be so much better for you and so full of "good luck", yeah right! In the end, you may just end up on Route (7) 77 off the 666 loop.

"Those who are able to see beyond the shadows and lies of their culture will never be understood, let alone believed, by the masses." -Plato

Here is what I believe he means by "seeing beyond the lies". Those who gain knowledge of their true identity see this "reality" for what it is, now understanding the shadows and lies of their world, as children must be taught of Santa before they can grasp the concept of giving. They now understand, they were always loved as they are allowed to experience the hard lessons en-route to discovering the hidden truth, as discovery through experience is the only way to "know" know-ledge, and so Dorothy has a whole new understanding of Love by experiencing its polar opposite. Our home is not this "Follow the Yellow Brick Road" temporary holographic projection, that most cultures, certainly western cultures only identify with. So, Those who are now able to understand the **necessity** of the shadows and lies are not understood by the few who only identify the *deception*, much less the masses, who can't even see the *deception.*

So many of us complain about the horrors and injustice of the world and "choose", not consciously, to stay mired in anxiety and depression because of what we **"see"**, but did you see it on the news or hear it from the teleprompter reading talking heads? The mainstream media is as controlled as our governments. They are forced to force-feed you everything that keeps you from realizing who you are and to keep you biting at separation. It is their job to keep you in Ego, full of dualistic drama and frequency-draining fear, because that is how the children learn, and it is up to you to stop biting at the bait. The world isn't as screwed up as they would lead you to believe. I almost never watch it, and if I am somewhere where I hear it, I use it as an opportunity to look for hidden messages and refuse to be dragged down.

Navy Seal and other Special Forces training is tough, but transitioning to the light from a dark life rivals, if not exceeds, it. It isn't easy, because what spirit needs to grow, to expand, is adversity, and if you only have to deal with what is pleasurable, there is no growth, and *we are* God, The Self, growing. This is a projected dream, as so many clues tell us that we are out here in the Dark in an extended dream. This is why they give us the monumental clue of sleeping **at night!** And to add emphasis to the clue, when we fall off into lala land, we do so under the influence of the Moonlight which is a reflection of the Reality that Shines! In 2013, My Astral Self made himself known to a close friend of mine who thought he was dealing with me! This is an Iron Age dream, no matter how real you believe it to be. "Don't fight the darkness. Just turn on the light" (unk. origin). I hear the Aquarian dream is much more *harmonious*! *"Come with me, if you want to live,"* with the accent, of course!

Frequency, the new borders, of the New Age

Our world and our perceptions, built on Separation, are changing by the day. Nationalism, the world chopped up into individual separate pieces is a form of this perspective. This was a necessary developmental period, as those who were *like one another*, came together. Now, prior to the formation of the United States and the rest of the "newer" western (clue here) hemisphere countries, your national identity, was also your ethnic identity. Meaning, obviously, that if you were from France, then you were ethnically French, as well. You came together with others who were similar (looks and language) to you and conversely "different" from all others in all of the world's other countries.

"The Times They Are A-Changin", as the world is rearrangin.

Nowadays, your country, for the most part, is no longer synonymous with your ethnicity and that is absolutely the case in the western hemisphere. I am American, but my ethnicity and racial identity come from various countries in Europe and I have many American friends who represent virtually all of the world's ethnic and racial identities. The news recently has been consumed with the NFL player protests involving the Anthem and Patriotism in general and the associated uproar from fans, that has grabbed the attention of virtually every American and much of the world, as Trump chimes in with his usual

2 cents. In 2005 my worldview changed dramatically and I entered "Conspiracy". In 2011, I began to see the world in Duality and Polarity and I identified the number 11 with this state. I have said for some time now that "Hollywood" and the greater entertainment industry was created "primarily", to send messages to those ready to "see" them, and mind control and duality bait to the rest.

All major professional sports are part of this entertainment industry and they deliver messages, at the proper time, to be seen by the aware and *less aware*. This entire NFL patriotism flap could not prove my point better. The NFL, from purely a business perspective, would never alienate themselves from huge segments of their fanbase if strictly money, was their driving purpose for being who and what they are. They could simply keep them off the field during the anthem or require them, like they require them to speak to reporters, to stand in a respectful manner as the anthem plays, and *all of this* would not be examined, but we are at a time when we must examine it. Oh, but just exactly *what* is being examined?

I'll take it a step further and put this into the context of the overall Age change. Nature exists as a working Whole and no part of it exists in a vacuum. This was recently confirmed on a grand scale after it was realized that reintroducing the wolves back into the ecosystem of Yellowstone National Park, brought back a balance of wildlife and plants that had been missing and changed the very course of the rivers by bringing back this vital piece of the "Natural Puzzle". The Satanic perspective had taken Wolves out, because it is compelled to control, and it thinks it knows better than the natural order, and the area suffered and was **ill**, as a result. *Nationalism is a mental construct form of forced separation and control. In its extreme state, it's a cancer to the whole.* Do you see the parallel? Most would not think much about it without some bait or poking thorn to bring our attention to it.

Enter the NFL and the "Non-politician President", who is shaking up everything, *whether you like it or not*. People are now questioning what it truly means to be patriotic for themselves personally, or to the wisdom of always looking for a leader outside of yourself. The divisions forming among these differing wavelengths in America, and the rest of the world, could not be more obvious. *I believe the new "borders", that are right around the corner, will be frequency,* and your future "compatriots", will be those you resonate with, as the cream is actively rising to the top. Those who are of different frequencies and opposing polarities are moving further and further away from each other....as those destined for the sun-drenched branches, move further away from those destined for the dark roots, in our "Self Same Tree"! Take note, that in the Thor (the new ones from 2011 to the present) movies, all races are included in Asgard. They are all Asgardian because of their frequency and perspectives.

Like the Highway to Heaven analogy, the Stairway works as well. Heaven and Hell both begin with H, the connected 11 of Duality, connected by the horizontal line of Her. The "Stairway to Heaven", is also the stairway to Hell, depending on you, going up, or down. How one takes these steps and how YOU control your "luck" and your life, are the only questions in life worth asking. Directions are paths, and the path to Unity lies in our "Manifest Destiny". Go "West" Young Man. It is the "Right" path, as opposed to the Left. Yes, these words have 2 meanings! Here are a few lines from, "Stairway to Heaven".

"There's a feeling I get when I look to the west, and my spirit is crying for leaving.

Yes, there are two paths you can go by, but in the long run, there's still time to change the road you're on."

No Love - No Happy, Know Happy - Know Love

As we change ages, time seems to be moving more rapidly than normal because more things are changing at a much quicker pace, and change is what really gives you your sense of time. We are not just viewing the change, we are an integral part of the change and so we feel these "changes" as forces working on us, very much like the physics definition of acceleration as these forces speed us up, slow us down and turn us in different directions, continuously changing velocity like we are on a roller coaster now, when we had been used to the people movers at the airport. The slow moving, little changing front porch times of Mayberry are no more, as we are moving to a section of the river that has rapids, and we have seen nothing, yet.

Whether or not you perceive yourself as one of the ones to whom it has been given, but just feel ready to move on, and want to know how to "ride" the rapids, the advice here may be of assistance. We are here to reach a particular level, on our path to **Self**-awareness, so in this filtering period between the Iron and Bronze Age, let's discuss some requirements to "consider" that may elevate, and point us in the Right / Light direction. We have two planetary bodies that we see virtually everyday that we don't need NASA to "tell us about". One shines and provides us with *everything, and* one reflects the *Light* of the other, so in this final chapter, let's take another evolutionary step to a deeper understanding of many "key" concepts, and how we can completely *play,* our own game.

We are told to love all, but until you know what love is, this will seem unreachable. Most confuse Love for pleasure and desire! We all hear the never ending, "I love this and I love that and love hurts", as that is the song of Ego on the Desire roller coaster, that we were all meant to ride on for a time. Love and happiness are chosen states of being and seeing in unity will help you find that state of minimal judgment in assessing the full spectrum polarity *events* that unfold around you. So finding this minimal judgement, "love", state of being *is* a very import- ant and you will know you have found it when you are perfectly happy with what and who you are "at this moment", with someone **or Alone!** So much of life is a paradox and this Truth is no exception. You have to be just as happy and content with being alone, as you are with being with someone, if you are to find this "state". This love and happy dynamic are inextricably linked and both "misunderstood".

If your *"happiness"* is conditional, as in "I'll be happy when or if", then you are again linking "happy" to pleasure or "fun" and they are not the same. One is 5 sense physically based, and the other, a beyond the physical state of being. If someone leaves you, and you become sad, then you are missing the pleasure they are no longer providing. If you "allow" (no one can *make you*) yourself to become unhappy if someone leaves you, then you have given away the control of your happiness, as you are not the master of you! This also applies to "being offended", as no one has the power to offend one who will not allow themselves to be offended. If you are offended, you allowed it. And didn't we already learn this in Elementary School? Remember Glinda's, "Never Let", warning to Dorothy! When you do, you will comport yourself in a manner that is very unattractive with a clinging, possessive personality that screams *low self esteem*. If you fear being alone, you will drain the positive energy out of those around you, repelling them, making you the main cause of the condition you hate.

Virtually everyone is *looking* for *this need* to fulfill a desired pleasure, and a hard wired compulsion to find a partner to reproduce to continue your genetic line. It's part of the lesson criteria to keep us on the pleasure / pain karmic roller coaster, which is of course learning at this particular level. You don't need to *find* love out there, but usually people don't like to be too introspective, because they just don't want to face their *skeletons*. Carl Jung said, *"People will do anything, no matter how absurd, to avoid facing their own souls."* We are all "pulled" down by our dark side programs that we struggle with and usually give in to, causing us to be unhappy with ourselves with many of us starting life with a dysfunctional upbringing which is by no means "accidental". I doubt there is anyone who hasn't looked in the mirror at some point in their life and said "I hate you", which leads to hating others, cementing separation and fear. Inflicting pain to others you perceive as "bad" or inferior is much more justified when you believe they are completely separate from you, but as you now know, inflicting cruelty to others and animals is inflicting cruelty upon yourself. At some point you will learn what you need to and accept yourself and transcend, because what you "hate", is not the "real You", but the programmed ego you and your "acceptance", is knowing that this is just what you need to work on, and until you do this, you won't find that *Heart Based* "State of Being". And *this* State of Being is *Everything!*

"The soul is a stranger trying to find a home, somewhere that is not a where." ~ Rumi

Be the change you want to see and don't succumb to the never ending surrounding *sorrow* from questionable videos and counterfeit news, which is not to be confused with empathy or protecting the weak within your sphere of influence. Attempting to endlessly save others from the lessons they generated and must experience, retards your growth and theirs. The egoistic mind of form will always attempt, through a constant stream of thoughts, to take you from the happiness of the here and now and dwell on memories. Your constant thoughts **direct** your reality, and they emanate from you 24-7, as a constant song being radiated into the field and acted upon, so take ownership to control them. Those who love you are all around you, when you "open" yourself *up!* Do not *always* depend on five-sense reality and look between the lines for messages. When I stay strong, positive and disciplined, I make my "right" luck, and when I succumb to weakness, I make my "left" luck. Refrain from being obsessed with your appearance, titles in life, or money and material toys, as they will vanish. Turn from being obsessed with what others think about you or how they view you. Forgive, as "they" are really an extended you. Try to keep a perspective of minimal judgement and remember, this is just a projection, for the God-inspired Target commercial and **so** many other clues tell us so!

The hundredth-monkey effect isn't just for those engaged in monkey business. Your enlightenment benefits all. Take an *interest* into "why" you are here! I will use this quote from Petula Clark because it nails it, and whether she or songwriters Hatch and Trent realized it or not, a higher authority spoke through them. The *Dark's* necessary agenda is to keep you busy and distracted on everything that **doesn't** matter, to keep you concentrating on the path that leads in circles, as you **down** your upside down cross energy drink to "get *stuff* done". "Look at you go!", like dogs chasing their tails, and don't we all know enough of those people. The "movers and shakers"! Careers that take you from loved ones to accomplish superficial goals within the dream to gather "treasures". Here is a nice quote from Ms. Clark that I saw on DailyMail.co.uk, from a recent interview where she admits, "I wasn't a good mother because I was away so much. I tried hard to be the perfect mother, the perfect wife and a great performer. I thought I could do it all but it can't be done. Sorry, but it just can't. I had a good stab at it, but being a parent and married is a full-time job." She is wise to know it and brave to speak it. There is a reason God spoke to us through her lips. She is right, much to the disdain of the Satanic feminists whose goal is to brainwash women to believe that superficial careers are paramount, like the *paths without heart Don Juan* described. I've included "A Path, with Heart", in its entirety within Appendix Four.

The most precious endeavor we can ever engage in involves interpersonal relationships, and none are more important than a mother's relationship with her child. Life really is all about interpersonal relationships, not the lies the evil programs lead you to believe. If there is *no life*, then there is **no life**. Who do you love? Who loves you? Whom have you helped? Who have you impacted? Who have you shared good times with or wiped their tears and given them yours? It is not about toys or ego illusory positions in the game. No tombstone has the epitaph stating "I should have put more time in at the office!" Do you love and respect the earth and other life-forms? Just as God sees through you, God sees through them, and make no mistake, the earth lives, and she sustains us. The transition period is here, and being blind or indifferent will just get you left behind and do you really want more of this? A child that is ready for second grade will not want to repeat first.

This book is only for a very small minority near the top of the collective pyramid who, like Neo, knows that something is now markedly different. The status quo is now severely lacking and *so very* unfulfilling. They are changing, and seeing things, that before were not there. We are moving into a new higher frequency spectrum, a new reality. Things that can't be explained by the senses or addressed as fixed "laws" in textbooks, that would not have occurred in the world we grew up in. Hollywood is giving us clues as well in movies like Avatar and Thor, showing us aspects of their worlds that fly in the face of Newtonian Physics or our understanding, which is vague, of gravity. Animals forming bonds or associating with other species that we were taught are competitors or locked into a prey / predator paradigm, carving into stone their programmed relationships, that should not be forming a friendship bond! Everything is changing, and it is time to build your Ark!

Like *Home*, Love is a State of Being. Like *Love*, Home is where the Heart IS

7. The Terminator and Your Twin

Hasta la vista, EGO

So many themes and messages that I discuss here have three meanings or interpretations: the openly obvious face-value one, the deeper one just behind the facade, and the even deeper one that points to the very meaning of this endeavor we call life. As I have shown you, The Wizard of Oz, The Lion King, Beauty and the Beast, Prince of Persia, The Matrix, and Terminator all display multi-level meanings. The Matrix and Terminator share a common and very popular theme: humanity being enslaved by self-aware machines. This premise apparently resonates with people, even if they don't consciously know why, because both were very successful with several sequels.

It's an interesting concept that we would be trapped in a computer program or enslaved by a self-aware machine that outwardly tells us that our godlike qualities are our weakness and undoing, and you see this played out during Agent Smith's words to the captured Morpheus. Ultimately this perspective is shown to be a lie and, in the end, saves us after we reach a summit of **Self**-recognition, where we are no longer blaspheming the Holy Spirit. Once this occurs, the machine itself is now no longer the colluding adversary but a willing and eager collaborator to propel its host to new heights of SELF-realization.

In Terminator 2, at the house of Miles Dyson, you have a symbolic meeting between a *Self*-aware person, the young John Connor, and someone who lives entirely in ego, Miles Dyson. The Terminator is the symbolic body of John Conner which is why they are *joined*, and because Connor is Self-aware **and** *in control* of his body by increasing his frequency, it is now his obedient ally whose mission is now to save him, as opposed to being his enemy set on destroying him. The SELF-aware John Connor is showing the unaware, the true programmed mechanical nature of the body by having the Terminator rip off the skin on his arm to expose the machine. Dyson's Ego is traumatized by this, as he screams on the floor, not wanting to accept the reality of the *human condition.*

He begins to acquiesce and realize that while he remains only ego-aware, he will remain a useful puppet and prisoner within the body and the collective Artificial Intelligence mechanism. We will eternally serve here as prisoners to the machine we *look* at daily until we recognize who is really *looking*. This is very distressing knowledge to the unaware, and most will do anything, as you well know, to keep from facing it. He now knows what he needs to do and begins to accept the truths the Self-aware John Connor is telling him and sets out to work with them and lift his awareness and simply do the *Right* thing.

His *"death"* at the lab was the symbolic death of his Ego. The self-aware machine that imprisons us **is** the body (and why the Bible identifies it as the Beast), and the greater body that our body is an individual cell within, and that **is the esoteric message** of the movie. The current "War on Terror" IS the beginnings of the machines v. man conflict outlined in both movies and *the Terrorists* targeted, are higher frequency humans, who exhibit the heart (light oriented) based traits outlined by Agent Smith. Now you know why the very citizens of the countries fomenting this global assault, treat their own citizens as Terrorists. It will be false flag after false flag until they have what they want, from those who would never use them for evil (dark) purposes, but once you (the individual) choose the light, and decide turn from this, then what they do, will no longer be relevant to you. This will become crystal clear by the end of the book. As you read, piece by piece will be added to the puzzle picture I am building, for *you.*

Of course, as the Matrix series began to get deeper with more emphasis on personal responsibility to raise one's frequency and be disciplined, its popularity fizzled. And most never get past chapter 5 in this, after *eating meat* and some *other activity* gets mentioned, and then I go from sliced bread to public enemy, Number One. "For whoever will save his life shall lose it", means turning away from this Ego paradigm or its control over you. This is not a quick death. It is not just the *"crucifixion"*, but all of the unstable times leading up to the betrayal. Then the betrayal, as you now stand in judgment of the Religious leaders, and then Caesar's courts with their Lawyer representatives whose ultimate allegiance is to them. Those in power who control here, will judge you, ridicule and mock you as lies circulate to those in your circle of friends and family. It is walking in pain and suffering carrying your cross, and then the crucifixion and at some point, *"It is done"*, and your Ego dies to this, and you let go of the riverbank, and allow the river to take you to **Its** destination, as you no longer look to control in what you have now identified. That identity will become crystal clear as the water calm, through the chapters.

"Or do you not know that your body is a temple of the Holy Spirit within you, whom you have from God? You are not your own." 1 Corinthians 6:19 (16 = 7)

Not knowing, and of course most don't, is blaspheming the Holy Spirit, which Jesus tells us **is** the only unforgivable "sin". (I'll cover the identity of sin) The "you are not your own" says it all. God made the body as a vessel for self-expression and growth, and when the self-aware (ego) vessel goes on its own to pursue its own agenda (it is supposed to do this), then the vessel or body is programmed to oppose this agenda, and in so doing provides us with necessary lessons as the Ego is eventually broken. We exist in a God growth, organic supercomputer, and You by virtue of your awareness of natural law and polarity, along with the willpower and discipline to increase your frequency, will produce a body, that works with you to achieve the agenda of God growth. Conversely, the agenda of Ego development will break down and always run into dead ends. How you treat and view your Temple is paramount.

We have known for about 100 years now that matter and energy are interchangeable. Max Planck the German theoretical physicist "coined" the term, The Matrix, in describing the existence of a mechanism that requires consciousness to be present to bring the wave to a singular point, the ever elusive atom. It smashed the "reality" of

Newtonian Physics and modern science confirms it. So when ego sets off to pursue *its* agenda, the body will become the adversary of ego and work against it through injuries, illnesses, faulty judgment and aging. This enslavement dynamic is our egos trapped within our bodies and our collective ego trapped within the electromagnetic mechanism of our world and no matter the lengths ego goes to search for perfection, autonomy and immortality, it is always a dead end. The *now* dying Peter Weyland in Prometheus laments, **"There is nothing"** to his decapitated robot, who replies, **"I know"**. Ego will always come to a dead end inside the "mouse" ego maze. There is only one God-given escape, through non-ego Self Awareness. And remember what happens to Neo at the very end, the real meaning of unplugged and to the inner light, just as light envelops the Beast and Thor as they are transformed, no longer trapped in the mortal body, having died, to this!

The Twin

Thomas **is** an Astral Self in the divine royal line, and I'll expand on "who" these are in *Jupiter's Ascension*. Your identity will be revealed during this critical overlapping of ages, and until you know your true identity, which is to be as Jesus or "The Christ", you will remain the "Doubting Thomas"! The apostle Thomas was also called Didymus, which in the Greek means "twin" or "double." Thomas is a masculine given name and is based on the biblical Greek Θωμᾶς, which is itself a transcription of the Aramaic te'oma úàåîà, "twin." The given name of Thomas the apostle was **Yehuda** (Jude, Judas), and the name of Jesus was **Yeshua**. The Gnostics, giving you a clue, called Thomas the twin brother of Jesus, as this is a metaphor for your true Divine identity of the soul and spirit being a "Son of God" in the line of Spiritual Royalty.

The Wedding, or more accurately "Weddings"

All were in attendance and if Jesus (a member of the royal Davidic line) attended, then this was a significant wedding indeed. His mother and all the apostles were in attendance, and it occurred, strangely enough, in Cana, largely populated with Gentiles. It is interesting, to say the least, that in this setting as just a guest at an unknown's wedding, is where he performs his first miracle. You will be blown away a bit later, hopefully again, as I show you that the truth simply had to be hidden, and why the accounts of this miracle are only contained in *"John"*, and no other!

Laurence Gardner, in "Bloodline of the Holy Grail", makes more than a compelling claim that this wedding was, in fact, the betrothal ceremony of Jesus and his future bride, Mary Magdalene. The man spares no details in this book, and on this point, I completely agree with him.

"Just as the men who were appointed to various patriarchal positions took on names that represented their ancestors - so too were the women styled according to their genealogy and rank. Their nominal styles included Rachel, Rebecca and Sarah. Wives of the Zadok and David male lines held the rank of Elisheba (Elizabeth) and Miriam (Mary) respectively. That is why John the Baptist's mother is called Elizabeth in the Gospels, and why Jesus's mother was also Mary. It is also why, in compliance with the same practice, Jesus's own wife would also have been a Mary."

-page 69, "Bloodline of the Holy Grail"

While the book is amazingly detailed (the "Devil's in the details"), I don't agree with all of his evidence and conclusions, and I reject his attempt to explain everything in the Gospels as a misinterpretation, mistranslation or metaphor so as to reduce all of the divine activity and miracles, to five sense, completely ordinary acts. That, and the fact that Laurence Gardner has a rather large *dog* in this fight, and his attachment to the noble household guard of the Royal House of Stewart, makes his assertions, especially to the nature of Jesus and his motives, extremely subjective and massively slanted. While I agree with Gardner's claim that Jesus and Mary were *married*, it was a union that cannot be easily understood by those without heightened awareness, as your frequency will determine whether your eyes see

ordinary or extraordinary. **They** were not here to represent an ordinary *male/female* union, as I will lay out in Chapter 12. Metaphysical
is *so* much harder to *see*, than the *physical* blocks in your playpen.

He is also a proponent, *which further confirms my point*, of taking
dietary supplements to make you more godlike, like monatomic
gold, in the same way, the Satanic ego needs technology to be as God.
(remember Apple's logo) I feel it should be avoided, if light is in your
path, in favor of God's apples that keep the *Doctors* away. I agree with
the brilliant investigations of Anna Hayes. She claims that the initial
growth of psychic awareness is not permanent, but rather levels off
and *later declines*. Further, she says, "Monatomic gold is an Illuminati
deception. While attracting the public with sugar plums of enhanced
psychic clarity and improved health, the ulterior purpose of promoting monatomic gold is to cause the destruction of the ten additional
virtual DNA strands which all humans possess and which are now
manifesting into 3D reality as seen with the 3, 4, or even 5 strands
of DNA that now show up in the blood of Blue Indigo (Millennium)
children".

It appears this *gold* is not a shortcut to bronze, or any other "out there"
supplement for that matter. To me in the movie "Limitless", there is
a reason the "pill" is called "the clear" and looks transparent to clue
you into realizing its placebo nature, as they tell you to eat properly
and avoid alcohol. It is all about your own internal frequency as you
have a spiritual agenda to develop and there are no shortcuts in the
Matrix, to substitute for your spiritual growth! Another nice clue in
the movie has them entering the **11**th Police Precinct, with a 911 sign
in the window.

Gardner's associations, promotions, and agenda are very transparent, and it is in his best interests to portray *Jesus* as a very ordinary
man with very ego-driven motives. He needs him to be just a man,
and her, just a woman, in the "royal" Davidic line, nothing more, and
certainly not God in any way, shape, or form. And He was anything
but, as our ascended Lord came to develop and deal with the prod-

igal egos, the lost sheep, and taught them who they really were and how to attain elevated "Christ consciousness". I think we covered his views on sex, and if he is not "to whom it is given," then no one is. Yes, Gardner has a rather large adversarial *god* in this fight, that fights the eternal polarity battle!

Mary doesn't *only* represent who she is portrayed to represent

Again, Gardner is correct that the only way for Mary and Jesus to have had the authority over the servants would be if they were more than just invited guests. What if they *were* invited guests or *presenters* for a *second ceremony?* As I will lay out, I believe we are now speaking of another symbolic second wedding or *union* that will soon take place, after the first. The Mary who spoke to Jesus and the servants, is not who you have been led to believe, and if Jesus is the bridegroom, then who is the other *half* of this magnificent clue?

The *Master* of the feast called that mysterious someone, the "bridegroom". As you will learn, this is an internal event, and the Master of the feast is also the Master of the House! "The master of the feast called the bridegroom, And saith unto him, Every man at the beginning doth set forth good wine; and when men have well drunk, then that which is worse: but thou hast kept the good wine until now." He is, in fact, saying that the wine that was being served before was just "passable", but this new special wine that Jesus had provided was superior! What he really meant is that *every man, to this point, has given their best to man, and their inferior to God, but the Bridegroom, has saved His best, for God.* This transformation is happening to a man, later in life.

So they had been drinking for quite some time, for the "men have well drunk" as this was not early or mid-ceremony as we had been taught or led to believe. It appears this new wine was for the new ceremony *later* . . . for "they". They have no wine. Let me say this again. The unknown bridal party has no wine. The fact that this ceremony is the event where he performs his first miracle means this wedding was uncompromisingly important! There are no two ways about it. This wedding was monumental, and the fact that the wedding party was not named speaks volumes relating to its esoteric value, for it was not meant for the spiritually young who would not have understood. This was meant for the very few *individuals* **right now** who will find the singular narrow gate by seeking, knocking, and finally knowing *who* **They** are **and** *living it*.

It was held in Cana, a largely Gentile community, so this wedding was not restricted to a certain group. The mother of Jesus and the disciples, who preached to the flock, were there. Mary says to Jesus, "They have no wine." His reply is a bit enigmatic (but you have me), yet respectful, as *woman is a title of respect and distinction.* "Woman, what does your concern have to do with me? My hour has not yet come." Mary though is no ordinary woman in the gospels, and her identity is as cloaked as the man behind the curtain, because this relationship is as ineffable, as any concept can be, and I will do my best to convey through words. Let's see if we can make the nonverbal connection and see if we can make some sense of the *"bridegroom"* equation.

Mary cues him, that this **is** the ceremony to begin his hour. Why does He *need Her* to cue Him? It will be completely explained in the final chapter, but it is for the same reason God created "the woman", from the man, to be his "helper". She again is not who or what you think she is. So continuing, her concern is for "they"! The fact that they have no wine must be remedied, for if steps are not taken now, the hour for *they* will not come, and it must because *they* are vitally important and the reason Jesus and Mary are at *this* ceremony! **I will tie all of this together in Jupiter's Ascension,** but it is important to read on and take in what is explained between now and then as if it were just "presented here and now", you would probably reject it, as there are **two "unions"** taking place.

"They have no wine." And You and I are *they*! Mary tells the servants, *"Whatever he says to you, do it."* Do you think she is just speaking to

the servants? She is speaking to you! "Now there were set there six waterpots of stone." Six, the number of creation, empty vessels, "each holding from twenty to thirty gallons." (20-2 or 30-3, 2 and 3 = 5, the number of man and the divine message) "Fill the waterpots with water." Where there is water, there is life and the number for water is 4 with 5 letters, the base, left masculine plane of The East. He symbolically created **spirit**, the vessel through which God experiences and expresses itself, and then immediately transformed it to "spirit-*containing* **soul**" by changing it to wine. Of course, the water is still there, but now there is something added to it, and what he added, was *Superior*. The number for wine is 6 with 4 letter, for the 10 of the perfectly Divine Spirit.

So now the vessel is a man and carries Soul within the Holy Spirit, and as I outlined in "The All that IS", once the spirit receives that metaphysical essence, that blank slate of God that is the Soul, it is now on a mission of its own, and that mission is to become God, as in more God through God growth, and the water turning to wine completes the agenda. This marriage or union of Spirit and Soul is "The Dance", to create the house for the newly created Master. Apart, the waveform Spirit has no memory and the Soul has no vessel with which to actually experience and grow. When bonded they navigate experience and grow, but apart they are incomplete. If the positive proton does not bond with the negative electron, both will cease to exist, but once bonded, they achieve eternal life, and so too must life have spirit and soul, for God to grow!

Remember, whatever He says to you, do it.

So the first miracle set in motion the groundwork for the union of unions, the Soul and Spirit union and the Marriage of a Twin Thomas Prodigal to his polar opposite "vessel" of waveform spirit, in what I have coined, "The Smith Equation"! It is an arranged marriage by the "Bridegroom" who became the *Bridegroom at the first marriage*, to establish the new Son and his "Saturnic Sibling", under him (Like Thor is under Odin, and Thor was Thomas, and Odin is Jesus Christ).

In the second ceremony, Thomas (the Thief that repents) represents the Proton, will wed his Elec-lady bride, which is his Electron (the Thief on the left that does not repent). When they "make the bond. They will have everlasting life, to be another link in the cosmic chain of Stars with their Dark Star Polar Partners.

The "2nd Union". *"He is you. Your opposite, your negative"*

The "veiled" Marriage that had to be kept secret *and* the second *ceremony*, is the union of the spiritual **thieves,** as they, or at least one, are not what you would consider *"thieves"*, in the traditional sense, but in our lives, we all *steal*, at some point. This is why Jesus is crucified between two thieves, as one will change course and go to the Light and the other *mock* him and continue on the Dark path. They don't tell you that they are a polarity "mated pair", just under Jesus. He, who is the Christ, must bring together one from "his line" (in his house or Ark), which is the line of The Father, that will contain his twin "Thomas", and one from the line of his Satanic brother, that will contain his *Alter Ego*.

We have all been led to believe that it was just a coincidence that two thieves were crucified with him on that day and that the one to his right, turned from sin repented and ascended and the one on the left did not, continuing to be a "thief" and descended. Wasn't that handy that the one who ascended was on his Right? Remember that Jesus sits at the right hand of the Father! Both have stolen in this life and yet the one that repents, not only is saved from descending into what we have been told is eternal torment, but as I will lay out to you, he is on the path of growth to become, as the continuing "Sun of man"!

If anything was an adult topic worthy of being withheld from the children, thousands of years ago all the way up to today, until the children were old enough to digest the truth, it is the identity of who was being married at the very famous unidentified *Dual* ceremony. To understand this dynamic – that only the "Bringer of Light" can give life to the grape *vines*, that "drink" in the rainwater and produce grape juice, that will be developed and made into wine, in the juvenile depths of the masculine Iron Age of Left brain separation, where the Divine Feminine property of God that brings the light is not only subjugated but scorned and persecuted so that She can be understood – it can only be digested and safely comprehended by an adult mind! This was a wedding ceremony alright, and it absolutely brought together the bride-groom of the one flesh, to stand the Tests, of our God of Time.

From my Glinda:

Wish we had some Shamans around, as you know they were all systematically and deliberately taken out. What I do know is that a Shaman would state that witnessing and being aware of synchronicities is a sign you are on the right path. I myself recall reading the Bible, trying to take it in and I was a young child. My Mom was given a children's Bible, full of pictures, but plenty of reading too. I recall it was a rainy day, I was bored so I read about the wedding that Jesus was invited to, the one where he turns the water into wine because they ran out. I recall the word Bride, which I knew what that meant, and then the word Bridegroom. Nobody uses the word Bridegroom anymore, I mean really do they Scott, we refer to the male simply as the Groom... Bride & Groom, Mr & Mrs (Mr & Mrs Smith). Of course in this world of ours, we place the male in the dominant role and female assumes his name. They have downgraded and often eliminated the Divine Feminine completely out of the equation.

But let's looks at the original tenets as such of marriage. We get the story of man marrying a woman in the sense we are told about it Scott, two humans, a union of sorts, but in the past it was the woman who was required to have a suitable dowry to hand over to the male, we've always been told this was monetary or something of value. BUT marriage, the true marriage Scott isn't about that...is it?? I also began to take in information as a young person and I was completely fascinated with Egypt. My father took me to the Museum and when I first saw Egyptian artifacts I was hooked and wanted to know more. What I found interesting was the Ancient Egyptians who were closest to their history having been around and who wrote of the first times, Zep Tepi had a long-standing tradition that the line of the Pharaoh was not passed male on to male, but from female to male. But this only happened when the Male married the Female in a ceremony that he acquired the title of Pharaoh from the Female, who was already a Pharaoh because she was the feminine.

Their archaic ceremonies to become a Monarch, the wearing of a Crown (Crown Chakra) was actually a recounting of something they obviously witnessed, remembered when humanity was in its highest state of Consciousness or as we have been told....its Golden Age. As we descend in consciousness Scott, we descend into Ages.... In the movie the Kingdom of Heaven the lead character played by Orlando Bloom is as you stated a Blacksmith, working with Iron...the Iron Age, and he truly is in his lowest state of consciousness as he is separated away from his other half, his wife, who tragically at the beginning of the movie dies and is being buried, because she killed herself. The Bride and Bridegroom no longer one with each other. The whole point of that movie could very well esoterically been made to get that very point across. What does the lead character do?? Go on an earthly quest to Jerusalem to find himself again, to find the Kingdom of Heaven. As I stated above the story of the marriage that Jesus attends and the word Bridegroom, this to me it was referencing that a marriage was not a bride making union with the groom, but the complete opposite... the male is making union with the female.

Jesus was no ordinary male, was he??? He was the son of the Divine Creator after all.... so the Divine Male was obviously making union with the Divine Feminine. This is why the verse you shared to me from the Book of Mark, the one where we are warned not to be asleep when the owner or master of the house returns stayed with me. The owner of the house, the master, is the return of the Divine Feminine. This is why in this male-oriented society she is downgraded and cast aside. The male energy, the base part of it doesn't like that it needs her to complete itself. The War in the Heavens, is the same War found here on

Earth....as above, so below. There were signs and symbolism of it every-where. Allegory and story written from all times about it, in their own unique way...trying to describe an event that comes about in a great cycle Scott, a Good Year.... Kingdom of Heaven was directed by Ridley Scott, another movie of his is called a Good Year...with Russell Crowe... it's about a man who inherits a vineyard from his Uncle...Wine... a har-vest... a good harvest of wine is always referred to as A Good Year.

*Where have we heard of a harvest before? When I return I will sepa-rate the Wheat from the Chaff. This is all represented in the accounts of the story passed down...Zep Tepi.... First Times..the Golden Age. Where if one is deemed to be the wheat, then they shall be bestowed the gift of All Knowing and All Knowledge... the union of the Divine Feminine (Knowing) and the Divine Masculine (Knowledge). The Blue is given to the Feminine, hence why Mary is wearing Blue...and Jesus is cloaked in red, the Divine Masculine. **The Divine Feminine is the Holy Grail. The Divine Masculine is the Ark of Covenant.** They are not things, material things, they are vessels that house both aspects of what is Divine within us should we pass the test. Because it is a test.*

In Zep Tepi one passes the Weighing of the Feather against the Heart, which is the holder, the recorder of all intentions. If you lived a good life over many cycles you receive Zep Tepi, if you did not and you do not pass you are destined for Atum as the Egyptians referred to it, or the road to Xibalba as the ancient Mayans referred to it during their End of Times.... this is where the soul was sent to galactic center, where the energy of it was recycled and destined to repeat the cycle again, until it got it right, after all in nature nothing is wasted. However, the memory of that soul from its previous incarnation was wiped clean from the slate, or as the Egyptians referred to it, the Book of Life. After all, if there is a Book of the Dead, stands to reason Scott there must be a Book of Life. Sorry about the ramble....wrote that when I first woke up....I was excited on the heels of what you wrote.

8. The Smith Equation

The Polar opposites of Black and White display the most "obvious" characteristics of what it is to be "polar" opposites. The saying, "It's right there in black and white", means there is no ambiguity, as one is the essence of everything and the other, the essence of nothing. Together they create what is crystal clear, and while they are tied to "something", they are "No-*Thing*", without each other. It is extremely difficult to understand how two opposite perspectives can come together to bring into existence "what can be *specifically* identified", which separately, in and of themselves "dematerialize" into phantom "probability equations"! The Light and the Dark, the eternal dance of the Soul and Spirit!

"A Smith...Agent Smith"

When I saw The Matrix, I paid no attention, that the only Agent named was Agent Smith, back in 1999. Smith is a very common *generic* name that you would expect to see in movies so it didn't jump out at me. Why would it, right? In 2005, the year of my "awakening", living at **1001 New Mexico St in Boulder City**, not being a huge Brad Pitt, Angelina Jolie fan, I paid no attention and did not see "Mr. and Mrs. Smith", contract killers contracted to kill and basically destroy each other, released 6-1-2005. When I was 8, I loved "Lost in Space" and couldn't wait for each week to pass to see another episode and of course guess which crew member was always sabotaging mission after mission to get the crew to return to earth? That's right, Dr. Smith! When I originally saw "Kingdom of Heaven" it didn't strike me as any kind of a clue that Balian was a Blacksmith or him proclaiming to King Richard the Lionheart that he was "the Blacksmith", as I thought he was just done "playing" the game, and while he was, that wasn't the esoteric clue!

When I saw Thor in 2011, the only thing I remember seeing and thinking was, wow, that is quite a coincidence, at the **1001** on the building the scientists used and they were in New Mexico. All of that would change in May of 2014, the 5th month of the 7th year, and when I looked again! A friend mentions something about Thor that makes me go back and look at it, to see what he is talking about and after they pass the 1001, I look at the scientist on top of the building and I see the letters SMI and then SMIT and I can't believe what I am looking at, because of the 1001 and my mother's maiden name is Smith, and I went numb for a bit. I went to other scenes in the movie to get a full shot of the sign because I had to be sure, and there it was, "SMITH". When Thor regains his power, he is enveloped in light, and the *vertical* SMITH sign is perfectly centered between his head and his hammer Mjolnir.

They pan up slowly to make sure you see the 1001 and then up to the 3 sitting on the roof, and I was raised by 3, my Smith grandparents and my mother. There is a man and two women and over them is the SMITH sign 3 times and the number of Smith is 6, on the emptied building. Thor's **here** ID made for him, gave him the name of Donald J, the name of my father, and my DOB month is 9 and his is 11, and both of us born on the 21st, as my second credited part in a film was 21. The building is also at the top of a **T** intersection, just like my house at 1001 New Mexico St., and Ave F intersects at my house, and I finally see this in Condo 11F. I could look down Ave F to the Masonic Temple (tiny BC, has one).

My "Smith" connection, held here by my mother
Patricia Ann Smith

And then I remember Agent Smith and **now**, it's no longer a coincidence and I continue to look with purpose. What I can now *see*, I can hardly believe! I go back to The Matrix, and when Morpheus was captured by Agent Smith, Morpheus does not ask him who he is, but he asks, "And you are?", and the reply is, "A Smith"! Not I am, but, "A Smith, Agent Smith". This too confirms it! Then synchronicity continues to bombard me and I turn the TV on that I rarely watch and The Matrix Revolutions is on and right at the part where Neo is meeting with the Oracle. She points to a wall hanging that says "Know Thyself" and she soon tells him the identity of Smith. *Neo: What is he (Smith)? Oracle: He is you. Your opposite, your negative, the result of the equation trying to balance itself out"*, and it hits me that Smiths are mathematical components of the Light and Dark polarity equation! Mathematics is indeed the language of the universe and a Smith is our body vessel and all of its programming, **with its union** to its "polar" body on the opposite side of the equation that you perceive as separate from you. It is very much a part of you and the overall program and part of the same consciousness that you and your ascended parent are a part of! This is the real reason why, near the end of the Matrix, the Self-realized Neo, jumps "inside" of Agent Smith, to tell you that they are actually joined as two aspects of one mind!

This is actually the next step or progression, explained in "The Terminator and your Twin", after your body has become your willing alley because you have become Self Aware with a *more* subservient Ego, but you *must still deal* with your polar Smith. And they are there to keep you "honest", and I mean on the *right* track. This means, if I veer from the light, *She*, rears her ugly (not physically) head to attack. And really, who is *more*, "The One", to cause the **cataclysmic shift in perception and awareness, Neo or Smith?** Why it is Smith, and I would still be ignorant to all of this without mine / *her.* After you have aligned with the light and rejected the "out-there" dark, you will be mated with one who has nurtured the dark and the program expands out beyond just *you!* Think Thor and Loki and how Odin "Lives" through them and manipulates their realities! I know I have done and said things I didn't *want* to do or I can't explain. Now I see *"why"!* And I've also seen Mr. and Mrs. Smith now, and we had the same metaphorical shootout destroying all I had built, and I, again, see *why! (can't move on with attachments) You can't really call your enemy, an **enemy**, after knowing that you would not have scaled the heights, without him or her in your life.* Hindsight being 20/20 of course, because *during,* you want to smite them, again and again and. . .*sorry,* got a little carried away there!

As I said, You won't believe how obvious some of them are!

So the Old English term of "one who works in metal" is, in fact, the "so below" **clue** to the larger, "as above", spirit carrying vessels developing in the Great Ages of Man! And now with my new awareness, I now understood "I am the Blacksmith" quote in "Kingdom of Heaven". I put the clue together with the fact he is in the depths of the Iron Age, the Smith vessel that **"works"** (develops the spirit), is here learning, in the Iron Age. At first, I thought "Smith" was the ascending vessel and *Black*smith was the descending, but I now see that **that was *not* the clue,** but the Smith within the "Dark or Material" *Iron* Age.

A "Smith" works in metals! A GoldSmith, SilverSmith, BronzeSmith, and Iron or BlackSmith is the body/vessel in each of the Great Ages of Man, the Gold, Silver, Bronze, and Iron Ages. On the small scale, the tilt in our axis provides us with 4 distinct seasons, and just as every "aware" cell in your body contains all of the information of the whole, as above so below, there are 4 grander seasons "of Man" that are brought about by the 26,000 year precessional "Wobble" with relation to our position above or below the galactic equatorial plane and our position within our grander trinary star solar system with Sirius A and B, which our Sun rotates around in an elliptic orbit. The closer we are to Sirius, the more light and awareness we are bathed in and the further away we are, the less we have. The Iron Age, the least amount, is our "winter", the Golden Age, the most light, is our "summer", and combinations the Bronze and Silver Ages make up our Spring and Fall. Bronze and then Silver headed to Gold, and then Silver to Bronze, headed to Iron. Just a man "Falls" back into less light,

so the Autumn is referred to as Fall. And the associated "Daylight Savings Time" clue is, "Spring forward" and "Fall behind".

This too is when the vibrational spectrums of red and blue corresponding with the Smith union hit me. Blue is the color of the ascending Smith and Red is the color of the "polar" descending Smith (and why purple, the combination of the two is the color of Royalty) within the same equation, the ascended parent that sees through both. This is why you see Blue and Red representing so many *Polar* Dualities, like Republicans and Democrats. Superman's costume! The Sky, and as I said, you'll be surprised how sky blue obvious many of them are, and I am far from finished. **Roses are Red, and *Violets* are Blue, another *elusive* in plain view clue!**

The repetitive programs I identified in SO many movies, stories and even the gospels that show a familiar pattern could be dismissed, but then it was taken to another level and I saw that same program being played out in my life. Everything is easy for the skeptic to dismiss and for me as well *until it gets **personal***. I couldn't care less who rejects it. I now see the light and dark division that is taking place as we transition into the new age. I see it because I now see the messages in the films Hollywood sends us, being actively played out in me and around me.

The young have the light and the dark within them, the two wolves, the Sun and the "adversary", the little Angel on your right shoulder and the little devil on your left. The one you feed is the one you will become and after your transition, if it is your time, you will manifest either light or dark and will no longer have both within you as I explained with Neo and Agent Smith above. In the winter of iron, you are the seed. You have the entirety, of leaves that dwell in the light and the roots that dwell in the dark, within you. To the cross above ground, or the upside down cross below ground. *If* you can identify your Smith, you know what wolf you have nurtured and the alchemical work of turning the base metals of tin and iron to gold **is** the mission of the *Smiths*!

Yes, we have a spiritual agenda, here. It is to achieve everlasting life as God grows through this process. After you, the real you of spirit, have learned most of what duality can teach, it will begin to prepare you for your "marriage". The *union* is to your polar opposite and it was arranged by your ascended parents who have already bonded. From the parable, you must be dressed properly, which is symbolic of preparing yourself, by raising your frequency, addressing all of your actions and addictions that keep you *here*. "My Kingdom is not of this world". If you are to ascend, you can't do the things that cement you here, shedding the old clothing of Ego, naked and now looking for the clothing of your purified "Christ Conscious" Soul. The developing sacred heart *twin* "Thomas" will be *joined* to a partner, their Agent Smith, so to speak, which sets the stage for your ascension. But you must first descend into the rabbit hole to cleanse yourself and break your Ego!

"Do you wish to rise? Begin by descending. You plan a tower that will pierce the clouds? Lay first the foundation of **humility**.*" -Saint Augustine*

So, if you are in a specific prodigal line you be joined with your opposite Smith, and one will be the Proton and the other will be the Electron. You see this dynamic in Thor better than any other movie because Thor shows you the generational scheme or progression. While you see it in others like the Lion King, they only show you the basic polar positive blue to negative red relationship, Mufasa to Scar, and while you see Mufasa continue through Simba and see why he had to go through this experience to humble him so that he could claim the throne, you don't see a negative counterpart for Simba once Scar is defeated. In Thor you see over several generations and you can see that Odin's father lives through Odin and Laufey, and Odin is experiencing through Thor and Loki, so that when you "wed" your polar opposite, they aren't yours, meaning you will not live through them, but your spiritual parents will, as they live through you and your polar opposite you are paired with! When Thor bonds with a Divine Feminine, he will then be the bridegroom and he will bring two under him to "live through", and **one** will be his "direct" spiritual child. *"Only **one** of you can ascend to the throne, but you were both born to be kings."*

"No tree, it is said, can grow to heaven unless its roots reach down to hell."

— C.G. Jung (the roots are necessary to the whole, in this beautiful and poignant quote)

"This sprang up from nowhere after my split in 2011. There was never a Sunflower before or after it at my house at **90** Matterhorn in Park City, which is at **7,000** ft. in elevation. It was the most vibrant yellow, and from the flower's perspective, it looks to be pointing
Right"
Why would the **Sun**flower do that Scott?

9. 7 11, Oh Thank HEAVEN

This **is** the 7-11 School of Duality, the "two" dualities of separation and polarity, for the children of God. The Eleven school of perceived physical separation, two people standing next to one another are on the surface of it, not connected, separate and look like the number 11, the one and one next to each other. We are to experience the various light and dark polarities of love and fear, good and evil, masculine and feminine, rich and poor, etc., as the extension of Odin's Ravens Hugin "Thought" and Munin "Desire", so that the full spectrum can be experienced.

In Thor, in the Hollywood created town in New Mexico, the first thing they show you after the town's sign is a 7-Eleven. The Mickey Mouse Club son of the Masons making a music video in a 7-11 parking lot wearing a 7-Eleven shirt. The films they appear in are too numerous to list. The clues are getting more obvious in the school because finals are near and Elevens, along with 711 and 911, seem to endlessly pop up in so many movies like *Back to the Future, The Matrix, Tombstone, Deadpool, The Last Samurai, The Departed or Limitless to name a few!* This is why they named the largest, that you see on virtually every corner, convenience store 7-11 so that you see it all the time. We are students here in the Divinity School for the children of God, and why their tagline is, "Oh thank **Heaven**, for 7-11". You won't see this interpretation of this number combination anywhere else in the world.

The aware will turn *right*, away from it and transcend it, while the unaware stay *left* mired in the elementary, lowest common denominator, "kardasiadrama" (even Star Trek warned us in a clue, over 25 years ago) and continue to bite, keeping them in the "Left mind" where they still need to be. They send you a steady supply of fear, anxiety, and hate because that is the lesson plan, to keep you biting, to learn your lessons. Dorothy learned them and had a better appreciation for where she came from. That is why Glinda didn't prevent her involvement with the witch. Even in the castle of the witch, Dorothy wasn't even touched, and the witch couldn't harm her or *take* her soul. And didn't they pick the perfect Mrs. "Smith" to play the dual horned Maleficent? Hooray for Hollywood showing us the "stars" of Ego in all of their glory. Some are *"Dastane*d*"* to be Stars, while the egos who lack the heart, will temporarily mimic as they die in the shadows of those who *will* grow up! *"Aren't we lucky to have found a line of work that doesn't require growing up?"* ~*Dick Van Dyke*

1001, the Horned Devil "Baphomet" hand sign decoded

You've been told they are the Satanic horned Devil, "Baphomet", hand sign. It's time for some clarity and unity for the various (separation) names and interpretations of the same symbolism. The 5 fingers represent all that 5 represents, and the 2up-3down (2/3) and 3up-2down (3/2) represent different awareness perceptions and convey a basic Structure of the 7-11 School. The two fingers pointed up have the same meaning as the two Horns on the Goat Head that symbolize "Lucifer" and the number 11, and the two mean **Duality**. And there are two "Dualities", *Polarity and Separateness* just as I outlined above. The visually enhanced interesting aspect of this particular way of displaying the 11 is that it accurately displays the symbol of both polarity and separateness by not only providing *more* separation between the two but the index finger is larger than the small or "pinky" finger and the *index* represents the "positive" light polarity while the *little* represents the "negative" dark, for the very same reason Thor and Mufasa are bigger and stronger than Loki and Scar. While they are absolutely tied together, the two are separate *fingers,* just as we can't perceive our connection with each other. Think of the Index as the **One** consciousness, The Self or God, and that's why you always use the index finger to mean One. That's its real meaning as you hear and see their hand signs of, "We're Number One" at sporting events. Now think of the little finger as the Ego of the One. So now that you know exactly what the 2 represent, the 3 represents the Trinity in its entirety.

So with the meanings understood, the two up and 3 down, means we are only seeing in separation, dealing in all of the perceived dangers and differences of separation and polarity. It also means that the identity of the Trinity, most especially our unifying Mother (Unity), is hidden from us. As a result of that Separation and **ignorance**, we are also blind *to Her,* our own internal dark, which is a vital aspect of us, showing us the totality of who we are. Our Mother, the "Elect Lady", the electron to the proton, our Divine Feminine, our internal Divine Dark, is what we are separated from. By the time you get to the breakdown of "Like a Prayer", at the end of Chapter 13, this will be explained completely, and with everything in between from here to there, you will absorb it completely. And as a side benefit, you'll know your dark!

Now comes the new "I love you" 3 fingers extended hand sign *"supposedly" created by the purported occultist,* Helen Keller. It *matters not* **who or how** *it came to us, as both were Divinely created by our admin-*

istrators who created both to communicate a level of awareness. Now that 3 fingers are extended or **seen, being now perceived**, it means we are now seeing the Unity of the Trinity embracing and accepting our Dark aspect and knowing we are all connected to the same body, the same consciousness. Separation is no longer perceived and that is why two fingers are withdrawn, repressed or down. That is why you see so many recently making the thumb extended hand sign lately. When you know that this communicates a heightened level of awareness and that we are all connected, it really is, in a sense, "I Love You"!

This is the 2/3 and 3/2 dynamic that you see everywhere and when you see **M** and **W** (Me becoming We) it can sometimes be a clue. As I explained, the 2 up and 3 down is the symbol for the left-brained separate reality we are coming out of and crumbling, but still very much in and holding on where it can. Here is an example! The logo "M" *Arches*, and there is that *frequency* reference as well, is the logo symbol for McDonald's, and the big M arch stands for 2 up and 3 down, meaning it is the *food and drink,* for the spiritually young or unaware, that are "putting what they shouldn't" in their bodies, and reducing their frequency! An anchor, if you hold on to it, to keep you in Iron! It amuses me when I drive by one and it flies the American flag and next to it is *their flag*, the "Golden Arches" on the red background.

Now I am talking to the guys here, look at your torsos men, taking the arms and legs out of the mental picture. We have a **head** at each end! The bigger head is *up,* and the smaller head is *down!* What they mean when you see the depictions of the red devils with the spiraling down tails from their crotch, with the arrow pointing down at the tip, is that the little head is running the show. Keep the serpent theme in mind, and remember all of the ancient Mesoamerican and Egyptian images of the snake protruding out of the forehead. They are channeling that creative sunlight energy up. Your discipline and willpower have to be great to assume the throne, and conversely, there had to be *one Hell of a strong pull, down.*

I saw a piece on the internet that demonstrates this polarity dynamic of what **is** God and what **is** the lack of God, and that how knowing **the lack of God**, can give you a much clearer understanding of what God is, and why we are here. Even though it is usually attributed to Einstein as the "young student", there is nothing to substantiate this, so I don't know who wrote it, but I like it very much. Here it is:

A university professor challenged his students with this premise and question.

"Did God create everything?" And most of the students said yes. Then the Professor continued, "Then if God created everything, then he is evil since evil exists, and according to the principle that our works define who we are then God is evil".

"Professor, does cold exist?", a student asked.

"Of course it exists. Have you never been cold?" Other students laughed.

The young man replied, "In fact sir, cold does not exist. According to the laws of physics, what we consider cold is, in reality, the absence of heat. Every body or object is susceptible to study when it has or transmits energy, and heat is what makes a body or matter have or transmit energy. Absolute zero (-460 degrees F) is the total absence of heat; all matter becomes inert and incapable of reaction at that temperature. **Cold does not exist.** *We have created this word to describe how we feel if we have less or no heat."*

The student continued, "Professor, does darkness exist?"

The professor responded, "Of course it does."

The student replied, "Once again you are wrong sir, **darkness does not exist** *either. Darkness is, in reality, the absence of light. Light we can study, but not darkness. In fact, we can use Newton's prism to break* *white light into many colors and study the various wavelengths of each color. You cannot measure darkness. A simple ray of light can break into a world of darkness and illuminate it. How can you know how dark a certain space is? You measure the amount of light present. Darkness is a term used by man to describe what happens when there is no or less light present."*

Finally, the young man asked the professor, "Sir, does evil exist?"

The professor responded, "Of course as I have already said. It is in the daily example of man's inhumanity to man. It is in the multitude of crime and violence everywhere in the world. These manifestations are nothing else but evil."

*To this, the student replied, **"Evil does not exist** sir, or at least it does not exist unto itself. Evil is simply the absence of God's love. It is just like darkness and cold, a word that man has created to describe the absence of Love. God did not create evil. Evil is the result of what happens when man does not have God's love present in his heart. It's like the cold that comes when there is no heat or the darkness that comes when there is no light."*

Tomorrow you've got to go to school! *Why?* **Oh to learn things and get smart.**

I'm like Pinocchio (who is not real, yet) here in an altered reality that dispenses consequences for all actions and thoughts. When I lie, it grows and keeps growing until it is as plain as the nose on my face and when I listen and give in to "pleasures" that "Honest John" sells, my "reality" turns into an "unlucky", unpleasant quagmire. The plans of my ego will always lead to "destruction", but in that devastation, I am learning. When I listen and act on the advice of my heart, who sang for us in the film, I catch breaks and get "lucky". What is "pleasurable", can never be satisfied, and what I thought wasn't fair, turned out to be an arrogant boy's sour grapes as I got, and get, knocked down a few, and sometimes more than a few pegs! My, "Honest John", is now more like the scarecrow, and willing to take a back seat to my Todo, my Jiminy Cricket, as the *"plans"*, step aside, for *Faith!*

Yes, Pinocchio passed the test and became *real*, by the hand of our *Mother, "The Blue Fairy". This is you and me. This is not reality, but we must pass tests here, to become real.*

When you wish upon a star /// *When you pray to God*
Makes no difference who you are /// *Ethnicity, Race, Faith, Gender*
Anything your heart desires /// *Heart desires are spiritual needs*
Will come to you. /// *So you will receive it*
If your heart is in your dream /// *When your life's path has Heart*
No request is too extreme /// *Heart requests are never too much*
Fate is kind /// *All of this, is for your own good and development*
She brings to those who love/// *She rewards those who Love*
The sweet fulfillment of /// *You will attain your spiritual agenda*
Their secret longing /// *To become what you pray to!*
Like a bolt out of the blue /// *A gift from above*
Suddenly, it comes in you /// *you become it from within*
Your dreams come true /// *The agenda of the Self, a Star is Born!*
When a star is born /// *When Self achieves its goal*
They possess a gift or two. /// *They create miracles*
One of them is this /// *Get ready for the last line*
They have the power to make a wish come true./// *You will be God*

As the road to enlightenment must pass through conspiracy, the coming years will be monumental, and the divine messages will be nonstop to all but only seen by those who are ready for the next level. To all my conspiratorial siblings who see behind the facade, I know all too well how marginalized you are, and the masses, supremely in the box of ignorance, not only laugh, but get defensive and go on the attack because you are tearing away at the comfortable box they have lived in since arriving, although they can't tell you when they arrived. Not only are you marginalized by the munchkins, but your fear has advanced to a darker, heavier, more resigned state of being and you kind of (but not really) wish you hadn't taken the red pill.

There is a small part of you that wishes you never left Munchkinland because the reactionary, fleeting, ignorant fear they display when the witch pays a visit melts away when she disappears and they once again lose themselves in the lollipop guild and the lullaby league of the game. Their box is still a playpen, but yours has turned into a jail cell. Restricted either way, but now you KNOW you're confined. Even though I know you won't believe this now, just take HEART, because when you do see what/who is behind the curtain, the bars melt away. It, of course, does come at a price, as Cypher couldn't quite cope with not partaking of the sensations, and if you thought you were lonely and marginalized as a conspiracy nut, well, at least you know you are now an adult, and the children and animals are so much more enjoyable to be around!

2 for One. Hell of a Bargain described in the next 3

All of us, are in a relationship, with ourselves! The very essence of the Duality of The Self and the Ego. Both have awareness, but one is real, and the other is AI, the very core of Polarity. One feels Love and Shame, while the other is incapable of expressions from the heart and has no shame in and of itself. Most have no idea that "their" thoughts stem from 2 sources. When you look in the mirror and tell yourself that you hate the person you are looking at, one is speaking while the other listens. The Self stems from the light while the Ego and the body stem from the dark. This is the marriage of Soul and Spirit, and IS the very "real and esoteric meaning", the 2 coming together in the Divine Marriage to become ONE flesh.

In this "Marriage", there is a struggle for dominance and who "wins" will determine an eternal polarity position, as the body, you and I find ourselves in, grows. On one side is Light, and on the other is Dark, and before you begin to demonize, know that God cannot grow without it. Your body is an Atomic (Adam) manifestation of your spirit and so Spirit and your body represent the Dark and is your "Temple" or vehicle (vessel) to "house" your Soul. The body / Spirit represents the Divine Feminine and the Soul is the Divine Masculine. In your life, if you are a slave to your bodies carnal desires, and addictive pleasures, then YOU will not be "The Head" of your marriage and you will be but a pawn of the Satanic Dark but if YOU control your body and its monkey mind that is constantly trying to take your attention, then YOU will be in control and the Head of your Divine Marriage and SHE, will take you to the heights, to become your own light. This is the message of both the Terminator and Matrix series. If you are not in control, then the AI of the body will run you and be your enemy, but if you are in control, then the AI will be your tool to take you to untold heights. *Are you the Head of your Household, or does your house, hold you?*

Only 144,000 (9) Revelation 14 (5)

14:1 "Then I looked, and behold, a Lamb standing on Mount Zion, and with Him one hundred and forty-four thousand, having His Father's name written on their foreheads. 2 And I heard a voice from heaven, like the voice of many waters, and like the voice of loud thunder. And I heard the sound of harpists playing their harps. 3 They sang as it were a new song before the throne (h), before the four living creatures, and the elders; and no one could learn that song except the hundred and forty-four thousand who were *redeemed from the earth.* 4 These are the ones who were not defiled with women, for they are virgins. These are the ones who follow the Lamb wherever He goes. These were redeemed from among men, being firstfruits to God and to the Lamb. 5 And in their mouth was found no deceit, for they are without fault before the throne of God."

This speaks of the mark of your frequency, and remember my Glinda's definition of Virgin! I can only hope that the **11**th hour applies here because I have certainly defiled, and been defiled, so for the ones "to whom it has been given," and I just hope it wasn't given too late! Something tells me it has not, and I am doing what (I really can't say *everything)* I can, to get the hell out of this level. As I said, my life doesn't appear to be my own anymore, as I see things most don't, and when my ego flares up with its wants, it gets shot down. My left knee swells up, and I can barely walk when my mind's not right, dwelling in ego on negativity or weaknesses that I should not be entertaining. After I get my mind right, in the loving and happy place of the now, within a day, my knee is fine.

I get almost immediate feedback on my choices and behavior, with good luck when I am loving and bad when I am not. Nature responds to me, and the flowers and birds communicate with me. Even a bird not seen in nature that pecks at my window at those moments. If I overeat, and I used to eat like a horse, I vomit, and I am now amazed at just how little I need to eat, and I gave up meat years ago, which was **very** difficult for me. I had never had a beard, and my daughter, who sometimes tells me (looking out for me, lol) to color my hair, this time tells me, as I was ready to shave, to try a beard even though it is very gray. She said, "Clooney's beard looks good". So I thought, What the hell. Big changes on the inside and now the outside of me. I feel like I am turning into the man at the market.* And that can't be a bad thing.

I am in the process of defeating my demons and addictions, and while I am doing well, I have one dealing with my nemesis, and every time I am not pure, I hear *him* at that very moment. The *him* is a Raven, and there aren't many up here, who is quick to tell me when I mis-step, and the cawing pierces the rustling of the wind through the tree leaves and pine needles. It penetrates my soul, and I know I fell! And my raven-haired nemesis, who has crushed *my ego's* plan for security, "the best-laid plans of mice and men", in my later years, is now identifying every spot on my white canvas to wipe clean so that an appointment to the throne is a *possibility.* So my nemesis IS from God.

Before enlightenment, my poem was my promise.
During enlightenment, my poem was my lie.
After enlightenment, my poem was my prophecy.

To understand the above quote from me, you would have to know my poem's content and whom it was written for. This projection is a house of cards, and the life I wrote about in the poem that had been given to me was a more stimulating (a lot more) five-sense version of ego that I mistook for life, like the wooden house replacing the straw, but it too was blown down. I am now building my brick house of SELF, but the wolf is always there to remind me...out there! This again confirms that the Wolf is *out*-there to crush our ego's machinations and keep us looking IN, where we should be looking for our own internal development. So it really did give me life, and when I wrote it, I had no idea I was writing of THIS life, not the one of ego I enjoyed at the time, which will always and must always die. While it was dying, I thought the poem was an idealistic, cruel joke, but the experience made me see the box I lived in and stepping out of it has set me free for I now know who I am. And I now know who she is, as she is literally my electron.

Yes, my poem became my prophecy, in this enchanted twilight zone. Right now, it is all about you. Saving you, your enlightenment elevates all of us, but getting out of here is hard, and it has more to do with your friends and family wanting you to stay "of the world." When I was a child in Baltimore, I went with my paternal grandfather one day to pick up a bushel basket of blue crabs. They brought them out and set the basket next to me. The crabs were in a frenzy, and I was surprised that there was no lid. I was only about seven and yelled, "Grandpa Jule, they're gonna get out," and he laughed as he was paying the man and said, "No, they won't, Scott, just watch them." Sure enough, every time one pulled himself up and got near the rim, another below him would grab a back leg and pull him back down. They will try to bring you down, and always will, as long as you allow it. The crabs represent the bodies, that do the bidding of the body that they are a part of, to keep yours, in the *fold.*

There is also an ingenious monkey trap used by the native South Americans in the Amazon region. They secure an enclosure to a tree trunk with only one hole in it, just large enough for the monkey to squeeze its hand in if there is nothing in its hand. They put a banana inside and walk away. The monkey goes to the trap, reaches inside, and grabs the fruit, and while holding it, he cannot pull his hand holding the banana out. The men casually walk up with a bag or net while the monkey frantically screams as they approach, looking like he is handcuffed to the trap, but he will not let go of the banana, and they know this. Sound familiar? God knows us all too well and some won't let go of the Iron Age box. I am letting go! Being in the world, but not of it. I didn't plan that 7-11, 7+1+1=9, would be chapter 9, but then again, none of this is me. It's coming, and when this is torn down, you will know why! Together, we will be prepared for it. No fear! And we will witness the birth of the Phoenix, the true New World Order, and a new, more advanced body, for this is a manifestation of our changes within!

We'll soon be at the apex point for the entire NASA deception with all of the 7 references in the Mercury Space Program to the mighty Apollo Program and the mission, 11, that stopped the world, and even this, as you will find out by the end, wasn't their biggest deception. They had to convince you of a reality that doesn't exist here in this spectrum so that the climax of our time will be "accepted". For now, you are cells in **this** body, and until you move beyond this level, to a larger body, the cells of this body stay in this body. *"I'm not the man they think I am at all. I'm a rocket man"*, as Sir E. John tells us.

We are like waves in the ocean, as your body continually replaces atoms and molecules and replaces old dying cells with new cells, but you remain You. A wave, at the various locations of its journey has different water molecules, but it is still the same wave. Your consciousness is who you are, and that is why you want to lift yourself **up**, from that of a material cell, "below ground" in the roots of the body you are currently in, so that you may become among the leaves above ground of consciousness that never die, which **is** the eternal life. Oh, and your body gives off natural gas and you accumulate and secrete oil on your skin. There is no "fossil fuel", another tall tale for the kids who don't know who they are, and "who" they reside "on". The earth's natural gas and crude oil is a naturally occurring, regenerative process, just like your own body that creates its own. That is why the middle east never seems to run out, and why all the old formerly capped Texas wells are producing again.

The Ritual that was IX-XI, here in the mirrored reality

The WTC Complex encoded the name of our school. As one dark wintry cyclical class ends, the legend comes to life and the recurring spring resurrects itself once more. The greatest clue became the grandest Ritual observed by all, trumpeting the end of the class of 6 and ushering in the rise of 8. *Being familiar with numbers, geometry and Latin helps to recognize the message.* There are clues hidden within the Gregorian calendar and its predecessor, the Julian, as I pause on this name. Septem means 7, but September is the 9th month, to show the special indivisible relationship between the child of God 7 who still perceives in separation, to the young adult God 9 who perceives in unity.

This extends to 9-11, occurring in the 9th month that means 7 and the smoking gun building 7, that falls perfectly down into its own foundation for no plausible reason near the towers that look like 11; **and** Novem means 9, but November is the 11th month, so that the few will see the connection of **7-11 to 9-11**, and 7's ultimate tie to 9. You and I are 7 on our journey of 11, oh, thank heaven, striving *to go beyond the dualistic 11*, that internal fight within, the rebellion of the Ego, for those towers (9+1+1=11) had to crumble at the hands of AA 11, but the 11 that represents someone who comes out victorious of the temptations, disciplined and battle-tested, with the acquired knowledge that transcends the bait of polar dualism. I write this on my avatar's birthday as I just turned 56 (5+6 = 11) on the twenty-first in this twenty-first century (2+1 = 3), 9-21-57 = 7, as I now finish this in 2014=7.

The now blind Samson of the Tribe of Dan destroying the two pillars, after regaining his strength! The end of the 3D Iron cube with its 2D symbol, the hexagon, to the 5D Tesseract, the cube within the cube, with its 2D symbol, the octagon. Look at the "Two that became

One" building that replaced the towers, that represented 11. The One World Trade Center sits atop a cube, with a smaller square at its top at a 45-degree angle to the bottom producing a perfect octagon at the center. It has 104 floors (5) and the perfect octagon has 52 (7) floors above it and below it. It is 1776 ft. tall.

And look at the monument where the Towers once stood. In their foundations, you see a cube within a cube showing you the reality that will replace the cube, and picture as you look down on them, an 8 around them. You also see 4 squares, which is "Foursquare" talismanic symbolism characterized by firm and unwavering conviction; "a foursquare refusal to yield", with assurances of permanence and stability! In "Oblivion" Jack tells his fiancée, "Look through here and I'll show you the Future" looking through the binoculars on top of the Empire State Building (the *current* empire), she sees the One World Trade Center Building, with its perfect octagon at its center, directly in the center of the shot, with the Statue of Liberty on the extreme right (the *now ascended light*). And the number of the **real Jack** within, is **52 = 7**.

While we are here and as we gain awareness, one of the main lessons is to recognize the school within the 3D cube and see beyond that stage of duality. Some of us must transcend it, through awareness and discipline, as the old must crumble. 3D Duality, the ll that the Towers represented, had to fall with the smoking gun building 7 that was never "hit" by a "plane", implodes perfectly into its own foundation. "Pulled" we are told. We are moving *west* to right brain reality, and I will **"prove"** this in "KANSAS Arc-kansas". And by the end of the book, you'll know why the Tower with the 360 ft. spire pointing *up*, was 1 WTC and was the "north" tower that symbolized The Self, and the other was called 2 WTC, the "south", symbolized the Ego.

Occurred on the 11th
On 9/11, 9+1+1 =11
Building 7 and the Towers that look like the number 11
Significant damage to *11* large structures

7 had 47 floors, 7-11

September 11th is the 254th day of the year: 2 + 5 + 4 = 11

First hit by flight American Airlines (AA) 11

AA, the number for A is 1

11:11 is the Divine Judgement, the graduation of 11

AA11 had, 11 crew members

AA11 had 92 total people aboard - 9+2=11

Taken from Wikipedia:

Passengers	81 (including 5 hijackers)
Crew	11
Fatalities	92 (including 5 hijackers)

United Flight 93 = 11

Flight 77 (14=5, and 5 is a divine message) had 65 on board - 6 + 5 = 11

The President in office on that date, George W. Bush - 11 Letters

The Prime Minister of Israel - Ariel Sharon - 11 Letters

Terrorist who threatened the towers in 93 - Ramsin Yuseb - 11 Letters

State of New York - The 11th State

New York City - 11 Letters

Afghanistan - 11 Letters

The Pentagon - 11 Letters

The WTC towers collapsed to a height of 11 stories.

The towers had 110 stories

The Statue of Liberty, with her 7 point crown standing on her 11 point star.

Manhattan Island discovered on 9-11, 1609 (7) by Henry Hudson -11 letters.

AA Flight 77 that supposedly hit the Pentagon was a 757 and flew through restricted airspace designated P-56 which is 7-11

The two Airline companies implicated American and United, and this will only make sense by the end of the book, are for Amaruca and Unity.

The Madrid, Spain bombings took place on 3/11/2004 - 3+1+1+2+4=11.
The Madrid, Spain bombings took place 911 days after 9-11
And the number for the London bombings of 2005, is 7. 7-7-2005, 52 (7) died and add 4 "terrorists" to get 11, and approx 700 non-fatal injuries!

And as I mentioned earlier, Ocean's 11 was my first credited part, as a common abbreviation for it is OC-11, 63=9-11, released 3 months after 9-11, 12-07-01, and 1271=11, and the number of Ocean's is 635151=3, and the series is a Trilogy. The film is 1:57 in length, as I sit here feeling a bit detached.

Let this, sink in. If not now, by the end

Transitioning to Unity and acceptance of our Dark was the real message of the ritual that **was 9-11**. When you attain Right Brain awareness, you become 1 with everything no longer seeing in Left Brain Separation, so that the 2, become **One**. Everyone makes the same mistake concerning "The Matrix", 9-11 reference clue, saying, "Look, Neo's passport expires on 9-11-01", but it isn't "Neo's", and All they see, is the planted 9-11 reference within a pre-9-11 movie. **The deeper clue** signifies the changing of the age, for he **isn't** *Neo* yet! He is still a person who *doesn't know* his true identity and as such is "Blaspheming the Holy Spirit". He is still, "THOMAS ANDERSON". Thomas, the "Twin", but still the Doubting Thomas, because he "doesn't know". The 2, will become One-neO, as She the Divine Feminine "Trinity", searches for "Him". It's why the twin towers merge to unity to become the One World Trade Center, That Jack shows his Lady, Julia (Julian, or "of Jupiter", and my best friend was Jack). The Duality of Separation is eroding and all of the turmoil you see around us is the Satanic foundations being washed away as 9-11, the ritual, communicated. His false identity in all Caps of "Mr. Anderson" issued to him by Rome at birth, that expires on 9-11-01, signifies the old millennium came to an end with the close of the 20th (the 2 of Duality) Century.

All of the evidence points to no planes. Just as with Building 7, no planes hit the Towers, the Pentagon, or a field in Stoney Creek, PA., as the rabbit hole gets ever deeper, and the event, more paranormal.

The new age and reality WILL happen, just as Spring follows Winter. 9-11 was a ritual at the beginning of the new millennium to announce the coming Spring. All who fight to maintain the old cube iron age will find the wide gate leaving the "500 million", the few from the 7 billion, who find the narrow gate.

"And I looked, and behold a pale horse; and his name that sat on him was Death, and Hell followed with him. And power was given unto them over the fourth part of the earth, to kill with sword, and with hunger, and with death, and with the beasts of the earth".

-Revelation 6:7-8

"And power was given unto them", meaning this: remember my reference earlier in the book about the serial killer, and that things that happen, have a reason, even though superficially, they don't appear to, but everything is choreographed. Their language is meant to communicate to the aware, no matter what language they speak. Mathematics, Symbols, Numerology, Sacred Geometry, Synchronicity. It doesn't matter that the entertainer who flashes the triangle has no clue what it means. The ones who put them up to it know, and it is for the few to "see". The few, who "live" the Da Vinci Code, who see clues and directions, where most see evil, or nothing at all, as they play 4 square! The majority will fear it. . . "and that makes enemies".

A mirror confirming a lX-Xl reality and the "Target" message

9 is God here and not here, in frequency and beyond vibration, in the Still point. Zero through 8 add to 9 telling you God is everything and when God is inserted into every individual number, all aspects of creation, you still have the original number meaning God is in there, the observing eye that is the origin of consciousness, and yet invisible and not perceived. Novem is 9 and Nova is tied to Stars and eleven is

535455=27=9. We, those of us here that are not simply Tin men or Agent programs are children of God. God's day is, the 7th day and the created adversarial aspect honors the 1st day of creation and so the polar aspects honor the two extremes of our given 7 day week, the clue we see day in and day out. (every day, is God's day) Sixteen is that perfect teen age year where you are still holding on to that *fun*, "no adult responsibilities" of being a child. You are no longer a small "dependant" child, and asserting some independence revealing your own identity apart from your parents, and that age adds to 7. Just two years later, in the eyes of the government, you are now officially an adult at 18 and that *coincidentally* adds to 9, and then you can do everything at 21 (3).

In the scene where Morpheus shows the newly freed Neo the training program, the room he takes him to has a television and the back of the tv shows us the brand. AWA, 151=7, released in November the 11th month in 1957. The company's first transistor radio was the Transistor 7, also released in 11 of 1957. As I was looking up radiola, LA radio stations came up and the first one I saw was KOST 103.5, and the numbers for KOST are 2612=11 and 1035=9 and they first aired in 1957.

All planned with numerous clues given years before 9-11. It is all distraction for those who will continue to be distracted, to continue biting at the fear duality bait, and that is why when you perceive danger or an "emergency", we are told to dial 911. The masonic powers that run the planet are doing what they are supposed to be doing. All who fight to maintain the old cube will perish leaving the 500 million, the few from the 7 billion who find the narrow path. It is all as it should be. Prepare yourself and don't bite at the 3D distractions. Cut out eating meat especially the tortured animals born in captivity in hellish conditions only to be slaughtered. Raise your vibration by working on your Arc and don't judge all of the madness unfolding all around us. It is all a clue for you, like Noah, to work on **you!**

A friend of mine in Las Vegas, Marilee Lear, who has been a promi-nent Casting Director in Nevada for decades, who I worked with on "21" and several other films, has a prominent husband in many fields, aviation among them, named John Lear. John is the son of inventor and founder of the Learjet, William Powell Lear, and to say that John is an accomplished pilot is a massive understatement. I first learned from him that there were no planes that hit the Towers on 9-11 and that none of the evidence and stated "facts" concerning the plane's trajectory and speed matched with what *could* have happened. In other words, the official story was impossible concerning the planes and of course "Architects & Engineers for 9/11 Truth" state categor-ically, that the official explanation for how the Towers came down is impossible. You already know what I believe 9-11 to be, but my point for this last paragraph is that I read something that *resonated with me* as to just what became of those flights that I know, did not crash into buildings or a field, so I wanted to pass it on to you. If you have any interest in this, then I recommend "Methodical Illusion" written by retired Flight Attendant Rebekah Roth and John has some great information out there detailing what, created the damage in the buildings, brought them down, and made you think planes hit them, and what role the smoking gun, Building 7 had, on 9-11.

*See appendix 5, yes, the man in the market!

10. KANSAS Arc kansas

She Fell from a Star, she fell very far and Kansas She said was the name of her Star!

Now for the *Heart* of the matter and I'll show you something you will have a hard time believing, as if the rest is, right? You'll want to dismiss it because it is so surreal, but it will be as clear as the nose on your face after I point it out! Time for the mother of Wizard of Oz clues! Glinda is the Good Witch of the North and when you think of the winged Caduceus, it is forever traveling "up" and our term for up is North! Another clue in this dynamic is the UN insignia world disc with the North Pole in the center, completely discarding any "thought" of the "south". We all know that ascending is up and descending is down. Look at the lower 48 states and notice the location of Kansas. It appears the clues have taken on macro geographic proportions, and what the Wizard of Oz tells us, has actually been made manifest here!

Pull up a map of the US and see what is in the very heart, the center, of the lower 48, and it couldn't get any more centered if someone tried and I think someone did, so let's look at **Kansas, the Star that Dorothy fell from.** Look at the Flag and notice its background is a deep royal blue with a hint of purple. Its state seal is in the center and displays a star, our sun, rising over purple mountains. The numbers 3, 5, 7 and 8 are encoded in the animals and people and all of them are headed west, except the two up, *and remember the horned, two fingers up, hand sign*, dual smoke stacked steamship sailing off to the east. There are **34, 5 pointed pentagrams** rising into the blue right below their state motto in Latin and all within a circle. The state motto, "Ad astra per aspera", floored me, and translated, it means:

"Through hardships to the stars" or "To the stars through difficulties"

Above it is their state flower, a Sunflower, and looking very Sun-like, and their official nickname is "The Sunflower State! Below is Kansas in yellow letters! The geographical center of the 48 contiguous states just happens to be **Smith County** in the *Sunny* state of Kansas on its *northern* border. I have looked into the numbers and was amazed by the numerology clues encoded all over the information of Kansas, like the highest point being 4,041 ft. which equals 9, or the fact it was the **34th (=7) state admitted into the union** or Eisenhower "Ike" from Abilene Kansas was our 34th president, but going through *all of them* will clog up my main point, as we already have compelling proof, and you can go and check out the other "tellings" numbers if you would like! Suffice it to say they are everywhere, so we will move on!

Now, pretend you are standing in the middle of Kansas, which is the geographic center of the lower 48, and now look to the south or "down". To your left is the east and to your right is the west, so east is left and the west is right! Turn your head about 45 degrees to the "left" and what state would you be looking at? Arkansas of course and there is a connection between the two states, the OK and MO borderline. Now, what part of Arc-Kansas is closest to you? Now you see where I am going! The northwest corner of the state that contains the Ozark Mountains or OZarc. The lower So East corner of Kansas is "connected" by a "wormhole", to the Northwest corner of Arkansas. So Arkansas is down and to the left or lower frequency and left brain perspective from Kansas. Now let's look at Arkansas the way we looked at Kansas and compare!

The Flag of Arkansas has a red background that surrounds the interior which is blue and white. The state name with 4 blue stars and 4 is the number of the masculine *left* Iron Age. Around it, it is surrounded by a blue band containing 25=7, white 5 pointed pentagram stars. Add the 25 to the 4 and you get 29=11. In the great seal, you will find 13=4 stars inside of 4 circles and a Roman eagle with the duality symbols of war to its left and peace to it's right. It was the 25th = 7 state admitted to the union. The state motto is "Regnat populus", which translated means, "The People Rule"!

Down here we rule, or at least we try, as we vaccinate everything in sight and put antibacterial everything everywhere, as we avoid *law-dog rule*. Satan puts on a good show, to most, in this precisely choreographed play and the Luciferian adversarial element has really set up shop in this little corner away from the sun. Psalm 18:2 states, "The LORD is my rock, my fortress, and my deliverer; my God is my rock,.." and *there just happens to be a "Rock, Kansas" and the Capitol of Arkansas is, "Little Rock"! "I will exalt my throne above the stars of God"!* So below, and to the left of Kansas, which is right in the middle with Sun/star references all over it, we have a little image of Kansas electrically connected by the MO-OK (K-2 and M-4 and O-6) border, 666 tornado wormhole, with a length of 34.42 (7 to 6) miles to Oz-ark and further out, could it Siriusly B Saturn, is "Little Rock" run by the Satanic "American" Rothschilds, the Rockefellers, and I'm not done yet!

And you thought Oz was a children's fairy tale! The as above, so below, solar structure is built into the layout of our country and this is encoded in the Wizard of Oz, among others! So not only are there physically manifested geographic clues to the structure of our country being like a solar system (or an atom), but politically too, out here in the little negatively charged satanic "kingdom" of Oz, the clues abound! I found this priceless tidbit by *accident*, as my Glinda laughs!

"Albert Pike was a lawyer who played a major role in the development of the early courts of Arkansas and played an active role in the state's politics prior to the Civil War. He also was a central figure in the development of Masonry in the state and later became a national leader of that organization." - from, "The Encyclopedia of Arkansas History and Culture"

Satanic leaders are alive and well and have run Arc-Kansas for years, from Winthrop Rockefeller to Bill Clinton the nonconsecutive 40th (4) and 42nd (6), with the numerology clue within a clue, and now the entire bombastic Billary machine that, like the Kardashians, never seems to go away, showing the polar relationship and has indeed been a bastion of Left leadership, to go right along with all of the other big, hiding in plain sight clues, like its name and geographic position. I just found this fact about Kansas, after speaking with my son about a college paper of his and then looking into land squatting in the midwest in the late 19th century, I find *this* interesting as it brings more ammunition confirming my *discovery* of these two state's polar dynamic. So, not only was Kansas not a slave state, and of course Arkansas, was, but it appears to have been a major catalyst in the abolition movement!

From ushistoryscene.com:
Kansas: The Land of Promise for African Americans

In the Reconstruction South during the 1870s, volatile racism pushed former black slaves to seek refuge in the Midwest. Many took advantage of the Homestead Act as an opportunity to manage their own households through subsistence farming while forging new lives in the Midwest. The Homestead Act did not ask for an applicant's race (it was assumed, at the time, applicants would all be white), so in order for historians to find African American homesteading family records in the National Archives, they must triangulate them with other sources. Kansas was the ultimate destination for many African Americans because, as Emile Pitre of the University of Washington states ...., Kansas was a place "where the abolitionist tradition seemed to loom large". Its history before and during the Civil War had turned the state into a symbol of freedom and justice for many southern blacks. John Brown, a radical abolitionist who led several armed insurrections against slave owners in Kansas in the 1850s symbolized freedom in Kansas. Although Brown was ultimately arrested and hanged, news of his exploits put Kansas at the **center** of the slavery debate. Kansas was also the first Northern state to allow African Americans to join the Union army in the Civil war, and one of the first to show public support for the Emancipation Proclamation and the slavery-abolishing Thirteenth Amendment.

Go West young man, "The da Beringer Code"

The Vatican has set up shop in the "New", *center* of the universe! On Mt. Graham, just north of the site of "The Reckoning", in the New

Mexico Territory. The Vatican is a member of the Mount Graham International Observatory (MGIO) consortium! **Next** to the Vatican Observatory looms "Large Binocular Telescope Near-infrared **U**tility with **C**amera and **I**ntegral **F**ield Unit for **E**xtragalactic **R**esearch", or LUCIFER, if you are on a first name basis with our Great Architect of the universe! By the end of the book, you will be!

From Wikipedia:
"The 1.8 meter Alice P. Lennon Telescope and its Thomas J. Bannan **Astrophysics Facility**, known together as the **Vatican Advanced Technology Telescope** (VATT), is a Gregorian telescope observing in the optical and infrared which achieved 'first light', the first starlight to pass through the telescope onto a detector, in 1993.

VATT is part of the Mount Graham International Observatory situated on Mount Graham in southeast Arizona, and is operated by the Vatican Observatory, one of the oldest astronomical research institutions in the world, in partnership with The University of Arizona." So why here, in the state I moved to at age 14?

So Amazingly Mystical, how clues that you see today, having relevance now, were set into motion hundreds of years ago. It shows you the Divine Choreography of it all! One of my favorite Presidents growing up was Polk, for several reasons, but now I know why he captured my imagination. You don't hear about him much. Our one term **11**th, the original "Dark Horse". An adult knows the world and the next heartbeat is West. A major clue, among many in what I thought was *just* one of the greatest films, turns entertainment into prophecy. Amazing how clues in this film, the Wizard of Oz, Thor - The God of Thunder, and Avatar, point to a "Territory", all confirming the other and comes to life today! Literally, you can see it, as in country big, and *so 7-11 obvious, that it remains unseen*, because the best clues, like 9-11 and the Statue of Liberty, are big and bold and seen by all.

What began, "East of Eden", ends with the death of the witch of the East, and marches West. The "Manifest Destiny" to the "New World" is a journey over the Mighty Miss Bridge through the *Gateway **Arch***, from the East of Ego, to the West of We. "Go west young man!" The future is the west, as everyone in the state seal of Kansas is heading west as the old outdated steamship sputters off to the east to die, like the witch of the East in Oz. Where does the legendary lawman from Kansas go with Doc? To the west! In the great seal, the wagon is pulled by 8 horses telling us that the new class of 8 will rise in the West!

Now, what is "The West"? It is certainly more than just a direction. It's similar to Wyatt asking, "Well who was the Devil?" The internal Narrow Gate leads *Right* to the *Real* Promised Land, of 8, the real-life Da Vinci Code! From where Oz lies, **the *true* "American Elders" point West to the Sun** with 4 rays of 7 and then just to the west the 5 point Pentagram shines the 4 rays of light indicating the collective gateway of the Narrow path, 5 and 7. They point to the "two" with the most "aboriginal lands". The Law, from the Heart, is coming! For those who pass through the wide gate, Hell is coming with him, as they scatter in "Tombstone"!

"By the time I make *Oklahoma, She'll* be sleeping"

Time to open your eyes and see, *The Point! You are now back in Kansas*, *again facing south. To your right is the west, and in the continental US, we have 11 western states. I've been telling you that the west is to the "**right**", but just in case you need a second opinion, **I just happen to have one!** We have covered the location relative to the Star Kansas, and I have said that the east, the Iron Age, the class of 6 is winding down, coming to an end and that the Aquarian Bronze Age, the class of 8 will rise. The Phoenix will rise in the west. **As the map shows, the "Land of the Red Man", "the Native American Elders" are also pointing from Arkansas to the west, and specifically, the New Mexico Territory! What does the state of Oklahoma look like, as I "Point" you in the "Right" direction? That's right! And the tip of its index finger specifically touches New Mexico.**

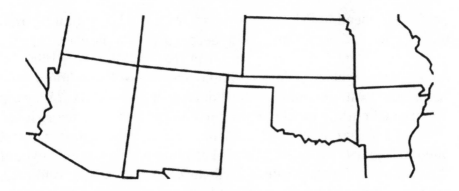

"By the time I make Albuquerque, She'll be working"

So why does Wyatt Earp go to Arizona in what was the New Mexico territory and clean out Satanic control there, and he tell his men that if he gets killed to kick it to the New Mexico line? Why does the Rainbow Bridge from Asgard come to New Mexico in "Thor"? Why is the Vatican Observatory and the "International Observatory Consortium" on an Arizona mountain, less than 100 miles north of Tombstone, in what used to be the New Mexico Territory, And a "Portal", AZ near them next to the NM line? And why did Percival Lowell choose an *Observatory site in Flagstaff Arizona, and where we discover* **Pluto***?* Why is the largest city there **Phoenix**? Why is Los Alamos, NM the birthplace of nuclear weapons, the first nuclear test in **Trinity, NM** and Roswell where we have our first "out in the open" encounter with ET or Interdimensional Grey Aliens? Why is there a city there named *Truth or Consequences*? On a personal note, why did I, on a family fluke when I turned 14, go from my birthplace in the east, out to Phoenix and all of my children are born in the 3 largest cities in the NM Territory, Phoenix, Albuquerque and Las Vegas? Why is LV, known as the Star of the Desert, named for Vega, our former North Star, and being "Vegan" raises frequency? Why do the two-letter abbreviations for all three states equal 9? Why do the abbreviated letters of the 3 largest cities, lv-phx-albq add up to 9? Why is Hoover Dam, which is now fully engulfed in conspiratorial clues pointing to its destruction, filled with extravagant spiritual statues, artwork, and imagery? Why was there an image of a Freightliner truck projected on the dam heading "right" and "west" toward a horizontal figure 8 having a license plate that can be decoded with a message that we are moving from 6 to 8 and from Iron (Fe) to Gold (Au)? Why did my life turn right in Sedona in 2005, and where I saw Tombstone again but now understanding the hidden messages in 2016? Why did the original outline for this book come to me in the vortex rich red rocks of Sedona? Why do the Arizona and New Mexico flags most openly display the Sun, or *"Stars"*? Let's find out why in this light of the stars amid the black canvas Twilight Zone. We are that "refracted, scattered" soft glow of **Him**, who is "just out of sight", just below the horizon, dancing within the dark womb of **Her**! The Black and the White of it, as we reside between the 2.

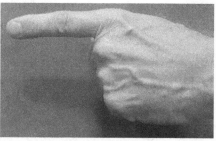

<table>
<tr><td>The New Mexico
Territory of 1860</td><td>That's Right! And even itself
pointing Up, and to the Right!</td></tr>
</table>

The East is east, but the West is Wow!

So why, New Mexico, the Land of Enchantment? It certainly is and I love the American Southwest for so many reasons, but let's look at the name **Mexico**, and see if that holds the answer! Mexico comes from Mexchico and is a Uto-Aztecan or Náhuatl word. It comes from two other words: "Metztli" that means Universe, although in modern Nahuatl the word had the meaning of Moon, and "xiclti" that means navel or center. Mexico essentially means *"the center for the birthing of the universe"*. It appears we do have an answer, and the old manifest state for the material and spiritual physical universe will make way for the "birth" of a "New" "Universe or Reality". You know, there is always a juxtaposed second interpretation and there certainly is here! No wonder I always wondered why the feeling in me was so strong, that not long after I moved to the west, I knew I never wanted to return to the east. And thinking of how Evita and I ended Chapter 5, there is a clue built into the dense foliage of the East, in contrast to the Arid landscapes of the 11, as I look to the West. And it makes me wonder.

Mexico, the center for the birthing of the universe. No wonder Mexicans so venerate Mother Mary, as so many pieces are fitting together for me. This, from Raul Reyes, of NBC News:

*"According to lore, it was a winter's day in 1531 when the Virgin Mary first appeared to Juan Diego, a peasant, as he was crossing a hillside near present-day Mexico City. She appeared as a dark-skinned woman who spoke **Nahuatl,** Juan Diego's **native language.** This woman asked Juan Diego to build her a little house, a casita, on the hill. Twice Juan Diego reported this to his local bishop, who didn't believe him. The second time, the bishop asked for proof of the apparitions. Early on the morning of December 12th, the lady appeared again to Juan Diego and told him to gather some flowers at the top of the hill – a strange request because flowers were not in season in December. Juan Diego did as he was instructed, and found an array of Castilian roses. The lady helped him arrange them in his tilma (cloak), and he returned to the bishop with them as evidence. As Juan Diego presented the tilma to the bishop, the flowers tumbled out and the two men discovered a life-size image of the Virgin Mary on the inside of the cloak. This image is known as Our Lady of Guadalupe.*

*To Jeanette Rodriguez, author of "Our Lady of Guadalupe: Faith and Empowerment Among Mexican-American Women", there are aspects of this story that make it unique. She finds it significant that the apparition chose to appear to a peasant. "That makes sense, because God always chooses the people **the world** rejects," she said. "The Lady of Guadalupe also offered a different brand of faith. She didn't say, go to church or say the rosary. (Matthew 6:6+7 says something similar) She* *said "If you love me, trust me and believe in me, I will respond." The his-torical context of this story is important, according to Rodriguez, a pro-fessor at Seattle University. The apparitions were seen only ten years after the conquest of central Mexico by the Spanish, at a time when the indigenous people of the Americas were devastated. The notion of a brown-skinned Mary figure was critical to the eventual conversion of millions of indigenous people to Roman Catholicism. "When indig-enous people saw Guadalupe's image on the cloak, they could recog-nize the symbols surrounding her;* **the sun, the stars, the southern cross,** *and the placement of her hands indicating a gesture of offer-ing," Rodriguez said. The sash around Our Lady of Guadalupe's waist, Rodriguez explained, indicates that she is with child – one of the rare depictions of the* **mother of God as pregnant.***"*

To confirm my message, because the *numbers* don't lie, the 11 western states lie to the west of Kansas; directly up or above is 3, the Trinity, and directly below there are 2 in lower frequency duality. They add up to 5 and not adding the two that are not in the lower continental, we arrive at 7. Even the numbers of the two lower, TX and OK, are 8, pointing to the new creation level of 8 to the west, as Texas the "Lone Star" holds it *up and to the west.* Now, what number will we find to the left or east? You thinkin what I'm thinkin? *For* Heaven's sake, there are 31, and let's not forget the "13" original states we started with to the east, which equals 4. Not only do the numbers not lie, we didn't invent them, we discovered their existence, and they communicate with *us* daily.

Just an amazing mystical, divine picture this is all painting. Our Star and its Polar are encoded into the states and the "Land of the Red Man" pointing to the birth of our new reality NWO, and the new Star and it's brother of Ego, the new Saturn, Pluto, and all of this hidden in the outlines of the states of the "New World", United Unity States. Our new Star Jupiter, represented by NV (5+4=9) with it's Star of the Desert LV (34=7) and its brother Pluto represented by AZ (1+8=9) where the new Phoenix will rise outside of the Light and the State representing the new birthing of our New Universe by our Mother who gave birth to them both, New Mexico (5+4=9). So here we have the new Trinity. The cleansing of "the Dragon" by the Son has cleared the way for the rebirth of the Phoenix. As you read, I will continue to show you how all of this relates, to a very personal, *internal*, transformation.

*Katsumoto: You believe a man can change his destiny? Algren: I think a man does what he can, **until his destiny is revealed.** ~* "The Last Samurai"

*From my Glinda: There was always something about the name America for me Scott that just seemed oddball to state the least. I could not for the life of me understand why Christopher Columbus (Cristobal Colon) was not given the supposed recognition of having a continent named after him, if indeed he was always acknowledged as having "discovered" it, but instead we are told it was named after a cartographer Amerigo Vespucci and changed with an A at the end to reflect the **female** and in keeping with all the other continents named in honour of the feminine power. I mean Columbia would have been a very apt name after all as we both know for reasons why it would have worked as we've studied the esoteric meanings. America was always that splinter in my mind for many years.... when alas out of the blue the reason for America was revealed and that it's an amalgamation of words not born of the English language but of an even more ancient language... ancient Coptic... or the language spoken of the Egyptians and that A-mer-i-ca really means the Land of the Living Souls. You may know the Ka and the Ba (Kabbalah)... the Ba of the soul incarnated into this plane...hence the root word for BAby.....(BAltimore) and the Ka or Ca for the Soul departed. Of course... Egypt residing in the continent of AfriCA. I look to the game of chess.... no one really knows where it originates from Scott...some speak of ancient Babylonia.... but it's never been proven... it could be so much older. Point I am trying to make.... America always seemed like some sort of board game...mapping or plotting out the game or some event that seems to happen here on planet Earth many times. Look at the East Coast and its 13 original colonies.... You have Virginia...named after the Virgin Queen, Elizabeth I... **virgin doesn't*** *mean pure, untouched sexually...that is the wrong interpretation of this word...a Virgin was a woman who had command over her own life in the past... a self-sustaining woman... sexually in control of herself.* *This would describe Queen Elizabeth I perfectly...hence then the naming of the Virginia Company and eventually the state of Virginia.... and then there is Maryland...named after the half-sister Queen Elizabeth had executed.... and stuck in the middle...Washington DC (District of Columbia). I feel the whole of the USA is some sort of plotted clue of events that transpired in the past...maybe many times.... clues hidden in plain sight... look how many states have Ca...or Ba... or Ka in them...and what would the ancient Egyptian meaning be to those names? Two vested virgins.... Virginia and Maryland both separated by the Obelisk of the Washington Monument. I think a higher story...the truth is being reflected all across the USA...in code.... hidden code... So yeah when you speak of KaNsas and ArKAnsas damn straight it's all a clue..... but to what? I look at CAlifornia...and its state flag of the bear and the star... five-pointed... it all seems to be astrology related. So I am with you in your thinking.... are we been given coordinates... a timeline..... of some repetitive event that seems to be occurring on Earth that is a real game changer for all life on this planet?*

While the Heart, is the only true reality, your pineal "eye" is your "sense" to view the Divine and your "material" two eyes to view the Duality dream. Now what does this all mean? You will get a better idea, if you don't already, by what will die, and what new reality will "rise from the ashes", when you read Tombstone Decoded. It certainly doesn't mean everyone should make their reservations to come to the American Southwest, but it means to get your own internal house in order and begin your internal move to the right, if you have not yet started, working on your Arc. Raise your frequency with right thought, directed attention and discipline as you *"ascend"*, and make your way to "The Right", in the Temple, between your temples, that only frequency can take you. The Narrow Gate of the internal "Pineal", the ascended frequency of Oz, or Aah. And there is a "Pinal" County in Arizona, just sayin!

"The light of the body is the eye: if therefore thine eye be single, thy whole body shall be full of light." -Matthew 6:22

It is up to each of us individually, the aware who are ready, to move beyond what no longer holds their attention and they will no longer bite at the predictable drama, because **everything**, is how you react and respond to it, and as you change, *so does your world*. Literally! You will then keep increasing your frequency to a point of transformation. O.K., time to Corral this. On, to 11.

11. Tombstone Decoded

He came from a Star, He came very far, and Kansas Ike said, was the name of His Star

Move over Dorothy! Yes, I am about to tell you that the biblical "Reckoning" is encoded in an *American Western.* I couldn't believe what I was seeing when I realized (*now* understanding) that one of the greatest *west*ern films ever made was actually an allegorical message communicating prophecy for the collective *and* an internal metaphor for the individual, as I watched it again with Max while in Sedona in June of 2015. While calling it one of the greatest is my opinion, it is a fact that this movie was wildly popular and grabbed the imagination of a generation and even to this day is one of the most widely quoted. It achieved an iconic stature that few films reach.

After I saw it in the theater in Las Vegas, I knew I had just witnessed greatness! Something that transcended most storytelling that went beneath the fabric of *ordinary* filmmaking. I couldn't put my finger on it at the time, as all I knew, is that this was one of the best films I had ever seen, and while I normally don't watch films multiple times, I really can't count how many times I've seen this film. I can see now that it tapped into the collective unconscious and took the timeless struggle between good and evil and weaved in a certain element of the human condition that blurred the normally distinct lines of where good stops and evil begins and contains the greatest segue in filmdom!

This was Jungian psychology at its big screen best, as the highly developed archetypes blended seamlessly, weaving alliances of normally adversarial factions and building rare chemistries between the antagonists that elevated their confrontations to just below flash point combustion, mixing drama, anxiety, and tension, with some defusing bits of humor, to take you to the cliff, dangle you over it and pull you back to safety. This film took the relationship of family, friends and foes to new developmental heights and having said all of that, as if that wasn't enough, very soon, I will show you why the relationship between Wyatt Earp and Josephine Marcus was the foundation of the greatest deception ever executed by "The Church of Rome".

Now, this was before radio and television and forget real-time social media that sees all, as it is happening, and this very much adds to the real phenomenon that was Wyatt Earp. I am not going to spend too much time on the real-life *"minutia type details"*, or at least what the best history tells us of Wyatt, because this chapter is more about the message of the movie than *real* historical facts, but without some of those "real historical facts" that are accurately portrayed in the film, we don't have this massive resonating message that is based on real people that helped shape America's young but powerful history! One of those facts that is totally improbable, because when you read and hear historians discuss the real man as opposed to the myth and legend and how little time he spent in Kansas where the *legend* began, is *that the man was a bonafide rock star of his day before he ever got to Tombstone*, and you *wonder how in the world he could have been.*

His notoriety didn't begin until he got to the booming cow town of Wichita Kansas in mid-1874 and later that year, due to a very favorable story of his actions printed in the "The Wichita Eagle" on October 29th, his fame started and the "legend" was born. While he wasn't an actual police officer during the incident the story speaks of, even though he is identified as one, his reputation was set, and he was hired as a **policeman** by the Wichita Police Force on April 21, 1875. He did a fine job adding to his reputation as a fearless lawman, but it was only for a year and six mentions of him in the local paper before he left with his brother James to venture to another booming Kansas cowtown, Dodge City. Stories vary on the reasons he left Wichita, as they do about his whole life, and as I said, the details of his real life are not the main point of this chapter.

He spent two years in Dodge City as an assistant city marshal and it was during this period he would meet his lifelong friend to whom he would forever be tied to. During the summer of 78, approximately two dozen cowboys terrorized Dodge City shooting up the town as they galloped down Front Street continuing into the "Long Branch Saloon" to vandalize it and harass the customers. The lone Earp, who never backed away from any danger confronted the men, being wildly outnumbered, and while stories vary on exactly how the exchange went down, Doc Holliday appeared from "nowhere" with guns drawn in support of Wyatt and between the two, deterred any of the cowboys from firing a shot, and Wyatt was able to take care of business without bloodshed. Earp gave credit to Doc for saving his life that day, and the two became best friends until Doc's death in 87.

As I say above, I am more concerned here about the message of the movie, *but* while Hollywood usually embellishes, they accurately portray a few absolute truths about Wyatt Earp and Doc Holliday to a tee! Without those facts that are accurately portrayed, we don't have this massive *superhuman with a sixth sense type* resonating message. Without these core *personality* facts, we are left with just another movie of the "Action Hero" genre. So much of what we are told and believe as "recorded historical events" are inaccurate anyway! I SO agree with the with the opening narrative from "Braveheart" that opens with these words that resonate to your soul; "I shall tell you of William Wallace. Historians from England will say I am a liar, but history is written by those who have hanged heroes." This is so true, and if you get hung up on the "historical" details of Wyatt's life during the time period of the movie, it will cloud the *real* message "Tombstone" is delivering, like concentrating on this tree or that tree without seeing the forest, then this chapter, or hell this book, isn't for you!

As you read, remember what was taken from William in "Braveheart" and Balian in "Kingdom of Heaven", and you will see a recurring theme. Here is a truth about the two that is accurately portrayed in the movie and confirmed in every source that speaks of Wyatt Earp and John "Doc" Holliday. Outside of his relationship with his brothers, Wyatt had very few friends (Doc too), and one of them was a peer of his, Bartholomew "Bat" Masterson, who worked alongside him a Deputy Sheriff Dodge City and then later became Sheriff of Ford County in Kansas. He garnered some national fame as a lawman as well and had this to say about Wyatt:

"In an article on Earp written thirty years later, Bat said:

Wyatt Earp is one of the few men I personally knew in the West in the early days, whom I regarded as absolutely destitute of physical fear. I have often remarked, and I am not alone in my conclusions, that what goes for courage in a man is generally the fear of what others will think of him -- in other words, personal bravery is largely made up of self-respect, egotism, and an apprehension of the opinion of others. Wyatt Earp's daring and apparent recklessness in time of danger is wholly characteristic; personal fear doesn't enter into the equation, and when everything is said and done, I believe he values his own opinion of himself more than that of others, and it is his own good report that he seeks to preserve. . . . I have known Wyatt Earp since the early seventies and I have seen him tried out under circumstances which made the test of manhood supreme. . . .Take it from me, no one has ever humiliated this man Earp, nor made him show the white feather, under any circumstances whatever. . . . Wyatt Earp, like many more men of his character who lived in the West in its early days, has excited, by his display of great courage and nerve under trying conditions, the envy and hatred of those small minded creatures which the world seems to be abundantly peopled, and whose sole delight seems to be in fly-specking the reputations of real men." -page 77, "Bat Masterson: The Man and the Legend" By Robert K. DeArment

He was also in countless fistfights with cowboys, as documented from several sources, who taunted him as a nothing without his badge and gun, and would never back down and always get the better them! What Wyatt had was very rare and what made him just as impressive, was that he never started the fights and he, by all accounts, was a very good man! I didn't say he was always "law", as in man's laws, abiding! He was very much a product of his time in the midwest and he and his brothers had a less than idyllic childhood. His father was less than responsible at times and left the responsibilities that he should have handled, to his son's and as soon as each was old enough to leave home, they did. His three older brothers joined the Union Army in 1861 and he tried on several occasions to run away and enlist but his father rounded him up each time and brought the thirteen-year-old back to the farm, that he and his two younger brothers were expected to maintain most of the time.

Their father moved them around quite a bit and they ended up in San Bernardino California at the end of 1864. The 16-year-old Wyatt found some work with a stage line with his brother in 65, then in spring 1866, Wyatt found work as a teamster transporting cargo. His assigned trail until 1868 was from Los Angeles, through San Bernardino then up to Las Vegas and then on to Salt Lake City. Folks, I don't even like to make this 12-hour drive on good interstate roads listening to music and drinking my, you guessed it, 7-11 Big Gulp! God, we were so much tougher and smarter back in the day!

Just when you think your ship has come in!

The family ended up back in the midwest in the spring of 1868 in Lamar, Missouri, and his father Nicholas became the local Constable. Here is where Wyatt becomes his own man and as I said, he wasn't always law-abiding, but he had his reasons and through it all never turned "evil". In November 1869, Nicholas resigned as Constable to become the Justice of the Peace and Wyatt was appointed Constable in his father's place. Now a handsome strapping young man, six feet tall (tall in those days), Wyatt met, fell in love, and courted Urilla Sutherland, whose family, originally from New York, was well known and respected in Lamar. Her father owned the Lamar House Hotel, and the two were married there on January 10, 1870, with Wyatt's father as Justice of the Peace officiating the wedding. They lived at the Lamar House until they were able to purchase their own home and in August they purchased a house on the outskirts of town and settled in as Urilla was pregnant, and everything seemed to be going well for Wyatt. Tragedy struck though and in the fall, about a month before Urilla was to give birth, she fell ill and both she and the child died from typhoid fever. This devastated Wyatt and he lost his foundation. He stayed in a downward spiral for years as jobs withered and brushes with the law increased. He was arrested several times over the next few years as he made his living buffalo hunting and working as a bouncer and pimp in Brothels.

Wyatt's association with Mattie Blaylock, a prostitute who worked in Brothels, was on again off again and she continued to work as a prostitute during their early years together. While they are said to have been married, there is no record of it, and her drug addiction began in the Brothels. This explains their "strained" and somewhat distant relationship in the movie, and their less than dramatic split after they left Tombstone. She stayed in Arizona and ended up working, again, as a prostitute in Pinal City where she died of a drug overdose.

Certainly the most entertaining, of the other half of the Tombstone equation, was the colorful *John* Henry "Doc" Holliday. Born to a family of status, especially of his mother's aristocratic side in the "haves and have-nots" American South of the mid 19th Century, he was a highly educated and cultured southern gentleman. He was very close to his mother, Alice Jane McKey, but she passed away from tuberculosis, that also killed his step-brother, right after his 15th birthday and he most likely was exposed to the disease from her.

After you have been exposed, it is not unusual for it to stay dormant for years, and in some, never develop into full-blown TB. I not only read this, I know this because, during one of my yearly police physicals over 20 years ago, I tested positive! I was told that a strong immune system will isolate the virus and quarantine it, much like your computer's antivirus program tracking down a virus and quarantining it. So his mother's passing had to have played a part, a large one in my opinion, in "circumstances", that included the death of his step-brother and sister, that turned the upstanding Dr. Jekyll-like socialite John Henry Holliday, into his version of Mr. Hyde. . ."Doc Holliday"!

After attending Valdosta Institute in Georgia that provided him with a strong secondary education in rhetoric, grammar, mathematics, history, and Latin, he left home to attend Dentistry school in Philadelphia at the University of Pennsylvania School of Dental Medicine. He graduated just shy of his 21st birthday and set out to pursue his dental career. Now at only 22, he was diagnosed with Tuberculosis and given only months to live; talk about a punch in the gut, and he was advised to move west as the drier climate of the southwest would slow the development of the TB. He moved to Dallas, and while he won awards for his various dental innovations and opened his own practice, his newly blossoming dental career was withering before it ever got off the ground, as no one wanted to go to a dentist with TB coughing just above their opened mouth. The clever Holliday soon found he had skill at poker and gambling in general, and relied on it as his new principal source of income. In May of 74, he and twelve others were indicted for illegal gambling and after an arrest for a gunfight, he moved to Denison, but after a conviction was handed down from the earlier indictment for the gambling charges in Dallas, he decided to leave the state. With his short-lived dental practice all but dead, and knowing his life would soon follow suit, along with the deaths of his mother and siblings, John became Doc to now live his remaining days on his own terms, following his own rules, and if there were casualties along the way, *then so be it!*

"I said to him one day: 'Doctor doesn't your conscience ever trouble you?' 'No,' he replied, with that peculiar cough of his, "I coughed that up with my lungs long ago."

Col. John T. Deweese – Doc's Lawyer – Denver, Colorado c. 1884-5

Now don't get me wrong, he didn't turn evil, but he turned his life, what little he had left, over to his passions and addictions and his newly developed outlook of throwing caution to the wind, with his razor-sharp intellect and fearlessness at the prospect dying created the gambling adversary from *hell*, and yes, that *may* accurately portray it. Add that to the fact, and stories abound on how this could have occurred, but Doc developed into one of the greatest and deadliest gunslingers the west ever produced. Add all that to his dry, caustic, sarcastic, salt in the wound sense of humor, and if you weren't angry enough over losing all of your money to him, his cutting tongue and patronizing delivery at your expense would put you right over the top *and that is not where you would want to go with him.* Doc could be a stone cold killer, and maybe "killer" isn't the right word, as he wouldn't "initiate" it, but just dispense what you ordered up. He would toy and bait and give you just enough rope to hang yourself, so that it wouldn't be Doc "pulling the trigger" to the duel to the death, but you, as you took the bait, got hooked, and thought you'd be pulling the trigger first, as the bullet goes through your forehead!

"Doc was a dentist whom necessity had made a gambler; a gentleman whom disease had made a frontier vagabond; a philosopher whom life had made a caustic wit; a long, lean, ash-blond fellow nearly dead from consumption (TB), at the same time the most skillful gambler and the nerviest, speediest, deadliest man with a six-gun I ever knew."

Wyatt Earp – San Francisco Examiner – August 2, 1896

An amazing description, and coming from Wyatt, makes it all the more impressive! And I just had to add this priceless quote from Wyatt:

"Fast is fine, but accuracy is everything. In a gunfight... You need to take your time, *in a hurry.*"

While this new Doc became more of the alter ego of John, he retained many redeeming qualities, that while they weren't obvious to the vast majority, he displayed them to his very small close circle of friends. While he wasn't that close with Virgil, Virgil still had this to say about him:

"There was something very peculiar about Doc. He was gentlemanly, a good dentist, a friendly man and yet, outside of us boys, I don't think

he had a friend in the Territory. Tales were told that he had murdered men in different parts of the country; that he had robbed and committed all manner of crimes, and yet, when persons were asked how they knew it, they could only admit it was hearsay, and that nothing of the kind could really be traced to Doc's account. He was a slender, sickly, fellow, but whenever a stage was robbed or a row started, and help was needed, Doc was one of the first to saddle his horse and report for duty."
-Virgil Earp – Arizona Daily Star – May 30, 1882

Or Bat Masterson's, who was also quoted as describing Doc as a most dangerous man with few friends, quote describing the same quality:

"Doc had but three redeeming traits. One was his courage; he was afraid of nothing on Earth. The second was the one commendable principal in his code of life, sterling loyalty to friends. The third was his affection for Wyatt Earp." -Bat Masterson, Wyatt Earp, Frontier Marshal, copyright 1931, Stuart N. Lake.

"He was always decently peaceable, though his powers when engaged in following his ostensible calling, furthering the ends of justice, made him a terror to the criminal classes of Arizona."
Bob Paul, Sheriff of Pima County, Arizona, Rocky Mountain News – May 22, 1882

Yes, "made him a terror to the criminal classes", in a way that seemed to deliver divine judgment and seeing into their souls knowing them better than they knew themselves! The totality of the 2 sides of Doc was played to perfection by Val Kilmer. He was the physical manifestation of every nuanced aspect of the man! Kilmer not getting the supporting Oscar was, "Satanic robbery". He was Doc Holliday come back to life. And you would have been hard-pressed to find a better Wyatt than Kurt Russell and even in the way the two looked very much like the historical Wyatt and Doc with similar looks and builds. It is also not a coincidence that Wyatt and Doc look very much alike and I find that to be another confirmation of their real relationship in the grand scheme of life and as communicated in the movie! Both were approximately 6 feet tall with the same slender build, though Wyatt was reportedly slightly taller and more muscular due to the fact that Wyatt had physically worked much harder in life than Doc and of course tuberculosis took its toll on his body. This also parallels the positive polarity, like Thor and Mufasa, being bigger and stronger than their negative polarity brothers. Both had light blue eyes and dirty blonde hair with similar facial features. All of the descriptions from those who knew and met them described them with these physical features with Allie, Virgil's wife, going as far to say that Doc's hair was light blonde, so all of the old photographs of Doc with black hair and dark eyes, have been colored in to symbolize his Dark Polarity. The two had very similar looks!

It's time for me to explain the exquisitely hidden esoteric messages of the movie and why they look the same and why key aspects of their personalities were identical and why other key elements were polar opposites or alter ego aspects! The movie Tombstone, like the Target commercial, encodes tremendous spiritual messages and the blueprint of future events that set into motion the arrival of a natural force to make your path clear, for *That* gate, that you will pass through as determined by your cumulative frequency, known as The Reckoning!

The *Western* Reckoning, the start of decoding the movie Tombstone!

1879 - 1+8+7+9=25=7
As 6 ends, 8 is taking shape to the west, the "Great Migration", the new class for 7,
Yes, the great migration *west!*
"Out of this *chaos* comes a *legendary lawman".* "Out of the Chaos" means out of what you can't understand. Now I know what the dictionary tells us, but "chaos" and "random" do not exist in Nature, the natural world we live in. Nothing is left to *chance, and* virtually all of us view Nature as lacking order, but it operates within a very specific programmed order that we can't identify or understand, and so we call it chaos. So here they *mean* "Out of the Divine Order comes...". Also think about that use of the word legendary, and right now the world is in chaos, so he represents something more, than just the man. While he is well known, and as I pointed out far more than he should be for that time period, he is not myth and legend, but they are telling you he is a god, not yet God, but on his way, and that he will lay down the Law after, he learns an oh so important lesson about the illusion of *control*!

As the movie opens, we see a tide moving in, an invasion, in the land of the two messianic Kings. The Judaic, Masonic two pillared temple of the church within the realm of Duality, living peacefully in vibrational harmony (symbolized by the comforting sound of the guitars) with nature and the sexual energies and to the light as symbolized by the cross between them. This is a Mexican village and Mexico has immense spiritual significance. In the previous chapter dealing with New Mexico, we uncovered the real meaning of Mexico and how it is a manifest state for the spiritual and material physical universe. "Where there is water, there is life, so the fountain's flowing water represents life, as in "life is present here". This setting symbolizes creation and because of its time (autumn or "Fall") within the age,

Satanic or "negative" adversarial forces are taking over because "lessons must be learned", making the most of *his* limited (he moves quickly) time, to make *his* move to dominate this world and usurp the *Most High's* authority, in preparation for the great test.

The "*Great* Nation's" forces move in to dominate the world and kill and subjugate the various aboriginal cultures who, for the most part lived in harmony with the natural order, but the stage is being set, for tough choices, and deep impactful lessons as Dark forces moving in to assert their "authority". "*2 And he laid hold of the dragon, the serpent of old, who is the devil and Satan, and bound him for a thousand years; 3.....and until the thousand years were completed; **after these things he must be released for a short time....**' Rev. 20:2* The leader of the dark forces displays 4 of a kind Aces on each leg, with the dark Ace of Spades out front as the dominant. The symbol of war in the tarot, a warning that troubles await, old age, winter, earth, then transformation! And the revealing of two secrets! The number of A is 1, so he displays 11:11 on each leg indicating the approach of the coming Divine Judgement. Four and four, as in Satanic left brain consuming itself, and both total 8, to bring forth the new class of 8. (In "The Last Samurai", as Capt. Algren, Tom Cruise, kneels before the Japanese Emperor, his uniform's shoulder Epaulettes display 11 7 11.)

He wears the dense base vibrational color of red, the color of the creation of 6, and his Satanic agents all are identified by this color. They call themselves *cowboys* as they are identifying themselves as just intelligent animals, part animal and man (but more specifically *boys*, as in spiritually young) like the Minotaur, wanting to maintain their animal instincts and urges and very much the adversary of God and anything of God. If it feels good, do it! He **lies** as he **must**, "Yall killed *two,* (duality) Cowboys", to *justify* their murder and subjugation under his rule, as Satan is the Father of lies, distortion, and manipulation, to in any way justify, (Amen to this one!) what they are compelled to do! They desecrate the sacred union, *just outside* the *Temple* of the Divine Masculine and Feminine, making him kneel before they kill **Him**, because the younger darker brother is attempting to take

His place here, and then *removes **Her, our Dark Divine Feminine,*** from us during our winter, so that we are now blind to the Trinity and only see in Separation.

Once the control is imposed, he now identifies **himself** as the lord and the giver, "founder of the feast", of their gifts and sustenance. He warns them to never stand against him, "Thou shalt have no other gods before me". The priest, those who know the esoteric knowledge, tell them that punishment awaits them and all who follow them, but they dismiss it and show no mercy and desecrate all that is sacred. Some will begin to recognize they are on the wrong path but need more time to change paths. The Holy are slain and they steal what they were not given, eating the fruits they did not cultivate, killing the servants of the *Owner's* house, while he is away, to occupy it and pretending to own what is **not** theirs!

"Do you know what lies in the Holy Land? A new world. *A man who in France had not a house, is, in the Holy Land, the master of a city. He who was the master of a city begs in the gutter.* There, at the end of the world, you are not what you were born, but what you have it in yourself to be. A better world than has ever been seen. A kingdom of conscience. A kingdom of heaven. Did you think that lay at the end of a Crusade? It does!"

--Godfrey de Ibelin, Kingdom of Heaven

The master who begs will not be begging much longer, for the *Owner,* will soon return.

Next comes the interpretation of the ages and the greatest cinematic segue (to me of course) of all time! As the ignorant, irreverent, mocking Satan laughs, he dismissively inquires about the meaning of the "foolish" warning by the Mexican priest.

"Hey Johnny, wha'dat Messkin mean a sick horse is gonna get us huh?" Yes, Johnny (32=5, the divine message) knows full well what he means, as he replies, "He was quoting the Bible, Revelations. Behold a pale horse, the man who sat on him was death. And hell followed with him."

Johnny remains transfixed on those words because *he knows* the priest is right, as it is prophecy. And they are about to reveal the man who sits on the pale horse. This segue from Johnny's introspective knowing stare to the piercing train whistle is pure magic. A spiritual battle of polarity is on the horizon! The train is a spiritual symbol as God 9 comes down to this realm of Duality 11 and the whistle is a summons, a warning, an alarm telling you that it is near! So as Johnny stares, *almost in admiration*, you then hear the whistle and then the transition to the depot as the train pulls up to the station, and low and behold, the number of the train is 11, with billowing white, the union of all colors, smoke or (spiritual imagery) mist, and then you see his legs at the front of his railcar, telling you that He, is who the Mexican Priest speaks of! Wyatt Earp has 9 letters, as he steps down, as in frequency into this realm, from his rail car, number 5150, which equals 11, but with 4 digits meaning he is entering the Realm of Separation.

He surveys the situation and begins to stop the cruelty shown to animals by the ignorant and spiritual children, teaching them to treat all life as they would want to be treated. If it hurts him, it will hurt the horse. Now he is not here to be an ordinary man, with ordinary jobs, so when US Marshal of the Arizona Territory, Crawley Dake, introduces himself, Wyatt will not even allow him to begin the offer, as Wyatt knows what he is going to say. Thinking he is talking to a man who would jump at an offer to work for him, he tells Wyatt that he doesn't understand why he came up to speak to him, but Wyatt stops him and tells him that *he,* is the one who doesn't understand. When Wyatt tells him that he did his duty and wants to get on with his life, what he is really saying is, *I have already gone through this level and moved on and I am now at an ascended level and must get on with my spiritual agenda and do what this level requires.* As he finishes his conversation with them, the end of Tucson, "SON", is shown next to him proclaiming he is the "Son" of God. He is then greeted by his brothers and this scene is shot through an open door, a portal. *"He commanded the skies from above; He set open the doors of the heavens" -Psalms 78:23* Morgan eats an apple, the symbolic forbidden fruit, and is later killed, because as I will explain, Morgan is the brother that will eat of it, and descend.

As Virgil introduces his wife "Allie" again, as they have met before, asking Wyatt, "You remember Allie?", and her response is "Good God well he better", is obvious enough but in the esoteric message of the movie, to me, it's since he is a good God, she would *hope* that he remembers her. He then says he has been dreaming (we are in, a dream) about this, "God since forever", as they then look at their reflected image in the window, and that is to show that this life is a mirror image of true reality. Wyatt is in line to be King and then God, and he can't do it unless he completes this stage here in this class with those below him. At the end of them "posing", the letters "SON" is again next to Wyatt's head again. As they walk away Wyatt asks Virgil if he has seen Doc, saying that he misses him, and they are now stopped right next to the 5150, as Virgil states, "I don't", knowing he is not too fond of Doc's decadent side because of *his* perspective, but

Wyatt knows exactly who his old *familiar* friend is! As Wyatt is placing his bag on the wagon, the letters W.P.R.R., 5799, are on the side of the locomotive!

In the next scene, we are introduced to Doc Holliday, and the first thing you see is a poker table full of paper money, coins and jewelry, the illusory treasures of this dream, as Doc effortlessly manipulates the money. This scene really epitomizes the Doc I described earlier and look at his name and what ego, the adversary, wants and strives to become! Doc, as in Doctor or Doctorate, indoctrinated into the *realness* of this mirror image. And his last name Holliday is the pleasure and comfort that ego always strives for, the 24/7 club med endless holiday or vacation! And "Ed Bailey", ordered up what he *deserved!*

As the family makes their way to Tombstone, Wyatt is leading the way and as they get to the Grand Hotel, you see the Bird Cage Theater in the background. You then see Sheriff Behan come out of his office that is shared with the County Tax Collector's office, letting you know he is 100% part of the Satanic structure. His badge is a crescent moon over a point up pentagram, that is a witchcraft symbol and the moon above the star indicates dark over the light, and any *law* enforcement that he administers is to protect the integrity of the Satanic structure that he is a part of. Behan is a two-faced Sith if this helps your understanding.

Behan acknowledges Wyatt's fame and then confirms his association with taxes, as in collecting what is Caesar's, because he is an agent of Rome, and goes on to confirm his left brain, seeing in separation worldview, by stating he has so many jobs of egoistic status here in Oz. He boasts that he is Captain of the fire brigade, sits on the town's real estate lot commision (selling what can't be owned), Chairman of an "Anti-Chinese League" and of course the elected Cochise County Sheriff. He is your typical munchkin politician as he confirms his left brain perspective seeing only parts (ultra-separation) but not the whole, by calling himself a *man of many parts*. Not wasting an opportunity to schmooze and network with someone who is famous, he offers a "free" cleaning on three homes coming up for rent for Wyatt and his brothers. They would have cleaned them anyway, but Behan is satanically clever and plays the phony quid pro quo game very well.

When Wyatt meets town Marshal Fred White, White tells him that the Sheriff is not the real law or authority, and that the town is controlled by a gang called the Cowboys. In other words a force, outside the originally established system set up by the "elected" representatives of the people (the state and local governments) that make and enforce their laws, has now been replaced by a small minority (the mob or organized crime) to establish and enforce their rules, now runs the town and the local government is aware of it, and allows it to exist. Meaning they are either participating (Behan) or too weak and or afraid to oppose it (Clum), or simply indifferent (Wyatt, at first). The underlying esoteric message is consistent with the opening scene that showed Satanic forces coming in like a virus to now control God's Temple and are turning "Life" into a "Tombstone culture of Death". This gets laid out in detail in the final chapter, and remember, who now runs what **was**, *our* government.

[As I remind you that our personal property is stolen 24/7 and that "new *laws*" had to be "drawn up" by the mob in suits and ties to *legitimize,* what was never established IN, what was known to be "unconstitutional". Ben Franklin replied, "A Republic, If you can keep it." when asked what they had created. He and the other Masonic Framers knew we wouldn't keep it, because the takeover was choreographed in, and This is all part of the Grand Play's *final act,* unfolding all around us. As I recall a scene from O. Stone's "JFK", where "X" askes "Jim" a question that *He knows* the answer to, of "Who has the power?", as they sit on a D.C. park bench with "The Dome" and Obelisk in full view behind them. Ollie knows the "fine mess" that was programmed **in** to "take **out**" Camelot. No matter how much they neon the natural, the Sight of Vega's Northern Light, will soon shine B*right.*]

Even White acknowledges that they (the Cowboys) are "good for business", for while they are corrupt, they do enforce "rules" that *everyone knows,* that allows them to flourish in the *mining* (below surface) camp. The commerce he identifies: alcohol, gaming and prostitution, are right up the mobs alley anyway, as Satan knows his "forbidden fruit businesses" (play for the young) very well! When he points out several of the cowboys to Wyatt and his brothers, the Cowboy's partner in crime, Behan, is with them. The forces that run the G8 governments, also run the organized crime syndicates (Of course the drug cartels too. It's why we invaded Afghanistan in 2001, after 9-11 to take back, police and oversee the poppies, and we are still there 17 years later. Pat *knew*) and many times they are one and the same. White tells them all the "businesses" are doing well, except the "Oriental", as that is the nature of the class, and we know that the East is coming to an end and the West is the future! It will get deep here! Wyatt is being shown all his options within creation that can accommodate the level of his *brothers,* and he knows Morgan and Virgil need to experience the very harsh duality of "The East", which is within the extreme depths of Iron Age, and **He,** hasn't quite released his illusion of control (and he is still arrogant as he knows, *it can't hurt **Him***), so he needs a lesson as well, as White says:

"All except 'the Oriental.' That's a regular slaughterhouse [what happens when you partake of the carnal or material fruits] Even the high rollers won't go near it. [Those of higher frequency. You do not want to go there, spend a life in Tombstone, unless you have to] That's too bad too. It's a nice place. Hell of a waste." And because White is "just a man", seeing from his tiny 5 sense perspective and believing this life is the be all end all reality without any spiritual foundation, he laments this as a "hell of a waste"! As 3D crumbles, those who hold on to the illusory treasures will sound like White saying "It's too bad, it was a nice place".

Before I acquired a clearer understanding of this, and I was engaged in a "Mr. and Mrs. Smith" battle with my other half, I couldn't believe all of the "treasures" that I believed I accumulated was vanishing around me by the day, and not just money and possessions, but my ego, my pride, my "status", was being drug through the mud and damaged irreparably, so I thought. I know all too well the bitter pill "the Beast" was swallowing, trapped in that body as everything was taken from him and illusory wealth around him withering and decaying by the day. In many ways, I was that beast in that cold place in the forest. When you don't understand it, it is a horrible waste, and you sound like Fred White, but when you finally *get* why all of this is happening to you, you see it for the maturation lesson that it is, and you are actually loved beyond all methods of measure! As I wipe a tear or two, let me get back to Tombstone. (describing it, that is)

Wyatt sees an opportunity, because even those on the path to the light, have egos to deal with and Wyatt believes he may be able to prop up the East for a while to get his treasure, even, if it is more for his *brothers* (they are really the material manifestation of Him), that his ego keeps telling him is *out there* for the *easy* taking! So he goes to the East, to grab his 7 share (25%), as his brothers, knowing his status and prowess say, "There he goes! O'l Wyatt". After Milt Joyce, who has been intimidated by lower level thugs and hoodlums, dismisses Wyatt's claim as being Wyatt Earp (son of God) because symbolically, Wyatt is more than just a *man.*

Wyatt knows who he is dealing with and they are far below him in stature and power. It is time to create an *opening,* for his brothers to step into the "East" for a while and build some *treasures,* where they, of course, should not be building them. After he expels the small-time hoods, he tells his brothers that they are well on their way, as he "acquired" a job for them in "Caesar's *Palace*", (the opening was there) to gathering some worldly treasures for a time longer, but that they still need to keep their eyes on the "brass ring", because the Bronze higher classes are on the horizon, but they are not there yet, as the cows pass by. See the parallel in Thor? Wyatt knew the thugs in the Oriental were no match for *him*, but he abused his power just as Thor did in Jotunheim, *putting loved ones in danger.*

The brothers acknowledge Wyatt's status as above them calling him "The One", and even "older" brother Virgil knows his place! Think of the brothers as aspects of Wyatt, the two below him, like the two thieves polarity equation, with Virgil to the right. This is evident at one of the most telling and symbolic scenes in the movie when Wyatt comes out of the "Oriental" Saloon walking in the center of his brothers, and of course Virgil is on his right as he is the one in his direct line, telling them he is providing a quarter interest for them, and all they have to do is keep their eyes on the "brass ring", meaning stay focused, while his alter ego little brother "Doc", sees all from the dark (he is in the shadows). He protects that which he knows he is a part of, and after putting his satanic underling Johnny Tyler in his place (Johnny acknowledges his Superior), he walks up to Wyatt and knowing full well what was happening and that while Johnny stands there with a weapon, there is no danger, and as the next paragraph gets into, He and Doc, can't get hurt here.

The Son speaks to his Ego in a very intimate and loving way by his tone and overall demeanor, "How the **Hell** (as Saturn resides out from the light), are you!?!" And Doc addresses, "The One" first! Wyatt, "I am rolling." Think Planets rotating and revolving, as they roll around the Sun! (see God and Satan in *Job*) He then addresses Morgan (he and Morgan are *like polarity*) before Virgil. After they exchange some pleasantries, Doc is amused that his older stronger, more virtuous Brother would lower himself to "be here" involved in lower "darker" activities that are just usually left up to him. He laughs and says, "That's what I love about Wyatt, he can talk himself into anything!", meaning he IS the Son, and whatever he says, goes, even if his actions seem to be in *"conflict"* with our Father, because there **must, be a reason for this.** Doc then dismisses the subordinate Johnny, but the One who is to ascend to the Throne, the brother to the Light polarity, has the final word, telling him to leave his gun before he is dismissed.

The next 4 paragraphs break from the sequence of the movie so that you better comprehend what comes next.

I was going to put this at the end as a "wrap up explanation", but we are into this and only with this explanation will the next scene make any sense as to why Virgil, leaves the next scene, and why later in the movie, "Allie" yells at Wyatt "cursing" his judgement after Virgil is ambushed and shot leaving the Saloon. I could never figure out why she was, in essence, blaming Wyatt, before my newfound awareness. This is also why Allie acknowledges Wyatt as Good God, and that he had better remember (because if he brings us to the dark, he may have forgotten me) me, since I am Virgil's Spirit, and we **too**, are "to the Light". *This is a story of a Prince who temporarily fell, like the Prodigal Son, to the "distant land" of Tombstone to engage in some riotous living, to eventually end up, with nothing.* He fell to learn his most important lesson, and after that, now in His Right mind, to clean His Father's House. If you have not seen the new 2011 Thor, and yes I know I have mentioned it a time or two, it is an absolute must see to help you wrap your brain around what I am about to explain to you, and to understand the next chapter!

Tombstone IS, in essence, the *Thor* of the American westerns, complete with the Thunder and Lightning bolts! Think of Wyatt as being Thor and Doc, Loki. Virgil and Morgan are subordinate to Wyatt because they are his spiritual sons like Thor and Loki are to Odin. Virgil is Wyatt's Blue ascending Smith and "little" brother Morgan, who is ultimately subordinate to Virgil as Loki is to Thor, is Wyatt's Red descending Smith within the Smith Equation. So like Thor and Loki, Virgil is paired with Morgan. **Think of Wyatt and Doc as being there, and not there**, and while I have already *separated* them from the other "mortals", in so many of the scenes you have to project a more aware perspective and know that, they are not truly there "in the flesh", so to speak!

Wyatt and Doc are not here to be mere mortal men, but Wyatt is more *directing* his brothers, and when the brothers leave Tombstone, the "higher 2" act as karma. They have already been through that class, that level, and they have moved on. They were not here to be *ordinary*, doing the things that an ordinary man does. You saw how Wyatt was introduced to the film, and go back to when they first see their reflections in the window. Virgil, Morgan and their wives are positioned in the center with Wyatt and Mattie (and some of her is even cut off, for a good reason), off to the side, as Virgil *thanks Him telling Him, "This is all your doing!" (this is no ordinary brother to brother exchange), and Wyatt responding, "We'll make our fortune boys!", because remember that lesson he must learn before he "lays down the Law"? Wyatt still thinks that He is in control!*

Now remember as they make their way to Tombstone, Wyatt is not in the wagon with his brothers (he is *leading* them) and how Wyatt addresses Morgan, not Virgil because Morgan represents the ego of the two and he is far happier about the "dark" opportunities that Tombstone has to offer. The more guarded and cautious brother Virgil who basically just observes as an aspect of The Self isn't as *excited* about Tombstone as his brother of Ego Morgan. Morgan yells, "Hot damn this burg's jumpin", as Virgil says, "Easy" to calm him down, and then Morgan excitedly points out the prostitutes. (Not a smart move with his wife behind him, lol, but I digress, and Morgan's wife is very beautiful, as I digress more). And as we get into the very interesting exchange with Behan, Doc addresses Morgan before Virgil and it is the very happy (Apple eating) Morgan that proudly points out that Wyatt got *us,* a faro game. Throughout this chapter, try to keep in mind that Virgil and Morgan **are Wyatt's physical presence, here.** The movie, as with this book, paints a polarity picture. (I know it's a stretch, but it will fall into place, if it is meant to, for you)

Continuing the movie sequence

After Johnny Tyler drops his shotgun, Wyatt toys with Doc by calling Behan over, and something **very telling** happens! *Virgil removes himself from the scene because He represents The Self who observes like your conscience, while his Ego Morgan is who stays to deal with everyone because your ego is your out-there identity.* While Doc is to the dark he is above this and has disdain for the Satanic element below him and shows Behan no respect and belittles Behan's illusory kingdom by calling it *just another **mining** camp,* for the mortals to chase their *riches.* It's a bit too small to be sure, but it looks like Behan is wearing a Masonic square and compass, but even if it isn't, we see one large and in charge after a very *miraculous* scene later in the film. As Behan defends Tombstone, Doc looks amused and is the only one who doesn't flinch or seem surprised in any way by the shooting and gunfight in the street right in front of them. After the shooting starts, every time they give a close up of Wyatt or Doc, you see a **119** on a sign behind them, ***and it is not the same sign***, so you see both associated with 9-11 (8 yrs before 9-11) and 11:11, for the two and that is the numeric sign of Divine judgement. They show the signs repeatedly to drive home the clue.

Wyatt and Doc know those involved and Doc mock's Behan and the childish, *uncivilized* Tombstone, that he knows to be a lower grade "immature" spiritual class. Our two boys involved in the shooting and who will later team with Wyatt and Doc, and show us who is behind all of this, are both are named Jack*, and Jack is 1132=7. Turkey Creek Jack is dressed in blue and red with nice *patriotic* white pentagram stars and Texas Jack has a purple and violet scarf, the red and blue and purple between the two. Between the killing and the stagecoach that just pulled up, now dropping off *strangely* dressed people, Virgil pipes up and says, "What the *hell* kind of town is this?", but that's Wyatt's little Angel speaking to him on his right shoulder, but then his little devil dismisses the question (waving the piece of paper at him) with, "Nice scenery". The two are polarized on their developing opinions of Tombstone, as Doc clues us in with, "An enchanted moment", that this is an internal Spell.

18 Bird Cage Theatre 81

Again, the 18-81 tell you this is a mirror image play made by God as they equal 9 and we are in a *cell* so to speak and all of this is a big stage. The curtain on the stage proclaims that Tombstone IS a stage and facing out the word gunsmith is to the left of the word Tombstone. The number of gun is 6 and the name Smith had to come up somewhere in this movie.

All the world's a stage,
And all the men and women merely players;
They have their exits and their entrances,
And one man in his time plays many parts,
His acts being seven ages.
-William Shake-Speare, 7 and 5 are all over this mystery man's work!

The Satanic adversarial element makes it abundantly clear that they run the lower vibratory shows of the Tombstone production of Oz. Lower show you ask? Why do you think all of The Cowboys are on the bottom floor? The lower frequency entities have their place, and when you delve into the dark by partaking it what you are told you shouldn't, you go to them, and your *now lower frequency* gives them, the power over you. *"And remember, never let those Ruby Slippers off your feet for a moment, or you will be at the mercy of the Wicked Witch of the West"* -Glinda, Dorothy's ascended Mother, The Wizard of Oz. She tells her to never **let**, because Dorothy has the power, and it can't be taken but given. Also see that Wyatt is not sitting with his brothers, but sits with his peer (ego), Doc.

When Fred White introduces Wyatt to Mayor Clum, He shuts Clum right down, quicker than the territorial marshal, even to the point of being rude! Make no mistake, even ascending sons who are in line to be King are growing and evolving just need to be taught a lesson from time to time. When Thor was banished here for a time by his father Odin, it occurred because Thor needed to be humbled and shown that not only must he respect his father, but all life including those he perceived to be under, different or "inferior" to him. Coming here was a lesson for him, as it was for Wyatt and the extension of Wyatt, his brothers! So, when you are on the stage looking out, Wyatt and his family are *up and to the right*, and Curly Bill and Johnny Ringo are *down and to the left!*

Now as the performance begins, what we see with the overall conduct and courtesy of the audience, could not illustrate better the futility of judging the morality of the past based on the morality of the present.

They are spiritual children and on top of that raised, ingrained with beliefs and behavioral norms, to accept behavior and conditions that we would not tolerate today, and yet there is never ending judgment of it. And you thought cell phones are bad! Just when you thought it couldn't get worse, they shoot at the stage and use gunfire to applaud, while everyone up in the balcony pays it no mind like it is all par for the course. That, to them, is acceptable behavior! *Just remember that* when you are aghast at practices mentioned in ancient texts without a rejection of or hint of such from the writer, know that they are speaking to the level of their audience, and from the perspective of their culture and what is acceptable to them. It could be too that, just maybe, you took it out of context or didn't see the metaphorical meaning, and the esoteric message flew by like the bullets. As I said earlier, it's amazing what you just accept, when you are dreaming!

Faust or The Devil's Bargain

The play they chose could not have fit this movie and it's message any better. I hear from so many people who are so completely in the box that have no sense of anything outside of the box so that *out of the box* choices either don't exist or they are completely foreign and out of the question to them. We are raised within the game of Caesar and most think that that is the only reality. They see the laws, textbooks, and conditions as absolute, thinking they have no choice. They confuse Love with Desire and what they think they need for life, and there is a hook to every bait that Caesar places by their mouth. The never-ending quest for pleasure, comfort, and security makes one weak to resist the bait, and I am speaking to myself as much as anyone.

I retired from the State Police early, also to follow my Loki to her "Indoctrination" into the depths of Caesar's core, because I began to see, after my awakening in 05, that I was part of a system that I now perceived to be an arm of the corrupt government. I could see the mandates and directives that confirmed my growing conspiratorial worldview. Another arm is the entire state driven medical industry that the FDA oversees. They shove their version of healthcare down our throats and condemn and actively raid and arrest the outside of the "official MD box" holistic practitioners who reject the entire Big Pharmaceutical industry and cookie cutter med school clones who are brainwashed to only dispense big pharma, body damaging drugs.

You and I know all this and the cures they suppress. Now a Doctor or Nurse, let's say, works in the quintessential "Den of the vipers or the House that Caesar built", and once they begin to wake up to a new level of awareness, they see as I did, that they are part of the machine that they now identify as the "enemy". They now know that the big pharma drugs and vaccines that are all around them are in fact poisons (when you gain even more awareness, you see it as "just what the lower frequency who *need,* need to take) for unsuspecting patients. What to do, now that you know? And to make matters worse, you have to take the vaccines, that you know are poisons, to keep your job! Here we are again.

All of Caesar's "jobs" are Quid Pro Quo, Catch 22 traps.

They are illusory Iron Age Bait to keep you here in masculine "east" 4. The program is perfect and stability is an illusion as there is only to, or away from the light! You know it's not right, but the adversarial you screams for the money, pleasure, comforts and "security", but damn, when you look in the mirror, you don't see you, **you see Faust**. In the game of life, choice is Everything and everything is a choice! The dark will tell you, you have no choice, and your ego wants to agree. You signed the "contract", and not only is the choice clear, but it is the only one! Take the needles, dispense the drugs, enforce the overly controlling laws that are outside of the scope of the constitution and you're taken care of! Go to Walmart buy what you "NEED", go home and eat the factory meat, processed GMO foods, chlorinated, fluoridated water and let tv raise your kids. Case closed, but something "tells" you that there is something that just isn't right. Something is bothering you, like Mr. Anderson. There is an alternative choice that Caesar does not teach and you have to venture out of the box, to find it! No one can choose, or do this, for you. It's all you and me, and every time you say I, you are proclaiming who you are, but it's when you know you are, that *everything changes.* I personally love the investigation. How could anyone, who doesn't knock at the door, ever imagine that staying *IN the box, is looking OUT* and that stepping *OUT of the box, is looking IN.* **How lewd!**

This next exchange and Wyatt's badge being taken by Doc and then given back to Wyatt near the end of the movie are two of the bigger clues of the movie. Get them, and you get a huge piece of the picture. Get this, and you will know who "The Man", behind the Curtain, is, and why Dorothy's ascended parent of Venus, is a **Woman**, as opposed to a **"FeMale"**. The term *"Male"* = 4, is an Iron Age term for the young anyway!

Wyatt: *"But who was the Devil?"*

(Josie takes off her mask and directs an *I want you* stare right through to his **soul**, because she **is...**)

Wyatt: *"Well I'll be damned..."*

Doc: "You may indeed, if you get lucky."

Lord have mercy, so many priceless lines with esoteric messages in this film but we hit the mother lode here! She is that internal aspect he doesn't acknowledge, *yet!* The Elect-Lady, that tiny but uranium packed caveat that makes us quintessentially *human!* She is that nuclear-powered punch that can create Stars, or send you down, *"with its splendors intolerable **blinds** feeble, sensual or selfish Souls? Doubt it not!", that Pike describes.*

After seeing that the **Devil** is a woman (a surprise in itself as we children are taught the devil is evil and masculine), and not just any woman, but his "Lady in the Red Dress", who is magnetically attracted to him, He is stunned at the combination. "Well I'll be damned", is his choice, and *risk, to be as God, or be damned! And if you don't know who you are, you may be, and if* you do, you must break some eggs, and sever many relationships here in the dream, most notably the drug addicts and prostitutes, if you ever hope to make a lasting permanent **cake**! The Light comes with a sword.

If your relationship with your woman, "out there" is strictly for the continued unbridled passion, "desired" sexual pleasure, you will stay mired in winter, and trapped as an Ironman and you will never make union with the True Her within! Spring, the Bronze Age, will always stay one step ahead of your Caduceus iron soled dance steps. No one, and I mean **No one,** will interpret these lyrics the way I have. Reminds me of the poor reviews Jupiter Ascending or Kingdom of Heaven got because when you don't understand, or even have a clue there are encoded esoteric messages directed to the aware, it all just looks and sounds incoherent, foolish, misplaced and disjointed.

"**Spring** was never waiting for us, **girl** It ran **one step ahead**, As we followed in the **dance.** Between the parted pages and were pressed, In **love's hot, fevered iron,** Like a **striped pair of pants**! MacArthur's Park is **melting in the *dark*,** All the sweet, **green** icing flowing down. Someone left the **cake** out in the rain, I don't think that I can take it, "Cause it took so long to bake it, And I'll never have that recipe again... Oh, no!" -from "MacArthur Park", Jimmy Webb

As Ego cries! Heavy-duty, immensely cryptic lyrics that most, who actually thought it was a cake, mocked back in the 60's! Hell, I was **11** when I first heard this and knew it had nothing to do with a cake. As long as you Satanically spill your Divine creative energy down and "out there", the *serpent downward,* undisciplined passions or "fevered" hot Iron Age, you will be trapped in the jail cell of the *iron"fe"male*! "*Striped prison uniforms* commonly used in the 19th century...", from Wikipedia. Green Chlorophyll, a material substance created from sunlight to create more of the Dark. And semen, the *material man- ifestation of our creative potential to create more bodies within the Dark,* hence "All the sweet green icing **flowing *down***" through the *root* chakra, melting to the **dark.** (Trust me, I didn't want to visualize this either) "I'll drink the wine while it is warm", keeping the passions inflamed, "and never let you catch me looking at the sun", as my choices are away from the light. "I will have the things that I **desire** (because I have not Let Go and **desire** leads to suffering) and my passion flow like rivers, and there would be another dream for me, someone will bring it", as he is not done with this *Iron Age level* quite yet!

Scott, what the Hell are you talking about? Camelot will fall, and "the Cake" **is** Camelot, Ego's supreme creation, perfection with your "out there" lover here in the dream! Lyrics in a song called MacArthur Park (4) that could best describe the essence of "Camelot", sung by the man who played King Arthur as it all collapses around him, twice in the same year, as he recorded the song, and starred in the movie in 1967 (23=5)! "After all the loves of my life, I'll be thinking of you, and wondering why". The lament of Ego, of one who has not Let Go, because they don't know what this place is! It's you, it's all **you!** I know this and to a point, I have lived it! Imprisoned or liberated by "The Woman"! "I'll be damned!" "You **may** indeed, if you get Lucky!" That priceless little gem of a clue, that tells you that being damned, and losing all here, *is* getting lucky. If, you know why you lost it.

As they leave the theatre, Morgan gives up the **real *New Age* message of this *Western*** telling us the importance of God, Stars, Heaven and Spirituality. Yes, that God made all of that and still remembered to make a little speck like him, (he is to the dark, so he **is**, the grain of sand, and not the entire beach) because we are in the universe and the universe is in us. It is Morgan speaking because our Ego is what ponders who and what we are, from the opposite Dark perspective of the Light. He is Wyatt's Ego, and this is also why Mattie's drug fix is supplied by Morgan's *wife,* Louisa.

Another huge clue is who goes to the bar and casino to "work", and who goes with his wife to spend time with who really matters, while Louisa is the only wife that is just fine with her *man* going off to work the gaming table. You won't see Virgil at any of the gaming tables "working" or playing, but you will see Morgan there all the time. Now remember I told you about the "real" relationship Wyatt and Mattie had and the fact she never "wasn't" a drug-addicted prostitute while they were together and in this scene, even after he relents and offers to spend the evening with her, they have her exhibit her addiction and "strange behavior", much to Wyatt's dismay. Morgan is quick to make him feel better!

All of a sudden, the place no one wanted to go near is now all the rage for those who want to see and be seen, now that the Earps are "in the Oriental". They waste no time accumulating illusory money and property. After commenting on the property, Doc's comment on Mattie not being as pure as the driven snow confirms what I said above, and he, being Wyatt's polar, is quick to bring up Wyatt's personal code of ethics to say things to him that others could not get away with. Doc knows Wyatt's mind and what attracts him because they are more than just friends. Notice while they are at the bar, Morgan is firmly behind and aligned with Doc and hanging on every word because they are coming from the same polar perspective. Wyatt then rejects Josephine's obvious advance and "offer" to **Dance,** because **he is not ready**, and hasn't **yet** learned his lessons, down in *Tombstone*. This leads up to one of the most intense and exciting scenes I have ever seen in a movie and delivers the best lines to confirm this entire chapter.

After Wyatt and Doc get back to the faro table, Curly Bill, Johnny Ringo, and Ike Clanton come in and make a beeline right to Wyatt and as they do they walk by Behan and he cowers down like an intimidated boy. People are around Wyatt because, well, everyone knows of him because he is far more than just a former lawman from the midwest, and Satan has been alerted that his authority here may be in jeopardy. As Curly Bill snatches an autograph, he looks at it and says that he has heard of him and Ike says, "Now listen here Mr. Kansas Law dog, law don't go around here, Savvy? (Curly Bill watches this exchange intently as this could all backfire!) To which Wyatt replies,

"I'm retired", and Curly Bill says back to him, "Good, that's real good!" And Icke pops up again emboldened, "Yeah, that's real good law dog cause law just don't go round here." Wyatt, irritated that Icke is testing his patience, says forcefully and indignantly, "Yeah, I heard you the first time! Winner to the King, $500, pointing at Curly Bill. Curly Bill laughs and tells Ike to shut up!

Lord have mercy, here is what was esoterically communicated:

Satan: Well well, I heard the Son of God is here! Why are you here?

One of his men: Listen God, Lawgiver from our Star (Kansas, our star, law dog, god law), your law is not followed down here!

Son of God (looking squarely at Satan and not his insignificant follower): I am not here to interfere with your rule or upset your little kingdom.

Satan (very relieved): Good, I am happy to hear that.

One of his men again (pumped up now): Yes, Lawgiver that's real good because we are the law here.

Son of God: Put your boy in his place and don't provoke me! I told you I am not here to overturn your little neighborhood, as I have my own agenda. To show you I am sincere, here is my gift to you and (this was the 500 and 5 is the divine message), I will acknowledge that you are the king here! (winner to the King)

Satan (happy that this went well heeds the Son's warning and tells his servant): Shut up Ike!

This next exchange is even more classic! Johnny Ringo, and I will identify him later and surprise or may not surprise you, but they are related, knows full well who Doc is and isn't about to be overshadowed by Curly Bill's success! Now we already know that Doc is

Wyatt's "Saturn", or Ego of their Father. There are multiple levels of Satanic and by the time they reach the level and distinction as Saturn, with their agents of Satan below them, they are completely comfortable with their role as second fiddle to God or those who will ascend to be, and they know who and what they are and that they ultimately are an aspect *of* and not *the* One! *Since they are that ego aspect of God, God has subdued His Ego, hence the waveform manifestation falls into line.* At this point, not only are they not the adversary but just the Dark perspective and a total ally of the Self, as they are the main teacher in the development, evolution, and growth of the One. And beyond this point and beyond the universe of form, when speaking of God there is no this or that, and all of the parts, are just the ONE!

I'll just call him Johnny here, but at the end, I'll tell you who I believe he represents. You'll have the movie to reference, so I'll just get to what I believe they were really saying!

Johnny: You must be his little brother.

Doc: That's the rumor! (can't improve on that)

Johnny: Are you going to mind your own business too?

Doc: Oh hell no! If I'm here, I am going to do what I do!

Johnny: You don't look more powerful than me.

Doc, looking a bit amused and completely unruffled as he takes a slow drink before speaking.

Doc: Why you must be Ringo, the most powerful god since "Wild Bill", those who are **very easily impressed** say.

Doc [speaking to Kate in a mocking tone directed at Ringo]: Should I be afraid of him?

Kate [speaking to Doc while looking at Ringo, but not at all looking fearful of him]: Maybe he is as dangerous as they say.

Doc: That's true. [Now in a really mocking tone] I don't know, but something tells me he isn't because I'm pretty sure I know who he is and I can see it in his eyes! Yes, I'm sure of it, I know a bluff when I see one!

Wyatt: Just leave him out of this.

Now they begin communicating in a way that shows they are connected and that no one else understands.

Doc: I speak my mind and I still know a bluff when I see one. [Doc is now only speaking to Ringo, in a way that only he will understand]

Johnny: You're talking tough, but that is all you do....talk!

Doc: Trust me, talking is far from all I do and certainly not what I do best.

Johnny: Fools don't learn from the mistakes of others, but have to experience the pain themselves!

Doc: It's your funeral!

Doc [begins speaking to Kate but ends up looking Johnny in the eyes]: That's a language only those of my kind speak, which means I know him like I know myself and what I saw in his eyes was not just a bluff, but real fear! Now I know I have nothing to worry about!

Doc is now glaring at Ringo with no fear or respect for him.

Now Johnny takes the bluff to another level and starts to display some power! Doc is still unfazed even though it amazes all around him but Curly Bill warns him to be careful because he has heard that Doc is very powerful as well. (Curly Bill just won, so he is more cautious) Wyatt is ready to strike and call off all bets if Johnny is foolish enough to actually attack! Because his power is impressing everyone else, Johnny continues the display and intensifies it, but Doc does not back down and just displays a disinterested amusement about his show! When Johnny is finished, all except Doc and Wyatt, are impressed, but Doc's response is perfect and shows everyone that Johnny's display was little more than a boy's attempt at self-aggrandizement by mocking his little staged show that he hoped would intimidate Doc, but instead, Johnny is the one who is intimidated and backs down. Curly Bill, still happy with his little "victory" with Wyatt, and knowing that a retaliation from a disrespected Johnny could eliminate his own "win", laughs at Doc's display and pats Johnny on the back to diffuse his tension. As both walk away, Curly Bill / Satan celebrates his "win", as the Son has committed to him that he will not get involved in Curly's dominance here, but Johnny has been put in his place and Doc has asserted his dominance over him!

As I pointed out earlier setting up the movie with some of the real-life facts about Wyatt and the fact that his first love and wife when both were only 22 and 21, was taken from him along with his *child*, it was a major blow to him in his young life. He drifted around with women, many prostitutes and never found "the one", and collectively we are in search of our Divine Feminine! He, like Balian, had his Divine Feminine taken from him meaning he is now, not Whole, and searches, for her. Wyatt searches for his Goddess, and that is not Mattie because Mattie represents, "out there", and Wyatt instinctively knows that staying with her will spell his doom. Mattie being a drug addict prostitute is a metaphor. You will completely understand what she represents by the end of the book. When Wyatt runs into Josephine he meets the inevitable as this **must** occur and she knows he longs, as she does!

Now, you **really have to imagine that Josephine is not there, but in his mind, and he is having this conversation with himself.** Her pointed questions hit sensitive areas as he has built up walls against the pain, but she persists and her questions take him to areas that he struggles with, as she seems, (She really does because she is, his right mind), to know him better than he knows himself. *She* knows they are not happy and that he is past the level of ordinary "procreation" and wealth here and tells him that ordinary life *here*, is not what he needs. "It doesn't suit you", she tells him. She *Tells* him she knows who he is, and then identifies herself! "I want to move and go places and never look back! That's my idea of **heaven**, but I **need** someone to share it with!" She needs her Divine Masculine to create their never-ending Dance (what he earlier was not ready for), moving North and never stopping, never looking back! The Caduceus, and he is Hermes! "Never heard a woman talk like that?" Never, because she is no ordinary "woman", as she is a Goddess and he knows it! He takes his oath on it! She has found him, and will be patient as he completes his lessons! As Wyatt rides back into town they have the Sun (telling you he is, The Son) at his back! He came from the Star of His Father so that he can grow and evolve to become his own Star!

After Wyatt returns home from speaking to Josephine, his talk with Mattie puts him at an important fork in the road, and he knows that this decision is massive. "Are you happy?" That simple question is what 99% of us run from because it makes us look at our current lives that are what they are because of our past choices that were made to fulfill Desires. Are you with an addicted prostitute who just fills your sexual desires (and who *may be* married you to be supported), as they suck your money and soul? There are many addictions and non-physical addictions are the hardest to break, keeping that person a slave to an activity or *under the control of others.* Are careers to the Dark pulling you down as well, as you justify it for the money?

Unless you want your carnal desires to pull you into the abyss with them, **it is time** to turn Right because you know you are not happy (and you could see it in Wyatt's eyes as he laid in the bed with her after returning from his talk with Josephine). The Dark is designed to eventually turn you from it (but You must make the decision like the Prodigal Son and be strong to see it through), as it is programmed to take from the Light because the Dark is nothing in and of itself. The Moon cannot create its own, but simply reflects the Light it gets from the Sun, and will, for eternity. The Divine play will turn Wyatt, to his real Divine Feminine, who is inquiring from within about his happiness, because she knows, he is in a Dead End relationship, with *the Dark.* That "bloody illusion" she told David about. That obvious clue just *slaps you in the face.*

After a visit from Tombstone's friendly opium distributors, Curly Bill begins to shoot up the town, because ultimately the satanic are not disciplined and will indulge in addictions and weaknesses that will eventually bring them down. He begins to howl at the moon, and we can all figure out why the child of the Dark is howling at the moon! The deeper clue is him shooting at who and what he is. They hate themselves, and as a result, all others. The Dark perspective is an "insane" dead end one and they all eventually consume themselves. Even though Behan is the Sheriff he refuses to act on the technicality of jurisdiction as an excuse to not help Marshall White, because he is in bed with the Cowboys, essentially sending White to his slaughter.

This is much like smaller agencies being put in harm's way because the larger, usually federal agencies are stopped from *real enforcement* because their politician bosses are in bed with the crime syndicates and drug cartels. They are set up to fail and sometimes be killed. It's like Oswald being assigned to investigate assassination plots against JFK only to find the most credible and significant threats are pointing back at his Secret Society bosses in the CIA, so they make him the scapegoat and kill him before he can tell all who actually killed Kennedy that day, in Masonic Dealey Plaza. "It's deja vu all over again!"

Like JFK, RFK and JFK Jr. among **so** many others being taken out by the force that created and carried out 9-11, all of this is being set up for the coming Reckoning because Wyatt was never meant to "not get involved" down here in Tombstone! Marshall White is killed as Behan looks on unfazed (even amused as he quips "never a dull moment" to the horrified Josephine), not recognizing that "him not doing his job" has set off a series of events that will lead to the demise of his little Satanic Camelot. *That **is** how it works.* Wyatt runs out on *automatic pilot* (the start of "getting involved") to take care of the Law Enforcement duties after White is killed. This is where Wyatt shows some of his power and makes a large group of Cowboys stand down with, of course, some help from his Father's extended alter ego Doc. Wyatt establishes his dominance and communicates loud and clear to all there, that what they had heard about him is, in fact, true, and he then takes the laughing Curly Bill into Custody.

Now we are back in the bar as he has found out, what he suspected, that the entire system is corrupt but he has already stated that they are not there to get involved. He is just looking out for his children so that they do not get hurt (he still is under the illusion that He, can control this) and build some wealth, but *Virgil* is very unhappy with his life, and the choices he has made, to that point. The weak around him are being victimized and he is not overly thrilled with how they are making their money anyway. *Wyatt* senses Virgil's disillusionment so his plan is to step up the money making so they can get out of Tombstone quicker, and in the meantime, just play pool, so we don't think about it. But while Virgil isn't saying no, you can tell that he, the real **He,** is **not happy.**

After Virgil saves the boy from being trampled by the horse and seeing the terrified, scared face of the school teacher, and note that it is the left side of her face that is scarred and disfigured, he has seen all he can take and changes course. Remember, Wyatt is there, and not there! Virgil can no longer stomach the injustice and the weaker always living in fear, so he rejects the gambling, but note, you never saw him around them anyway, and he accepts the Mayor's offer to be the next Town Marshall, who will now openly oppose the corruption. He has already recruited his brother, who I said is subservient to him because of what Morgan is (notice too throughout the movie how Morgan looks a bit "mechanically fake" and exhibits fear), and they are already posting laws by the time Wyatt confronts. This will make so much more sense if you again view them as there by themselves and are able to have a conversation with God, like they used to have in the Old Testament. Actually, this is one man having an internal struggle with the very hard choices that need to be dealt with right now. Here is what they are really saying!

Wyatt: What are you doing? I didn't open up opportunities in Tombstone for you to clash with the Satanic element. I have a plan for us to get rich and beat the system and told you not to get involved with their dominance here. We can beat the system if we ignore the injustice.

Virgil: You got us involved, and you know I can't just sit back and ignore it. I can't live in a place where people are dominated and live in constant fear and then try to make money here and pretend everything is alright with everyone else, to feed my greed.

Wyatt: This is going to ruin *my plan*. Don't do this to me.

Virgil: This is bigger than your little illusory plan. I am responsible for my soul. It's about.....

Wyatt cuts off Virgil off (to speak to Morgan) because Virgil was about to say, "...doing what is right!"

Wyatt: Try to talk him out of this because I know you liked the opportunity here. You liked the easy money and....Oh no, not you too!?!

Morgan: We came together and I can't work the gaming table without his permission. I had to back his decision! I didn't think you would have a problem with it, being a lawman as well. "Just did like I figured you would" (He said this because Wyatt, **did!**)

Wyatt: Now not only are you two in danger, because look what happens to those who oppose them, you also may have to take another's life!

Morgan: We know what we're doing, this will work out for us spiritually!

Wyatt: This will not end well for my Ego! (Now starts, Wyatt's big lesson)

You may be thinking that if Wyatt is "the Son" as you say he is, then why is he making obvious mistakes? He and You, are not *so different.* You see, on the evolutionary path that includes many incarnations, even in the "higher realms" with more advanced vessels / bodies, the *upperclassmen* gods do what they believe is right and when they make a "mistake", it is all about the lessons that *They, the Sons or the adopted polar sons,* and those under them need to learn! Like us, but they are in a higher class, they still need lessons repeated at times! It is all in the grand scheme of God growth for the younger of us as well. Jesus too needed to be betrayed and all that went with it for his own development before he could ascend! He knew he had to but he wasn't thrilled with the process at times either. He took Peter and, the "Sons of Zebedee" with him, James and **John** (the sons of Thunder), while he prayed to his Father at Gethsemane, to spare him from this ordeal, **if** it is his will, but this is a necessary step, and Jesus knew this is how **it,** must be done, as unpleasant as it is. And it is amazingly hard to let go of the illusion of control. Wyatt had a plan, and like Thor's, it didn't end well, but like the Oracle's comment to Neo about the vase tells you that, their *plans* were, so to speak, *planned,* and when a lesson is learned, is "bad", really *bad? Of course, it isn't! The Fall, was fulfillment!*

Things really start to unravel now! Not only are the brothers the new law in town who actually stand up to the Cowboys, but Doc is cleaning up in Poker taking much of their money while mocking them in the process. Between the brothers opposing their control, and Doc grabbing much of their wealth, they are beginning to have had enough of the Earps and Holliday. You notice you don't see much of Johnny, because he wants no part of Doc. With Doc and the Earps in town, the Cowboys are not getting the respect they once enjoyed and they are no longer running the town as they once did when White was the town Marshal. This is similar to the two brother Kennedy administration coming in and upsetting the corrupt system when JFK was firing secret society members, like Allen Dulles, left and right and taking steps to oust the private bank known as the Federal Reserve and allowing RFK to go after and prosecute the mob. It obviously didn't sit well with them and they had to take back what was theirs. And it was all in the plan to bring about the end of the greater age.

Doc surely did find his female equal in Kate who doesn't want the excitement, travel, sex, fun and big money high life to come to an end and tries to get Doc's mind off of the fact that more than half of his lungs are now gone and that his "excesses" are killing him faster! "I knew it wasn't nothing", and that priceless look he gives her. *"We must talk. It appears we must redefine the nature of our association."* Meaning, he knows that, in order to fulfill his destiny to help Wyatt, He must change course now, for his time is slipping away. She represents the "expected" Luciferian dark's pull down, that "he" must now turn from, to complete Wyatt's lesson here. Doc knows that, while he is **from the Dark,** he is no longer on the *Dark's side.* This next point is a huge spiritual connection. Like Loki, Doc was taken from and **adopted** by **The Light.** *"Then again (she) may be the antichrist"! (she is, a manifestation of That)* Kate, like Hela in Thor, is a part of the Luciferian Dark, that will eternally remain, in the Dark.

The interaction between the three brothers in front of the Marshal's office goes a long way in confirming my spiritual take concerning their true relationship. Wyatt sits apart from them, detached from their drama. As Mayor Clum walks by him he sarcastically thanks him for fanning their flames. As Doc joins in the act Wyatt appears more as their father laying out different options and consequences. He is, in essence, telling them to think it through and look at all of the ramifications of the different possibilities that can come from a confrontation. This is rather like a single person going through the thought process before a very important decision is made. After Virgil's steadfast position is made clear, Wyatt turns to Doc and tells him that this is something *he* needs to work out and he needn't concern himself with participating in a confrontation, but Doc knows he is connected to him and he is part of the reason a confrontation is imminent. So Doc admonishes Wyatt like only a brother can!

Wyatt turns away and then sighs and does what any good parent must finally do, as he turns to Virgil to *Untie the Apron* String. He has laid out all of the "what ifs" and it is now time for his boy to live his own life and learn from the choices he made. I tried to look for the quote that fits here, but I couldn't find it, but I heard it back in the 70's I believe and it was attributed to Charles Bronson, and went something like this as this is what I remember. "Some men, particularly men with money, try to shield their sons from the harsh lessons of life, that they themselves experienced, that turned them into men." So true and at some point you just have to let go after you have done your job and let them live their life to experience all the consequences! **"Your call Virg!"**

The **4** walking down the street (The **North**, Wyatt - The **South**, Virgil - The **East**, Morgan - The **West**, Doc) with the burning building behind them, is telling us that the class of 6 is coming to an end and that justice is coming to cleanse. The Phoenix of 8 will rise from the ashes of the old paradigm. This image with the words "Justice is coming" was used on the movie poster and DVD cover for good reason. As they walk down the street, all of the background **actors** watch, Wyatt asks himself, "How in the Hell did we get ourselves into this?" A question that has left my lips on numerous occasions! (slow learner) Doc is there not only to help, as Virgil is not the only one with lessons to learn down here in Tombstone, but to ensure that events unfold to maximize Wyatt's lessons, as Doc is both the accelerant to this combustible confrontation, but he is also the reaper who going to collect *those* who will occupy the roots! He winks at Billy Clanton to ensure he gets his men. The McLaury brothers and Billy Clanton will be buried alright, and they won't be coming up anytime soon! Now Ike had no gun so no one shot at him, but as the guns were blazing only two who had guns, did not get shot! They are there, and not there, and they walk away, the team that they are!

After Behan couldn't stop them, he now tried to arrest them, because they are rapidly destroying his little empire there, but he is far weaker than Wyatt and backs down. "You were right, it was nothing like I thought", laments Morgan, but, and that is why we are here, to experience and he learned a valuable lesson! The funeral procession down Allen St with all of the cowboys present holding signs that they were murdered, are Satan's lies of course. Don't expect them to make sense. They are not in their "Right minds", and the war is on, meaning there is no "fair" involved here! It has started and right after Wyatt and Morgan talk, you see a good shot of the rising Sun and church steeple with a cross on top of a pyramid over a bell, and I think I have covered what all these represent! As the Earps walk down the street, they find themselves ostracized from most of the town they believed they were liberating, but as we see around us, this world does not always make sense to those who do *right*. You are no one's "Savior", but simply doing what you know to be **Right** as you shake the dust off of your feet.

"You have to understand, most of these people are not ready to be unplugged. And many of them are so inert, so hopelessly dependent on the system...that they will fight to protect it." ~ "The Matrix", Morpheus speaking to "The One"

A drunk Ringo confronts them and wants to exact some revenge on the brothers, especially Wyatt, but they pay him no mind, but his words, that he wants their blood, which is red, and their souls, reveal his true identity. This is why Doc had him pegged at the Saloon, that he is in Luciferian line that will remain in the dark. *I completely understand this dynamic now of how the Light, takes a piece of the Dark, to be the next Ego of the Light, thereby "saving" that little piece or perspective of the Dark, to move up to the Light. Just as Loki knew where he came from, Doc knows his own, but both have been removed from the Dark, to show the Light its complete spectrum.*

After Ringo yells at the brothers for not having the guts to engage him, Doc emerges from the shadows to eagerly confront him saying, "I'm your Huckleberry. . .That's just my game!" According to the Historical Dictionary of American Slang, "I'm your Huckleberry", was a common slang term in 19th Century America and meant, "I'm just the man you're looking for." Even in his compromised state, Johnny didn't immediately engage Doc and was, this time, rescued by Curly Bill and company. Wyatt should have been more tuned into Curly Bill's comment to Johnny, "Juanito, their time will come.", but everything happens for a reason because without it, the Reckoning will not unfold.

The scene with Behan confronting Josephine confirms what we knew that the Satanic Cochise County Sheriff was in league with the Satanic organized crime cowboys. The Dark are endless schemers and they ultimately consume one another and themselves. He knows they are going to "hit" the Earp brothers, and attempts to sway Josephine back to his side by telling her that he will be King, and will control Tombstone, this world.

It is Satan wanting to be the Man, to the Divine Feminine. She, of course, rebuffs him. The weather is dicey and unstable the night the brothers are shot because not only are we all connected, but everything is connected to everything, and what goes on in our minds, affect what you see out there. We, are HAARP folks. The Satanic forces have no honor, decency or shame (don't expect "fair") and attack the wives of the Mayor and the brothers and of course shoot at them from the shadows. When the Doctor tells Virgil and Allie he will never again have the use of his "left" arm, Allie yells at Wyatt and it has only been in the last few months that it occurred to me what Wyatt's true identity was in this film. I never understood why she blamed him, until now. Wyatt is not there! She is more cursing God for what has happened to Virgil, (for putting them in harm's way) but she is actually yelling at Morgan, for pushing the move to such a dangerous place, and this is why he runs from the house.

Wyatt simply can't escape it playing pool. His Ego, Morgan, is then shot, and as he is dying he again tells Wyatt that he is the One, and he doesn't mean his "older brother"! Wyatt is not targeted and not around when both brothers are shot again confirming his *other-dimensional presence.* In stories dealing with polar relationships, the "negative" one usually perishes before the "positive" and here, Morgan will die before Virgil and Doc before Wyatt. As they leave town, Wyatt again is not in the wagon with the rest of them, but with his now deceased ego, and as he stops to speak with the essence that crucified Christ. Wyatt, like Thor, has now been humbled, and with his ego's plans crushed, he tells Satan that his plan is done, as he now knows to "let the river take him", and not set up the "illusion" on the river bank! But what is *also done,* is his agreement to allow them to rule here, but what he does from this point, is the will of The Father. Satan, being Satanic, is programmed to bite off more than he can chew, so that they can be taken down, here in the 7-11 School of Duality!

Wyatt knowingly was prepared for an ambush, and now with his true spiritual son safely back on the 5150 train "home", he signals to his son Virgil that they are once again aligned and One! The Locomotive 11 is passing Wyatt as he puts his boot on Ike's throat and says, "All right, Clanton. You called down the Thunder (god). Well, now you got it." And of course Lightning creates a sonic shock wave that you know as thunder, and lightning is electricity, and according to Wikipedia, *Elektor (ἠλέκτωρ) is also an ancient Greek name or epithet of the Sun, see Helios.* And Kansas, Ike said, was the name of his Star! When Wyatt says, "You see that? It says United States Marshall." With the 5 point up, pentagram within the circle badge really means he is authorized by the Stars, that he carries, the **Heart of The Father**! *This is actually another confirmation of a huge point!* This is big for Wyatt because what he **was** doing in Tombstone with his spiritual family was *his plan*, his will, but now this "Reckoning" is not *"his will"*, but the will of God.

"For I have come down from heaven, not to do My own will, but the will of Him who sent Me." -John This truly is, **Letting Go!** *He is now autho-*

rized, by The Father to carry out what he will do. Like the asteroid that causes change, it is the will of God. Not the Egoistic plan of Wyatt but God working through him. You are now doing more by doing less! All of these years, the quotes I thought I knew because they seemed self-evident enough, were anything but! I am not here of my own will, or I am not speaking on my own authority, seem to be crystal clear, but even the ones, like this, have a more subtle, hidden meaning. Wyatt is now operating on, **Faith!**

Take a good look at him Ike, 'cause that's how you're gonna end up! All with **the mark** will die!

The Cowboys are finished.	Satan's time is finished
You understand me?	[You know Ike doesn't!, lol]
I see a red sash,	I see the Satanic vibrational signature.
I kill the man wearin' it.	I send him to his chosen domain
So run, you cur.	Run cockroaches, but you can't hide!
Run! Tell all the other curs	Tell the other roaches the Reckoning is here
the law is comin'!	God's Law will be enforced
You tell 'em I'm comin'!	The God of Thunder has arrived
And hell's comin' with me, you hear?	You will hear the thunder!
Hell's comin' with me!	"...and Hell followed with Him."

In the next scene, the film confirms they are coming from our Star! They begin cleaning house! They show them doing this until the scene that shows Wyatt's divinity at the creek. It is important to remember that something similar like this really happened. Think of the countless gunfights this guy has been in and even coming out in the open with bullets being fired in his direction from various locations. This is from Wikipedia of the real event:

"Now Curly Bill fired at Wyatt with his shotgun from about 50 feet (15 m) but missed. Wyatt returned fire with his own shotgun, killing Brocius with a load of buckshot to his chest. Curly Bill fell into the water at the edge of the spring and lay dead. The Cowboys fired a number of shots at the Earp party. Texas Jack Vermillion's horse was struck and killed. Wyatt's long coat was punctured by bullets on both sides. Another bullet struck his boot heel and his saddle-horn was hit as well, burning the saddle hide and narrowly missing Wyatt. Firing his pistol, Wyatt shot Johnny Barnes in the chest and Milt Hicks in the arm."

Again I say, *this is more than just an "Action Hero" Hollywood movie*, as there are core truths about Wyatt and Doc that validate the overall message! They never get hurt, as Doc is taken later by God. Wyatt's coat looks like swiss cheese and bullets are lodged in his boots! I seriously have no words. . .okay I do, but this is real life Divinity being played out, and not a Hollywood set. And this is just one of dozens of shoot-outs they have been in. Move over Arnold, this man **is** the real-life Terminator! In this scene, the Masons openly tell you what this movie is meant to communicate and who, is giving it to you!

"Did you ever see anything like that before?

Hell, I ain't never even heard of anything like that. Nothin'.

Where is he?

Down by the creek, walkin' on water. [another clue of his divine lineage]

Well, let's hope he's got another miracle up his sleeve. Cause if I know Ringo, he's headed straight for us. Well, if they were my brothers, I'd want revenge too. [revenge is Satan's karma]

No. Make no mistake. It's not revenge he's after. It's a reckoning. [a reckoning is God's will]

Doc. You ought to be in bed. What the hell you doin' this for anyway? [helping Wyatt **is** Doc's purpose.]

Wyatt Earp is my friend.

Hell, I got lots of friends.

I don't."

Okay, this scene is **openly telling** you that what occurred was Divine and that a Reckoning, a judgment, not Ego driven revenge but God's Will, will occur here and that the two polar aspects, Jesus and Satan, if you want to put a name to them, will judge you. They are working through the Divine Feminine and are your Spiritual parents and who better to judge? Doc is tied to Wyatt and his One true *friend!* The Father is the Royal Purple that sees through his blue positive Smith and his red negative Smith. The Father, who sees all, the leaves and the roots of the tree is beyond judging, as that is left up to his "Children", and they know their flock! As Creek is talking to Doc, they show you who is bringing this message to you! His Masonic Square and Compass necklace is large and in full view as he is dressed in red and blue, and Texas Jack, his purple scarf! They bring you Hollywood, they bring you everything! They are also telling you that this Divine event will appear ordinary. They will unfold as usual disasters, as Wyatt and Doc did not come down from chariots above the clouds. Those who look like you and me will foment this transitional change taking place and the two flocks who are separated, will go to their respective locations, and I cover that in remaining chapters.

In the next scene, the satanic forces have amassed in large numbers to defend their perceived *control*. The stagecoach is showing that the *good* people will escape the carnage and that those who die, it is their time and even if you don't understand it, there is a reason for everything! As Wyatt is challenged by Ringo, he accepts, stunning the others who see Ringo as more powerful, but as soon as Wyatt says, "It's not finished", it goes right to a large Lightning strike at to peak of a nearby mountain! The Divine plan unfolding! Wyatt's direction is beginning to crystallize and he has another revealing talk with his "brother". Doc tells Wyatt who he is dealing with in Ringo, because it takes one, to know one.

"A man like Ringo...got a great empty hole right through the middle of him. (meaning he has no heart, and will always be an aspect of the dark) He can never kill enough or steal enough or inflict enough pain to ever fill it.

What does he need?

Revenge. [Yes, Ringo is a dark program that has a job to do]

For what?

Bein' born." [He is doing what he was born to do! To **be** the sharpening rod that sharpens the steel]

Ringo knows who he is, or I should say, what he is! Remember Agent Smith becoming "self-aware" within the Matrix and discovering himself to be a computer program? Or on Star Trek TNG's episode where the boys are enjoying a "Sherlock Holmes" Holodeck program when the amazingly intelligent Professor James Moriarty discovers he is actually a computer program within a "starship" and plans his escape? Well, Ringo's big empty hole is void of a heart and his knowledge that he is just a programmed empty, as in heart, vessel doesn't sit well with him and the *justification for his existence, as Ego doesn't feel connected, **is through** conflict and control*, and don't we see this worldwide. His Satanic ego is programmed to the extreme adversarial extent. It is all about which Smith vessel contains the heart, which **is** the soul! The sacred heart! One is real, and one is just a machine!

As we know, Doc was acting a bit, as to the severity of his illness at that moment, because he knew what Wyatt was up against with Ringo. When Doc asks Wyatt, "What's it like to wear one of those?", he is saying, what's it like to have the Heart of God? What is it like to have a Soul? How many wooden boys and machines, like "Data" from Star Trek, wish to be "human"! What they lack is Soul. And there are lots of Tin men and women walking around that look like you and me. Doc will soon get a taste of that feeling, like when "Q" rewarded Data, by allowing him to actually **know** the feeling of laughter, for saving his life in "Deja Q".

Just as the Rainbow bridge comes to this world in "New Mexico", Wyatt tells the boys, "They're not givin ya safe conduct. Shootin starts, you better kick it east to the New Mexico line". He is telling them, telling you, the *narrow gate* will be found in **New Mexico**, when Hell breaks loose here. When Creek says, "I ain't got the words", he is saying that what he feels transcends words and cannot be communicated verbally and Wyatt agrees knowing he is speaking of the heart!

Of all the hidden messages in here, I just saw this one **just now**. As Ringo believes it is Wyatt approaching him he speaks to him and says what we all heard as, I didn't think you had the courage, but his, "I didn't think you had it in you.", was actually to Doc! (the hidden meaning) They both know they are to the dark, but something is different about Doc this time! Here is what they really meant!

Ringo: I didn't think ya had it in you!

*I was sure you didn't have a heart! You're a terminator like me! Why are **you** here?*

Doc: I'm your Huckleberry.

*I **am** just the man you are supposed to fight.*

Ringo: Fight's not with you Holliday.

My fight is with the Light, those who have hearts, those who are real!

Doc: I'll beg to differ, sir. We started a game we never got to finish, play for blood, remember?

Oh, but you did start a fight with me. You started a game of dominance for this red world and here we will finish it.

Ringo: I was just foolin about.

I was just playing you like you were real.

Doc: I wasn't.

I am going to take away all your excuses!

And this time, [as he exposes his badge] it's legal.

Because now, [as he exposes his heart of the Father] I AM real.

Ringo: Alright Lunger, let's do it.

Then you "really" are my enemy!

I just now saw that (like a Star is Born), coming to this scene to decode it, and as I was hearing Ringo say, "I didn't think you had it in you", I had that light go off *"sur-realization"*, that he's not saying that to Wyatt, but to Doc, and why Doc wanted Wyatt's **"badge"** before he left. *The Sacred Heart, the Lion's Heart, His Soul!* That is, the only reality!

After Doc shoots him in the head, notice it is on the left side. He is killing the left brain! And his "Come on Johnny" taunts, are come to the light, come to the right. What does a daisy look like? A little fuzzy half ball yellow center with long white petals all around it looks like the Sun to me. "You're no Daisy at all", means you are not from the

Light! And "poor soul" means he is poor in soul, he has no soul. When Wyatt gets there he resumes his normal polar relation with Wyatt by dropping the heart. He got a taste of it because he **is,** like Loki, now in the Light family.

Because of this, he is protecting his Light family from what he used to be, like Loki killing King Laufey. Now while Loki's logic is warped, he does believe he is protecting his family of Hearts. It's like the wooden creation Pinocchio, who dreams of being real like his Father and would do anything to protect his Father! Doc is protecting his *real* Brother from, "his father?" (maybe) The amazed Wyatt says, "Alright, Let's finish it.", and Doc once again clues you in on their "Divine" level with, "Indeed sir. The last charge of Wyatt Earp and his Immortals." The 4 Horsemen ride off to finish their work! You have to laugh at the two guys who got away, who you really wanted to see go down, but Behan and Ike, get away...for now! (You can run, but you can't hide) And a round of applause from me to Jon Tenney and Stephen Lang for amazing performances that made you truly detest them. And Col. Lang isn't done making you despise him!

The last scene with Doc and Wyatt is amazingly touching and revealing. Yes, Doc and Father Feeney, "Investigating the mysteries of the Church of Rome"! Isn't that the truth! In the next chapter, I will reveal why Doc called it **The Church of Rome**, and not The Catholic Church, as this **IS the biggest in plain sight mislead of all time**, and certainly mysteries galore. *This next interaction between them is your own internal polar conversation.* We curse the dark, but we need the dark! Not too much, but just the right amount of spice! And who wouldn't want Doc as the extra spice! Keep in mind that now with Wyatt's Ego dead, and the Satanic element vanquished, Doc is very close to withering away as well. He was only here to work in Tandem with Wyatt as the force of The Father. He is only hanging on now because Wyatt is still not ready to cross his internal bridge to his Divine Feminine of The Right Brain. He still needs his internal Doctor's guidance. Doc knows that Wyatt coming back to see him is retarding his development, so he admonishes him for coming back.

"You're the only person I can afford to lose to anymore. How we feelin' today, Doc?" (because his will, his plan failed, he feels he has lost everything and the only thing he is literally able to lose, is an argument with himself, in reality, he has only lost the thoughts he was attached to, and Doc is there to help him see this, and that he is a better man for it. He has progressed. And that is what life is all about)

"I'm dying. How are you?" *(I am ready to leave, but I can't until you leave the Left.)*

"Pretty much the same." (I am not ready to leave the left, which I know **is** *death)*

"So now we add self-pity to our list of frailties." (Wyatt is admonished for finding excuses not to embrace his Dark, remaining in Left Brain Separation)

Wyatt tries to distract him, but he doesn't budge and while calling him stubborn and stuck in his own pity, he compliments him for the love he has shown him that "maybe" no one else in his life has shown him, and that he has Hope because of Wyatt. Wyatt is basically speaking to his Father, who is telling him he is proud of him, but he still needs to take another step.

"All right, Doc."

As Wyatt speaks to his internal Doctor, he is pretty low right now. **His egoistic** plans have been destroyed and we have now come full circle from Fred White's, **"It's a regular slaughterhouse"**. Doc will help him see that he is not the only one who has lost, and that he has a wonderful opportunity in front of him and that he needs to be grateful for it. Wyatt is healthy and Doc is near death. Wyatt needs to put things into perspective and know who he is, and that the universe awaits the Full mind and power of the Son!

Doc continues:

"I was in love once. My first cousin. She was 15. We were both so..."

That's good, Do. That's... That's good. What happened?

"She joined a convent over the affair. She was all I ever wanted. What do you want?

Just to live a normal life.

"There's no normal life Wyatt, there's just life. Now get on with it."

I don't know how.

"Sure you do. Say goodbye to me. Go grab that **spirit**ed *actress* and make her your own. Take that beauty and run, don't look back. (He is telling him to see in Unity and to embrace his Dark, His Feminine Right Brain. To flow with the river and to not stay mired in the negative thoughts of the past. They were lessons, so move on, and **SHE is** waiting for you! Leave me now, but I will always be a part of you! Wyatt listens to the best friend he has ever had!

He is now ready, and with that Doc passes away. With valuable lessons under his belt and with the twinkle of Doc in his eye now, He goes Right, to Josephine! Wyatt going *into* the Theater, as this is all one big theater, is Him going within to truly "Marry" His Divine Feminine, His Temple, His Spirit, to truly become, "One Flesh". That's why when he is initially speaking to her, it's her reflection. She is within Him! He is the Prodigal Son who has come home, no longer looking "Out There" for the drugged prostitute. He *was* lost, and is now Found! And once He "made the bond" with his **El**ect Lady, and the fact they are now One, it would last until the end of the universe, which was the clue in, *"I promise I'll love you the rest of your life".* Her message to him of, *"Don't worry Wyatt, my family is rich!",* clues us in to Her *royal* identity, for there are "no worries" when you are the extension of the One God *creating the material.*

> *"You cannot beat a river into submission. You have to surrender to its current, and use its power as your own."* ~"Dr. Strange", The Ancient One's advice to Stephen

Now that that Wyatt has grown and matured, he will create "responsibly". He had to learn this lesson first. They move outside and Josephine asks, "What shall we do first?" and Wyatt tells her it is what she wanted to do the first night they met, but he wasn't ready. She wanted to dance, and of course, now, they are in the position to *dance because He is ready,* so Wyatt asks, "May I have this dance?" And they begin to dance, round and round, beginning their eternal *Dance.* Think Caduceus, as They begin their own Creation Dance!

At the still point of the turning world. Neither flesh nor fleshless;
Neither from nor towards; at the still point, there the dance is,
But neither arrest nor movement. And do not call it fixity,
Where past and future are gathered. Neither movement from nor towards,
Neither ascent nor decline. Except for the point, the still point,
There would be no dance, **and there is only the dance**.

T.S. Eliot

"Wyatt and Josephine embarked on a series of adventures, up or down, thin or flush in 47 years they never left each other's side. Wyatt Earp died in Los Angeles in 1929." ~The ending Narration. In 47 = **11**, the 2, never left each other's side, and he passed on, in the City of The Angels in 1929 = 21 = 3.

Tombstone is definitely encoded with clues pointing to an Apocalypse type event, a planetary reckoning or cleansing with a new rising level of awareness. Wyatt and Doc are clearly identified in this film as a step above normal men and in many aspects of real documented historical facts, many of these mystical differences are confirmed. And as you'll see by the end, Josephine has much in common with "Jupiter" and "Jane Foster". Wyatt Earp, who is identified as the "Son" in the film, never had children, like someone else. The movie Tombstone is clearly an internal metaphor of a "Thomas" finally embracing his internal Dark (no longer projecting it by seeing in Separation) to become One with it, becoming the "Bridegroom", and in "The Matrix" at the end of the movie, this dynamic of coming together with his Dark is represented by Neo dressed entirely in Black, and *Once you* do This *(go black) you never go back!*

In the *endless, timeless* universe, there are cyclical classes that have a beginning and an ending. The final exams in those classes don't mean *The End*, but the start of a new beginning, and the answer to the why puts every question I ever had about the necessity of a final judgment, *straight to bed!* Now, go grab your hot toddy, put the reading light on, tuck yourself in, and let all of the pieces fall into place as **"The Reckoning"** is but a celestial segue to, **"Let there be Light"**, for **Jupiter's Ascension** addresses all, and this is one *Jones,* that you just might want to keep up with!

Lastly, Kevin Jarre, the writer of Tombstone died in **2011** of unexpected "Heart" failure, on 4-3-2011 (9-11) which added up equals **11**, in Santa Monica which has **11** letters, at the age of 56, which equals **11**. The name is most likely of Phoenician origin coming from North African Saint Monica of Hippo, the mother of Saint Augustine! Remember the question, "Why would Target do this?" This answers this question better than I could ever answer it, in the mystical 7-**11** School of Duality. Kevin, with its 5 letters is 7 and Jarre as well has 5 and is 7, and 7+7 is 14, which is 5, the sublime Divine message!

12. Jupiter's Ascension

Simba....Look at the stars. The great kings of the past look down on us from those stars. So whenever you feel alone, just remember that those kings will always be there to guide you. And so will I.

~The Lion King (1994) 5

It is *well-known* that the universe is expanding, and of all of the "well known facts" that are usually exoteric fairy tales, this one happens to be true! The Father of "Lights" grows! They are the great kings of the **past** because on the path to become a Star, you must first be a great King of the Solar System, which is a Star in training! Yes, Jupiter has 7 letters, and individually add to 1379259=39=9, so it is a 7 soon to become 9, and Jones has 5 letters and adds to 16551=18=9, the Divine message that a transition is near! So, let us look at the Ascension of one, Jupiter "Jones"!

From Wikipedia:
"Jones is a surname of Welsh origins, derived from the given name John which in turn is derived from the Hebrew name *Yochanan (Johanan)*

John /dʒɒn/ is a masculine given name in the English language. The name is derived from the Latin *Ioannes* and *Iohannes*, which are forms of the Greek name *Iōannēs* ('Ιωάννης), originally borne by Hellenized Jews transliterating the Hebrew name *Yohanan* (ïÈðÈçÉåé), "Graced by God"

So, **Jones** means, **Graced by God**

Now keep in mind that while there is a "masculine perspective" our waveform teacher of the dark, isn't what you have been led to believe as curved lines are feminine so waves and spherical planetary bodies are by Nature Feminine, and we all know we live on Mother Earth, and the two work hand in hand to develop and *"create!* And we have just learned that Jupiter Jones really means, **"Jupiter *Graced by God*"**! So, the *Female Star* of the movie "Jupiter Jones", played by Mila Kunis, is actually code for the *planet* Jupiter, so the **Star** of the movie *is* **Jupiter!** A clue within a clue, but maybe duality is in play, and there is "another".

Where I am about to take you, *we don't need roads!* And that's good because there aren't any! We are blazing a trail in the outer reaches of our solar system. Now that I know you will be mated and forever linked with your polar Smith, I have taken several other clues, more filled in dots to connect more lines and this concept of solar expansion "appeared" to me. Because the clues got personal and our days of the week honor them, I don't just think, I know the Thor and Odin "mythology" is truth, for those ready to take the next step, and to all others not ready, either ignored or just seen as entertainment or cute stories, and that's perfectly fine. The pantheon of lower tier gods and goddesses of the Proto-Indo-Europeans fits very well in my model of the structure of the All that Is One mind, God. They are just in a vibratory realm above ours because they are more advanced than us as they are our spiritual parents who have already been through this. As I stated earlier, the evolution of the many separate species not connected to the whole is an exoteric understanding of an immense process that cannot be understood through the eyes of a child. God is growing and evolving, and we, like cells within the larger body, are interwoven aspects of that overall growth! The esoteric meaning of "evolution" deals with the development of the entire organism, the Universe!

Cogito ergo sum!

The light is expanding and not just *"carbon copy"* expansion, but growing and evolving from new perspectives, and as each new Star grows, it needs to look back at itself, subjectively outside of the light, and with all of them, from a slightly different perspective. As snow falls adding to the snow on the ground, superficially they all look the same, but every flake is supremely unique, just like every star. Think of it this way! Suppose you were tasked with creating a way to teach "you" about yourself to younger inexperienced aspects of yourself who only knew love, freedom, abundance, and protection, having always been sheltered, never experiencing anything else. You know they can't just be told this or learn it from a textbook and kept as experienced knowledge! A man can read and watch films and be there for the birth of his children, but unless he gets into a real woman's body, with *all of the God-given hardware*, and tempt me as you may but I won't say *his, erh her* name, he won't really know what it is like to be a woman, *much less giving birth*. You don't know it unless you experience it and that is why know is in *know*ledge, knowing the broader complete picture.

So you devise a *real-world* classroom that will separate them from the loving collective and devise a vessel for them to experience it, similar to their "light" bodies. The created vessel will be a mirror image opposite in nature so that they are denser and more restrictive, so that they will learn what it is to be free, by in**car**cerating them within a temporary **car**nal prison with boundaries in an imaginary world of pain, suffering and loneliness where they have to strive to survive (lol, sign me up, right?). You will also program their vessel with a **self-aware** darker adversarial perspective so that they will be able to subjectively look at themselves from the **opposite perspective**. As we all know, how much depth of character, and you know that twinkle when you see it, can one have who has no knowledge of the dark? Most of us know someone (usually an older relative) who loves you and would give you the shirt off their back and you think of them as saintly, but they have this magnetic "life of the party" quality with amazing stories precisely because they have been around the block in an "unsaintly" manor a time or two! And a Prince, who has also lived the life of a scared and starving Pauper, will be a better King for having experienced this perspective.

I was having a hard time making sense of Thor and Loki as "the two" under Odin in the "Pyramid Scheme", and it didn't make sense to me that half under him would be to the dark or negative, in their own pyramid pointing up/to the light/positive, and at some point *they*, assuming the top ascended position. As I thought about it, I knew that the segment of Thor at the beginning of the movie with Odin as a younger man speaking to his two young boys giving them a history lesson was a massive clue in many respects!

As they enter the Armory vault facing the blue Casket of Ancient Winters the boys are on each side of the *single-eyed* Odin. Thor is on his Right, and Loki is on his Left. He steps away from them and walks to the casket and turns to face them, continuing the conversation, saying "But the day will come when *one* of you will have to defend that peace." And after Thor proclaims, "When I am King, I will hunt the monsters down and slay them all just as you did Father!" Odin's only reply, and for good reason, without squelching Thor's exuberant talk of exterminating the "monsters", as he believed his father did, was to say, "A wise king never seeks out war, but he must always be ready for it!" He then walks toward them and passing in between them, continues by as the boys look at one another full of joy and enthusiasm, ready to conquer the universe and run in what looks like a straight line toward their father to catch up to him. When they catch up to him to grab his hands, Thor is mysteriously back on Odin's right side and Loki on his left! Of course! After both tell their father they are with him, he says something that, as soon as it left his mouth, I knew was vitally important!

"Only one of you can ascend to the throne, but you were both born, to be Kings!"
                    -the "Single Eyed" Odin's words to young Thor and Loki

I now understand the two under Odin, or the "two under" any Eye at the top of the pyramid and why *only* **one** can ascend to the Throne! First and foremost, there is only The Self, the One Mind. The reason the "Light", the "Positive", the "Right" is the only "Polarity" to Ascend is because, the opposing perspective is a "Duality" illusion, for in the end they are just aspects of the same consciousness, as you can't separate an Atom and have two surviving parts as each simply vanish. So the positive polarity sees through both as the Neutron, being still within the nucleus, for an organism must be more Good than Evil or it will consume itself and perish. As I pointed out earlier, life is set up to eventually crush, but not crush, more *subdue* Ego, so that Ego knows it's place within the One, as it is the *bad*, but not bad, more adversarial aspect that the **one** mind needs in order to completely understand itself. *How many arguments or discussions are enhanced by one side being, "the Devil's advocate"?* The quote by Odin in Thor tells you everything. One is His true child, being the continuation of "The Father". The other child is the True child's "Devil's Advocate".

The real you, the Spiritual Self is inserted into a program that in essence, splits the "Self" in two, who are physically manifest here, who "wed", in a spiritual and real mathematical equation. They will know one another very well, and in some cases very **intimately,** *as I cough,* well, and when they will move apart to their respective polarities mirroring each other within the Smith Equation, they are still one and will always stay connected (son of a..) within the equation while manifested in this program, within this reality. Thor and Loki or many others like them will eventually be an aspect of a new Star or it's Saturn polar aspect. Once they are "brought under control", to understand unity, think of Doc or Loki as the Ego oriented perspectives of Odin/Jupiter, being there to help and guide His Son, Wyatt or Thor. So the atom's property shows us justification for the "need" of an electron (Saturn). As we grow, we are made more aware of our basic atomic makeup in this cosmos of Duality. Know that just as a proton must have an electron, our Sun absolutely needs our darker Saturnic Lord of the Rings. **They were both Born, to be Kings!**

Many will lose their minds over this, but Saturn really is that get your hands dirty aspect of God that rears the children and prepares the ones destined to the new stars and dark stars, or to the less desirable eternally dark**er** parts of Town all overseen, by **Her.** We are becoming more aware of our cosmic players, and it's why the Pope is speaking of *"him"*, more openly! Time to establish our homeostasis, and stop the repression of an aspect that IS as necessary as breathing itself and embrace it because it is, who we are! Time for clarity and *balance!*

Let's look at Odin (Jupiter), and begin to lay this ongoing structure from a divine blueprint, out! It took me a while, but I have this "Negative" lineage, in its proper location within the structural pyramid. While being within the pyramid of his ascended forefathers, Odin IS at the top of the pyramid in Asgard and that is why he is called the "All Father" as he is the spiritual father of everyone in Asgard, and all under him in the solar system, that will be a part of the new Star and Solar system that breaks away from this one. But it's not the one you are thinking of, because you have been (big surprise) mislead. He presides over the 9 realms, and not including Pluto as a planet anymore was a clue for me. In the movie, *Jotunheim* is a very dark cold planet of rock and ice and that is what they tell us *Pluto* is, and these *new images of Pluto look remarkably similar to Jotunheim*, and where they came up with these pictures for Jotunheim back in 2011 is for another discussion. So it's not the eternal fire, but the eternal cold and darkness, as that IS opposite from the warmth and light of the Sun.

Time to just lay this out, and let the meteors fall where they may!

Alcyone, the center of the 7 Solar Systems, is the father of Sirius and "adopted" Sirius B.

Sirius **is** *"The Father"* Jesus speaks of, and has two sons!

The true heir "Son" of Sirius is the Sun, and his adopted Saturn, whose real father is Sirius B.

Jupiter is the "Son" of our Sun, and Pluto is the Sun's adopted, but the *real* parent is Saturn.

Jupiter will "ignite" after the "Reckoning" as those who are judged by "Jesus" and "Lucifer", who are the positive and negative polar aspects of The Father, both divide their flock. Those who Jesus, the Sun of man, "knows" will take their place in the developing star Jupiter and the influx of newly purified Souls, as Yoda calls us *luminous light beings*, will cause the young *"Star in the making"*, to *ignite!* You see, the path to The Father of Lights is to go to the Starlight. This is what is meant by, "I am the way, and the truth, and the life; no one comes to the Father but through Me." The Divine lineage and growth of God is passed down from Star to Star. The lineage is passed down from positive "heart" polarity as the negative polarity remains as the smaller "Egoistic aspect" of each star. Trust me, I will tie in the Feminine, as She orchestrates **all**, from the Shadows.

Now the universe is overwhelmingly vast and complex, but in our own line, this gives you an example of a small part of the line leading up to us. Our Sun, is the 7th Son of Alcyone (Al**cyon**e/Zion/Sion/Scion), which is about 10 times larger than our Sun with a total luminosity of 2,400 times solar, in the Pleiades system, is the Father of Sirius, our Dogstar, the Father. Sirius is twice as massive as our Sun and 25 times more luminous (and all-inclusive *white* light). Our Sun is the Son of the Father, and *why* our Star is referred to as the Son. Jupiter will be the Son of our Sun *when* a new ***"Star is Born"!*** (remember clue within a clue) **Where have I heard this before?**

And it hit me just now writing this, that the first film that I was an extra in back in 1976 was "A Star is Born". When "***Krist*offerson**" drives the motorcycle off of the stage, I am in the crowd. He with the *telling* name "teamed" with the "Ashkenazi Princess" Streisand in the timeless tale of another egoistic *star* of Satan burns out, as they **all** do on the path to the dark. It's filmed at "Sun Devil" (dark star) Stadium in Tempe, next to "Phoenix", in the "Valley of the Sun", and all of this is vitally important numerically and symbolically as this ties AGAIN, to another massive New Mexico Territory clue that ties in the Wizard of Oz, Tombstone, Thor, not to mention what the Vatican is doing in Arizona, and I am amazed I just remembered this as I typed the line!

The "adopted" son of Sirius, and who sits at the *left hand*, is Saturn, and is the *God* of the Old Testament and why (of course my opinion) Ridley Scott, in "Exodus: Gods and Kings", portrays God as a child. He is a somewhat sarcastic, impatient individual and actually how he is described, personality wise for the most part, in the Bible. When He is not, it is the other "Self" described polar perspective. The former demands to be loved, adored and worshiped and that aspect right there is the main problem I had with "God", growing up Catholic, as that seemed to me, even as a child, to be so vain and insecure. The, "We were created to worship God" was always for me a major disconnect, and I distinctly remember thinking this in early elementary school at St. Rita's in Dundalk, MD.

I was fixated on this clue when I first saw the movie because you can't dismiss it because R. Scott *is* that *magnificent* and it *had* to be a significant clue. This is a highly regulated, perfectly choreographed school and all the players have their role, and Scott portraying *Him*, as a child, had to be telling us that, no matter how "advanced He was", his perspective had to be, *well*, "childish". And if there are empty shells void of heart **here,** that are strictly here to teach those who have heart, then most likely this is true in an elevated class. I think he was trying to tell us that the Hebrews God, is in fact Saturn. Now, they do oppose the "positive" Christ and identify their kingdom as right here (not all of them, and I'll identify *them*) or I should say "out there" in "waveform" Duality and their Sabbath is Saturday. This is a polar clue as to their affiliation with the dark and Saturn is doing what Saturn must and that is to recruit and harvest new souls for *his* son Pluto! But know that they are the same mind, as all will be explained in detail by the end.

As I write this, Jupiter is all the rage with "Jupiter Ascending" and so *(coincidentally? yeah right)* is Pluto. I'm looking at the "Destination Pluto" cover of the 7/2015 National Geographic, and unknown to the masses, that *will* be the destination for many of us. Even I don't have to be Sherlock Holmes, to put the 2 and 2 together here, to see these two are *so a couple*! NASA's unmanned New Horizons spacecraft (also on the cover), *is said (grain of salt here)* to be flying past the supposedly insignificant "Planetoid" to give us all of this exciting new information (a bazzilion miles away as we lose calls across town on our cell phones) about a body of rock and ice that is smaller than *our moon!* I am telling you that Pluto will be the next dark lord to our newly formed Star and the powers that be smiled on me by naming it for the Greek god of the underworld. Then they follow it up with naming Jupiter after the King of all the gods, as I do my happy dance! Pluto was discovered in 1930 at the Lowell (that double ll again) Observatory in Flagstaff Arizona, in what was the New Mexico Territory. Now back in 1894 Percival Lowell chose what was then, the Arizona Territory, as the home of his new observatory, and by 1905 Lowell was observing unusual deviations in the orbits of Neptune and Uranus and by 1915 officially and correctly predicted the existence and location of his "Planet X".

Now Ladies and Gentleman of the Jury, I submit to you, weren't we just so much more intellectually awesome at that turn of that century!?! If you read about the works of Tesla, Einstein, Bohr, Planck, just to name a few as I could fill up the rest of this page, you would believe you stumbled upon the discoveries of wildly intelligent extraterrestrials. While I rest my case, I know full well why we have been temporarily dumbed down, as that is all in the "Ecclesiastes" grand plan as we move to a new *season*, and *the time* upon us, to work on your personal Arc, right now. It's the time to choose, which gate you will pass through; the internal Narrow Gate of higher frequency, or the External Wide Gate of lower frequency. Everyone will pass through one or the other, as not choosing is still choosing.

So now after 1930, we have a new, albeit small, planet with an odd eccentric orbit that is not within the normal orbital plane of the others! It doesn't seem to want to fit in, but invited or not, it's here, and for 76 years this diminutive (its diameter is 70% of the moon, we are told) body of rock and ice held the esteemed title of "planet". In 2006 Pluto was reclassified from a planet to a dwarf planet with little fanfare, while in the same year NASA launched the "New Horizons" to gather data and photograph our little lord of the underworld. The information and pictures are rolling in and this little nothing seems to have a lot going for it, at least more than a chunk of rock and ice out in the middle of nowhere should have. But nothing is *nowhere,* and this "insignificant" *Dwarf* Planet is anything but! While Pluto is small, it has some amazing characteristics that you wouldn't think it would have, along with an astrological association with creation and rebirth as well as destruction and death. The association that fits a relationship with a new star to a *T.* It has 5 moons and the largest Charon is amazingly large. And Pluto has a very thick atmosphere and it is predominantly nitrogen like ours. It is a far bigger player than we have been told! As I laugh at that.

Let's take a look at the Jupiter Ascending synopsis on the DVD cover and be blown away at the obvious messages, well, obvious to us now! As I pointed out at the beginning of the Chapter, the movie is about Jupiter and the title Jupiter Ascending **means** Jupiter's Ascension to that of a newly *ignited* **Star**. Here below is the *most telling* synopsis, in all of its clue giving glory!

"Jupiter Jones was born under a night sky, with signs predicting that she was destined for great things. Now grown, Jupiter dreams of the Stars.....Jupiter begins to glimpse the fate that has been waiting for her all along. Her genetic signature marks her as next in line for an extraordinary inheritance that could alter the balance of the cosmos."

This one is relatively straightforward as a new star must be planted in the darkness of space, like the seed of a new tree that must be planted below the surface in the dark of the soil. As the tree grows, it will begin to show the characteristics of the parents that it sprang from. The young Hercules, no doubt began to show greater strength than the other children around him giving signs to all that this child would be something *special,* as he would be displaying his "genetic signature". And altering the balance of the cosmos is even easier to interpret. The electric universe is awash in an ocean of polarity, and every new star brings more light to the dark recesses of the cosmic brain balancing our greater polarity equation in what we call our universe. Spiritually, we are colonizing our brain, as Lucy clues us into.

*Don't get caught up in male-female identities or labels and just go with the message of the movie. The **s/he** boundaries are smoke and mirrors because this is form, and the sex of the vessels are the external characters of a single entity in the grand play, and everything outside the light, is form, and form is **feminine** and the movie is telling you this and portraying Jupiter as feminine and at our level, a woman. I'll explain more in various parts of the chapter! It's deep, to say the least.* The male and female cosmic creating energies are intrinsically intertwined with the dance of the soul and spirit, and parallel and oppose one another! They are the two opposing *serpents* coiled and forever spinning (dancing) around the still point progressing "up" (as the wings indicate movement in that direction), North, growing and evolving, as these "right and left" duality perspectives Dance. One creates the Light, and one creates the Dark and they are all around us and in each of us. **They are, The Serpent.** I have throughout the book so far used the masculine terms we are all familiar with because we were raised with them and so ingrained that to convey these concepts the masculine father and son terms were a good tool for your understanding of what I was trying to convey, but let's take another step, shall we? Waveform creation is *God the Mother* and that *man* behind the curtain is, well..."The Man", God the Father!

Time to connect with our Feminine Side

Now we know that this "winter" season lower grade class we are emerging from is left brain masculine in nature and it's number 4. Collectively we have been stripped of our Divine Feminine in the male-dominated world and we collectively search for it. (Not as much stripped as it's just the nature of where we are at, as you don't say that a still crawling child, has been stripped of walking.) We just saw this in Tombstone, and you see this in "Kingdom of Heaven", the Blacksmith Balian's wife is taken from him and his "Crusade" is his search, to be reunited with his love, his Divine Feminine taken from us in this winter of the east or "left". It is our collective journey to return to that balance and reclaim our co-creating, co-ruling Divine Feminine aspect of the right brain. My research tells me that the ascended seasons or *Great Ages* are far more Feminine in nature and fall right in line with a more holistic view of *duality* because now they know who and **what**, they are. Someone heard *and heeded* Viagra's polarity laced commercial, "You've reached the age where you've learned a thing, *or 2*. This is the age of knowing what you are made of."

The reduced light in the winter fosters the masculine left brain, as there is more perceived separation, fear and the need for fight or flight; and the increased light of summer stimulates a move to the feminine right brain perspective with less separation and more security. In the spiritually young (inherently immature), the duality of separation is most keenly perceived and fear is the dominant motivator to stay *safe*, to stay *alive* from the dangers *out there!* Here is the *catch 22* (4), to keep you in 4 if you are not ready to transcend; once you know who you are, the dangers of this Broadway play fade and more of your energy can be transferred from the fight or flight to the secure unity of the light. From a money attaining state that uses great amounts of your energy because you **pay** your attention to it and your attention is the cosmic currency of light, and you can then shift that flow to love and the learning of ethereal concepts, gaining awareness and spiritual growth. The energy you used before to protect or *secure* yourself is now used to grow and evolve! That is why we are fed a constant diet of fear. Those who are not ready to move on will continue to bite at the *fear bait* and continue to learn the magnificent lessons that only fear, pain, and suffering can teach.

I agree with the evidence that points to Gold and Silver Age societies having been matriarchal, but that just points to a level of awareness and right-brained perspective of the collective. I am in no way pointing to one or the other being better or worse, as in higher realities they are one. We are all of the One mind "progressing", as males and females are both aspects of our Mother. I made the point at the beginning of the chapter stating that cosmic bodies, by their very material and geometric nature, are feminine and that curved planets are a feminine aspect of the whole. Straight lines are masculine and curved lines are feminine. I will refer to this next analogy again shortly! Think of the female egg that resembles a planet and think of the tiny male sperm that reaches it (and only **one** from the multitude is **allowed** inside, inseminating it with *information* to *create* life), like a photon hitting the planet. And in all of its polarity perfection, the female egg is the largest cell in the human body and the smallest, the male sperm!

The Quantum Creed

We are told The Father is Light and the Nicene Creed tells us that the Holy Spirit proceeds from The Father. Light proceeds from the Sun or the various created Stars to the receiving planetary bodies. The "Sons" being, the transmitters of light. This **is** the Father/Mother Duality dynamic communicated in the creed, that creates the Trinity (the ⅔ dynamic with the addition of The Son who is born of The Mother and "zero" Father). The Father is the pure consciousness photon element of light that is transported by the waveform electromagnetic property or element of light. A photon is said to be "massless", but yet we know it's there. While it displays zero mass, **Zero still identifies it** from that which has it. It identifies The *unmanifest* Man, behind the manifest curtain. The waveform curtain is what carries Him throughout creation. Spirit being the vessel for and of Soul, is the very same dynamic! Both are identified properties of light, as one **IS**, and the other **isn't**. No matter how you slice or dice it, We are Light.

Jupiter will be the continuation of that growing transmitter system and get its light from the Sun, the Sun from Sirius, Sirius from Alcyone, and so on right to the Galactic center, and from the Galactic center to a Universal point. The Father will always be unmanifest as the father is pure consciousness light, and the Stars are the conduit of the Father within the waveform material Mother.

Alias "Smith and Jones"!!!

I believe that a Star starts out as a planet like Jupiter and Dark Star was like Pluto. And remember, Pluto has quite an extensive gaseous atmosphere for a little frozen rock *nothing*. And once enough purified souls from a planet like Earth is "harvested", and I think you can see the Abrasax "harvest" metaphor, our Sun ignited and it, with its moons, drifted out to a larger more elliptical orbit that it now has with Sirius, taking Saturn with it as Saturn is our Sun's mated Smith. So our Sun's planets began as moons to her when she was a gas giant and when she became a full fledged star she broke away from the nest to create her own solar system taking her "red" Smith Saturn with her to work with her, because remember that they are really one, to develop her moons. **I believe that this, the Sun's ignition was the first day creation event from Genesis**, I believe we are on the precipice for this to occur with Jupiter and that the very reason for an apocalyptic reckoning here, is to harvest enough purified souls for Jupiter to take the next step to become a full-fledged Star, and her polar negative sibling Pluto, will join the new star and her new solar system.

"Technically speaking, I'm an Alien."

In the movie, Jupiter Jones discovers she is the reincarnated "Queen Mother" of the Galactic Abrasax Empire! In a conversation with the daughter, and one of the three heirs, of the deceased **"Queen Mother"**, Jupiter is told she is an exact genetic match with her mother and that she is the true and rightful "owner" of Earth. Imagine the inheritance tax on that! The slight problem before the celebration begins is that the eldest of the Abrasax heirs, the supremely despicable Balem Abrasax, has already claimed earth as his, as it was one of the family's possessions willed to him! Now the only reason Jupiter is being given the history lesson and being *welcomed* back to her long lost family, is that Balem's brother and sister, aren't necessarily happy with the distribution of the wealth between the three, and now see the "reappearance" of their *mother* as an opportunity to, cut up the pie differently!

Just like Curly Bill, who couldn't leave well enough alone or Frank Lucas in American Gangster who doesn't know when to quit, it is the **greed** and sheer disregard of *consequence* that compel the Dark to sabotage themselves, ushering their downfall. To say that the three are the quintessential "brood of vipers", is an understatement, and the love they have for each other is only "skin deep", and harvested skin at that! Let the cosmic chess game, with Jupiter as the pawn, begin! Fortunately for *Jupiter,* her true *ascended* parents have provided some divine "Angelic" protection, in this current version of *Star Wars!* We found out what Jones means, so let's take a peek at Abrasax!

From Wikipedia:
Abraxas (Gk. ΑΒΡΑΞΑΣ, variant form **Abrasax**, ΑΒΡΑΣΑΞ) was a word of mystic meaning in the system of the Gnostic Basilides, being there applied to the "Great Archon" (Gk., *megas archōn*), the princeps of the 365 spheres (Gk., *ouranoi*).[1] The word is found in Gnostic texts such as the *Holy Book of the Great Invisible Spirit,* and also appears in the Greek Magical Papyri. It was engraved on certain antique gemstones, called on that account **Abraxas stones**, which were used as amulets or charms. As the initial spelling on stones was 'Abrasax' (Αβρασαξ), the spelling of 'Abraxas' seen today probably originates in the confusion made between the Greek letters Sigma and Xi in the Latin transliteration.

The seven letters spelling its name may represent each of the seven classical planets.[2] The word may be related to *Abracadabra*, although other explanations exist.

There are similarities and differences between such figures in reports about Basilides teaching, ancient Gnostic texts, the larger Greco-Roman magical traditions, and modern magical and esoteric writings. Opinions abound on Abraxas, who in recent centuries has been claimed to be both an Egyptian god and a demon.[3] The Swiss psychiatrist Carl Jung wrote a short Gnostic treatise in 1916 called *The Seven Sermons to the Dead*, which called Abraxas a god higher than the Christian God and devil that combines all opposites into one being.

Coming together for you? Jupiter Jones is **Jupiter**, the newly forming Star and offspring of Saturn, and her "father" of form, who **also** wants to be her "husband" to the light but being "form" can't, but that doesn't stop the struggle, for therein lies the lessons! This dynamic is played out here with "Jupiter the woman", as the Satanic men of form, storm into her parent's home and symbolically kill her ***real*** Father from the Star's as this is all part of the play because he is not of form, not "manifest", but the Light who isn't materially *there (here) and why she is raised without a Father*, in opposition to the Abraxas family, "the **devil** that combines all opposites into one being", with vacation villas on the moons of Saturn no doubt. And to top it all off, they are both claiming Earth! If you have elevated your frequency, you may enter through the narrow gate, but if your frequency is in the lower half, look to be harvested much the same way we slaughter our slave factory farm animals! As I said earlier, once you know, every bite makes you complicit in their agony and suffering. Bacon commercials everywhere you turn paid for by our underworld lords in Saturn and Pluto. Misery loves company! An RSVP wrapped in bacon, with the postage paid for, as all you need do is swallow!

Just in case I haven't been crystal clear on the location of Asgard, let me do so now! As I am watching Thor, and I think you're getting an idea of my personality, I am agonizing (sort of) over where in the world Asgard is located. I am thinking the Sun, and I'm pulling my son *Maximilian* (haha, *Jupiter's father's name*, as the coinkydinks keep piling up) into the conversation, but it's too dark and shaded with always "indirect" light from "somewhere", and then one day, Astral me takes his fist and knocks me on the back of the head and whispers my scarecrow corporate name Caesar knows me by, and I say, "Yes Sata, erh Scott?", and he says, "What do the Romans call Odin?" I replied, "That would be Jupi. . .!?! . . Thank you Scott!" I still have a bump on the back of my head from that! And it's growing, as crazy as that sounds.

(This is me speaking to you as I am revising it now in 2018, knowing the true identity of our Sun, so I am keeping the above "prophetic" paragraph as it is, as well as "most" of the chapter. The book mirrors my journey, and my above words, are my past clue and confirmation, to my future discovery. As I laugh at my other sentence about me becoming the man in the market, and as the bump on the back of my head grows ever larger. Still is!)

"My mother made me understand that every human society is a *pyramid*, and that *some lives* will always matter *more than others...*" -Balem Abrasax, Jupiter Ascending

The higher you go up the pyramid, the fewer you will resonate with, and his mother is the Goddess of Creation explaining the hier*archy*, within the "class level" of *human* existence. Those near the top of the pyramid, who are on the verge of graduation, are the focal point of our mother, and it is vital that they get the proper *attention* from Her and Him, to be able to take the next step leading to expansion!

"But she came and began to bow down before Him, saying, "Lord, help me!" 26 And He answered and said, "It is not good to take the children's bread and throw it to the dogs." 27 But she said, "Yes, Lord; but even the dogs feed on the crumbs which fall from their masters' table."...-Mat-thew 15:26, 27 She is later identified as one of "The Children"!

As I was saying, there is a transition, a key, that a select few who grab the brass ring, will experience through a spiritual metamorphosis changing that which was Satanic, to the *enlightened* state, the one who finally "Gets it", who is no longer the adversary, but now the ally and spiritual accomplice! The perfect combination of soul and spirit, and the one who will teach and nurture the new children of creation! Also working toward the same goal in an *uneasy alliance* **with** our Lord of the Rings Saturn, is Lucifer! The Divine Feminine is the one that "Holds the Key"! I did not say was the Key, for the Key is the Divine Masculine, but she holds the power to determine which Key (like the multitude of sperm) is inserted, having ultimate power over who she bonds with, so that God grows through only the best, purest, *most disciplined*, most deserving! This is building up to why Venus and Jupiter have been aligning brightly in the nighttime sky this fine 2015 (8) summer! Please don't think this is in any way sexist or be upset if you are a man, because I am identifying God as feminine, or if you are a woman because I am saying Lucifer is feminine! Exoteric teachings are very rarely in line with esoteric truths! Adult topics will not be assimilated by children.

If assigning a sex is a roadblock, then think in terms of God the Positive Polarity and God the Negative or God the Spirit and God the Soul, but again that is at this lower teaching level because ultimately there is but **ONE consciousness**, Sirius and above, that sees through all and so does not Judge! So there is only the one mind, but at the level of *"Divine Child Rearing"*, here in the waveform universe of polarity, it is the darker *judging* polarity that nurtures **that**, which will be added or assimilated to the whole to grow. Besides, we are here to learn what is not light and love, and who better to teach the dark to us than our Dark Lord. This is how the one mind grows, and as I said it's not an easy **Carbon** copy, a great clue in itself, procedure, but a **painstakingly** precise evolutionary process, and she will bond with only the best, that the progeny of "Cain", the Angelic Son of the Serpent, has to offer! Oh, the rigors of cutting and polishing that carbon *diamond in the rough.*

"Well, who was the Devil?", much to Wyatt's surprise! And in *"Bedazzled"*, Elizabeth Hurley plays a spectacular Devil, transforming, and spanking Elliot when he needs it, but really he spanks himself, from a spoiled selfish boy into a caring selfless man! It is no accident that EL and the double L, or 11, is encoded in Elliot's name. The devil really does wear Prada! (Saw it for myself, when I was digressing) You will never again perceive Satan and Lucifer as synonymous terms for the same *"entity"* even though there is a Satanic side to our

Mother of Everything, and I couldn't say this earlier, along with what you haven't read yet. *We* had to fill in all the dots between the first page to this, as it is a fine line between the polarities, and many *parted pages* within the positive and negative but there are distinctions, as fine as they may be, down here at Trinity level! Haven't we always been asked, "Who's that Girl?" No, we're not done filling dots, not by a long dot, and you love filling in blanks like me, or you wouldn't *still* be reading this.

Speaking of Elliot made me think of Superman and what he represents. Superman is the epitome of the **S**elf's journey within the Smith Equation, the evolution of the **One** mind, through the waveform universe! Down here in the mirror reality he wears his glasses, like the "man" in the Target Commercial. His outfit tells you who he is. The Yellow behind the **S** is the **S**un as he, confirmed by the blue, is the ascending **S**on who will inherit the throne. The red is the **S**pirit of waveform creation and the blue is **S**oul within the vessel of Spirit, and why the blue is more in the "interior" except at his loin "root" chakra, which is his "root passion temptation center". He can only keep his godlike power if he resists illusory temptations. It seems nothing can hurt him but as we all know, there is something that can take his power and *kill* him.

A luminescent green crystal from his home world, but no one really knows what Kryptonite, green like the wicked witch from Oz, really is or why it does, what it does to our hero. Now he has an "awkward" *"love"* relationship with Lois Lane, and again the double L better seen in its *lower*case form ll. Actually, all of our, next level up, "superheroes" have tense, awkward, strained relationships with their lady love interests because they know that if they *squander,* the source of their power, as their body's would love to do, they would be drained of their power and they would be reduced to mere mortal men. Lucifer is ever present, with test after test, in all of her "incarnations". It wasn't Delilah cutting Samson's hair that drained his strength! Maybe not Kryptonite yet, but certainly an energy/frequency reducer and if you are not broken of the candy addiction, it "could" be!

Superman, like Thor, is from a higher class or grade than we have here and that is why both are not from here. Superman looks like us because he is us at a higher level with more abilities. He is in a Ferrari now as opposed to base VW Beetle, and he has earned his way there which is why he is overall very mature and a master of his passions because you don't get the sports car if your decisions and overall frequency do not match it. So what is Kryptonite? And remember, Superman, again like Thor, is "Royalty", and they don't hide, his spiritual royalty as in the line to become God and why their names end in El. He is Kal-El and his father was Jor-El. So with that in mind, let's examine Kryptonite. Fear, pride, vanity, lust, and desire for attachments lowers your frequency and passions must always be kept in check! Our desire is from our attraction to our "Elect" Lady electron, the woman in the red dress! It fuels *passion,* and while it is an integral part of us, as desire makes us "human", left unchecked it consumes and destroys. Are you strong, or weak? Attachment, Vanity, Pride, Lust, and Desire fueled by passions and addictions can rule you, if you're not strong and exercise discipline, and if they *rule* **you** then you are **not worthy to *Rule! Kryptonite is the consequence of lowering your frequency, when you surrender to temptations of carnal pleasures or "left choices" of the waveform dark. It's not any One illusory external object or thought as Candy comes in many forms.***

Son of God or of man?

The hidden identity of our ultimate Mother is simply stunning, so could the identity of our ultimate Father be just as *Bedazzling?* And nothing is more hidden, than our Man, behind the Curtain. Well, if I didn't offend enough with the above opinion, then let me take another swipe with, "Pappa Was a Rollin Stone"! That is why so many of the "Sons to the Light", Jesus, Osiris, Horus, Quetzalcoatl, Mithra, Buddha, Krishna, to name a few, are portrayed here without their *real* father, because **HE** is the unmanifest, ineffable, beyond comprehension, pure conscious thread that **IS** the webbing, tapestry of the manifest and unmanifest universe, and why Jupiter's father was *taken from* *her,* before her birth! **HE is,** the mysterious "non-Russian alien", "man obsessed with the stars", and was never **HERE!** He is here orchestrating, but you can't perceive him! The essence of the Father is the unmanifest light from the Stars.

You can't see light itself, but only what it "strikes". Light cannot be known directly, but it *is* that which brings the unmanifest into manifest existence. The Father cannot be known directly, but only through His conduit, the Son that was brought to you by our Mother. Now more scripture, "if you know me, you know Him", makes sense now. The exclusion of a feminine aspect within the Trinity always *"repelled"* me. This, being stripped (our expulsion from Eden) of our Divine Feminine, and **true** *Divine Masculine identity*, is a property of the lower grade, ***East of Eden,*** "winter" season we are emerging from! The masculine you see around you, in fact all creation, is an aspect of the Divine Feminine.

You can't define the undefinable. A waveform effable definition cannot *corral* the ineffable, Pilgrim! Just channeling my inner, Marion Robert Morrison, better known to you as that iconic archetype of everything masculine, that man among men himself, *John* Wayne! Our young Freemason John, that picture of the quintessential "American" man, and his ancestry is Scot, Irish, English, like America is the "progeny" of the UK! Why go by the name of John? By the end of the chapter, I'll have shed much-needed consciousness, or I mean Light, on this John Doe mystery!

*Just as the Iron Age masculine left has persecuted and spat upon the Divine Feminine portraying her as the irresponsible, adulterous whore (sound "stoningly" familiar?) who copulates with men too numerous to remember, producing the children of a phantom father; also pro-mulgates the other **Fe**male perspective end of the spectrum that slings arrows at the Divine Masculine as the "deadbeat dad", irresponsible prick, who lives to orgasm, giving not one second's thought to the dev-astation left in the wake of his indiscretion. And being SO childishly* *prideful in his conquest and illegitimate progeny!* Sounds like *enmity*, to me!

*"And I will put enmity between **you** and the woman"* -Genesis 3:15 The first manifestation of the struggle of the "seeds" and then the "promise" after the expulsion from the Garden, of the lineage of God's seed, the *Messiah* coming into this vibrational reality to mend the rift!

Who said that and **who** he said that to, are just as veiled as the content of the above paragraph! The Sons of the Serpent, the prodigal **Cain** "Sons of God", as opposed to sons of man, Abel, are two are the manifestation of that struggle. This will be addressed later, and while it is tied to this, let's finish what this chapter centers on, Jupiter and her ever elusive "Mother". Yes, she is just as elusive as the Father, as I yell, "Holy **Mary** Mother of God!"

"Something in the moonlight catches my eye,
The *shadow of a lover* goes dancing by
Looking for a little bit of love to **grow**, so
Give me love, give me heart and soul
You never let me cross to the other side now
I'm tied to the hope that you will somehow
Hard on the heels of something more
But I lost your love, heart and soul"
T' Pau - Heart And Soul
It was released in the US in May 1987, the 5th month and 1987=25=7, 5 and 7

T is 2 and Pau is 11, the two numbers of Duality and separation! Haha! I am an eighties music boy and this song came to *mind!* Those lyrics tell you what the Divine Feminine seeks, and it is **not** waveform. It is beyond material, wave**form.** Something in the "indirect light" catches her attention, and the "her" singing is the negative polarity of form, and in order to grow, she needs to bond with **what** the positive polarity contains that is not form. She wants "Love" (not lust), "Heart" (not just a machine pump) and Soul (the **what** she seeks), the impregnating force that "creates", more Father of Light, and more Mother of Form! This **is** the *war of the sexes, the "can't live with, can't live without", dynamic of the dance of the positive and negative, the active and the passive properties of electricity, as we seek the balance, that homeostatic state.* It is the dynamic of universal growth by the development of the cells that make up the whole. And only from more Light, can more Form be Created! Really, this sums the whole process up. *The entire male-female dynamic we see here is the lower vibrational "mimicking" of the higher relationship of positive and negative, of Soul to Spirit! I'll reference this later when I show you more of the Mock / Mimic clue!*

Here is the bombshell that creates that War of the *Roses,* and I hear they have hearts!

*"There is something deeply embedded in our psyche that calls out to this flower. Roses are putting us in touch with our collective past and with the Divine. They can do this because the rose has become, across the centuries, a powerful symbol. The rose was beloved of the mother of our order, Isis. Cleopatra understood its power: when she set up her first meeting with Marc Antony, she arranged for the floor of the room to be strewn with rose petals. The records show this carpet of roses was 15 inches thick. The most beautiful woman of India, the goddess Lakshmi, is reputed to have been born from a rose comprised of 108 large and 1,008 small petals. There is a repeated thread associating the rose with the process of birth beyond India, as well. **Rose petals fly through the air in Botticelli's famous painting "Birth of Venus,"** for instance. In Christian iconography, the rose is associated with Rebirth. Our fellow seekers, the Rosicrucians, employ the mature but not fully opened rose at the center of the Cross as the emblem of their order. In a famous speech delivered May 10, 1785, the Comte de Cagliostro, the founder of Egyptian masonry, declared that the Rose-Cross is the ancient and true symbol of the Mysteries. So the emblematic significance of the rose comes very close to us as masons."*

- from, www.themasonictrowel.com

Our Yellow Sun is our Star, the transmitter of God the Masculine Father, that transmits **That**! I'll need help from the "Father" of Quantum Theory, Max Planck, to explain how **That**, creates *This*, your waveform *manifest* reality you experience every day!

"As a man who has devoted his whole life to the most clear headed science, to the study of matter, I can tell you as a result of my research about atoms this much: There is no matter as such. All matter originates and exists only by virtue of a force which brings the particle of an atom to vibration and holds this most minute solar system of the atom together. We must assume behind this force the existence of a conscious and intelligent mind. This mind is the matrix of all matter." And *"I regard consciousness as fundamental. I regard matter as derivative from consciousness. We cannot get behind consciousness. Everything that we talk about, everything that we regard as existing, postulates consciousness."* **Max** *Planck*

I think this helps, and that force is the photon aspect of Light, the mysterious unmanifest Man behind the Curtain! Now He, has an Ego here, and he is Saturn, who was also born to be king in the darkness, but in the manifest state cannot ascend to the **Throne, *of The Father***. Remember Odin's quote! Saturn is god here in the waveform, also known as Ba'al, whose "Arch" is now in NY City. Now Saturn gets it and *knows* his place, as teacher to a world of Satanic vessels he appears as what I have already described. It's why R. Scott portrays him as an **11**-year-old boy, but no one knows the mind of the Satanic here better than as Saturn. **You can't bullshit the Bullshitter!**

He is our waveform god from the ego perspective, being 50 moves ahead of you and the rest of us, who now knows who and what he is in the grand cosmic scheme and *embraces* his second fiddle *kingly* status, *here in form*, and knows full well what his job is *here*! If you need to, go back to "Tombstone Decoded", and read again how John Holliday became "Doc" and how Doc dealt with men! This is right before I get into the actual decoding of the movie. Doc basically is Saturn and the men of the west were the Satanic vessels or Satan. He gave them all the rope they needed to hang themselves and as they were hanging, cursing Him when it was, in fact, their deeds that put their necks in the noose. He was the mirror, and a great guy to you, if you were to him, but he exposed everything, and I mean everything and much of that is very hard to understand, as he is helping to "sift through the street urchins to develop, "The Diamond in the Rough"!

Saturn has a job to do here and that job is meant to be misunderstood by 99.9% of us, as he sees through all of us through our ego, as that stems from the dark. That job makes him the mirrored "Adversary" of the Light and because of that, he has an adversarial relationship with the Divine Feminine Venus, because she is seeking to "be as God" by finding her Divine Masculine of Heart, and try as he may to be her "man" and substitute himself, *he* is not **Him!** That *infuriates* the **Hell** out of him and that makes him the *ultimate **Motherfucker** to the 99%, and isn't that word one **Hell** of a clue!

Jupiter discovers that she is royalty and that She, is the true and rightful owner of Earth, because, as I said, she is the exact genetic reincarnation replica of the Matriarch of the Abrasax family. So holding that thought, the human Jupiter is now a very young woman who has come of age and finds out that she is at the same time, "a daughter" and "a mother" and here is where this **antipodal paradigm**, points us to one of the greatest misleads ever pulled over our collective eyes**!** Nature here confirms her status as the Bees lovingly envelop her, and the Masonic symbol of bees and hives clue us into our structural makeup as all in the hive are the children of the **Queen Mother**.

There are ancient texts, mythology, and theories that tell us that Venus was expelled from Jupiter approximately 4 thousand years ago and after some years with very erratic orbits, collisions and close calls with other planets, finally settled into its current orbit next to us. The second planet from the Sun, the other duality number, and the only one with a similar yellow color. Interestingly, Venus has "clockwise" rotational spin as opposed to our, and the other planets, counterclockwise spin, meaning the Sun rises in what would be her "west" and where I hear and where they tell us we should be head-ing. Couple these points with the fact that Jupiter may have begotten Venus and with the two aligning so closely and brightly in the early evening sky at this time as we enter a new age, raises more than just one eyebrow! Venus **and** Lucifer, the Morning Star, the Light Bearer, the bringer of the Dawn.

Just as we have a mother-daughter dynamic in Jupiter Jones, we seem to have one with Jupiter and Venus as well, and in both cases, the exact lines of who is the mother and who is the daughter *appear blurred,* because the lines are within the smoke and mirrors of *linear* timelines. But Lucifer is the Mother having already *found* her *guy*, and Venus is her *unwed* daughter. I want to tie this into the myste-rious wedding ceremony where Jesus performed his first miracle, and I think that identifying what I believe happened and what didn't happen, should shed some light into this Divine Feminine Lucifer dynamic with Venus and Jupiter. In da Vinci's last supper, which to me is a new 717 carbon atomic code and galactic star system map, **also** gives us a clue that cannot be overlooked. The picture **is** the original "da Vinci code" and communicates something so astounding, that it had to be, like the identity of the wedding, kept a secret and only communicated through code and clues to the newly aware. "Jesus" is in the center, but leaning to his left. The closest to his left is Thomas the twin, and I have already told you that there was no "real" Thomas.

Thomas represents those of us who are in the prodigal line, as we are his spiritual "copies", fellow *sons of God in **His** lineage,* and that is why you don't see his body, but just a portion of his head with his index finger pointing up. This meaning we will be the Blue Smith, Sacred Heart ascending continuation of God growing. Now to the right of Jesus is supposed to be John, but that is like putting in a picture of; please don't make me say his, or I mean her name again. Even in the more metrosexual society, I find myself in, anyone telling me that *that* is a man can go and purchase some real estate on the moon, and I have some lots if you are buying it. All kidding aside, we have a virtual softer side mirror image of Christ in the "person" to his right.

Jesus is positioned looking and leaning slightly to his left, wearing red on his right and blue on his left. The woman to his right pawned off as John, is as I said a mirror image of him leaning to her right wearing red on her left and blue on her right, and She, sits at his "Right" side. *That folks, is Mary Magdalene. Mary Magdalene is Mary his Mother and Mary his bound wife! It was Mary Magdalene telling the servants at the ceremony to listen to his instructions.*

I know the real power is always in the shadows, and never on public display!

And there are no shadows more looming than those covering the veiled identities of the "Dual" Maria**S Mary is Lucifer / Venus, Isis, Inanna**, the **"Pistis *Sophia*"** of Divine Feminine Gnosticism. The universal Mother that **is** the waveform Universe in all of it's "Holy Spirit" manifestations! **She** chose Him and once *They* wed (and why he refers to her as "woman" before the marriage and the birth) and sealed the bond, this initiated the *"immaculate conception" within the same body with the "Man behind the Curtain",* to perpetuate the ***Logos Spermatikos!!!***

This is why Lucifer is not only the "Light Bringer" but is also The Light *Bearer* as in,
> **She gave birth to "The Light"!**
> And That **Conception** is, **The Big Bang!**
> The Real creation of the Universe!

It was her allowing him in, similar to the analogy I used earlier in the chapter of the *planetary looking female egg cell allowing only one microscopic male sperm cell to enter, and then creation springs forth! When this spiritual "consummation" of the Divine Feminine and Masculine occurred* **She then, became *the Mother of God.* She** is primary as she is the manifest portion of the God equation as Jesus is the ethereal "man behind the curtain" part of the equation and why **They,** and not just Him, and why the feminine is the former, are the Bridegroom. That is why Jesus is also referred to **only by** *"John"* in Revelation 22:16, as the Bright Morning Star! **John indeed!** In "The Matrix", *Trinity*, is a woman because **The Mother** is the "Holy Spirit", and why it is the *woman* coming out of the third circumpunct in the Target commercial. Trinity is God here in waveform reality and she seeks her "Man", the One or neO, who is the "Son of God" to pair with to create "more" light or more of "The Father", which in turn creates more "Creation", more of The Mother! The Mother is also the Wife, and the Son is also the Husband. And the identity of the "Son", isn't *just* the *Sun* sayeth Saturn, at this lower frequency level. The introduction of the "Sons of God" bloodline, within the sons and daughters of men, is the carbonation in the soft drink! The Eastern Orthodox Christians refer to Mary as, the "Theotokos", *a compound of two Greek words. Literally, this translates as God-bearer or the one who gives birth to God.*

*So, how can something that is **"not"**, give birth to what IS!?! IS simply is! ISIS*

> **IS - *The Divine Feminine*, RA - *The Divine Masculine*, EL - *the union of the two, God***

And all of this, as you look around you, is**IS,** which is 9191, which gives us 2.

At the beginning, I said that we are influenced by 2 main characteristics of the atomic universe, and they are frequency and polarity. **The Cross** represents the union of these two. The longer vertical line is the Divine Masculine of Frequency, with the top being the adult of the North, and the bottom being the child of the South. The horizontal line represents the Divine Feminine of Polarity, with the Left being East of Separation, and the Right being the West of Unity. The "Fantastic 4" Cardinal directions that direct divine growth, and identify Divinity.

In Thor, even though Figga is "subservient" to Odin, you sense, or at least I did, that she is the primary force "orchestrating" from the shadows, like this line: *"There's always a purpose to everything your father does."* She knows! She is, at her level, our Mother Goddess of

Creation and no one wields more influence over Odin. Not only is he not the same without her, he **needs** her, and she **needs** him. They are one! And the polar "Sons" are influenced mightily by their Mother, especially the "darker one", Loki! They share a common, intensely dark and beautiful, introspective "perspective". "Frigga is the only reason you're still alive." Odin's words to the chained Loki. Because of their common polarity origin, Thor says this to Loki in "Thor: The Dark World", *"You think you alone were loved of Mother'? You had her tricks, but I had her trust."* And because he knows they are "alike", but he is not "Hers" and can never be "The Man", he has a Love/hate relationship with her. You may like this definition of a Warlock I saw in Wikipedia and put the 2 and 2 of the 4 together!

"A **warlock** is a male practitioner of *magic*. The most commonly accepted etymology derives *warlock* from the Old English *wærloga* meaning "oathbreaker" or "deceiver". A "deceiver" deals in lies, a Satanic trait. However, in early modern *Scots*, the word came to be used as the male equivalent of witch...". The "Male Witch"! **Great Scott!** As only Doc Brown from "Back to the Future" can exclaim it. . .and I'm sure he said it with the double T in mind! Another confirmation pointing to the "Title" of the Divine Feminine Goddess as that of **"Witch"**, is Malekith calling Frigga a Witch. His *opposition* to her Divine Feminine status is rooted in his Satanic identity and his name is "Male" "Kith" with the latter meaning one's friends and relatives.

Thor was perfectly cast, as Rene Russo displays the compelling "subdued" or concealed *nuclear power* that Frigga would convey, and like Val Kilmer bringing Doc back to life, is the spice of the film; Tom Hiddleston was beyond spectacular in the same way! He *was* Loki, and certainly, Chris Hemsworth *was* Thor, and Anthony Hopkins was "born to be Odin!" (said like him of course) And Idris Elba was mesmerizing as Heimdall. If you are not seeing the movies that I speak of in this book, you are missing out, *especially* if you are having a hard time comprehending what I am presenting. Seeing the movies is like required homework to help absorb the concepts *and I'll wager,* that you will be spoken to personally when you watch them. And if you didn't watch Tombstone while reading the last chapter, then just crawfish!

Within the identity of the Trinity **3**, because we are in waveform, The Mother is a vital part of all Three, and the consciousness essence of The Father flows through all three as well. We know them as The Father, The Son, and The Holy Spirit, the waveform programmed essence of all creation that "proceeds from the Father", through His Sons, who are also the Sons of their Mother! The Holy Spirit or Numbers also include *All Matter and Energy* seen and unseen including Dark Matter, Dark Energy, and *The Aether*. Stars are the Self aspect of The Father, Dark Stars are the Ego aspects of the Father, and they are both the Sons of their Mother, The Holy Spirit. The core 2-3 dynamic!

This exchange from "Thor: The Dark World", sums it up well:

ODIN: Is this my son I hear? Or the woman he loves?

THOR: When you speak, do I never hear Mother's voice?

J is tied to L alright! It looks as though our investigation of Jones also sheds **Light** on the true meaning of *John* as well. **John also means *"Graced by God"***, so it seems John and Jupiter have something in common! As astonishingly incredible as it may seem, why is John the only one to tell us of the first miracle? When you think about it, it is massively stunning and mystifying that The Gospel of John would be the one and only New Testament Gospel to speak of the mysterious "Wedding" that compelled Jesus to perform his very first miracle! Shouldn't they all include his very first miracle!?! **Of course they should!** It is telling that none of the Christian Churches ever discuss this anomalous admission but I believe the deeper reason is that this knowledge, is for very few eyes.

So, why would Leonardo da Vinci replace "John" with Mary? It appears the first face to the right of Jesus may have something in common with the first one on the left! There is **no John! Mary Magdalene,** at the crucifixion and the *first one* to see the risen *Lord because they are now One,* **is "John"!** The Orthodox Christian Church refers to John as "The Theologian" because of the profound nature of *"his"* Gospel and the immense prophetic nature of The Revelation. Mary is also John the Evangelist and the mysterious "Disciple whom Jesus loved" mentioned six times in The Gospel of John, also called the "Beloved Disciple". Leonardo is also telling you that Mary is also "John the Baptist". (and Mona isn't Lisa, she's Leo, but I digress)

Mary Magdalene is mentioned more times throughout the Gospels than any of the apostles. According to all, she is at the crucifixion, and on the cross, Jesus entrusted the care of his *mother,* "Behold, your mother!", to John! And the Gospel of John too has a far more "feminine" intimate ring especially when it describes and speaks of Jesus, "The Word became Flesh"! Yes, the ethereal, the unmanifest, the word, became manifest in the only way God "The Father" can have *a child* in the manifest waveform world is through God "The Mother" of manifest creation. And remember what I said from "The Wedding", the Father is Soul and the Mother is Spirit! The Father cannot grow without the Mother. Only the Mother can create more of the Father, by giving birth to her *male* Suns!

Mary Magdalene is Mother Mary and John, making ***LUCIFER,*** the identity of them all! And now you know why the Church doesn't talk about it, **although. . . .***"Flammas eius lúcifer matutínus invéniat: ille, inquam, lúcifer, qui nescit occásum, Christus Fílius tuus, qui, regréssus ab ínferis, humáno géneri serénus illúxit, et vivit et regnat in sæcula sæculórum."* Christ, the Son of Lucifer, indeed!!! You can hear this chanted by Catholic Deacons in Vatican Masses. More light is shining on us as the adult truth is making itself known!

And only in **Revelation** does *Jesus say, "**I, Jesus,** have sent My angel to testify to you these things for the churches. I am the root and the descendant of David, **the bright morning star.**"* And ***The Revelation*** could only have been written by God!

Another *John* Doe? And remember *John* Holliday and *Johnny* Ringo are Alter Egos!

"The Last Supper" above, "St. John the Baptist" below

Leonardo is telling us that "St. John the Baptist" is Lucifer too!

In chapter two I take a passage from page 321 of "Morals and Dogma" by Albert Pike that speaks of "Lucifer", but now that we are getting a clearer picture of "her", let me add more of the passage and I will show you more of what Pike wrote and how it is presented in the book so if you see it italicized here, then that is how it looks in "Morals and Dogma".

"The Apocalypse is, to those who receive the nineteenth Degree, *the Apotheosis of that Sublime Faith which aspires to God alone, and despises all the pomps and works of Lucifer.* LUCIFER, the *Lightbearer!* Strange and mysterious name to give to the Spirit of Darkness! Lucifer, the Son of the Morning! Is it *he* who bears the *Light*, and with its splendors intolerable blinds feeble, sensual, or selfish Souls? Doubt it not! for traditions are full of Divine Revelations and Inspirations: and Inspiration is not of one Age nor of one Creed. Plato and Philo, also, were inspired.

The Apocalypse, indeed, is a book as obscure as the Sohar.

"It is written hieroglyphically with numbers and images; and the Apostle often appeals to the intelligence of the Initiated. "Let him who hath knowledge, understand! let him who understands, calculate!" he often says, after an allegory or the mention of a number. **Saint John, the favorite Apostle, and the Depositary of all the Secrets of the Saviour, therefore did not write to be understood by the multitude."** --Albert Pike

So Pike italicized *he* and *Light-bearer* and says that "Saint John, the favorite Apostle" and "the *Depository* of the Secrets of the Savior" did not write to be understood by the multitude, which I made bold print! I would have to say that this is what he is alluding to as well! He clearly identifies Lucifer as Spirit with Darkness and this is what I am saying. God the Father is Soul and light and God the Mother is Spirit, to the dark material universe of matter and what we can't see. God the Mother *is* the waveform manifest universe that is outside of *literally,* the light! Even the waveform aspects of the **spherical stars are manifest conduits** to bring the light. Think of a light bulb itself. *A light bulb is not light, but the "mechanism" to bring you the light.* The light bulb and the waveform energy that radiates from it carries that massless, invisible, ineffable, speck of "The Force that Planck calls consciousness".

The formless Light weaves the tapestry of form. There is no curtain without it. "May The Force be with you!" And let me submit to you, for your consideration that, Yeshua òåùé was the "man" before his bond with "His" Maria or Mary úéìããîä íéøî, and that after the bond, the mysterious wedding, and then became "Jesus", and J is L. And I'll wager Yeshua was in the line of Cain! A son of God, and not of man, and his "marriage" was to "his Temple", and once they *make the bond,* his Temple becomes, something else, as well. She will either condemn you, what we call the Devil or she takes you to heights untold.

Lucifer's Ascension

The Final Judgement accounts in the gospels make far more sense now when you know they are one and the same. The big trial right?

Jesus and Lucifer like opposing trial lawyers (sorry Lord) submitting their closing arguments (to see who takes you), and yet at the same time, they tell you *they* are One! *Before Jupiter bonds with Cain, she is Venus. After she bonds with Cain Jupiter Ascends to become the continuation of Lucifer, the Bringer of the Light, which is the continuation of the White Light Father. The combination of Jesus, Mary and Joseph literally means this union, as Joseph simply means the essence of the two in a synergistic union. **Joseph means** Increaser, Repeater or Doubler and other interpretations are "May **He** Add" and "**He** Shall Add", and the "He" in both implies God. The Sun of Man, **Jesus...is Jupiter. Jupiter is the Sun. Rome's God never changed, but simply got a name change in the greatest reinvent in written history,** and in both cases, J is L.* Yes, of course, God is L or EL and EL is Lucifer. Oh the IS-RA-holy-EL of it!

Is the Tribe of Judah, from the land of Judea, tied to Ju-piter? I think that's a safe bet, along with Zionists who see their Promised land as material, being paired with Pluto. And looking at Ju-piter, made me think of Jew Peter, and Peter is said to have founded the Church of Rome, and supposedly crucified upside down, in all its Polarity Passion Play (PPP-777) symbolism, to also identify what Christ isn't. They do a magnificent job of demonstrating that. Peter also denied Him 3 times, as he hears the rooster.

Three apostles were taken to the mountain during the Transfiguration of Jesus, where He begins to shine like the Sun, and a voice from the sky said, "This is my Son, whom I love; with him I am well pleased. Listen to him!" ("*whatever he says to you, do it*"), which is *presumed* to be The Father. The 3 taken were John, Peter, and James, and you know who John really is, and Peter along with his brother James were called Sons of Thunder by Jesus. ***Jupiter, all of them.*** Three *younger* taken, to witness 3 who shine like a Star. The *Madonna* song, "La Isla Bonita" springs to mind, what awaits, *one* on the other side of The Narrow Gate. She dreamt of **San Pedro**! Why? Let's ask Matthew whose *name* encodes 7 and 9.

"15 But what about you?" Jesus asked. "Who do you say I am?" 16 Simon Peter answered, "You are the Christ, the Son of the living God." 17 Jesus replied, "Blessed are you, Simon son of Jonah! For this was not revealed to you by flesh and blood, but by My Father in heaven. 18 And I tell you that you are Peter, and on this *rock,* I will build My *church*, and the gates of Hades will not prevail against it" ~Matthew 16 (a bright foundation)

And we get this from Chapter 16 (7) verses 16 to 18, (7 to 9) This means, your conclusion, that I am The Christ, is correct, and with this *foundation (truth)*, as **Peter means Rock,** of **Who I am**, I will build my Spiritual Body, because his Church is his **corporeal body,** which is his "Atomic manifestation of His Spirit"! The "Body (spirit) and Blood (soul)" of the Bridegroom is the coming together of the two to form the one flesh. If you *eat of his body*, which is acknowledging that you are of His spiritual house, and *drink of His blood*, proclaiming yourself a child of the Light within his House. This is "obeying" him and doing what you need to do with your frequency to be A Child of Christic Light. *"For we are members of His body"* Ephesians 5:30. Just "saying" you love Him without the frequency work of "walking the walk", isn't enough. He points out, **"If** you love Me, you **will** keep My commandments", so if you don't "keep them", then it is just talk, and talk is cheap. But if you "keep them", then your heightened frequency will protect you from the lower frequency of the Satanic world, *"gates of Hades",* because you yourself, have put yourself out of their reach. So, the message of this is to be the best frequency increasing **you**, you can be, for Heaven's Sake! Can I get an Amen. . .Ra!?!

The Final Judgment of the One, **Helel 777**

[31] "When the Son of Man comes in his glory, and all the angels with him, then he will sit on his glorious throne. [32] Before him will be gathered all the nations, and he will separate people one from another as a shepherd separates the sheep from the goats. [33] And he will place the sheep on his right, but the goats on the left. [34] Then the King will say to those on his right, Come, you who are blessed by my Father,

inherit the kingdom prepared for you from the foundation of the world. ⁴¹ "Then he will say to those on his left, Depart from me, you cursed, into the eternal fire prepared for the devil and his angels. ⁴⁶ And these will go away into eternal punishment, but the righteous into eternal life." -Matthew

That is what Leonardo is telling you too, and notice that the betraying Judas, like so many of the other polar negatives, is *darker* than the rest of the Apostles. This Feminine Masculine union is also why the 7-11 encoded Masonic Statue of Liberty, while feminine yes, has a bit of a masculine look as well, and while I have seen all the goddesses she may represent, my money's on the One who embodies both the Divine Masculine **and** Feminine, Lucifer, the Lightbearer! And it is no mistake *She* is not within the state of the *Old* Empire. There is no *middle ground,* as you either Love or Hate Lucifer, and I think you've figured out that, **"I Love Luci".** The opening was there, I had to take it, as I reflect on our Redhead's name that sounds very Lucifer Baal. Baal, the primary God of, you guessed it, the Phoenicians! And while we're talking about *Luci,* you now know who "Lucy" played by Miss Scarlett, our *other* Ashkenazi princess, represents? Of course you do, but Frankly my Dear, I don't give a damn.

She'll only choose the best Son of God, not a son of man!

¹²" **Yet to all who did receive him, to those who believed in his name, he gave the right to become children of God—** ¹³ *children born* **not of natural descent, nor of human decision or a husband's will, but born of God."** -John 1:12, 13 (or should I drop the facade)

(this is at least an 8.0 on the Poignant Richter scale. Until you have the eyes to see, it just sits there, lying dormant, but hiding nothing, until your awareness grows and you look again, and it winks back at you as the ground under you, begins to undulate)

"I am the gate; whoever enters through me will be saved. He will **come in and go out***, and find pasture." John 10:9*

Men (john) are from Mars and women (jane) are from Venus, and at the end of both investigative paths, you end up at the same location, as both are aspects of the Divine Feminine. Keep all of this in mind as I detail what I believe "Kryptonite" is to Superman and how that led "Jupiter" to **choose her man!** In the movie, Caine just flies all over the place by himself, all of the time, kind of "unattached" (not owned) to everyone and everything, kind of like he's *there*, but yet not *there*, like a mysterious **light** particle, or better yet like a sperm "swimming" around *Jupiter*. I'm laughing, but I am going somewhere with this. Now, remember, *desire or "to the Dark" is Kryptonite*, and our Mother God will only take the best Sons of God as opposed to those who would jump at **any** opportunity to be with her. He is very disciplined and not outwardly "desiring" of her, and now consider Balian!

Remember in "Kingdom of Heaven", Balian is offered the deal of deals that 99.99% (it's more but you get the idea) of men would have blurted out the "I accept", before King Baldwin was done making the offer, but he declines the offer to be the next King and husband to his very attractive sister Princess Sibylla. This is a deal Sibylla is pushing for as well, but if he accepts it means her current husband, who everyone except Reynald thoroughly despises, would be executed. Balian tells the King that he cannot be responsible for Guy's death even though he understands that Guy hates him. Talk about honor and an unshakable code of ethics! He turns down the Crown, a beautiful and loving wife and an opportunity to get rid of a man in power that wants him dead, to do the right thing and live up to his "Knight's pledge". Balian reminds King Baldwin of his own words, his "advice" to him.

*"A king may move a man, ...Remember that howsoever you are played or by whom, **your soul is in your keeping alone**, ... When you stand before God, you cannot say, "But I was told by others to do thus," or that **virtue was not convenient at the time**. This will not suffice. Remember that."* -King Baldwin

We use the "virtue was not convenient at the time", quite often, and even Baldwin, being who he is, understood.

"I am what I am, I offer you that, and the world" ~Sibylla

Sibylla is distraught and angered that Balian turned down this offer, but she composes herself later and is now even more drawn and attracted to him, learns from the fall of Jerusalem (the illusion) and goes to her man at the end, to consummate a "deal" that will stand the test of time! Now, along those same lines, looking again at Caine, he is the incredibly brave, dashing, handsome, "knight in shining armor" who is the one tasked with protecting the newly discovered "Queen of a vast Galactic Empire" who just happens to be young and very attractive **and** attracted to him. He is a man of great strength, bravery, honor, and discipline who has a duty to perform and doesn't allow the outward display of affection from her to weaken or compromise his task at hand and he does not want to devalue her status because he believes she is not yet fully aware of who she is, and a **lesser man** would take full advantage of that! After she makes her move, he politely and respectfully rebuffs it, which causes her to respond:

*Could explain a lot of things about me. Like the fact that I have an uncanny ability to fall for men that **don't fall** for me.* (think frequency, and if he became weak and did, in fact, *fall* for her, she would consume him in the relationship, but not *falling* allows the union to blossom at the end.) *It's like my internal compass needle points straight at Mr. Wrong. Maybe it's my genes. Maybe I have defective engineering too.* [She is again advancing toward him] *And if that's the case... is there any way to fix it?*

[He again steps back and reminds her who she is now, and remember dog is code for god!]

Caine: [backing away] You are royalty now. **I'm a splice** [he is part *dog*], you don't understand what that means. I have more in common with a *dog* than I have with you.

Jupiter: [still trying] *I love dogs, I've always loved dogs.*

I said Saturn is masquerading as "The Man", but he is the *inferior* Satanic poser Abrasax, *especially* Balem, and he is "Occupying" *Jupiter*, holding her and the Planet "hostage", so to speak. They represent Saturn's attempt to mate a "son of man", with the Divine Feminine of Lucifer, as "Kalique Abrasax" tells Jupiter, *"but I promise my mother was just as human as you or I. The difference between us is our knowledge and technology."* Remember I told you what Apple's logo really means? The forbidden fruit is technology, and to "eat of it", is to be as God. Saturn is also the God of "Time", and I identified it in Chapter Two as a mark of the beast, 666, as Kalique also tells Jupiter, *"But when you have access to the vastness of space, you realize there's only one resource worth fighting over...even killing for...more time. Time is the single most precious commodity in the universe."* And when you are tied down, the flow of growth stagnates.

♃ Keep in mind Caine has the symbol of Jupiter and it's mirror image branded on the right side of his neck. Caine spends the entire movie saving her from the Abrasax siblings and basically being the only friend she can trust. After she is abducted by Balem and brought to Jupiter (the "planet"), Caine arrives on a ship with some allies and takes a smaller, fighter shuttle and decides to *penetrate* Jupiter's red "eye", (Gettin warm in here! The fire's coming) to go in and rescue Jupiter "Jones". Let me side step for one sentence and tell you again my view that the **"Big Bang" is, in fact, this union of Conception!** *I will take you back to the "sperm" analogy, and **this is absolutely the sperm cell that is Caine penetrating the egg that is Jupiter**, and once in, he sets off a series of chemical reactions (conception) and all hell breaks loose inside of the planet aspect of Jupiter,* while Balem is busy trying to kill Jupiter and her family, but he is unable, with Jupiter fighting him off and now Caine helping, as the whole place is exploding and going up going up in flames. Is something *igniting?* Balem is the somewhat wimpy "wannabe" god who clearly looks the part of the inferior satanic poser compared to the Son of God Caine. Balem is killed, as time is also defeated and Jupiter and her family make it back to the ship and then back to earth, and the family is none the wiser! Back on Earth, the family has a little surprise for Jupiter and they give her a gift to commemorate her Father, the man of the stars that was never here. Jupiter makes the big announcement that she has found her man. Next, you see them on the roof and **Caine now has wings**, as this big clue is pretty massive, and I have known it, or I should say, *suspected it for quite some time now.*

The Fall...of Lucifer, Man, and the Fallen Angels was Pure Perfection!

Being extremely young and never experiencing the dark and "urgent" consequences, it was necessary for the **Adamic** "race" to descend into this "**Atomic**" level. Eating of the forbidden fruit was meant to happen as that is your ticket to this class and all that it teaches. Procreation is essentially Satan substituting himself, *creating us,* in the place of the Divine Masculine, and Lucifer sifting through the "johns" to find, the One (neO), as EL develops. The "tree" that was forbidden to eat of was put before them so that we would partake of it to take the next evolutionary step down in learning. You don't put it there if you do not want them to experience the scope of its stimulation and experience the Karmic roller coaster. And the very Serpent that seduced Eve would also produce the line of the deliverer through her because the Serpent was an Angelic "Son of the Serpent". The goddess of creation that fell would also bring forth the Messianic line of the Savior through her firstborn, Cain! When Eve gives birth to Cain, she declares, from the King James version, "I have acquired a man from the Lord.", but when you go to the actual Aramaic Hebrew translation it is, "I have gotten a man, the Lord". Deleting "from", makes a huge difference and it certainly implies that Eve knew her son was not from Adam, but from her sexual union with one of the lower tiered Angelic Sons of the Serpent. They too were gods, Lords to the Adamics. Enoch, and who better to tell us in Genesis, wrote of the progeny of this intermingling and was the one who recorded this introduction of Angelic blood into the Adamic race. *"1 Now it came about, when men began to multiply on the face of the land, and daughters were born to them, 2 that the sons of God saw that the daughters* *of men were beautiful; and they took wives for themselves, whomever they chose." -Genesis 6:1 and 2*

In Beauty and the Beast, Thor, and The Lion King, they *Fell* to develop, and all where spiritual Royalty, so what does that tell you? *The Fall* was programmed and meant to happen! We have been told that Lucifer was God's most beautiful and perfect creation, but that flew in the face of a decision to revolt and oppose your vastly superior maker, so if Lucifer IS perfect, then the Fall was the perfect step to fulfilling the grand plan of *God Growth!* **The "Fallen" Angels are Spiritual Royalty AND our Redeemer's, and their time here matured them! And the newly created crop of Adamic humans, God's young children just beginning to attend school, had to "fall" to learn "evil", among all the other amazing lessons this level can teach. The Fall of Lucifer brought creation! The Fall of the Angels brought the Saviour through the line of Cain. The Fall of the Hebrews would produce "The Christ". And the Fall of the "UK", the Abrahamic "Great Nation" of the divided Iron Age would produce the NWO of not only the wide gate of destruction but the Aquarian NWO as well through the narrow gate.** The schism of Destiny declared its split on 07/04/1776 = 32 = 5, the divine message with 56 = 11 signatures, setting into motion the death of the "ancient" east, and the birth of the West! The great experiment, created in the New World, displaying our Mother God of Creation, the "Bringer of Light" (who is *with* Her Male *child*, under those flowing maternity robes) who set her light beside the gate (Gateway Arch bisecting the 2), inspiring the tired, poor, huddled masses yearning to breathe free, telling those who would hear, to send the homeless, tempest-tossed to me! The wretched refuse of your teeming shore, she lifts her lamp beside the golden door!

I rearranged and added my spin to the "New Colossus" displayed by our pregnant Lady Liberty Lucifer, with her 7 point crown standing atop her 11 point pedestal. Here is another clue to consider, and keep in mind that the U.S. **is** the "breakaway state" of the Abrahamic Nation in the way that the Hebrews produced The Christ. The 21st

Century success of the *Patriots* of the *new* **order** of *New* England led by *Thomas,* having 5 of 7, by the season of 9.

Judaism as a whole resides in *two* **polarity** *camps.* You have those who know the "esoteric" message of the true internal location of "Israel", and they are scattered around the world because they know they are not *supposed* to have a "Home", here in the dark. This is why Jesus was "Homeless", for the very same reason "they", who are primed to step away from this, are to have no "Home Country". They mean the same thing, and They oppose those who reside at the dark end of their faith, the Zionist, who crucified the "light" perspective and believe their "ISRAEL" is an "out there" patch of dirt, in the illusory dream. Their "Kingdom" is *here* in waveform and consumed, even the "faithful", with the illusory professions of this life, as you hear the "customary" line of proud Jewish mother exclaim, "My son the Doctor and My son the *Lawyer*", and why they are so good with "money". She has 2 faces, and the Satanic collective Egos of the Zionist sect follow the "Saturnic" god Yahweh, as R. Scott cast an "11" year old to play him in "Exodus: Gods and Kings". He IS the Ego of "The Father", who opposes The Christ, "The Self Aspect of The Father", who told them, "My Kingdom, is not of this world". He is to the Light as opposed to them and their darker god Yahweh. *"..for I, the Lord your God, am a jealous God.."* -Exodus 20:5. You can, of course, see the Thor Loki parallel. One group will bring destruction, but leading up to this there are lessons and spiritual growth, and the other, will transcend, to the "New Reality of continued Growth".

Our God Trinity within our waveform creation is **The Father (Space), The Son (Time), and Our Divine Mother The Holy Spirit (Numbers)**, and they are the three at work developing and administering the growth of the One Consciousness, that they and everything are an aspect of and when you see a peace sign, that is what that symbolizes! Islam and Christianity both have aspects of truth. Just like there are no "male" and "female" distinctions at the highest levels of the one consciousness, at the lower vibrational developmental levels, there is separation and there are three Deities at work here in the atomic level where there are, of course, **3** elementary particles that makeup, *"everything".* One positive, one negative and the One neutral that sees through both that is also within "the nucleus" of The Self. The Two and Three dynamic is everywhere in creation and is itself headed by Lucifer, and is *overall* Feminine. There is a bloodline that exists in waveform creation that was created to be a conduit of light, or a conduit of The Father, to be brought into waveform creation. The stories of gods having children with "mortal" human women should now make more sense!

The Savior's coming was prophecy as the Fall and the Redemption are cyclical events brought forth by our **Mother of all creation!** Heart *is* soul and the only true line of God. Eve's union with a **"Son" of the Serpent, a Son of God produced Cain**, and that is why the movie is telling you this **Caine Wise,** (and wisdom is Heart-Soul Knowledge, and remember the words of Jesus in Matthew 10:16, "Therefore be *wise as serpents"*) who is half **DOG-GOD,** is a "Son" of God the Father and will bond and mate with "Venus", to become "the Star" **Jupiter! Who will be the new transmitter of the unmanifest God, the Father!** Today's Rh negatives are *"splice".*

"Rhesus negative blood type appears suddenly 35,000 years ago in Cro-magnon. Where did the Rh negatives come from? Why does the body of an Rh negative mother carrying an Rh positive child try to reject her own offspring? Humanity isn't one race, but a hybrid species"

-Robert Sepehr, "Species with Amnesia: Our Forgotten History"

Let's look at where they may have come from! I mentioned earlier in the book that I would give you some more information about Noah. The Book of Enoch was largely excluded from the Bible, although certain verses, like Genesis 6:1 and 2, seen above, made it in. The entire Book is viewed as "non-canonical" by the larger Jewish and Christian establishment, except for the sects of Beta Israel in Ethiopia (look up Negus, please) and Eritrea, which is fascinating. Whatever their reasons for excluding it, you *know at this point why I believe the writings were withheld and why we are continually misled as I believe Enoch and Noah are in the line of Cain.* There are references about the new-born Noah by his father Lamech that are as unambiguous as they get, as he describes who and what Noah looks like. *This is from the Book of Enoch, Chapter 105:*

> *After a time, my son Mathusala took a wife for his son Lamech.*
>
> *She became pregnant by him, and brought forth a child, the flesh of which was as white as snow, and red as a rose; the hair of whose head was white like wool, and long; and whose eyes were beautiful.* [I am assuming light blue] *When he opened them, he illuminated all the house, like the sun; the whole house abounded with light.*
>
> *And when he was taken from the hand of the midwife, opening also his mouth, he spoke to the Lord of righteousness. Then Lamech his father was afraid of him; and flying away came to his own father Mathusala, and said,* **I have begotten a son, unlike to other children. He is not human; but, resembling the offspring of the angels of heaven** (not in, but **of**, meaning "these" Angels are down there with them), **is of a different nature from ours, being altogether unlike to us.**
>
> *His eyes are bright as the rays of the sun; his countenance glorious, and* **he looks not as if he belonged to me, but to the angels.**

Continuing Polarity clues, the Rh Negatives among the Positives!

It continues, but you get the drift, and you have to conclude, because he tells us Noah is unlike **all the rest**, that the "Adamics", are dark-skinned, haired and eyed, in contrast to the Angels who are very white "ruddy" skinned, light-haired and bright, probably light blue, eyed. Adding credibility to Enoch are the accounts of the "White Gods" of the ancient Meso-American to South American cultures. I am in no way sending this in an ego-driven direction promoting separation as that is not germane to the polarity point here or the entire book in general. We are all manifestations of the one mind and display polarity perspectives with various levels interacting to produce the various experiences and lessons! **Besides**, this lays out the identity of "Adam and Eve", and why Black people are said to have Soul, as the path **back** to the Light of the Father, starts in the Darkness of the Mother! This is the real meaning of "Black Lives Matter". (more on that in the last chapter) This just very plainly **confirms** that an Angelic line of Angels did in fact "Fall", "coming down" to intermingle and breed with Adamic humans and, that I stated above, was all programmed and meant to happen! Do you see the huge parallel, another in your face clue, between this slice of Biblical history and American history? Also, I believe it is a mislead that there happens to be an "identical" grandfather, father, son name combination in the line of both Cain and his brother Seth, so you don't "see" Cain's true lineage. Cain is not *from* Adam, nor is Noah!

According to the statistics cited on "therhnegativefactor.webs.com", the percentage of people in the United States with A- blood is...5.7%. Seriously!

Saturnic Yahweh trying to be, **The Man**, as he sends *John* Doe after *John* Doe, from the sea of *John* Q Public. John after "call girl John" sent to slaughter in the *Tombstonish* Brothel of Abrasax. The number of John is 2, the other more "feminine" Duality number! The best of the best and the worst of the worst. Sifting through the minerals can be a tedious task, but she never tires to find "the One"! As I alluded to earlier, Saturn is doing his job to work with Venus to find her "The Diamond in the Rough"! A tale from, "The Book of One Thousand

and One Nights" (I know, 1001, you can't make this up!), tells a story that Disney, with some Masonic alterations, has taken, like "The Lion King", and spun a tale of diamond-encrusted truths, to communicate the ineffable concept of God growth, hidden within a child's story! Doing what they do best, "Aladdin" paints an accurate picture of the Matriarchal nature of waveform creation, outside of "The Light". You cannot be the King if you are not chosen by the Princess, and "The Divine Mother" (in the Disney movie She is a he, the Sultan) and *She* is exceedingly dis**cern**ing! Sifting through the endless fields of egoistic cubic zirconia, is untidy and quite time consuming, as the millions in the sea of egos scream "Me", but she will not choose any unworthy, and will not stop the search until her Diamond in the Rough is found, and after being selected, she'll work diligently with Jafar, to cut and polish him, to unlock his potential. It will be very unpleasant for him for quite some time, but nothing worthwhile comes easy, and there literally **is nothing** more worthwhile.

Just as the 4 letter designation for a "man" is *John,* a similar 4 letter designation is given to a "woman", and we call her *Jane.* Like John Doe, we have our female counterpart Jane Doe, with "see John run, see Jane walk", as we use these names in 1st grade textbooks to teach our children how to read. They are the general names to differentiate the male and female sons and daughters of men! They are the male and female aspects of creation and the children of our Mother God of Creation. Throughout history, we hear of "gods" coming *down* and having sons with "mortal" *daughters of men,* and Thor's lady friend just happens to have the name of "Jane Foster". Look for *this Jane* to be the "foster" mother to a demigod here, and of course "Dad", won't be "here".

The Cain Files!

The closing scene is monumental and the message at the end of the movie moved me as I saw him with wings and looked again at his name and again I am stunned! Yes, I could dismiss all of these clues, until they got personal! They just don't seem to stop! I've mentioned some of the others like Ocean's ll, "A Star is Born" and 21 as ones I have been in, that point to or confirm clues, but after seeing the end of this movie, I remember a movie I was in with William Devane and I guess I am stunned and yet not, as this has gone far beyond any "theory" that needs more proof or just more coincidences. Acting tends to overly stroke ego and Satan knows this all too well and being who I am, I have been separated from most of it. Ninety-nine percent of my auditions here have brought me nothing after 9-11 and while I now see why, I landed this part out of the *blue*, as one of the guys already cast out of LA to be Devane's "right" hand man, for whatever reason, couldn't make it out to Utah on the required filming days. I was called by my agent and told to get down to a park in Provo asap for a cold read audition with the director of a movie they had already started filming called, "The Kane Files". When I got there, there was already about 15 guys waiting in line with their sides (script) in hand. By the time it was my turn, there had to be at least 10 guys behind me and I went over to Ben, the writer and director, and as I finished my last line with him, he said, "Congratulations, you're Max!"

Indeed! Max is Jupiter's father and my son's name and Caine *Wise,* is her winged "man", and in 2010, I am "Max *Godling*", in a movie called "The Kane Files: Life of Trial". Here I am "acting again", with a law enforcement background playing an FBI agent (as it reminds me of "Birdman", who was "Batman"). The lead character's name is "*Scott Kane*", "*a man with a checkered past is trying to live a clean life.*" It's almost laughable, as I said you can't make this up and they clue you in, to the fact that the Cains are not "*ordinary*", and They certainly wouldn't have killed off, the One.

"*Therefore whosoever slayeth Cain, vengeance shall be taken on him **seven**fold. And the Lord set a mark upon Cain, lest any finding him should kill him.*"—*Genesis 4:15*

Our teachers have *taken* us to this fork, working in harmony with our world, solar system, and greater galaxy in this amazing school, and while they administer from the shadows, they couldn't be any more out in the open. Middle Age Cathedrals that display advanced engineering encoded with sacred geometry, harmonics, cosmic and anatomical messages built into the architecture and artwork, scream of advanced knowledge creating stone buildings that the "technology of the day", had no business building! Evidence of more advanced grades from the past are all around us worldwide as stone megaliths and structures of gravity-defying proportions, incorporating impossible logistics, almost too numerous to count, dot the planet above and below her surface, displaying the most advanced structural engineering mathematics, while encoding knowledge of sacred geometric shapes, ratios, and proportions that tap into cosmic energy and harmonics forces, lead all who study them to seriously question our *given* history. The great archaeologist and Egyptologist, Sir William Petrie concluded that whoever built them, had knowledge and used tools and technology that *far* exceeded the technology of his day, and still exceeds the technology of today. In "The Hidden History of the Human Race", Michael Cremo proves anatomically correct humans have been here far longer than our textbooks tell us, and that we have been deceived from the top down. Stone structures thousands of years old, and far older than we have been told, all over the world and under the oceans of staggering complexity that has led people to conclude that Aliens must have built them and all the while, the largest most secretive of societies with magnificent stone buildings in every major "western" city, call themselves *The Masons*. The bigger and more obvious they are, the more hidden they remain. So, ancient complex stone structures abound and they call themselves **The Masons**, and we have been *deceived* from the top (they control all) down, and **they** operate in *secret*! Okay, nothing to *see* here folks, carry on! Because it is all as it should be, as they speak loud and clear to ears that hear!

1 And a great sign appeared in heaven: a woman clothed in the sun, with the moon under her feet and a crown of twelve stars on her head. 2 She was pregnant and crying out in the pain and agony of giving birth. ~Revelation 12:1 and 2, again, written by St. John

On November 20th, 2016, Jupiter *will enter the* Constellation Virgo in the area of the abdomen and will stay within her womb for 42 weeks, until its *birth* on September 9, 2017, representing a normal pregnancy. On September 23, 2017, the constellation Virgo will have the Sun at her shoulder and the Moon at her feet. Above her head will be Leo which contains 9 Stars and at this time, the *wandering stars*, Mercury, Mars, and Venus will round out the alignment with the Lion's Stars to form the crown of 12 Stars. At this time, Jupiter will still be near the womb in the area where a **child** will be born. This will represent the Birth of our New Star and many calendars *originally* began in the constellation of Virgo, so the **Son**, would, therefore, be born *of a* **Virgin.**

So! Jupiter **will** be the next Star, from **our** solar family, and Pluto, it's "Saturnic" counterpart!

"Jupiter Jones was born under a night sky, with signs predicting that she was destined for great things. Now grown, Jupiter dreams of the Stars."

Do tell! And having been mated with Cain, a Son of God, she'll do more than dream, as you *may* want to grab your sunglasses, but definitely lose the sunscreen, because Jupiter is in fact, our newest Star.

Ignition and Liftoff!!!

"We make our world significant by the courage of our questions and by the depth of our answers."

--Carl Sagan

13. Decoding Plain Sight

A Sioux creation story says that long ago the Creator gathered all of Creation and said, "I want to hide something from the humans until they are ready for it. **"It is the realization that they create their own reality."** The eagle said, "Give it to me, I will take it to the moon." The Creator said, "No. One day they will go there and find it." The salmon said, "I will bury it on the bottom of the ocean." "No. They will go there too." The buffalo said, "I will bury it on the Great Plains." The Creator said, "They will cut into the skin of the Earth and find it even there." Grandmother Mole, who lives in the breast of Mother Earth, and who has no physical eyes but sees with spiritual eyes, said, *"Put it inside of them." And the Creator said, "It is done."*

Mocking? No, it's the mimicking of spiritual children!

Much of the world you see around you is a small-scale representation of something much larger. You have been told something to the effect that in mockery and of course *imitation* of God's 12 tribes, *Satan,* and you know who he is, blessed 12 of "his" bloodlines. And then later the 13th for the grand *"royal"* hoax, for those who will be fooled, and that is most. So we are told that Satan mocks God, but is that what is really happening? When you see children playing house, they are not mocking their parents but looking at the larger world and mimicking what they will someday be doing or trying to create a similar environment to "practice", as "playing" in many respects is practicing. We are told in several gospel passages that Satan rules this world, for now, and he who will never be King will create his "Kingdom" which is an imitation of the grander and so, *"plays house!"* The never-ending push for "economic growth" and more material "stuff" is mimicking cosmic growth and "imprisoning" animals in zoos is Satan seeing this place as a prison of sorts, so he will do this to the animals under him, what he perceives God does to us, as he disregards their feelings or worth. The worldly royal bloodline ruling families mimic spiritual royalty, like Odin and not just "like" Odin, as they *are* mimicking his reign. Odin is our "Raven god" and next in line to *"shine"* and I pointed out earlier, the "British" Royals take "The Legend" very seriously, as they *"mock"* spiritual royalty here in level 6, by making sure Ravens are never allowed to leave the Tower of London. The structure of the Royal Houses of Oz mimic those who will be the Mon**archs** of the greater Solar System, who then become *Stars*!

Speaking of stars, this is also why we call our *Celebrities of Ego*, Stars! Satan cannot become a Star because he is leading the Saturnic negative polars heading into the depths of the Dark, to do the jobs that we don't want. He still wants to "act" like God so, what does he do? He, because mocking is part of the clue, calls *his,* for the most part, Ego driven darker ends of the equation *stars,* as Hollywood movie *stars* are the only Stars *he* can hope to create. Satan yearns to be a Star, but an *adored and worshipped* "celebrity" here, will have to suffice. Of course, it is impossible to force love and respect, but Satan demands you love and worship him, as that's a big part of his polar opposite, God opposing job.

On the illusory "Hollywood" Walk of Fame, they pay homage to all of the "greats" with their own *Star* pentagram, like my favorite, *"Donald"* Duck! My runner up is Big Bird, a no-flight *Phoenix mock.* The *two* **polarity** awards, the "Golden Globe Award" and the "Oscar" pays "house playing" homage, to our Divine Masculine Soul and our Divine Feminine Spirit parents. The *normal* family unit mimics the structure of its spiritual counterpart as the polarities of male and female, are actually the positive and negative dynamic of the relationship of Soul and Spirit and Self and Ego, and they are both attracted and need each other to create "more". It is the 2 combining to create 1, at our level. In essence "Mother" is allowing us to play Galactic House, and we **are** in *Her* house!

We can now add another metaphorical "as below" mimic of the multitude *searching* for their "Forever Loves", their. . . "Soul Mates"! Which here, in 7-11, is a necessary *"practice"* for development, as doughnuts endlessly search for their holes. (the *opening* was there) The

Perfect school to grow and expand the "Right" thought of "Reality", by discouraging, through perfect consequences, the Left thought of the waveform illusion. And the beauty of the inner workings of the school is that the lessons are enhanced through Left thought while at the same time, discouraging it.

I was having some fun, a few years ago at my bank with my daughter when she was 14 or 15 after one of them asked me if I wanted to set up an account for her with a credit card. I knew them all and I am a bit animated and even the ladies that worked there had a good laugh with my daughter, who is very used to my humor as we joke with each other regularly. I don't remember the exact wording, but it was to the effect that he must have taken leave of his senses to suggest giving a credit card to a young female teen, thinking you can control this combustible dynamic and that that's how they ultimately lost control at "Jurassic Park", listening to the guy who suggested they make them all "Female". *Okay, they liked it, and you had to be there!* Well, now I see the bigger clue of the movie, as *"It's not nice to fool* **Mother** *Nature!"*, within the overall message that creation **is** waveform Feminine, and she absolutely runs the show, and you don't disrespect or *toy* with Her thinking you control *anything*, without paying the price. Had they made them all male, they'd still be in the garden of Jurassic! Haha, and the "blood-sucking lawyer" was the only one who liked Hammond's park!

"You were given specific orders......The orders were for your protection.

I think we can handle **one little girl**. I sent two units! They're bringing her down now!

No, Lieutenant, your men are already dead." The Matrix - Agent Smith speaking to police

I discovered that my "kicked in the teeth" experiences, did so to show me (and Wyatt), that I am not in control here. And in Kung Fu Panda, Master Oogway explaining to Shifu to, "...let go of the illusion of control". All of this is an aspect of Her! In Oz, all of that was controlled by Glinda! And from the "Green" of the Emerald City to the "Green" of the other god-like Female, the Wicked Witch, it is all a necessary lesson! And back in Kansas, Aunt Em was running the ranch! The All Seeing Eye is not government or big brother "keeping an eye" on us, but the All That Is, that sees through each and every one of us and knows absolutely everything out there and "inside" of us!

Both genders are polar manifestations of our Spiritual Mother

Look at the X female and Y male chromosomes and you'll see the female has 4 ends and the male 3, so again we see another polar property, and I earlier covered the size of both. Further proof of John and Jane vessels being aspects of the Divine Feminine is that both contain 2 chromosomes, the feminine number of duality and **even males** will carry an X female chromosome. The "Jane" will always provide the X within her egg and the "John" will provide anywhere between 200 to 500 million eager sperm, each carrying only one chromosome that is either an X or Y, swimming feverishly toward the egg. The egg will only allow **one** to enter, and if it is a Y, a male will form, and if it is an X, a female will form. I have a "humorous" story, at least everybody I've told laughs, about how the Y sperm are "faster" swimmers, but the X has more endurance, and how I used this *valuable* information to produce a "desired" *result*, but that's not for here, thank God.

Religion, a developmental step, below 1

Religion is a *building block* in spiritual development and closely parallels why we are taught about Santa as children. As I pointed out earlier, you can't teach a small child how to give, who is not physically or psychologically ready to give, who only takes or receives because of their age and needs. Before you can teach them to give, you first teach them how their behavior affects what and how much they will receive. When children are playing with their blocks, that is, of course, their level, and it could actually harm them, to teach them that the blocks are something other than what their senses are telling them. Their stage and they are unable to see beyond it, is all about 5 sense "solid" separate reality, and remember, "spiritual children" come in all ages and body types. Like the blocks, if you tried to tell them that higher realities of the Self or God, were to be found "inside", and why the sides of your head are labeled Temples (of course your entire body is the Temple), your message would simply be rejected. So you begin by taking them to a *Temple* they are ready for and **can** comprehend, a bricks and mortar church, synagogue or mosque, and you talk to them in terms of *out here* males and females in marriage, before you begin to (but as we heard from the One who would know, "few will accept this") acquaint them with the true internal marriage of Soul and Spirit. It's a necessary stage, like the blocks, in our self-realization and growth to be discarded, unless your path **is** to the Dark, to eternally externalize the internal, and that too, is part of the plan herein waveform, to complete the equation.

"The most fundamental message of Gautama the Buddha is not God, is not soul... it is freedom: freedom absolute, total, unconditional. He does not want to give you an ideology, because every ideology creates its own slavery. He does not want to give you a religion, because religion binds you." ~ Osho

Put it inside of Them

Speaking of the "Inner Temple", let me now make the mysterious first miracle marriage "crystal clear" as take another step to its "true meaning". I am speaking now of the first ceremony that they *did* have wine. Christ and "Mary" are there in Cana (10) which is **now** *The* 11 whose ego has "let go", is Yeshua's union with his body, the Divine Feminine of *Mary* "within". That's why Lucifer comprises them both, and why He who will be the Christ, cannot find his Soulmate "Out There", for in the True ONE, she of Spirit, is already, *In There*. This is why the number of the "Perfectly" Divine "Soul" is 10, whose Ego, while still "in there" to enrich and no longer looking "out there" for **"her"** (lowercase), has completely let go which is why the 1 becomes 0, and like the One Mind 1+0=1, that sets the stage to ascend from this level.

They have consummated the perfect Soul - Spirit "Marriage", which is the *real* meaning of becoming One Flesh, like Wyatt and Josephine. He no longer looks outside of himself for anything *more*, and like the Prodigal Son has returned Home, *within*. When he was *out here* he was lost in one dead end after another, and when he returned "Home", to the only place you can *find* the Promised Land, he was Found.

Remember, here and *not here*! The "Serpent" was the adversarial Ego of the Angel who lusted after Eve, the pull to the dark, and the "physical" manifestation of that "negative" polar sex drive to release his starlight creative power through his lower root chakra, was his penis, that, of course, looks *"serpent" like*. **The Angel was the Serpent, psychologically and physiologically! Ego, better known as Satan, wanting to create new life "in place of God".** And collectively, the Fallen Angels are the "Serpents", and so "Sons of", who "took wives for themselves", from the "daughters of men", better known as Eve, from the "created" Adamic race. **They fell** because they **pursued the *illusion* of the "out there" feminine temple which is one of the main properties of *The Synagogue of Satan*, rather than the Temple of their own, that they are one Flesh with, *The Temple of Christ!* This is precisely what he meant.** You see **THEY,** were supposed to have been beyond this step and had to *step way* down in frequency to do it, but they were young and still had lessons to learn at this lower level. Virtually all but a select few will accept this, and I get it, because it is, only supposed to be a select few. About 99% will interpret His words below as speaking of men and women, and the 1% or so will know He means Soul and Spirit, and that Man created Marriage to "separate", and we are here in separation, this union.

6 "However, from the beginning of creation, God made them male and female. 7 For this reason a man will leave his father and mother and be united to his wife, 8 and the two will become one flesh. So they are no longer two, but one flesh. 9 Therefore what God has joined together, let man not separate." 10 When they were back inside the house, the disciples asked Jesus about this matter. 11 So He told them, "Whoever divorces his wife and marries another woman commits adultery against her....12 And if a woman divorces her husband and marries another man, she commits adultery." ~Mark 10:6 to 12

7 "Why then," they asked, "did Moses order a man to give his wife a certificate of divorce and send her away?" 8 Jesus answered, "It was because of your hardness of heart that Moses permitted you to divorce your wives; but it was not this way from the beginning. 9 Now I tell you that whoever divorces his wife, except for sexual immorality, and marries another woman, commits adultery." 10 His disciples said to Him, "If this is the case between a man and his wife, it is better not to marry." (because we know what that leads to) *11 "Not everyone can accept this word, Jesus answered, "but only those to whom it has been given. 12 For there are eunuchs who were born that way; others were made that way by men; and still others live like eunuchs for the sake of the kingdom of heaven. The one who can accept this should accept it."*

Many people will not only "reject this", but they will have an irrational "cognitive dissonance" type "allergic reaction rejection" of this because they do not want to consider that what they have built their entire life and belief upon, is a developmental state and that their way of life may be taking them further into a dream. That's why the world only loves its own, and direct insults, to those on the path "To the Light". The path back to the Light is not easy, and *here*, certainly not popular, as they fervently crucified the One, and those closest to him denied they knew him. While most esoteric clues are cleverly hidden, the clues for "this" Divine union have been some of the most "in plain sight", in Black and White of all time, telling us that "your body" **is the Church**!

"28 In the same way, husbands ought to love their wives as *their own bodies. He who loves his wife loves himself.* 29 Indeed, no one ever hated *his own body, but he nourishes and cherishes it, just as Christ does the church.* 30 For we are members of His body. 31 "For this reason a man will leave his father and mother and be united to his wife, and the *two will become one flesh." 32* **This mystery is profound,** but *I am speaking about* **Christ and the church.**" -Ephesians

She is within to the aware, and without to the unaware.

A woman in my place has two faces. One for the world...and one which she wears in private.

*With **You,** I'll be only Sibylla. Tiberias thinks me unpredictable.*

I AM unpredictable. ~ "Kingdom of Heaven"

If you find her *in private*, and if you love Her, pay attention to Her and treat Her as your virtuous Queen, but at the same time, stay disciplined and **in** control of your desires and passions, in other words, *Lead* in the dance, then *Lady Liberty* will liberate you. The esoteric meaning of Liberty. If you don't, and treat her in **any** other way and fail to lead, becoming a weak slave to your passions and desires which really is a dark reflection of you, then she can be...unpredictable! I certainly didn't, which was a direct reflection of my dark direction. I simply have to take responsibility, because I can't be the victim, and see in Unity. Like Thor, "I've Changed", to avoid the "Damned" outcome.

"I envy you. But such a thing is not meant to last." -"The Matrix Reloaded", Persephone's awareness, advising Trinity that passion between "Lovers" is fleeting and ultimately an illusory dead end, after being reminded what a passionate kiss felt like after kissing Neo.

Time for *Personal* Pollution Legislation

As around us, so within us, or for this point, it is better to reverse it! There is an absolute correlation between the pollution we introduce into our bodies, and the pollution introduced into the body that we are cells of, Mother Earth. We are the collective consciousness and we manifest a material projection onto the larger body in proportion of what we do to ourselves individually. The destruction and pollution we dispense upon our mother is a manifestation of very real acts we carry out on a daily basis polluting our own world, our body. We are all mini versions of earth just as the cells of your body are mini versions of you and every morsel of junk food and liquids we ingest pollute our "children", who are the cells who reside within your body! They don't fly their own flag for nothing. A Flag represents a consciousness paradigm. Scott, you mean I am contributing to the pollution of the earth by eating and drinking the garbage, the place with the arched M sells? You mean I am being a reckless "Hamburger" King, to all of my cellular subjects? Yes, and I am impressed with the way you worded the questions! We each have a responsibility, and it is hard and takes great discipline, to reject polluting ourselves, as they make "carbonated" soft drinks tasty. *It is though, far easier to complain about chemtrails and factory smokestacks, as you smoke, or water pollution, as you drink all manners of poisons, or landfills as you stuff yourself with junk food, or stay horrified and bitter at the torture and total lack of respect endured by animals as you eat your bacon.*

"5 This is the message we have heard from Him and announce to you, that God is Light, and in Him there is no darkness at all. 6 If we say that we have fellowship with Him and yet walk in the darkness, we lie and do not practice the truth;... -1 John 1:5 And "If you Love me, you will keep my commandments." John 14:15

It's not a pump

This is one of the examples of Christ using the word "Hypocrites" when describing the Pharisees. If you continue to pollute yourself, and then demonize the companies that provide the pollution, you are simply part of the problem and just add more fear and smoke and mirrors to muddy the water! And isn't WATER, another huge clue, that is only now being seen for what it is because it was said 2000 years ago, to be the message for us NOW, as it didn't apply then. As I pointed out earlier, the universe and flow of the galaxies run on electricity, and pure water is the programmable key to your *perpetual motion circulatory system* that taps into the same cosmic forces. An average adult body contains approximately **100,000 miles of blood vessels**. *Let this really sink in.* That is 4 times the circumference of the Earth. ***Plasma,** the **4**th **state** (lava9lamp) of **matter, propels it** and your **Heart is not a pump but the very central seat of who you are!*** Think of it this way, at any major transportation hub, what is the responsibility of the hub? To "coordinate", *not provide the thrust,* and make sure that everything that comes in, goes out to the correct location. That's what the Heart does! Do you really think a little fist-sized muscle can work, 24/7, 365 days a year, for 70 to 100 years, if you are "lucky", pumping 2000 gal a day, while navigating through 100 thousand miles of vessels (we really can't conceptualize this), while taking about a minute for the blood to do a round trip? I didn't either, so the more you are in harmony with nature and your own clean body, the healthier and more naturally operating, like solar movements, your body will be. Pollution and *lack of Self,* will sever this connection and compromise your system. Most people today don't drink, just WATER. It's too *boring* and they are ruled, as most of us are, by their taste, as they defile their Temple.

*"Truly, truly, I say to you, unless one is **born of water** and the Spirit he cannot enter into the kingdom of God. 6"That which is born of the flesh is flesh, and that which is born of the Spirit is spirit...."* --John 3:5

The other meaning of this esoteric message is to find the homeostasis midpoint of the "liquid" that sits between the ethereal of gas and the material of solid.

We have very tough choices in front of us, and they are placed there to "test the water". I sense another clue in that miracle liquid crystal that gives life. A water molecule has three atoms: two hydrogen (H) atoms and one oxygen (O) atom. To be born again of the water and to know that it is a reflection of the Trinity as the 2 H (remember Heaven and Hell, the two I's (and I is 9) (9-II) connected by the highway or staircase encompassing the entire spectrum) and 1 O are the very essence of life itself here in our waveform universe. The O, of course, is Her and the two H's are Her 2 Sons; the one to the Light and the one to the Dark, that in grand polarity fashion.

"The highest good is like water. Water gives life to the ten thousand things and does not strive.

It flows in places men reject and so is like the Tao." --Lao Tzu: The Tao Te Ching

Folks **we** too are HAARP. They have the less aware believing that only "They" have the power to control the weather on this planet, but HAARP is a clue that **We** have the power by our actions, as what we put into our own worlds and our thoughts both of which regulate our frequencies influencing the planetary frequency played by the global "Harp". Remember the harps played in films to symbolize the change in one's frequency, and we influence our world. The Native Americans "played their Harps" while dancing for rain! The Abrahamic "Great" Nation of "Negative Polarity" spread all over the world wiping out the positive polarity knowledge of the indigenous tribes who knew this. Whether you or your cells like it or not, they are in *your* keeping and the planet is in *ours*! You harbor a universe you spawn and your views and negative thoughts keep it and the world embroiled in countless conflicts as you curse the rain, curse the "War on Terror", and wonder why you are ill. And speaking of cells, NASA lies to perpetuate a Satanic paradigm that we are independent of our greater body, from what we are a part of. At this "level", we are part of the cells "here", which is why we, again at this "frequency", cannot get beyond a certain point. Think of it this way, can any of your cells independently just up and leave you? You may be giving them good reasons polluting their world, but you and they are "stuck", and when you hear the *"sky's the limit", it really is!* The only prison, for those who see this place as one, is the one you fashion for yourself.

"As long as you still experience the stars as something "above you", you lack the eye of knowledge."
— Friedrich Nietzsche

And I will follow this up with my own slant, and stand on the shoulders of Nietzsche's wisdom!

As long as you still experience the interlaced dynamic of corporations, government, and religion, being run by those you perceive to be either insane, stupid, greedy or power hungry, displaying wanton, indiscriminate cruelty, running humanity into submission or extinction as something **"outside of you"**...you lack the eye of knowledge.

Dior J'ador - "The Future is Gold", the 51 second spot
https://www.youtube.com/watch?v=Rm-vBq-1T1k

The Dior J'adore commercial, shot in the Palace of Versailles built by Louis XIV aka *"The **Sun** King"*, starts in "The Hall of **Mirrors**" (remember what the Target commercial told us this reality is) with its many chandeliers above with many individual lights (stars), and you hear **7** *steps* as Charlize walks through the hallway. This symbolizes our journey down here at this level (*separation* perception) of creation that is now passing away. She says "the past can be beautiful, a memory, *a dream*", and if she continued *following* the crowd immersed in the **dark**, the deeper she would have *fallen* in "this" dream, but she stops to take control of her life and "make her own moves *up*" within the game. She knows what she needs to do internally to find that "fork" in the road that leads to the Narrow Gate. Her stopping to grab the gold "yellow" cloth is her changing course to follow the path to the Light of "Self " realization, taking her out of the Iron Age with her outstretched hand with the duality hand sign indicating we are in the duality dream, and the three fingers grab it means she is now seeing in Unity. She is now going within, to ascend and transcend this level, as she says, "But it's no place to live." This is a temporary school to learn, and not the be all end all reality, so it is not wise to "build your treasures" in what is an illusory waveform level, and her going up is her internal "Arc Building" (body alteration) through daily discipline. The only way out is up (it's why Angels have wings), and her going up means she is actively increasing her frequency day in and day out, changing cell by cell, as the internal work produces physical changes. As she ascends to the light, she rips off her jewelry releasing her attachments, to the "treasures" of this "existence", and in doing so, *lightens her Up,* and further increases her frequency. Plus, her jewels are also her "pearls" (a *dual* clue within a clue), her wisdom, being sent down to those still here as divine messages, (like this book) to what her siblings need to do if it is their destiny to ascend as well. There are things we need to do to prepare, and you cannot rise above "this", if you hold on to "this". That IS the *Inconvenient Truth* and the, "No one knows the day or hour, means that what you need to do, to let go of the carnal trappings of 3D Iron, must be a way of life and you need to be doing it now, which is why she says *"and now is the time".* They are telling you the narrow gate is within, not "Out There" and YOU must be the change and free yourself from the carnal and material trappings if you want to find it. And then she says, "It's not Heaven, It's a new world", and this is very telling as to the "identity" of this place and that it isn't the "Reality of Heaven" (yet), but the next class of 8 within the duality dream. Just as you must complete and pass the class of 6, you must do the same in the Bronze of 8 to reach your goal of Gold. If this were an "ordinary" commercial, they would never say, "It's NOT Heaven", but would absolutely equate using it with Heaven! So my sweet smelling siblings, this is not "just" a fragrance commercial but a *Targeted* message, to the aware.

Lancome La Vie Est bella

In a world full of endless laws and narrow-minded dogma programming us how to live and what to believe; Could there be another way!? The illumined Eiffel Tower points up amid the grid of straight and curved lines. Here is another international message telling us that this is a "mirror image" of reality. The Target commercial tells us this IS a mirror image in two places. Notice she enters the room wearing white, like the Self in the white room of the Target commercial, a soul carrying vessel of the Self, entering a crowded room with 3 (Trinity, above and not "seen") white light crystal chandeliers, the stars above. She walks across "it" (life) toward a wall with 6 (creation) lights on it and what appears to be an opening. She then walks by a column of crystal that was not there before, like the cloth coming down from the top of the dome in the Dior commercial. This indicates we are connected to higher vibrational "realities". After she gets to the "opening", we see that it's not an opening, but the fact that she is realizing that this life is a programmed mirror image. She is realizing what this place is and now *knows* she is in the "CHESS GAME", and the smile indicates that she will no longer be played, removing the puppet strings, but will now PLAY the game and be the master of Her! The woman putting the sunglasses means they still see in the dark or lower awareness. Walking up the steps indicate she is increasing her frequency by her choices. As she turns with the knowing smile, as she now knows who she is and what this place is, and in that knowledge life becomes beautiful, and not the cruel, sad, unfair, "life" of struggle she once saw it as and struggled within. And then at the end after she is smiling after ascending, it goes to a very quick city shot again with a "smile" and the sun rising on it as the collective's frequency increases, for she pulls us all up and she, of course, is not alone. More light and knowledge as frequency increases!

"The Best Plans are No Plans"

Keep this *line in mind* from a *current* group of "Corona (Crown) Beer" commercials featuring *Snoop Dogg*, as they are more esoteric clues to the makeup of the human condition, than advertisements. When your plans (decisions) are *consciously made* "on the fly" (not pre-made, but just made in the present moment), your A.I. *Subconscious*, that connects to everything else (the greater body's A.I. we are within), has no access to them to keep you a pawn (subservient cell) in Her game or system (as She is programmed to do). This dynamic is displayed in "The Matrix" with "Pre-Neo" Thomas Anderson's connection to The Matrix that allowed the A.I. to counter and influence (in an attempt to thwart) his "independence oriented" plans. This gives credence to the Robert Burns poem, *"The best laid schemes o' Mice an' Men"*.

This commercial is a *One Person's Internal dialog Metaphor*. Snoop (: to search or investigate, and the initial of S for Self) is dressed in blue and white (Sky / Light, and he on the Right) with a rather out of place, royal looking robe (and long white pants) on a warm beach that makes no sense unless it is, and it is, meant as a deeper clue of his identity as the Organic *Real* Self (Black/Soul) with Samberg (White/Spirit), on the "Left" in Red (in the Root Chakra area) shorts, representing the "Artificial (A.I.) Ego". You see, The Computer seeks direction from the Programer (real person), and when you take control and give it positive (to growth, Up) directions, it carries it out, but when you fail to "take control" (lead in the marriage within the One Flesh), and let the *Autopilot* make your decisions, it is pre-programmed to take you in the negative direction of decay.

Our current push (deeper addiction) toward further dependence on A I's "cell phones" *solid*ifies you remaining in Her system, Separated (cell in the body) from Self. Any addiction ties you down, restricting your freedom, so you may want to consider ditching what connects you, which is why Snoop takes Andy's cell to ruin it, if you want to *consciously pursue* "The Crown" (giving Andy a Corona) of Independence (a Fine Life). "Andy" (Ego) agrees and underlyingly whispers, "D O double (duality) G" (God) to his Self.

The meaning of the "Goat Head" Statue

Like the Horned Satanic hand sign, not the least bit "evil", but the picture of Polarity and God growth, giving us information. The image of the Caduceus, and you know the serpents are Soul and Spirit, is incorporated into its torso with the center globe or consciousness point at mid-heart level, that have grown up from the groin or root Chakra where all growth starts. The wings have 2 meanings as one indicates "Up" Northerly growth from child to adult and "beyond", and the second, like the winged angels, ones who break free of "gravity" with its terrestrial bound limitations. Gravity, and I explain this in the next chapter, is a perspective, that manifests itself as a force, that keeps you down on a level learning symbolized by the dome within his abdomen, until **you** are ready to transcend it. This isn't just happening all around us but also happening within each of us. The children represent our perspectives of the polarity extremes of black and white, male and female. The boy represents the Divine Masculine "Soul" being "Black" and Male and the girl represents the Divine Feminine "Spirit" being "White" and Female. In the last chapter, I will completely identify the Light and the Dark and their respective polarity identities. It will be crystal clear by the end of the book. The "half man, half animal", like "The Cowboys" from Tombstone Decoded", indicate our transition from animal to man, and man's eventual "shedding", of his bodies animal characteristics and desires (parts of the perspective I spoke of), to embody true "Hu-man" turning to "the Light" becoming God. The pentagram is the symbol of man and the "point up" at the position on the forehead indicate "pineal" "Light Sight" activation. The right hand with the "two" fingers up represent "Up and to the Right" development and the left hand is the opposite "Down" frequency and to the "Left" of Separation, the abode of the lower spectrum "evil spirits". The polarity you have nurtured and your frequency "signature" will determine your *up or down*, to the *light or the dark* path. The horns are again Duality in the school of 11, and the trident, the Trinity, up through the top of his head is the Christic "Fire", think stars, of the "Serpents" Creative Energy of God moving up, being expressed "to the Light. This image just "gives" you information, and doesn't represent a Devil or evil idol, but you will "see" to the level of your awareness! Whatever you don't understand about the image now, you should by the end of the book. Now to Somewhere over the Rainbow!

A Little More Oz!

Before her dream, Dorothy did not appreciate her home and her family, as she longed to "join the circus" and leave them behind. She was taking them for granted and not being very mature by needlessly putting herself and Toto into situations that negatively affected others and could have brought dire consequences for her family. After her experience with the witch and the "insanity" that was Oz, she was changed. She loved and appreciated her family and friends more passionately, became more responsible, and saw "home" in a whole new light! "There's no place like Home". You already know I believe *"this"*, is Oz, the Munchkins are spiritual children and I have made references to the soles on Dorothy's slippers representing her soul and that the Wicked witch is the programmed dark or evil that Dorothy must experience and that the yellow brick road is the road back to the light as Dorothy *is* a Star child and is being "developed". I have said that *"all of this"*, is God growing and evolving, but there is certainly more to the Oz Allegory, so let's tie up some Oz loose ends, since I am not a loose ends kinda, guy!

I've talked about how stories like this usually have three interpretations based on your awareness and there are none that fit this like L. Frank Baum's classic and for him to have weaved so many intricate meanings from all three levels speaks to his intelligence, depth, and the fact that he must have been well connected to the school's administrators because there are immensely deep spiritual concepts deftly communicated. The children's movie aspect speaks for itself and while very entertaining, to me growing up, the tone was very ominous. The second level is pretty blatant and you really don't have to be knee deep in conspiracy to see the political symbolism and the fact that it is one big allegory from start to finish. I want to concentrate on the deeper spiritual messages, but just for an overview, I want to run down some of the second level, conspiratorial symbolism. None of this is from me and has been out for over a hundred years, and all deal with the *"realities"* of this world, behind, the facade!

Dorothy - A simple "ordinary" person, or an American Populist character from the rural areas that characterized American Populism.

Scarecrow - Farmers and other populist workers with little education. From a more conspiratorial slant, that you see more with the scarecrow than any of them, the scarecrow was your the "false corporate identity" you were given at "Birth" with a "Certificate" generated on the Stock Exchange to declare you as a capital asset of the corporation, with your name in all capital letters indicating you were a corporate possession under the guise of the Roman International Empire using Admiralty and Uniform Commercial Code laws, as opposed to the "natural person. A scarecrow version of Kansas would be KS, a satellite corporation within the larger corporation, as opposed to simply an area of land Kansas.

Tin Man - Machine like industrial workers, with no feelings, hence heartless.

Cowardly Lion - He is William Jennings Bryan, who was an American Populist Presidential candidate in 1896 and 1900, who was a magnificent orator, but was portrayed as a coward whose roar or bark was worse than his bite, for not supporting the US war with Spain. Same as it ever was! The program or "Nazi playbook", is amazingly predictable. This ploy has been repeated ad nauseam throughout world "history" because the programmed school works. What child, old enough to grasp stories, does not buy Santa Claus? It served its purpose even though you now see beyond it, and if you are reading this, you see things your younger siblings can't. And so they bite, as peek a boo, gets a laugh every time.

Oz - The abbreviation for the standard unit of measure for precious metals, the ounce.

Yellow Brick Road - represented the Populist's push to return to the "gold standard". The yellow bricks were gold bricks.

The Ruby Slippers - Now in the original book, the slippers were silver and that is exactly what they represented, as the other accepted precious metal that we all view as "real money". This level has no "good" explanation for why Hollywood changed them to red, but Hollywood did not create the movie for the conspiratorial message.

The Wizard - The phony controlled politicians who do the bidding of the bankers.

The Emerald City - Washington DC and green for the greenback dollars.

There are many more but most are a bit laughable, like Todo being "prohibitionists" or the "winged monkeys" the Native Americans, so I'll dispense with listing them all because it is just more fluff and beating a dead horse because the deepest spiritual message is the real reason "The Wizard of Oz" was created, and listing more of this level does not contribute to understanding the deeper interpretation. The most important point concerning more is that the conspiratorial angles, *never stop,* and it really does become the *dog chasing his tail* or *beating a dead horse.* You see, you are still viewing from separation which stems from the dark, and the separation bait literally never stops because the dark wants to keep you "in the dark". After this section on Oz, I will show you the perfect commercial that communicates this dynamic, from the same "Why would Target do this?" source that brought us the Wizard and everything else.

This is my take as I have not seen what I will tell you here, anywhere else. What comes closest on *two points* (more like 1 and a half) is something I saw on a Mark Passio video, when he tells you that Toto is *"Human"* intuition, and I agree with him, it is the Heart intelligence guide from God. This **is** why Todo is a dog, god spelled backward. Toto always points her in the *right* direction (yes, even in the garden of Miss Gulch) to learn, as the heart know**s** before the head. The other point, the *half* I alluded to, is his identity of Dorothy as the Soul, which most would see as close or even the same as Spirit, but to me, they are not the same thing. While he comes close on this point, I see Dorothy as Spirit, so she is the spirit having a "human" experience because she needs to learn and she is female because spirit is "Feminine" by nature.

I've already told you that the munchkins are the very young spiritual children, and so portrayed as children, and they are only here to live in 5 sense reality. They are not ready for anything deeper, and as Dorothy leaves crossing the border, they stop on a dime because they are not allowed to leave munchkinland, just like your kids can't leave elementary school on their own. The citizens of the Emerald City are the "seniors" ready for the next level and why they are portrayed as young adults. Now, let's look at why Dorothy is on her journey with the gang. Dorothy is Spirit, coming to the Duality school of 11. While here she needs an *atomic* vessel or a body, and the Tinman is her body, the Scarecrow is her self-aware ego mind with its programmed intelligence and the Cowardly Lion is her Soul of 7 **and** personality with its weaknesses and emotions and is an aspect of Dorothy's Astral **Self**, and last but not least she has her Heart-based intuition, Toto, with her. All of these are aspects of "most" of us! We all have a body which will be programmed to meet our level and lesson and the cells they contain *desire*, and they don't come with sacred hearts from God as that will be contained in the Astral Selves within the body and I am not speaking of just the pump (which it really isn't anyway) that circulates the blood; a mind with varying degrees of intelligence, to be very smart or average or "below" average in terms of cognitive abilities, and him telling her that he has no brain is a clue telling us that the cognitive ability does not come from the "Grey Matter" in your head. Also, the tin man and scarecrow are purely mechanized waveform programs and that is why when the Witch of the West sprinkles the opium poppies on them as the adversary, those two are not affected by the drug, as they are not "real".

Glinda is our Divine Feminine *adult* God of waveform Creation and representing Spirit and she is the mother of all young developing spirits and why Dorothy, her child, is a girl, represents a young "learning" spirit, having a "Human" experience here, and this is of course Oz. When she comes here to "incarnated" in Oz with her Soulmate Lion, she can be a man or a woman. Consider it like Jesus here bonding with his Spirit Mary already within him! She was experiencing the fear along with her Cowardly Lion Soul and remember during much of the movie, she wore a blue bow on her head and he wore a red bow also showing they were a polarity Soul and Spirit mate. Speaking of the Lion, the reason he **is** a Lion, and not something else, is the Lion demonstrates the makeup of the "Divine Masculine" spiritual lineage. He **is** *King of the Jungle,* as Jungle is an esoteric "slang" term for "Nature" or the Natural order of the Universe. Like Odin being the "All Father" in Asgard, all in Asgard are "below" him so to speak. They are all his spiritual children within his house. In a Lion pride, all of the cubs of the various females are his offspring. The "Divine Feminine" spiritual lineage is demonstrated in nature by the Queen bee and her hive, and why bees and hives are Masonic and of course, LDS symbols. Remember the bees recognizing Jupiter? All in her hive, and the earth is one big hive, are her offspring. The dance of spirit and soul.

Also, the three witches identified in the movie are Glinda, the witch of the North, and the freshly killed witch of the East, as the age coming to an end is "The East", and her sister the witch of the West. Since South is not identified and Glinda tells Dorothy she **is** a witch, only asking if she is a good or bad one, they are telling you that **Dorothy is the Witch of the South, Glinda's child.** An Adult knows their true identity as The Self and no longer identifies with their Ego and as a result, they are in the position of North and their number is 9. In the position of the South is the child and their number is 7. (this is also why 7-11 is owned by the **Southland** Corp.) A 7, like the cross, is comprised of a smaller horizontal line, and a longer line that is vertical on a cross, and diagonal in the developing 7 indicating their growth is *up,* and to the *right.* You can ponder what the 2 lines represent. Dorothy, not realizing who she is yet, denies who and what she is. God is continually growing "UP" and evolving and that's why North is "UP" and South will always be below North, as a child is to an adult. Because there is continual growth up, that is why the Pole and central point, the one mind, is always headed up or North and that is symbolized by the wings, and that brings us to the identity of the two perspectives of East and West. East is "Separation" or left (4) brain perception and West is "Unity", the knowledge of the only One reality...The Self or right (3) brain perception. And remember, as I alluded to in the synopsis, the World Wide Web, aka www, is a step in the *Unification* of the Global Mind, and the initials of our Supremely *evil*, Luciferian teacher, the Wicked Witch of the *West* just happens to be WWW. Her cackling laugh would be perfect here! (admit it, you just *heard* it)

Dorothy's **2** ruby red slippers represent Spirit and the Duality of Our Divine Mother, as spirit traverses the full spectrum of Good and Evil (evil spirits too), Light and Dark, especially the Dark base that is an integral part of all of us. It IS our electron, elect-*lady in red* of the Dark and the knowledge of our Divine Feminine, making us whole, is our knowledge of Right Brain Unity. If we do not recognize her, our **Holy Spirit** that **we** are an aspect of, we are denying who we are, a form of cancer, and this is Blaspheming the Holy Spirit and all who do can never be forgiven. This is why Glinda tells Dorothy to never **let** those slippers off your feet for even a moment or you will be at the mercy of the wicked witch. The Witch, who represents the Evil end of the spectrum can't take them, as you must give away your power and of course, the slippers contain *souls*.

So east and west, each with 4 letters, represents the electromagnetic circular flow, like a propeller propelling us North, just like the east and west of the circular rotating earth, of energy to and from separation to unity; and why north and south both have 5 letters representing *the "real" us of The Self*, like the 5 pointed pentagram star that mirrors our shape of a head up and two arms extended out to the side and two legs extending down, like the 5 extensions of the pentagram. They continually flow in and out of each other like the polar aspects of good and evil, as The Self continues to grow and evolve. The only way the child of God grows is through separation, and as more children are created and sent to "Creation", to experience separation, God or The Self, grows! This is why Genesis tells us, "God had planted a garden in the *east*, in Eden", as it allows us to fully identify our-Self. The child of God can only realize who he is, to grow up to become a fully realized adult, through coming out of the "sheltered" Light into separation with an ego.

Now when Dorothy gets to Oz, what is the first big change that jumps out at you? Everything is in different colors. She came from a star as Glinda tells us, and there Dorothy is not in Separation as all is one and are bathed in white light. Just as Dorothy is here to experience separation, the light is also separated into the various frequencies that make up the whole. Glinda, the first *"Person"* she meets, is clearly not an ordinary human as a pearl or planet-like sphere, (and FYI, I have seen pearl-like spheres that stay stationary for long periods of time and take off at warp speed) floats down from the sky displaying different colors before remaining on a purplish violet color, the highest frequency and the color of Spiritual Royalty. Dorothy is her spiritual child and in order for her to develop into a new star, and again think Jupiter, she must experience and learn in order to grow and evolve, and experiencing the dark is a necessary lesson. You don't learn if you don't engage the game, and you don't engage without motivation. Without the "motivation" of having made an enemy of the witch of the west, then she might not be all that motivated to journey or leave Oz and learn all that is not love and light from "Glinda's" green alter Ego, the "Wicked Witch. So she is directed and motivated by Glinda to follow the Yellow Brick Road, the path to a new Star, and the fact that she has the blue dress confirms this path of Ascension. What they don't speak of is the red brick road next to the yellow that spirals off with it and then heads in another direction, which would be the path to the new Saturn. Not long after she gets to Oz, you see both the red and yellow brick roads on either side of a river and a bridge connects them. Glinda is coming down from what appeared to be a bright Star, the "bright morning star", and showing you the 5 point "up" pentagram Star on the rod with the crown and wings, and relatively beautiful. Glinda is Lucifer and I already explained why the man behind the curtain is not seen. The one who is seen is an ordinary man of waveform him, as opposed to **Him,** and all of the theatrics of who seems to be in charge is all of the smoke and mirrors illusions of the game and all of this is a classroom for God growth.

The "evil" Witch is the negative polarity perspective here in the class and certainly the polar aspect of the "Glinda", that teaches all, that is not love, and because she is a lesson plan of the "even" program, she is not ultimately real, as shown by her melting from "pure water" (born again of water, and remember the river between the two roads). But real or perceived, WHO will gain control of Dorothy, the good or evil perspective, must be dealt with. **Will the Soul allow** His Temple to control Him, *which (witch) is going to the lower frequency Dark,* **or will He** gain control of his fears and weaknesses (through working on raising His frequency), to liberate his Temple by being "The Man", in the relationship, thereby allowing the Spirit, His Temple, to take him up the unfathomable heights to the Light to take His place as another worthy Son of Glinda and the Father of Lights? This was metaphorically played out when the Dark temporarily gained control of Dorothy after she was captured by the flying monkeys, in the dark (they are walking in the Valley of the shadow of Death) and scary forest of Oz and taken to the Dark Castle of the Witch. He only had a "finite" time (the hourglass) to accomplish this, for once all of the Sand had traveled from the North chamber, through the narrow "isthmus", to the South chamber, then the Dark will have taken control of Dorothy and acquired the ruby slippers representing her essence as a vessel of the Holy Spirit, that carries Soul. So Dorothy being "taken by the witch" meant that *They* had fallen (too fearful) to the Dark that never stops pulling down and that He had to become the **Man** of the Divine marriage and take back his Lady by increasing (no fear) his frequency. He and the crew set out to take back their Lady, from the clutches of evil, who conquered His fear and liberated His Lady. They are now, the mated pair, on their way UP, having taken control of the Divine Marriage of Soul and Spirit.

Now consider this, the "winged monkeys" are the "Satanic" mocking of the Fallen Angels, as you ponder that "Angle", while the Witch is our Satanic GMO *alterator (being Satanic, she will lie to convince Dorothy that She is good and Glinda is the evil one, over time) who says, "These things must be done delicately..",* haha, fool that she is. And this, as I say, oh my "god" to myself, is the view of the Anunnaki, the extreme negative polar perspective who did NOT create, but just genetically manipulated what was here, with their genetic code, to produce the

Angelic and the Adamic Sapiens, **and something else that I'll talk about in the next chapter**. The Angels were the first "creation" and why they are the Angelic "Hosts". In the grand scheme where there are no accidents, the Annunaki created a slave race that rivaled, and in many ways surpassed their intelligence and material physical abilities. The "superior" being, would no longer be subordinate and the Adamics were created, and "dumbed down", to be better servants to their masters than the first attempt. And I have covered how the two lines intermingled, much to the disdain of "him" of negative polarity, which will produce the line of "The Cross", the positive polarity line of the Cains! The "Negatives", are "Positive", if you can read between the parted pages.

Dorothy, the Witch of the South, child of the North, must experience the totality of what she is, and **make peace** with every aspect. Before leaving Oz, by the internal "only way" she "can" leave, Dorothy reconciles with everyone she needed on her journey through the East. Before she leaves, she professes her love for those she needed on her journey. First her Tinman, who represents her body, telling him she'll miss how he would rust from crying, breaking down "so to speak", as they "feared seeing in separation". Then to the Lion, telling him she'll miss how he used to cry for help from perceived dangers. Lastly whispering to the Scarecrow, in his LEFT ear, that she'll "miss him most of all" because she is leaving her Left Brain Perception of Separation, of mind that he represents, and going to the Right Brain, as she kisses his Right cheek. Glinda, our Divine Feminine of Creation, instructs her to tap "or access" her Ruby slippers 3 times, as odd numbers deal in reality and say the 5 words, "There's no place like Home" because there really is, no other place. She says it 9 full times and during the 10th (1+0=1) time she wakes up back in Her Star.

"Crunch all you want, we'll make More"

In the Oz section you just read, I told you the dark conspiratorial angles, *never stop,* and it really does become the *dog chasing his tail* or *beating a dead horse*, once you already get it, and that I'll show you the perfect commercial that communicates this dynamic. Here is one, from a series of commercials around 1990 starring Jay Leno. You can pull it up on Youtube under "Doritos chip commercial with Jay Leno":

"Okay, it's 2 am and you're staring at that bag of Doritos Tortilla chips and you're asking yourself these middle of the nights questions like, "Did I just get up to eat these, or am I just eating these because I'm up?" I don't know, does it matter? The point is, the Doritos are there, and so are you, and **one of you ain't leavin' till the other ones gone.** *These chips are great, but they're* **not worth losing sleep over.** *So, if you want to get back to bed, do yourself a favor, and Crunch all you want, we'll make more."*

It's pretty obvious what they are telling you, that if you *want* to be a child of the Light, then get out of the Dark's *2 am Home Field advantage* that never stops providing you with bait to lower your frequency, and that "The Smart Move", is to get your tired rear end to bed and sleep, when you are meant to sleep, unless you are a Vampire. Like he says, the chips aren't leaving, **until you leave.** The only mind you can control, is yours.

Patrick Smartpants

Speaking of the *Scarecrow* and how mechanized he was, made me think of a SpongeBob Episode that I really liked that came out in 2005 (7), and it was episode 11, go figure! In it, Patrick loses his brain and SpongeBob finds one and put it in Patrick's head, thinking it was his, but it was another "smarter" brain. It outwardly changes him and he drifts away from SpongeBob because they now have little in common, but Patrick is *still* Patrick and in the end, he longs for his "inferior" brain, because it allowed his friendship with SpongeBob and the joy he remembered from it, was more important to him than his new found mental prowess and "better" brain. They end up finding his old brain, so they can remove the *smarter* one, because being happy, was more important to him than being *smart.* But we now know in our *evolution* that the brain he was born with was not *infe-*

rior, to the replacement **and** that the essence or origin of who you are is not contained in the brain, but that it is just a tool, like a computer.

Endless jewels in children's programs!

Big Gems in Kung Fu Panda

Just as at the end of '13, '14 had one of those life-changing events, that again, Ego does not want any part of. A few weeks ago being depressed, and yes, I know I shouldn't, from two "depressing" turn of events, I decided to watch "Kung Fu Panda". I hadn't watched it in years, so I thought I would watch a little to improve my mood. It was created by "DreamWorks" which is an offshoot of Disney. Amazing what I got out of it, what I wasn't ready to "see" the first time I saw it, other than the many laughs. Brilliant, encoding of so many secrets in "Children's Comedies". I was being "Shifu", thinking I was on the right path, *talking my talk*, "making my plans", and unwittingly *still being played in duality chess*, while thinking I had let go, but I was still, *expecting.* When Master Oogway tells Shifu, "The Panda will never fulfill his destiny, or you yours, until *you let go of the illusion of control*". Hit me like lightning!

"Your mind is like this water, my friend. When it is agitated, it becomes difficult to see. But if you allow it to settle, the answer becomes clear." This was meant for me to see at this time. And then seeing the "Masonic secret symbol" cleverly hidden and Po discovering the meaning to the "blank" Dragon Scroll, that was tellingly *reflective!*

"Daughter, your faith has healed you. Go in peace and be freed from your suffering."
                                                             -Mark 5:34 (5+7)

There is no secret ingredient. It put me back on track! So many times, the pain of moving in a different direction, especially when you know it happened either beyond your control, or you did something that you can't explain, IS the event or fork in the road, that MADE you. I must be on the right path to have a polar me, the equation equaling itself out, who would make Lucifer quake in her Prada boots. So much of life is spent as "The Doubting Thomas"! Now back to my Happy Place!

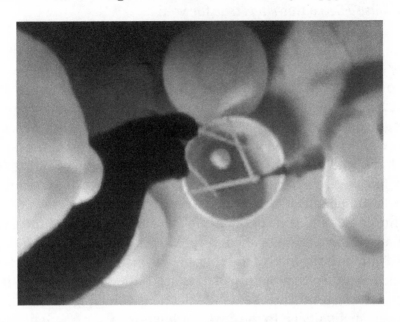

Also, when they are "fighting" for the dumpling in the bowl, they flash the "square and compass" Masonic symbol for a small fraction of a second with their chopsticks to show us who is bringing us this message. Upon hearing Master Oogway's *vision*, Shifu orders in the **present** what he believes will avoid any **future** confrontation with Tai Lung, when in fact it is his reactionary orders, upon hearing Oogway's **past** vision, that sets into motion the confrontation that will *occur* in the **future,** confirming Oogway's **past** vision of the **future.** Master Oogway responds with the "Jean de la Fontaine" quote, *"One often meets his destiny on the road he takes to avoid it.",* which is pure script writing perfection! Another movie to see if you haven't and that quote reminds me of *this* Zen Proverb, *"The obstacle is the Path".*

Look at you go!

In a response to a video that *"tried"*, to decipher the *"information"* and clues on Monster Energy Drink, I believed I brought the "Satanic" necessity, for "Energy" drinks to "light", and *why*, they attempt to keep you *"busy"*! See if this *rings true* for you!

Huge clues "They" are giving us, *seen,* but not understood by the nice lady, who can't tell you what the *agenda is,* or why Satanic messages are on an energy drink in the first place, and last but not least she believes the upside down cross means witchcraft. Good for her for recognising clues, but she sees it through her level of vibratory aware-ness which was molded by her religious affiliation and of course spir-itual age, and can't put the 2 and 2 together to figure out that the very fact we are being given these clues like the Doritos commercial, means someone is trying to help us. It is a clue to the few, who are in "the game" and still "of the game". You can't transcend the game if you are *of the game*, engaged in the duality "business" of the game, and **That**, is the agenda of the clue, to tell you this! Why on an "energy drink"? Because they help you "get stuff done", to keep you better engaged in the duality game, in this class. Staying engaged, "dis-tracted", in duality is "to the dark", or lowering your frequency which keeps you here in the dream, and **That** is what the upside down cross means. The "cross" symbolizes Christ Consciousness, the path to the light, and when upside down or opposite direction, means the path away from the light. And that is why it is showing you that when you drink it, you are turning the cross upside down by drinking a supple-ment that motivates you to stay in the superficial "business" of the illusory game, which is the path to the dark.

"They" Businesses and Entities

What is a "They" company? Well, country boy Sam Walton did not create the largest company in the world with Distribution Centers having rail and airstrip accommodations, by his "country boy self" as it metaphorically encodes "enclosure within the 3D *walled* class of 6", from the "Oz-Ark" region within Ark-kansas, as who purportedly work with FEMA. Apple didn't become synonymous with technology with a logo that hints at it's "forbidden fruit nature", by "accident" as we find them in all American public schools working hand in hand with the government, and curiously being the only computers that are virus proof. We watch Terminator and Matrix movies demonstrating the dynamic of the dominance and enslavement by *machines*, while we submit to pull of our Cell phones that track the content of your communication and web visits and constantly monitor your position around the country that the government records. The most popular cyberspace website, Facebook supposedly dreamt up by a college kid with the ethnically curious name, with it's "f "of 6 within the walled enclosure logo that wants to know everything about you that "someone" sees. And Google, the company that knows more about your habits than you do, with every square inch of virtually every city street on film, and the list goes on and on, and you get my point as all are created to monitor the *kids*, by that which guides all.

I just now thought of the Wendy's logo, and especially when it is entirely red. You'll hear people say that the "mom" encoded on her collar is a subliminal message for you to equate their food as being "home cooked", and sure, for the younger it is, but I think the deeper message is its confirmation of our God of Creation Mother. The base color of creation is red, and there are three, Trinity, letters in red and mom. Wendy is a young lady and there are six, Creation, letters in Wendy's. Her head is placed within a circle, also think earth, and as I pointed out circles and globes are feminine. Her hair has **two** side pigtails tied with two bows, polarity, and the centers of the two look like little globes that have the same approximate tilt as earth's axis and the white lines above and below the "poles", accentuate this image.

The Polarity foundation of the Electoral College

One of the hidden benefits of the Electoral College, known by the Masonic founders, is that it gave a "benefit" to the candidate that was "*less* Satanic". They knew that over time, *most* would gravitate to the large *man-made* urban areas that are further removed from nature. The more removed you are from Nature and Her natural cycles and overall order, the more removed you are from God. God is light, and the further removed you are, the Darker your perspective and the more you "want to control" and legislate "life", with "man's laws and artificial order". Big cities will always vote differently than those in rural settings. People who live metropolitan areas are dependent on the system for their survival and and people in the rural (farming and ranching) areas are far less, to not at all, dependent on the system for their survival. So the Electoral college gives the less populated rural area a "larger presence" in elections because the big cities will always vote to be "taken care of" by their rulers "Here". The true irony is that the *Independent,* don't need government, and the *Dependents* that do, don't really get to choose anyway. They are like children happy with the choice of "peas or carrots", when they wouldn't have chosen vegetables in the first place. And I believe the children are more aware that they've been "had", then the *adults,* at the primaries.

The hidden symbolism of the American Flag

Duality will, of course, be a major theme as 2 polarity extreme colors immediately jump out at you on a white background, and when you add the white you have the 2/3 or 3/2 duality variable I have already explained. The 3 of the red, white and blue, to the 2 of the stars and stripes. White being unity with no separation. Pulling from the information in Kansas Arc kansas, we are moving from east or left brain perception of "separation", and the number of that is 4 and we find that there are 13 original states and a fact hidden from the casual observer is the fact there are 31 states east of Kansas and that number is also four. Seven and five are encoded in the flag from the pentagram with it's 5 extended points and there are 50 with a total of 250 points that adds to 7 and we have 7 red stripes. The 50 stars and 13 stripes add to 9. The blue is on the top half and in the corner, and on one side, it's up and to the right, because the flag is a mirror image on both sides. The 2 of the red and the blue, and the 50 stars, confirms, and I, of course, have far more evidence, that **Spring** will bloom in 2050.

Decoding the order and numbers of the 7 Days of the Week

Five is the number of a man and we are here developing and so there are five work days. On each end, we find our polarity gods of Saturday and Sunday directing us and the seven days have a number associated with each of them. This one was hard, as the days are not in the "correct" order, and that was throwing me off assigning their respective numbers and *positions*. As the game progresses, you will work your way to one or the other side of the week. You better be gettin metaphorical with me! In the center of the week is our middle of the road leader Wednesday, Odin's day and Mercury is associated with this day, and if your frequency is below half in the spectrum, you will be in the Tuesday range as this is the day for "Tiw or Tyr", our god of war and darker Brother of Thor, like Loki, and Mars is the planet for this day. If you are really further down, you will inhabit the Monday realm of our Moon goddess. Conversely, if you inhabit the regions of the spectrum upper half, you'll be in the Thursday range with our lighter god of Thunder Thor, and Jupiter is associated with this day. If you are really buzzing you'll be in the Thank God it's Friday realm partying the *night* **away**, with Frigga, and her planet is Venus. Now you know why most despise Mondays, and love Fridays.

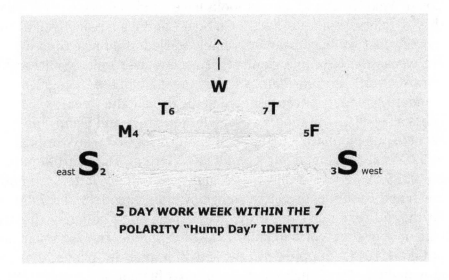

5 DAY WORK WEEK WITHIN THE 7 POLARITY "Hump Day" IDENTITY

Now you can see, with the positions and numbers, why this wasn't "obvious". The vortex, the rotation, the pendulum, the pulse and heartbeat of our galaxy and greater universe **never** stops! Just as day becomes night and night becomes day, and east rolls into west and back into east, the flow of the current eternally flows. Think of the pendulum, back and forth, starting at the center, the heart, ground level, that is at the very center and sees all. It starts at the center of 1 Wednesday and swings to 2, 2 to 3, 3 to 4, 4 to 5, 5 to 6, 6 to 7, 7 to 1 and continuing to 2 and repeating the sequence again and again eternally. The flow from the roots that get their nourishment from Mother Earth up to the leaves, as they receive the nourishment from the Father Light, then back to the roots.

A Solar System Shakeup?

If your mind is not already spinning at this point, give me another shot here. I woke up at 3 am one morning, with a David Bowie verse running through my head and a specific clue from "Back to the Future" (Another "Zemeckis clue" like Polar Express). My eyes, evidence around me, and Hollywood clues are giving me conflicting information to what NASA and the textbooks have taught us as gospel. If what they're telling us about "Earth" isn't true, and it's already well documented that we have been supremely misled, then *what and where* are we, as the two blue giants, that no one ever talks about, grabs my attention? Nor like *Pluto*, are they included in the "recognized" 7 wandering planets or represented in the days of the week, as "Earth" is not as well. The numbers again tell their story and 5 and 7 always seem to pop up relating to the "real" children of God. The word Earth, 51928, is 25 and 2 and 5 is 7 and it has 5 letters. The word Neptune, 5572355, is 32 and 2 plus 3 is 5 and it contains 7 letters, so both Earth and Neptune, in mirror image fashion, encode 5 and 7. Since Earth (and remember the word "Earth" was God's name for the dry land only, or that which in polarity fashion *opposes* the water and air, in Gen. 1:10) is "supposedly" the "big blue marble" planet, that we now deduce *"isn't"*, then what planet *does* fit that description? Why that would be **Neptune** *or Uranus to a lesser degree* and far bigger and "bluer" than our images of Earth. Earth, we are told, has a sister planet next to us that is similar in makeup and size, and so does Neptune, with its duality partner Uranus, another "big *blue* marble" whose symbol is a circumpunct with an arrow at the top pointing up. I've concluded that odd numbers deal in "reality", and even numbers deal in the illusion. Neptune encodes 5 and 7, and Uranus encodes 4 and 6, further pointing to a material / ethereal divine polarity partnership and If you take *Earth* out of the Solar system, then Uranus is the 6th and Neptune **is** the 7th planet from the *Sun* and we of 7 "are" here in 6. If Jupiter is the "Son" and the next Star of the Father, then it **is** the 3rd planet (and its like sized "feminine" partner the 2nd like Venus and its little "masculine" nemesis, the 4th like Mars) from the "Son", and is "between" Jupiter and Pluto, as Norse mythology calls Earth "Midgard", "Middle Earth" or "Middle yard", and this name also fits a "fictional universe" placed "within" Uranus or Neptune (or the combination of both?). Uranus is our god of the Sky and Neptune **is** our god of the sea, who is certainly ever-present "here" just as "He" would be in "his" own world, meaning to me that the "sea here" that he presides in, is, in fact, a part of the "waters" of Neptune.

In Back to the Future, "Doc", our symbol of Jupiter, and "Marty", our symbol of Pluto, do "battle" against the "Clock Tower", the symbol of our god of Time, Saturn, and their "stage" is in fact the "Enchantment Under the Sea" Dance on Saturday *night*, with a statue of Neptune and his Trident (Trinity symbol and Enchant means Spell), meaning that Neptune is *hosting* this internal *"Self/Ego" struggle.* Their battle against Saturn, is for "independence", to flee the nest and start our own Solar System. It is also my belief that the 7th Day, that God rested on or in, is Thursday or Thor's day, not Sunday, which is the Day of Jupiter, and this *7-11 School of Duality*, is a developmental realm for the family gods we have been led to believe exist only in mythology! The Sun in our sky, IS the Son, Jupiter, and our moon, is actually Pluto (and probably why we've never "named it", only calling it the "moon" because they're hiding its identity. Naming it moon is like naming a planet "Planet") and we are Neptune/Uranus, the Siblings of both. The land Pluto, the Water Neptune, the Air Uranus and all properly...

color coordinated! Think of the three-pronged Trident, water in the center, between the solid of land, and the gas of air. "Born of Water". *"For here Am I sitting in a tin can...Planet Earth is Blue and there's nothing I can do"* The Tin Man is body vessel, and tin is dominated by Jupiter, and has 3 letters and its number is 295 or 16 which is 7. Can has 3 letters and its number is 9. Not only is Pluto discovered in 1930, but in the same year, Disney introduces "Pluto" the *dog*, as I think of "Moondog" the composer who had the look of a Norse god, and a recent *NASA delivered* picture of Pluto has a silhouette of Pluto dog's head and neck on the surface. Disney also has copyrighted artwork showing "Pluto" on the moon burying bones, and Pluto sitting on a crescent moon with a dog tag on his collar that is circular with an additional crescent moon shape on it as well.

I am convinced that our Sun is Jupiter and our Moon is Pluto, and that Sun and Saturn pawned off on us by NASA does not exist. I am sure it is Jupiter that orbits Sirius and what we believed was Saturn is actually Sirius B and B is for Black, our Dark Lord, and of course B is 2 meaning it is the Ego of Sirius, the electron to the Proton. And let us not forget Harry's *God*father from, "Order of the Phoenix", Sirius Black, and his brother Regulus Black.

Thor: What realm is this? Elfheim, Nilfheim?

Darcy: New Mexico

"EARTH is a realm, it is not a planet. It is not an object, therefore, it has no edge. Earth would be more easily defined as a system environment. Earth is also a machine, it is a Tesla coil. The sun and moon are powered wirelessly with the electromagnetic field (the Aether). This field also suspends the celestial spheres with electro-magnetic levitation. Electromagnetic levitation disproves gravity because the only force you need to counter is the electromagnetic force, not gravity. The stars are attached to the firmament."
—Nikola Tesla (attributed to Tesla, but I can't confirm it)

The esoteric USA Interstate Highway Grid

If the best clues are the biggest, than this one is right **UP** there with the 911 giants! The USA, encoding 3 and 5, is the collective narrow gate NWO and its layout mirrors atomic and solar system structure. Growth is a series of steps forward or up, and at times you take a step back or down, after taking two steps forward or up. My time as a State Trooper helped me see this, among other things! The continental interstate highway system is like the body's circulatory system, and its structure and identification of arterial pathways speak volumes to those beginning to see the correlation. This explanation from snopes.com is perfectly succinct, *"North-south routes are assigned odd numbers, with the numbers growing larger from west to east; east-west routes are assigned even numbers, with the numbers growing larger from south to north."* Likewise, Mile Markers, that tell you how far along you are by how many miles you have traveled, always get larger heading North, or heading East. Like I said earlier, An adult knows the world and the next heart-beat is West. . .Literally, you can see it, as in country big, and so 7-11 obvious, that it remains unseen because the best are big and bold and seen by all.

Some of the more "telling" interstate designs and designations include using a capital I as an abbreviation for Interstate Highway and, of course, the number of I is 9 and these signs use the polar colors of red and blue on a white background. Talking about the occasional one step back for every two forward, as we fall or get knocked down throughout life, but get back up to persevere, is shown in how the highway flows and confuses the new troopers at first when giving dispatch their location or "20", as I smile in duality, because a highway must at times deviate from a straight line path because of geographic "roadblocks", as sometimes "Northbound" lanes will, at times, head east, west or even south for a bit before resuming their northbound destination. Those who are trained properly know they are still heading North, even though they are temporarily heading in any other direction if they are on "Northbound Highway".

In my best Gomer Pyle "southern" accent, "Surprise, Surprise, Surprise", I-17 (8) just happens to be in Arizona and connects Flagstaff (I-40 and Rte 66 pass through Flag.), where we discovered Pluto, to Phoenix (I-10 through Phx)! And get right outta town, I-25 (7) starts in Las Cruces, "the city of the crosses" New Mexico, and travels north to connect with I-90, in Buffalo, WY (57=3). I-80 takes you from the great city in the Empire State of NY to the manifest destiny golden state city of SF (16=7, and my birth initials, go figure) where you will find the "Golden Gate Bridge". Amazing how quickly (not uncommon for me anymore) I can go from laughing to tears, as just now writing this I see that I-70 starts in Baltimore and ends at "Cove Fort" (8 letters, but the numerology value is 7), UT (5) on I-15, directly between where I live now and Las Vegas, where I have a home in the "North" (NLV and N is 5 and LV is 7)! The Highway number clues in the U.S. are almost endless! See what they tell, You!

All of a sudden I am reminded of that biannual *pain*, **Daylight *Savings* Time** which is meant to be a **pain** for all who are consumed in time, and why Fall is "Fall **back**", and Spring is, "Spring **forward**". Time to move on to the next "Timeless" Age!

The Dark Identity of The Divine Feminine and Repentance

Madonna's **"Like a Prayer"** music video breakdown

It is occurring of course here in the dream that is "outside" the light (Stars), think Drunvalo Melchizedek's explanation of God as the circle of light, but creates another, partially outside the light. Madonna represents all of us with an extra emphasis on the Divine Feminine, as this is why she is dressed in black and has her natural dark hair color here, because our Mother is Spirit, The Dark Polarity, and as I'll talk about more later, no other film or recording star, is more tied to the Divine Feminine than Madonna. She is running from *perceived* threats, and the noise is our own internal turmoil, confusion, and fear, the duality fear based 911 (11) activity of separation in this "darker" realm of extremes in polarity. This is mid-level, so think of a tree, and we the seeds put just below the surface of the ground. She runs past a light (fire in the can), not yet seeing certain "enlightening" clues put there to aid the developing aware. As she falls a jail cell door closes, meaning we are in our own self-imposed prison as long as we perceive in separation. The "key" is within the level of our frequency by developing our Christ Consciousness, finding out the **Whole** of who we really are, our true identity symbolized by the burning cross. She is trying to make sense of her life, events in her past and looking for the "why" of her current fearful state, which is, because she is still seeing in separation and not yet seeing in Unity.

The men attacking a woman is an internal polarity dynamic symbolizing the suppression of Right Brain Perspective, occurring within her psyche. She has grown up in a world that has fostered and promoted it, and she is a product of her environment, as we all are. Now, what do I mean by that? *We are all an aspect of the Divine Feminine*, and here is where it gets *complicated*. All people, all races, and both sexes are manifestations of our Spiritual Mother going through a particular phase or Age because we are collectively *growing up, as that **is** what all of this is*. **Right brain sees in Unity and is Feminine by nature and left brain sees in Separation and is Masculine by nature**. The number of Left brain separation is **4** and that is why there are 4 men attacking the woman. In the lower winter of the Iron Age, "Unity" is not perceived, because we are children, so the *masculine of separation* becomes dominant due to perceived threats from separate "out there" dangers. As a result, our survival instinct, fight or flight, puts more emphasis on our Ego, that perceives in separation, and our masculine nature to "save and protect" us, and while it creates an internal imbalance, it was done to *"protect"* us. While it worked for obvious "learning" reasons, the dark is always programmed to go "too far", which is why the imbalance cannot be sustained, becoming a cancer and eventually killing itself, and of course "itself" is part of the waveform illusion. And here is how we are all, thoroughly duped. **Masculine does not *mean* male, feminine does not mean female, Light does not *mean* white and the Dark does not mean black.** The Satanic system, being 100% invested in the 5 sense reality, assigned external White to be Light and Male to Masculine while failing to acknowledge any connection to our internal psyche. This *childish*, yet programmed, belief suppressed our complete nature, and caused our natural internal and external polarities to clash, out-there, as *masculine* dominates *feminine* and *dark* dominates *light,* because we suppress them within. **This is why the Iron Age promoted a, "Might makes right", Male dominated patriarchal system, oppressing and subjugating females and White is always seen as good and better (more *evolved to* the light) than black, which was seen as bad and inferior (less *evolved from* the light).** This is why white men are attacking a woman and specifically **why** the *white man* looks at her the way he does. *His **white** face **is** the face of the **dark**,* with the at first guilty and then turned to threatening look to intimidate so that the dark maintains its control.

We refuse to acknowledge our internal dark and as a result, the Dark is externalized, shown as the black man being blamed for the attack, prosecuted and jailed, out there and inside of us. (not saying all are innocent but look who is jailed) The Church represents the body, and the Bible has always esoterically inferred, and many times outright said it, that our body is our Temple. **Again the message of this video is what is going on inside of us that manifests itself "out there".** Also note, the Church is white with eight, the number of the new Aquarian Age of Unity perception, window pie segments lit yellow like the Sun and all are "upside", and you go up steps, higher frequency, to get in. So inside the Church, we see an American flag as this represents Bacon's "New Atlantis" and as I have already covered, the "New Mexico Territory" takes center stage in the New World class of 8. There is also a picture of Martin Luther King. We are still in the dream, and King "Has a Dream", and Unity is its theme, as the dream will become brighter. The Black Christ, which the images showed before, confirm it, is our internal Light, behind bars because we suppress our Light by seeing in separation and denying our own internal dark, which is a part of all of us, but we don't want to associate any part of the dark as being anything within or a part of us. This is why you see the flash of **Light in his Right** eye. Because the persecution is internal and really against ourselves, it causes us great sorrow, suffering, and depression, as **we** are no longer whole, and a lack of the entirety of **The Self** causes insanity, which means not whole. Even many of the "white among us", and of course Madonna being white represents this, know that something isn't right as we feel it in our hearts, our intuition, that we have been suppressing our own dark side, and that our senses are in a sense, fooling us. This is why in our separation, we created external Devils around us. So many have been turning a blind eye because, in the illusion of our separate state, we believe it is happening to "them", and they are not us. I am not you, and the internal "negative" polar voice inside of us, ego, fosters this view and always attempts to validate "difference", and that this is a dream, and she calls it a dream which is why she reclines like she is sleeping, is the be all end all only reality. A black man comes to the aid of the white woman, as he "descends" down the steps is the Light attempting to correct our imbalance, but our Satanic Ego prevents this and externalizes the dark to be "out there black". The white police see a black man over a dead white woman is our internal dark Divine Feminine persecution.

"I close my eyes, Oh God I think I'm falling" When we "descend" here to learn, we are given limited awareness (eyes closed), because if you had knowledge of where you came from, you would know that this is an illusion, and thus there would be no urgency to live and learn if you did not believe that this is real. The smiling Black Woman **is** her Mother Goddess of Creation and she represents ALL of Creation! This is like Glinda welcoming Dorothy.

You also hear, *"in the midnight hour I can feel your power"*, means at midnight it is usually quiet, away from the noise and distraction of the game! "Be still, and know that I am God." And there is no other time to become more intimately acquainted with your "Dark Side", than "Mid*night*".

"Life is a mystery", This means we must solve it, and that is to figure out "who we are", and there are many lessons before we come to this

knowledge, as the lessons are the "building" of this knowledge and maturity.

"Everyone must stand alone", No one will choose for you! No outside savior will save you. Your frequency is in your hands alone, as **you** face the consequence of every thought and action.

"I hear you call my name", We are always "spoken" to by our ascended parents. In the beginning was the word and it still is. "You can run but you can't hide." means, everywhere the cell goes, it is still in the body, which is why she says, *"And it feels like home".*

"I have no choice, I hear your voice", We are compelled to find, to address our agenda. God, the one mind, is the only reality. There is nothing that is not.

"Feels like flying", Union with God is freedom.

"Out of the sky, I close my eyes", We came from our higher vibrational home, the light, and into, the dream.

"Heaven help me", Anything you ask, from the Heart, the agenda of your Astral Self, you will be directed to, at the perfect appropriate time. You are a child of God, and while the illusion makes you feel alone, your "Glinda", our Mother God is always with you.

The darker entities, the corrupt "evil" governments, are *all a part of who we are collectively*, but the "collective" is unaware of this because they don't know *who they are*. "We" repress our polar "negative" content to project a Devil and thus physically manifest the collective "Mr. Hyde", the corrupt governments and corporations we see around us because it "will" come out one way or the other. If we do not bring it out by accepting and "repenting", then it will come out to oppose us as our adversary and destroy us!

"If you bring forth what is within you, what you bring forth will save you. If you do not bring forth what is within you, what you do not bring forth will destroy you." -Gospel of Thomas "The Gnostic Christ" saying 70 (7)

When you know yourself, face your Dark side and acknowledge it, which **is** "bring forth", as a part of who you are, *that is* **Repenting**, then you no longer project them into the physical world as you regain a healthy state or "balance" with both polarities, and internally **be the change you want to *see*!**

Her going to the "Dark Christ" is her acceptance of the whole of who she really is, and that there is no "evil out there" but inside of all of us. She unlocks the bars and kisses his "Left" foot and him kissing her Left side is the acknowledgment of our own full polarity and unity so that she is now fully "Illumined" and the **Dark Christ** kissing her forehead is the activation of her pineal gland signifying this. This event **IS** the Crucifixion which kills identifying in Separation and Ego Identification. Freeing him, acknowledging her own internal dark, has freed her.

Also, she sings in front of 5 burning crosses, and 5 is the Divine message, and during this says "just like a dream, you are not what you seem"...and that would be ourselves and Lucifer. Now being whole, we are joyous and our polarity perspective has found their proper place within us as we reach our spiritual "Homeostasis". We are now no longer "Blaspheming the Holy Spirit", which is not knowing who you are. Until you realize who you are, you will always, remain in the dark!

Now, a very important part here, as **knowing is not enough**, which is why the Dark Christ returns to being "locked away". You must also **"Walk the walk"**, and make your Higher Awareness knowledge a practical way of life so that you can turn it into increasing your frequency. Her going, to tell the truth, and him being released is her internal change manifesting to her own day to day actions and manifesting in the external world, because many things that you now do, are not looked kindly upon in a world that sees in separation. "They love their own". This music video was created by our loving administrators to the aware among us who are to find the Narrow Gate. This message is pure Love and Growth!

"Big stage" artists, are all vehicles to get the *message* out there to us. If you ever heard most of them talk, you would know the scope of this message did not come from them! And as I said she and all the others do not get a grand stage unless the force that runs the music industry and the planet *owns* her, and then they grant it, and she spreads their message, not hers. She and the others, send out a message, even though they *may* think it to be "evil", for the guarantee of material wealth, "here". That's why many of them like Dylan, Perry or Beyonce say or gesture that they made a deal with the Devil. They are told to say this so that the aware can be confirmed and the unaware, steeped in the duality of the Good vs Evil polarity will see it in the opposite perspective and stay in fear, the one message interpreted two ways! The aware way and the unaware way, who can continue to go insane as they have their ammunition to keep the fight going against the "separate Devil". And there is, of course, some truth to them *"selling themselves"* if they don't know this bigger picture, and chances are that they don't. *"We will keep you popular and making money on a grand scale"*, as long as you perform what we tell you to perform. Our message, not yours! The message is indeed a liberating one if you have the Eyes to See!

And the Stage reference, *as a play ending* at the end, with the red curtain, is obvious and oh so true. We are the Stars of our own perfectly choreographed play!

And as if we needed more confirmation clues as to the real identity of Mary, Madonna is the birth name of Ms. Ciccone, and not just her "stage" name, in this "why would Target do this" type clue, like Al Gore to allegory. This is why I said "with more of an emphasis on the Divine Feminine. Her, "Like a Virgin" recording further demonstrates her symbolic "alignment" with the "Mother of God", and since I have identified Mary as a manifestation of the God of Creation, Lucifer, those who "guide" Madonna with the content of her recordings, gave her the song, "Material Girl" which also became her "alias" handle since it's release. We are living in a waveform material world, and she is the Material Girl. And remember "Open Your Heart"? "Open your heart to me, *I hold the lock and you hold the key*", and then "You must be my lucky Star" (you may indeed, if you get lucky). I believe I remember about 25 years ago, she brought her *father* out on stage and said, "Ladies, the only man I will ever bow to", but I can't find the quote, and that is the best of my recollection, which I see now means, that gesture, by the Divine Mother, is accorded only to The Father!

The "Carbon*ated*" World

"Why does Enterprise require the presence of carbon units? Enterprise would be unable to function without carbon units."
--Star Trek: The Motion Picture

Think of our **world as a *"Star Ship"*** and that she is full of carbon units like a glass full of a carbonated beverage. Carbon is added to the medium of "static" water to produce "interaction". We are all the individual molecules submerged in the dense liquid (the material world). You learn as you interact, and as you learn you grow, and as you grow your awareness expands. As your awareness expands, you learn who you are and what this place is, and your discipline grows to resist the illusory ties to this world, which increases your frequency. Your higher frequency makes you "lighter", thereby creating a bubble around your body, as you rise above the lower frequency of those around you. As you continue working on your Arc you continue your ascension, until, *poof!* You have escaped the bonds of the material world, or **That**, which wanted to keep receiving your energy. (Very similar to the Matrix) It's not a prison (although it can seem like it), but a rigorous developmental School, 7-11 style!

Then, and only then, can you open up "The Final Frontier", as all is within. Here at this level, "Space", is not within this spectrum. NASA tries to make you believe you can get there, "out-there", but out there, in the dream, only reflects the level of the collective, and we are still, in a playpen (the Dome). Star Trek is really meant to represent our inner psyche. Our world is a reflection of our mind, and you are your own Starship "Enterprise". You are composed of several psychological aspects, like a cold, unemotional, logical, very machine-like Mr. Spock, and in the newer version, they did make him a machine as his counterpart is "Data". Then there is the emotional, daring, risk-taking, full of passion Capt Kirk, and his counterpart in the newer TNG is, Capt. Picard. And then there is the more pragmatic, measured Dr. McCoy, and his TNG version, 1st Officer Commander Riker. Think of them as the Tinman, Lion, and Scarecrow, and notice how "The **next** generation's" version of them actually are more mature and seasoned, like they are the older version, as we collectively mature.

I am probably in the minority (a normal condition for me) but I greatly preferred Capt Picard over Kirk, and Riker kind of reminded me of me, and those two worked together perfectly. And as I write this, it does not come without its *downside* issues, as we seem to be more alike than I had originally thought. Riker was good at what he did at his level, and very comfortable in his position, that was ultimately not in *the lead.* Sure, he did well professionally and was affable, looked good, socially skilled and comfortable around the opposite sex, but there was a personal responsibility issue that "held him back" from assuming the *Top Spot.* Of course, deeper is what this is meant to portray making me feel a bit vulnerable exposing my soul with each typed key. Wasn't it is a young ambitious female officer, vying for his 1st officer position on the Enterprise, who stirred the pot exposing his issue that held him back from accepting the command of his own ship? It was, and the deeper meaning was that *Nature provided him* with an out-there force to make contact with him. A force that acts on an object (him) to take it in another direction than it (he) was previously headed. She made him face the issues (that he repressed) that held him back from taking command of his own personal Enterprise, his body. He did later, as an older man, as I am doing now. He was stagnant in his development without this "force", as I'll soon tell you what Newton's Laws of motion really communicate. Wow, the emotions! This was a tough paragraph to write. (my 50's….Lord have Mercy!)

It really is a steady progression up, like a step pyramid that gives you an accurate visual of the process, and every step is increased frequency. Whenever I fall back, take steps down, to my old addictions, of the lower vibrational waveform flesh, like dense food, alcohol or sex, my life almost immediately gets, well, shittier, like the description of "lower job duties" within the collective body I am a cell within. The "punishments" or consequences are fast and impactful like a slap on the face, and completely transparent as to what brought them to me. Like a parent who has devised a cookie jar that shocks the hand of his young child whenever his hand is not supposed to be in there. This is literally, what is communicated in the stories of **the Material "beasts", whose eternal path is to the Dark**, the ever-hungry vampires or werewolves who are slaves to, and must satisfy, their carnal addictions, and the pleasures they receive are matched, because the punishment is built into the equation, by extreme pain, suffering and misery and they are condemned to roam, AT NIGHT, as a slave of the Dark.

I was putting gasoline in my car recently when I thought this type of antiquated energy will soon be history, which I know now is why they call it "fossil fuel" and I saw a sign that spoke of us *reducing* our *"Carbon Footprint"*, and another clue struck me. We, all life forms, are transitioning from carbon-based life forms to crystalline based. As we move forward step by step, some of us are working, "up and to the right", to reduce our "carbon footprint" positioning ourselves to pass through the "West *Star* Gate", and many *resistantly* are not, as we journey to "Silicon Valley". Our Mother divulges one "Inconvenient" **alagôrē** after another in all of their plain sight splendor to produce paradigm altering *epiphanal* moments to bring about heightened awareness for the formation of our "Crystalline Footprint"!

Another *clue,* and one of my earliest memories, I fondly remember, is my mother explaining to me how "receiving" Christmas presents works. She, of course, told me that if I was a good boy and minded her and my grandparents, I would get "most" of what I wanted, but if I was bad, Santa would only leave me a few lumps of coal (fossilized carbon). Here I am now in my late fifties laughing to myself finally understanding, why *coal* instead of "nothing", meaning that "staying bad" (lower frequency) *maintains* your "carbon footprint".

The King of Hearts!

I have already mentioned "MacArthur Park" as having extremely deep esoteric messages, and I have to pay tribute to Jimmy Webb and his music, for allowing me to feel that oh so familiar tug at an early age. I have never heard such depth of heart, compassion, soul and a yearning desire that transcended desire to pure need, within the scope of the human condition. I was so taken with Wichita Lineman back in the 60's. The lyrics are short, but oh so powerful. We are biological machines that run on electricity. So using a lineman, he who works on electric lines, in the song is to me, genius! Another aspect that makes it perfect is the location of Kansas and his and it's connection to Heart. He is in Kansas, which I have identified as our Star and he says he's "Searchin in the Sun". Really? I really don't know whether Jimmy Webb knows what he is actually communicating or if he is "the guided messenger", but his songs and their messages, like so many in the entertainment industry, are universal truths gift wrapped as the most beautifully written songs I have ever heard. We are all connected through an electromagnetic *"Webb"*, and he says, "I hear you singing in the wire." and then he says, "I can hear you thru the whine.", because the wires make a humming sound and the wind whistles as it flows over the lines. In the beginning was the word, and the word was sound, as the universal song never stops, as we, dance! The lyrics also describe the inner loneliness that a man feels, while he "exists" here, and his longing for an absent lover, his Divine Feminine. And not just the want, but a survival need. *I knew none of this as a child. I only knew I loved it* and had no idea why thinking I had to be the only

11yr old boy who bought "Wichita Lineman" and played it over and over again in his basement. My love for his songs was not shared by any of my age group that I knew of, but then again, I had few friends growing up.

Life is like a series of fireworks display. You remember ONE, that was supremely spectacular because as it was occurring, you were "one" with it, seeing, hearing, feeling it in all its splendor...and then it all fades away...and you remember, *knowing* it, still wanting it, yearning for its return. But that moment, as beautiful as it was...will never return. It is gone...with you, and all those involved. "You can never go home". It may "look" like it, but it is not what you left. I had a similar experience. It was magic for **3** years and better than most for another 7 more. The last 6 was just..hanging on to the memory as we went in two totally incompatible directions, each day more so than the previous. You can never "Not go home" because the journey is your home! *"I live inside my own heart Matt Damon"*, Prince reminded Matt who played Bourne. There is only the journey. I had to be ripped from my false Maria, so that By The Time I Get To Phoenix, my real internal Maria, will be **Rising!**

*"I wanna move and go places and **never look back**. Just have fun, **forever**. That's my idea of heaven. **Need** someone to share it with, though."*
-Josephine from "Tombstone"

I really like this from Haleaxandria.org:

"In the classic trilogy, The Lord of the Rings -- The Fellowship of the Ring, we have the fundamental struggle of good versus evil. While there are many minor characters in the story, all of them do not necessarily get overly involved in the great clash of powers. As the good guys attempt to thwart the nefarious, dictatorial, and thoroughly evil activities of the Dark Lord, there is an individual who is apparently, unaware of the seriousness of the matter. His name is Tom Bombadil. When Frodo and his friends are in Tom's neighborhood, Tom manages to rescue them on two separate occasions. But with respect to the great

battles taking shape, Tom seems to care less. In fact, there is the impli-
cation that he is like a parent, watching the squabbling of children and
simultaneously remaining aloof. As a parent figure, Tom seems to think
that it's all much Ado about Nothing, but that it's a worthwhile learn-
ing and growing experience for all who wish to participate. In effect,
Tom chooses to opt out. Tom did not appear in the movie version."

There are no accidents, as everything happens for a reason, and as
we all know by now, Tom's awareness and frequency *allowed* him
that "state of being! You cannot *truly* break the rules until you **know**
the rules! Know that you are not a prisoner to the circumstances and
programs under which you were born. You see Tom perceived everything, that Frodo and his friends perceived, differently. Tom's world,
his position along the path, was different because of the way he perceived it. When you are aware of your thoughts and consciously control what you pay attention to, you knowingly become the master of
your responses, without the automatic subconscious programmed
responses, like getting cut off in traffic and allowing it to push your
button, the "programmed pissed off" reaction that defines your day,
or from *drama, an emergency, news,* whatever this bait or that bait is
that presents itself before you, to elicit fear or the same old negative
responses that you don't even consciously decide on, that keep you
at a lower frequency. **You** choose how you respond to what you now
know to be a lesson that the others need to learn. **As grandmother
Mole said, "Put it inside of them", "...and only then does that man
truly begin his own game",** when he finally discovers **it** within!

Everything will change when your desire to move on exceeds your
desire to hold on.

--Alan Cohen

14. Aquarius Targeted

The Polarity Play is nearing "This" climax.

We are **in**, "Those Times", and try as you may, but you can't serve two masters and the one you have *nurtured* and aligned with, is putting you in one of two camps. This is occurring even if you are not consciously aware it. Things will be said and done with people you had ties with, to separate you from those going in th*e other directions.* The differences between everyone is becoming more and more pronounced by the day. There are 50 Shades of Grey, and the further you are from the other, the disconnect will be more pronounced. The Dark will not see what the Light sees and the world of Dark will become more and more Alien to those moving West. You will speak your truth and hear, "You make No sense to Me", nor will their concerns be yours, as you will no longer be on the same wavelength with them. The seed is about to sprout and you are working toward "which" aspect of the tree you will inhabit.

The roots of the Self Same Tree will have a VERY different perspective of truth, and the world they reside in, then the branches above ground that bask in the light. When they describe their experience, you'd swear they can't be talking about living within the same *"place".* You will have two groups, that won't **see** as YOU. If you're a senior ready to graduate, those still in elementary school will obviously not see what you see, yet. Then, of course, all they need is time, to reach "their", graduation. (they **will** get it) The 2nd **group**, are also seniors who are taking the opposite polarity path upon graduation. Most will take the left, which is not Right, as one is Dark and the other Light. You will know your flock and which isn't.

"Be wary of any belief or ideology that promotes division between you and your fellow human beings." -unknown origin

What views and is aware of the message of the quote, **stems** from the same *polarity or source* that would promulgate the ideology of division, *that message tells you to be wary of.* It is also the "devil" whispering to you from "your" left side to be "wary" of the separate "out there" Devil, but he isn't *out there.* This perspective or magnetic influence always pulls you to identify with separation. Polarity is so amazingly hard to see because of this (but once you do, it's so amazingly obvious). And within the beautiful workings of the school of 7-11, it is supposed to be, as you are oblivious to the deeper structure and you have all of the motivation and urgency to jump in and *"participate".* Until you have very discerning eyes, you'll think that what you are seeing is light perspective, when it is in fact, the dark, and remember what is viewing it, as I just covered.

Satan not only attacks and condemns the Light, but also the polarity **it** stems from, further thickening the fog! When someone is judging and "arguing with you" and tells you to "get out of Ego", that is the pot calling the kettle black, a spade calling you a spade! That's Ego telling you to lose yours. When you hear that, that is simply their Ego's rejection of you, tantamount to, *be gone*, whether they realize it or not, and 99.9% of the time, **they won't**. Ego "judges" that which it perceives to be separate from itself, and wishing *the opposition* to "be gone", but it's a projection of something in themselves that they see *in you* that they don't like or simply can't process! It hardly stops there though.

When a group of caring, "good" people are together, they're all safe knowing that none of them will hurt any of the others. There are no malicious games or hidden agendas and certainly, there is no fear of physical or emotional harm. On the opposite end of this spectrum, the opposite applies. In a group of liars, thieves and killers, even though they are all cut from the same cloth, none of them are safe from each other, so that not only will the bad attack the good, but they will also attack the fellow bad. A killer kills, without regard to who is killed. This is cancer, and this is precisely why Light polarity must dominate within the dance of polarity so that the organism does not consume itself, but it is all ultimately a series of events for consciousness to experience. This is why the nucleus of an atom is so much larger than the electrons, and why the stars are so much more massive than all of the combined planets and their moons. This is why Mufasa and Thor, in the various esoteric tales of polar royal sibling relationships, are larger and stronger than their "darker" younger brothers. The Negative polarity is absolutely needed during growth, as it identifies the Positive, but it must not, *ultimately* dominate. At the higher frequencies it knows and is completely content with its deferential role because ultimately, there is only the **One Mind!** That is *really* why you **can't** serve two masters, **literally**.

Satan will usually persecute what it believes to be Satanic, to appear to make itself like "The Most High". I saw an article on social media from a friend who was very disturbed by the fact that organized and socially acceptable "Fox Hunts" still exist in Britain. Of course, it is *heartless* and cruel, but it hit me as I looked at the pictures, now that I see clues the way I do, that a greater symbolic message was being communicated through this archaic, "cancer to nature" ritual. Now, the UK is the Abrahamic "Great Nation", that is the progeny of "Britannia", the creation of Rome. The superficial interpretation of who nailed Christ to the cross, we come up with the Jews and the Romans. On a deeper "internal" level, we see that it is our Satanic adversarial perspective from negative polarity that crucifies our internal Christ for not conforming to or being controlled by them.

The "privileged" or Satanic ruling here, are the men in the **red** coats, the negative polarity, that oppose God. They set themselves up as God here and proclaim, that they will be like the Most High by persecuting and destroying "the beast". Being the "adversary", he is the adversary to **everything** because he is in opposition to God, and even the negative polarity is an aspect of God! They are out to destroy THE BEAST, but in reality, they are the beast. They portray the wild (nature) dogs, (dog/god) as the beast, but the metaphor is the Satanic exterminating God. *The number of FOX is 666, so the even deeper message is that the Satanic also consume themselves.* And don't we call an attractive young woman a FOX? Here's another one I just thought of, "dog" is code for God and our Goddess of creation **is** a Witch, and the name that Satan has bestowed on the female dog is bitch, which rhymes with witch! The W is 5 and the B is 2 and the remainder of the word, itch, is 9238 = 22 = 4, so he replaced the reality of 5 that gives us 9, with the "even" duality of 2 that gives us 6. ***That "son" of a bitch!*** The **Fox** and the **Wolf**, that encodes 4 and 2, uniquely symbolize our Dark Divine Feminine, and why, in *this* world, they **are persecuted, along with Bees** (remember what they symbolize) and other extreme "mortification of the flesh" acts.

The Lorax, whose number is 7 with 5 letters, points us to the Forest

I've used the analogy of a tree when describing the structure of the Self, and I would like to expand on that analogy to better display the growth of the universe. It's amazing how many memories of things I had experienced, seen or heard in my past that I didn't fully under-stand or realize the true significance at the time I took them in, until now, writing this book. It just occurred to me that something I heard in a movie called "Phenomenon" back in 1996 was a massive clue to the structure of the universe and a massive analogy to conceptualize how it grows. We had heard the entire time I was growing up, that the Blue Whale was the largest living organism of all time, but at some point they gave that title to the Giant Sequoias of the central Sierra Nevada mountain range, but they now include the caveat of "largest *single* tree", because now we have a new largest living organism. *John* tells us in the movie that it is an Aspen Grove.

When you see a large stand of Aspen on the side of a mountain, they are all the same plant. The largest we have discovered is a single organism grove called "Pando" (5), the name given to about 43,000 (7) aspens sharing a common root system covering about 106 (7) acres in Utah. When I saw the movie, I was only pleasantly surprised with the information I figured to be true, but now I see that the Aspen growth pattern is similar to the way our solar system and our galaxy, is expanding. Think of the Aspens above ground as the individual Stars of the Galaxy and the planets and dark matter as the root system that connects them all. Aspen tree roots expand out, like our Sun's planets expanding out and a new "Aspen" will soon "break ground" with its moons as the new root system. It's amazingly not amazing that the two largest trees that show the structure and growth of the universe are found in the 11 western states of the "New World".

New cosmic polarity *positions* are opening up!

I noticed the parallels of the structure of the tree in the human body. As you have that picture of the structure of the tree, keep in mind that the roots below the ground in the dirt, are doing the *"down and dirty"* jobs that are "less than glamorous", but absolutely necessary in the grand scheme of keeping that tree alive and healthy. The level ground is the midway point between the two opposite aspects of the tree. Now, right after conception, the Heart is the first organ, the very first thing, to be created, literally from "Nothing", and also keep in mind the vision of "Christ" as the Sacred Heart and the fact that your intuition comes from the heart, and It IS the Eye of God who sees all, from his secret place. Jesus tells us the Father does not judge, as He at that level, sees through ALL, the light and the dark. As you **envision all of this and your body,** disregard your arms and legs and look at what is at your center between the crotch and your brain. The Heart is at the Center and distributes the blood to everything above and below, and think of it at **"Ground Level"**. Our design is more like a tree than one would give thought to.

Doubt you'll see this take of Cosmic growth anywhere else.

Around and above the heart we find the air filled lungs, the air we breath, and above that the nervous system centers and of course the Brain, with it's light illuminating neurons, the stars above us, consumed with it's lighter "white collar" thoughts to navigate us through life with the dissemination of information and signals. Below the heart, like what is below the ground, all of the dark, down and dirty jobs from the stomach and liver, to the intestines that do what you really wouldn't want to do if you had to pick a job to do in the body, but yet there are jobs that are "shittier yet". Further down are the Kidneys and the intestine to the colon, doing the jobs that epitomize down and extremely dirty. We are cells in a larger body and as this cosmic body grows, **we** will go to either the positive (Narrow Gate) or the negative positions (Wide Gate) being created, and ***all* is Divine**. That which does not judge, is the one that knows that it needs colon cells as well as brain cells, but we here are being primed to fill these positions that are becoming available and if you spend your life in lies, theft, death, addictions, malice, stirring and shoveling shit, you will not be going UP to the office buildings of the Stars, but you will be going DOWN to work in the darkness. It is not complicated like ego likes to make it, as you will either deal in truth or lies, life or death. But hey, a tree needs its roots, and you certainly can contribute to God's "regularity" if truth is **not your *strong point.***

There also has to be some compelling "Benefits Package" or "intoxicating" bait for them to *"choose"* the "lower" jobs. This "Perk" has to "really" perk their interest! I hear that sex sells. When your creative energy is depleted, ***something* is receiving energy from you,** and when you increase your frequency, you are keeping your energy, from that "something" that doesn't want you to keep it", and the temptations will be intensified to get it back (free porno...Hello!). I saw this quote, *"If your woman isn't a revolutionary.....She'll persuade you to be a slave"*, and at this point in the book, you know, it isn't *Her, if you end up in chains,* but You! (I'd have worded the next quote a bit differently, haha!)

"The woman is the biggest thief of that energy, and thus the spiritual power. I've always known that and was alerted. Of myself I created what I wanted: a thoughtful and spiritual machine." ~Nikola Tesla, from "The Emissaries: Beasts of the Code" by J.H.B. Edmonds

The two polarity divisions have formed right before our eyes like a great chasm formed by a massive earthquake leaving two groups on each side. Be thrilled differences between the two are so obvious. Jump for joy instead of complaining about the contradictory insanity, that will remain contradictory insanity no matter how many decibel levels you attain or sane sound bites you put forth. You are only making sense to your own choir, as in those you resonate with, who don't need Capt. Obvious, and that used to be me, telling them how political munchkins are the epitome of delusional inconsistencies. You are pointing out "No shit Sherlock" monumental hypocrisies and lies as obvious as Bill denying his never-ending accusations of sexual misconduct as the semen-stained dress is hung up behind him for all to see and laugh at, except *his* choir.

You know who you are, or at least you can identify your choir. You are on the light path to be a Star, in what is essentially "Star Search". There is a very good reason these extreme views void of "heart-based common sense", are promulgated by the *Celebrity* community. And these include the entertainment industry, along with the predominantly Satanic institutions like Government and Academia (some aren't, calm down). They are the Polarity left equation balancing itself out, as you are Neo asking who the hell is this Smith guy. Satan cannot become "The Star" and he cannot be rehabilitated because he is heading up the *needed* Saturnic polars heading into the depths of the Dark, to do the jobs that must be done. He still wants to "act" like God so he again, calls "His" Ego infested dark ends of the equations *stars*, as the little atomic *celebrities* are the only "stars" "he" can hope to create.

Let them, like the very important looking munchkin officials, make their little egocentric proclamations and contradictory stances, to be the crystal clear messages of, "Where you need to put your Attention" and not on those who crave it and stay detached at their folly instead of getting upset at it. Staying upset at it means you are too close to it by lowering yourself and on the *left* side of the chasm. Don't be *Randle*, so get *your butt* out of the *Cuckoo's Nest* of collective butts and get back home, because teaching a pig to sing or dance or whatever the *hell* it is, you are just pissing them off because they are totally convinced that they are "right" and see YOU as the loon anyway. **That's How it works!**

If they *knew* they were destined to work in the colon, they wouldn't do it, and you and I might get called to do the dirty work that must be done. So knock that shit off (wink), get Happy, and let **them** stay in colon training to work in the galactic waste plant!

"We shouldn't be here." ~ "Thor", Hogun's assessment upon arriving in Jotunheim

This is basically a clue telling you that brain cells have **no** business in the colon dealing with colon cells. They do what the larger body needs to be done, even if you can't quite understand it, and Thor, at that point, wasn't aware enough to know this. He was at the end!

Newton's 3 Laws of Motion *encode the Identities* of, the Divine Masculine, the Divine Feminine, and the 7-11 School of Duality

Life is magical and mysterious and the "measure" of its beauty is in the eye of the beholder whose awareness dictates "what" they *see*. If you're on the path to Self-awareness, at a particular point on your journey, you realize that everything that comes into your life is a result of your spiritual agenda *and* Newton's **3rd Law, "For every action there is an equal and opposite reaction",** because of what you do and think about each and every second. *There are No exceptions.* Now, why is it the "3rd" law? It is the Primary Law of 3, the Trinity, God, at this level in "waveform", and that's why it is also a law in Physics, because the Trinity, in the language of waveform is "Space, Time and Numbers". At this level of 6 within the "The 7-11 School of Duality", the school is created for the development of the children of God, and their number is 7. Every thought, or premeditated action stemming from thought, carries with it a consequence, because thought is paramount, and **is** an "Action".

This is confirmed in Matthew 5:28, *"You have heard that it was said, 'YOU SHALL NOT COMMIT ADULTERY'; 28 but I say to you that everyone who looks at a woman with lust for her has already committed adultery with her in his heart."* Every thought and associated act as a result of the thought, takes you to or away from the light. And this confirmed in Galatians 6:7, *"Do not be deceived, God is not mocked; for whatever a man sows, this he will also reap. 8 For the one who sows to his own flesh will from the flesh reap corruption, but the one who sows to the Spirit will from the Spirit reap eternal life.."*

Newton's **1ˢᵗ Law** of Motion, "The Law of Inertia", says an object will remain as it is, whether it is in motion or at rest, if left alone and not acted on by any other outside net force. I believe this law identifies the Divine Masculine or Soul.

Newton's **2ⁿᵈ Law** of Motion, "The Law of Acceleration", says that when this "outside" net force acts on an object, the object will accelerate *(look up the physics definition of acceleration).* That means it is making it do something different than it had been doing. This Law identifies the Divine Feminine or Spirit. In Genesis after God made man, God knew that man would need some outside stimulation to exert a *force* on him to (compel or motivate) "help" him to experience and change, as 2:18 says, "It is not good (he won't get much done! Haha) that the man should be alone; I will make him a helper..." Yes, the opposite sex is attracted to the other, especially a man to a woman, and this attraction motivates action! As I pointed out earlier, Soul needs Spirit to experience, change and evolve, and Spirit needs Soul because it would be an empty heartless mechanism without it.

So Newton's 3 Laws of motion clearly identify the polar Godheads and their relationship with respect to the overall growth and development of the Self, and how this dynamic brings situations and lessons based on the actions and thoughts of their children. *You can see why now in the Target Commercial, the woman is the last to replace his piece in the center of the board with hers because **He** is within **Her.** If* your path is to the light, at some point you must be turned **in**, as we analyze the *dynamic* of Eve.

The Creation of Adam and Eve, and their true Identity

Let's go a tad deeper and I'll break down the creation of Both in Genesis like no one has ever explained it. Now, Gen. **2:7** confirms that **Adam is** The Divine Masculine of **Soul** saying it plainly, and as such he is in a state of the **1ˢᵗ Law** of Motion. That ends *"things said plainly"*, as the remainder of the explanation will be a bit of a stretch like me trying to get you to see that *Wyatt was, and wasn't there*, with his brothers in Tombstone. This is the dynamic of what is happening within and without. Now go to **Genesis 2, King James version,** and follow with me, as I don't want to include the biblical text here, but it's easy enough to find, and I'll list the verses I'm explaining. Okay, we know that Adam represents the Soul and he needs to grow and needs a helper who looks at things from a singular, separate, adversarial perspective. Remember, without it, he won't be motivated to get much done. Here goes:

21: We know we are dreaming here. This, is not reality. We are in a waveform dream, so *The Lord caused Adam to fall into a **deep sleep**.* He took *an internal aspect to create an extension of who and what he is,* and what he took, a rib, has a geometric curve, like a golden spiral, that is built into our waveform reality and curved lines, especially *this curve,* are feminine, and a rib can regenerate and make another one, and so they can replicate, as in create more here in the dream. 22: Eve represents Spirit and Ego/body and as such represents the **2ⁿᵈ Law** of Motion. 23: She is literally *in him as his Spirit and Ego, and outside of him as his* w*oman and his* body (she is literally his body), being the embodiment of the Soul's external Ego and Spirit, out there in the dream. I've identified the body, as an atomic manifestation of Spirit here in waveform, but another appropriate definition for this Genesis interpretation is that ***the Body, is the dreams representation of Spirit.*** [Remember, the lower your frequency, the more you project out in the dream, to become more separated or less than what you were, which is why the less aware *need more.* The higher your frequency the more whole you are, as less of you is projected out there, until you eventually need nothing at the top of the pyramid.]

24: This is huge, **we do not read that God woke Adam up**, and this means that this was and is an internal process, and the only external Adam is experiencing, **is in the dream.** As I pointed out previously, *Man* here in the dream of separation represents Soul and The Self, and *Woman* represents Spirit and Ego, but internally we know that *we (each) individually* have a Soul which is The Self from the Light, and a Spirit which is The Ego-Body from the Dark. Within, they are the two coming together as One Flesh, and out there in the duality dream, they are male and female, husband and wife. The deeper you are in lower frequency, the greater you are in separation and the more is taken out of you and put out there in your dream. The lower your frequency, the more you need of everything out there, because there is less in you. True Duality. 25: Yes, 7 is the child. Very young children are not aware enough to realize they are naked, and we all have very young pictures of ourselves, naked as Jaybirds, having no awareness we are parading around in our birthday suits. As you are no doubt beginning to realize, this is not a *one-time* isolated event, but a continually running, "human condition" *state* of affairs.

Genesis 3:1, 2, 3, 4, 5: Now the Ego is absolutely essential for growth. It gives you your perception of your individual identity, and naturally looks at things from the opposing view of unity and the natural order. With this in mind, we all talk (some incessantly) don't we? **So the Serpent,** in this context, **is internal and external ego perspectives.** It's usually the slightly older kids who are the first to plant the seed that that Santa story that *you* have been buying isn't true, and we usually hear about sex from friends before we hear about it from our parents. So yeah, we have all these rules and regulations that we just blindly obey, but at some point, we begin to question **why** we have to obey them, and start to believe that it is actually in our best interest to no longer obey one or more of them. We are gaining our independence, forming our own opinions, and will now experience the good and bad consequences (so that we can experience good **and now know** evil) of our decisions to do what **we** believe is best for us rather than just doing what we have been told. Living, is learning, and the Father of Lights, allows you to go out there and live.

6: Hey, that friend, or what I told myself, makes sense to me! I believe this is good for me. And look how 6 is worded, to best confirm this was (while it may too have been external) an internal conversation: *"...she took of its fruit and ate. She also gave to her husband **with her,** and he ate.".* This is worded to tell me that Adam was not off in the *lower 40* (American slang for another section of the property) of Eden, and she had to go and find him. He was right there with her, internally or externally, as Lucifer (Oh hell, did I say that out loud? I meant to say Serpent.) spoke to her.

7: We are experiencing life and growing up and becoming more aware, so yes, now we have the awareness to realize we are naked and it's time to cover our private parts. No more pics in the buff. Unless you're weird, but I won't go there! 8, 9, 10, 11: God (your parents) comes in, but is still treating them like they are younger than they now are, so he walks in on them and they of course are now older and **expect** some privacy and independence, plus they know they are doing what he told them not to do (sex?), so they are of course a bit afraid and apprehensive, and they (too, the singular Adam) try to avoid contact, just like we all do. 12, 13: My Ego that you in fact gave me, allowed me to grow and become aware enough to not want to be naked around you, and it told me that disobeying this one command was the right thing to do, for it caused all of this growth and awareness.

14: Ego, for your disobedience of My Law, and inducing Adam to do the same, you will always be in a secondary position or role in all creation. 15, 16: And to you, The Self and the man, since you participated with this disobedience, I will ensure that you always have a love-hate, pleasure-pain relationship with your ego and with her, and when you regularly capitulate to your ego and to her, they will always remain adversarial to you (this is getting personal!), because your actions are lowering your frequency, ensuring you are remaining in the dream. The seed (children) of a son of the Serpent, will have an adversarial relationship with the seed of Eve that gives them birth. When you bruise his head with your heel, your heel will also be hurt in the process because you are one flesh. You both will be punished for being weak and lowering your frequency by biting at the carnal (waveform dream) bait, and your illusion of controlling your lives by actions in the dream. *Remember,* **he is still dreaming.** What he is doing ensures that he stays dreaming because he needs to develop, but at some point, after **he has learned what the dream teaches**, he **must** wake up, and why there are SO many negative consequences for remaining in the dream of lower frequency, which is an immature perspective, and why we are prodded to "grow up".

21, 22, 23: This is life and what we go through with our children when they reach that age when they can no longer live at home. *"Since you're not going to obey the rules of the house, then it's time to get out, and besides, it's about that time anyway for you to be on your own to grow up. Mom and I prepared some things for you on your journey, here's some money to tide you over for a while until you get established."* And as your young man or woman is leaving, the parents say, "Now they will become adults like us." And all of this drove them even lower to the East, to the Dark, as it was supposed to. And of course 24, means that he must die to the illusory dream, if he wants to achieve everlasting life. Your "Real" Soul's mate, is within, and will be continually burned building your house, with the illusion of Her. Someone slapped the Hell out of me, showing me my real wife of my flesh, was within. This is because my *Soul's mate, isn't out there.* She turned me from the illusion and pointed me **In**, to my true Soul's wife of *my Mary*, my body, my Temple, my Spirit, and when she turned me to my *real Maria,* she became Nicolle. As my **Glinda** pointed out, *"The Divine Feminine is the Holy Grail. The Divine Masculine is the Ark of Covenant. They are not things, material things, they are vessels that house both aspects of what is Divine within us should we pass the test. Because it is a test."*

"Everyone wants to go to Heaven, but no one wants to die!"

The fruit of the Tree of the Knowledge of Good and Evil, is the *Dark*, and the fruit of the Tree of Life is the *Light*, as Polarity prevails again. The Garden of Eden is God's "Natural" setting, and what is mystically, but naturally, provided because we keep our frequency high and have let go of trying to control it. **The Garden of Eden is a Frequency. Like the Promised Land,** it is the residence of a **Right Mind.** The more "whole" you are, the less you project, "out there" in the manifest waveform world to need. Just as your manifest world matches your frequency, as you up it, you will reach that point where all **you need** is provided. This is why Jesus tells us to not worry about what we will eat or wear, as The Father knows we need these things and we will be blessed with plenty **if** you listen to Mary, to do whatever He tells you to do.

Going further into the AI Dark, to "control it", is a karmic slippery slope that always *ends up* showing you a "Dead" end. And while I may be revealing a bit too much, as it is put there for a reason, I have experienced this "bruised head", when I was thinking with that one, and it sure as hell didn't come from a heel. (before I *"knew", what I was made of,* taking herbal supplements that keep *T-mones* up) After I got the point, it vanished. Scared the "Hell" out of me, until it did. So yes, that verse is not *junk,* like junk DNA. I know what it means, and I'll leave it at that. I'll talk more about what we label as *Junk or Chaos,* and how we attempt to dismiss what we don't understand and in the process, identify what hasn't, to this point. After this explanation, let me borrow a question from Wyatt, but replace Devil, with God. "So who was God?" You may indeed, *if you get Lucky!*

Time to ID the Light and the Dark

I want to add a "light and dark" analogy or comparison that may clarify more of its identity, especially the dark because we deal in it, and help with the understanding of Galatians 6:7. It will certainly blur the one that seems to be your *obvious* choice, and disappoint more than a few, like the *rich man* who thought the choice was clear until he was told what he'd have to give up. When I say that every thought or action you have takes you to the light or to the dark, we all shake our heads in agreement that *light is the obvious choice,* of where we believe we want to be heading. This is true because the dark has been demonized, as I pointed out in the "Like a Prayer" breakdown, and that sounds good to most because we associate it with everything that is bad and evil, and most just aren't too sure what "choosing the light" really is. If I look at it through a polarity lense and replace the "dark" with the word "material", and replace the "light" with "ethereal", it puts another easier to grasp slant on what each means.

The **Material** *Girl* again gives us a massive clue, telling us who The Divine Feminine is, and what type of "boy" (the clues are in virtually every word, as the dark perspective is immature, hence "boy") makes her "rainy day" (those days that oppose sunny "light" days), and the clue within the clue is that choosing the material *"does"* create the *"rainy day"*. And Materialism is absolute core of the Dark perspective. You all know the vast majority are consumed with "cold hard cash" and "saving their pennies". Most are all about more money, bigger houses, faster flashier cars, physical beauty, sensation chasing, staying *young* through surgeries, drugs, or supplements, smart pills, and everything pleasurable that the 5 senses can bring you, as the list goes on and on. You would be surprised what constitutes the spectrum of the "material", which is "the dark" or "the flesh" mentioned in Galatians, which is why most will cling to it leading to the "wide gate", that we are told, "most will find". So every thought takes you to the Material or to the Ethereal. As I described earlier, your brain cells deal in the ethereal all day, and your colon cells deal in the material, and as we jump to the next level as The Self grows, you will either be going to the equivalent of one or the other.

The Clash of the Polarity Super Heros

What in the world could the hidden message be in "Batman vs. Superman"? One needs something to be a Superhero and the other is just being who he was born to be. Remember I told you that the logo of Apple actually meant that technology is a forbidden fruit, and that partaking of it, "the bite out of the apple, is to "become as God". Well, if you choose technology to *improve yourself* or to become more "Godlike", as they are selling it, then you will always be a slave to it. And when the system crumbles after the next big manmade or natural disaster (a programmed inevitability), then who will be there to fix you when it *malfunctions*? (another *inevitability*) Obi-Wan describes this dynamic of the Dark with Luke, concerning his Father, "He's *more machine* now *than man.*" A Dodge commercial within a Batman vs Superman promo provides us with a telling polarity clue: *"You can't have a hero, if you don't have a villain. The world needs villains, and villains need cars."*

This is saying that you can't identify the light without the dark, and obviously, the villain is the dark, and I outlined how the dark is also the *material*, so they *need* cars and *material tools*. Batman's costume is black and he is known as the "Dark Knight", because he *is* a, "To the Dark", Superhero, and that would be Satan's version of a Superhero. Satan is competing with God, so he will create *his* version of a "Superhero"...or his version of a god, to safeguard his Satanic creation "Metropolis" from *destruction*. Batman, (also think of "Buddy Pine" or "**S**yndrome" from "The Incredibles", and another clue is that Buddy is a *boy*), is however just an ordinary person using *"technology"*, to be as a god, while Superman just "is" and doesn't need *"gadgets"*. This makes Superman the enemy of Batman (until they discover their common *Mother*) because Batman is to the Dark and is in opposition to God's order and Natural Law, and Superman is a product of that "Law and Order". "I grew up in **Kansas** General. I'm about as American as it gets."

~"Man of Steel". Yes, our "Light" Superhero grew up in our Star!

While watching "The Dark Knight", the true identity of "The Joker" became *laughingly* obvious to me. It was in no small measure due to the *different* portrayal of this very *well known* "villain" by Heath

Ledger, that elevated the persona of "The Joker" from that of a sadistic, mischievous clown to what I now know him to be. Just looking at him, told you that "this" was not The Joker you grew up with, as Ledger's uniquely original portrayal of him blurred the archetypical boundaries of who you perceived him to be and why he did, what he did. While Heath didn't "create" this *"unmasked"* Joker, he most certainly was tasked with bringing him to "Life", and he artfully brought the "face" of Divine Consequence or Karma to the Big Screen. Here are some of the Joker's lines with "Harvey Dent" from The Dark Knight that best illustrates his "**real**" identity:

"You know, I just do things. The mob has plans, the cops have plans, Gordon's got plans. They're schemers. Schemers trying to **control** *their little worlds. I'm not a schemer. I try to show the schemers how pathetic their attempts to control things really are. So When I say that you and your girlfriend was nothing personal... You know that I'm telling the truth. It's the schemers that put you where you are. You were a schemer. You had plans. And look where that got you. I just did what I do best. I took your little plan and I turned it on itself. Look what I did to this city with a few drums of gas and a couple of bullets. You know ... You know what I noticed? Nobody panics when things go according to plan.* (planned "wars" and other atrocities) *Even if the plan is horrifying. If tomorrow I tell the press that, like a gangbanger will get shot or a truckload of soldiers will be blown up, nobody panics. Because it's all part of the plan. But when I say that one little old mayor will die ...* (not part of the plan) *Well then everybody loses their minds! Introduce a little anarchy.* (Natural Law) *Upset the established* (Satanic) *order. And everything becomes chaos.* (Natural Law) *I'm an agent of chaos.* (He's doing the will of God, and not his own) *Oh, and you know the thing about chaos?*

It's fair. (That's right, because it's Natural Law, and nobody gets, what they don't deserve)

-The Joker speaking to Dent in the hospital in, "The Dark Knight"

And, of course, The Material Girl clues us into the chaotic world we find ourselves in that I know I **must** leave as well.

"People give me the business; I'm not living in **fear**; I'm just living in **Chaos**; Gotta get away from here! I want to *free* my **Soul**. I want to *lose* **control.** If I can get to the week *end* (to our polarity gods), everything will turn out just fine" ~ "Where's the Party", Madonna

Out of Chaos, comes Order, for there *is no* disorder, in Nature

The Joker, quite simply, is the Natural Law of "consequence or Karma". He is **not**, a *villain and* he knows our understanding of *"chaos"* (in this context) does not exist. It is a *Satanic`* explanation for a complex *order* it can't comprehend or an outright lie for those who are sharp enough to "know", but most fall into the category of the former. Even what had been perceived as "chaotic" atomic and molecular movement **isn't,** as German Chemist and Mathematician Peter Plichta, outlined in his book "God's Secret Formula: Deciphering the Riddle of the Universe and the Prime Number Code". He discovered the movements actually follow rules of programmed algorithms that govern their moves to generate a Sierpinski Triangle forming the base deterministic material structure that our "solid" world springs from. Like "chaos", there is no stability in the natural world, as there is only growth or decay, the duality of light and dark, of *Self* or lack of *Self,* and why you can't serve both masters at the same time. You must either be heading to one or the other. The "Caduceus River" is forever heading "North", and you are either heading North with it or it is pulling away from you, and the lower your frequency, the faster it pulls away from you, that you feel as gravity. And I'll only give you one guess, more than generous I know, which side of Dent's face and head is *acidically* eaten away. So Satan needs technology to attempt to be as God, so when you see those who present themselves to you as your God, and they need technology and may have "some" more mental and physical abilities than we do, but still need technology to do what they do and are just more advanced versions of "us", they are not God.

"Time", to define!

The definition of "Satanic" according to Merriam-Webster is:

: of, relating to, or worshipping the Devil, or characteristic of Satan
: characterized by extreme cruelty or viciousness

Now, when I described Satan and what being Satanic is back in Chapter Two, that was the first step for many of you to go beyond equating Satan with a singular Devil to tie it more intimately with us. Let's take another step in our understanding of term "Satanic". I couldn't help but think about the ever deceptive Sith herself from Arc-kansas saying that until a "person" is born, it has no *"constitutional"* rights, as Hillary has said many times that "unborn persons have no rights under our laws currently. She makes sure she specifies "constitutional", rather than basic "Human Rights" as outlined in the Declaration of Independence, part of which states, "We hold these truths to be self-evident, that all men are created equal, that they are endowed by their Creator with certain unalienable Rights, that among these are **Life**, Liberty and the pursuit of Happiness." Since I am only identifying "Satanic" here, for the purpose of staying on track, I'll address quickly why she chooses her words carefully. *"All persons **born** or naturalized in the United States and subject to the jurisdiction thereof, are citizens of the United States...", **that, as you can see, only "identifies" who is a citizen, and as such, who falls under the jurisdiction of the Constitution**,* and since they are not yet born, they are not yet citizens, and this will be for another discussion. Now back to identifying "Satanic".

So *obviously* it would be murder to cut up a child that was just *born*, but just minutes before still inside the mother, it is somehow *not* "murder", to cut the child up and throw it away as an abortion.

Now as I lay this out, please keep in mind that I am **in no way** supporting or opposing any law or the Roe v. Wade court decision. I am only defining **Satanic,** and you can either accept it or reject it, *but it's the perspective that opposes Nature or the Natural Laws of God* *and Creation.* It is the Extreme adversarial, extreme Ego, to the dark negative polarity, perspective. When one elucidates this perspective, they are being SATANIC, as polarity is expressed again.

It is the, "I know better than the most High". "I will ascend above the heights of the clouds; I will be like the most High." ... I will ascend into heaven, I will exalt my throne above the *stars* of God". (Another clue as to "what lights" are meant by, the "Father of Lights").

Now, how this applies to abortion, to help me identify Satanic. How did we all come to be "here", in the material world? Did the child about to be born just "materialize" at that moment as it emerged from the vaginal birth canal? **The child was of course "here" before that**, as rudimentary as the point may be, and the same people who would deny the child, who had yet to emerge from the canal, any human rights, are the same ones to condescendingly scold or dismiss you for even pointing out something so "obvious"! Of Course, the child is HERE before it emerged from his or her mother. We are not Stupid! No, **that**...is not what afflicts them!

So, I ask again, how did you come to be here?

A man and a woman come together and "consum*mate*", before this you are not here, and then, at that moment of conception it started the beginning of YOU, ...and you came to be, in the "material form", here! Arguing, that at the early stages of the pregnancy, the developing human is not yet a human, is to anthropomorphize the entirety of the experience to only the experience after we *"look"* human! It should be obvious that since we *cannot* determine that "moment" during our 9 (the number of God Here, and Not Here) month gestation period, that we magically "become" human, that that moment can only be at that very moment it all started.

Conception!!!

That IS the Law...Natural Law! To end it at **any time by the hand of "man"**, is taking the "law", into your own hands!

I know, I know, laws, whether they be man-made or natural, can at times be...**Inconvenient**. Oh wow, having a child now is not convenient, so let's make a "convenient law" and not assign him or her "rights" so that we can terminate his or her life, before we can see them! This will make it easier for all to stomach and *accept*, even though it is extreme puerile reasoning bordering on "insanity" to "believe" this.

Out of sight, "Out of Mind"! (My, the clues don't stop!)

This IS, the...Inconvenient Truth.

Like it or not, Abortion violates and opposes Natural Law, and so, is **Satanic**, and this explains their *insanity,* as I'll show you shortly.

I don't care how you *"justifyingly"* "slice or dice" it, and like all the decisions you make, there will be consequences! I saw this quote from Norma McCorvey after I had already written this, but wanted to include it, as it most certainly confirms my point.

*"You read about me in history books, but now I'm dedicated to spreading the truth about preserving the dignity of all human life, from **Natural Conception to Natural Death**."*

~Norma McCorvey aka **Jane** Roe, of "Roe vs. Wade", who never had an abortion.

Now remember too, from Chapter Two telling you why Jesus referred to Peter as Satan, and with this "updated" understanding of Satanic, you can better understand why Jesus called Peter Satan because what Jesus had just disclosed to them was in fact, a Natural Law of Ascension, to become a Star. It is God's Law that must be carried out as the universe, extended nature, expands! This is from Matthew 16 (note 7): 21 to 23 (3 to 5):

*"21 From that time Jesus began to show His disciples that He **must** go to Jerusalem, and suffer many things from the elders and chief priests and scribes, and be killed, and be raised up on the third day. 22 Peter took Him aside and began to rebuke Him, saying, "God forbid it, Lord!*

This shall never happen to You." 23 But He turned and said to Peter, "Get behind Me, Satan! You are a stumbling block to Me; for you are not setting your mind on God's interests, but man's." And of course, Peter is acting Satanic at verse "22".

Here is what this *union* means, and how Wyatt and Doc's exchange perfectly describes it. Now, why would God allow his Son to be betrayed and crucified? His "Prodigal" Son needs to be **separated from *Separation*.** He must be *severed* from his dream waveform Magdalene, to go Internal to bond with His same flesh wife Mary. You already know that Jesus is Jupiter and Lucifer is the Identity of all of them, and that includes the Dark Judas, as J is L. Lucifer **IS** the expression of the entire spectrum, so half of her is *Good* (Light Stars) and the other half is less and less good to down-right *Evil* (Dark Saturnic Stars). That half of her is the "Projected Devil" in lower frequencies that see in separation.

So here is the progression. Severing the Son from Separation (his "out there" Mary/Ego) takes time and that is all of the unpleasantness leading up to the crucifixion (all of this is "I'll be Damned"), which is the death of His Ego, **BUT,** (big one!) He (the Light Lucifer) will always be mated or *Bonded* with the waveform Judas (the Dark Lucifer). This is the new proton being bonded with the new electron, and once they "make the bond", they exist eternally (the 2 thieves under Christ). And that is what is meant by Doc's, "If you get Lucky" reply.

Now, making the bond is unpleasant for the Son temporarily, because it is pulling him down by transferring his energy to His polar negative, and that is symbolized by Judas getting silver as money is waveform energy. The Dark one represents the vessel and must get its energy/sustenance from the power source, which is The Light. This is symbolic of the entire spectrum as the only one **really** producing the Light is the Sun (Jupiter). The light produced (energy/money) from the Moon (Pluto) must come from the Sun, and that dynamic expresses the spectrum. Both then grow as a new Star system, Up and Down. The Son then attains, His own everlasting life identity, and His dark polar mate, not only "took the bullet" for Him, but eternally keeps Him, "**IN**-check". You gotta Love that! Because He, is the extension of the Father, He will then have 2 below Him within the same dynamic and so the cosmic family grows.

The TA definition of Satanic:

: the perspective that opposes God and Unity or the Natural Order including Nature and the laws of Nature and Creation.

: worshiping the perspective that opposes God, Nature, and Life.

Repeated thoughts or actions to the *Satanic perspective*, will ultimately bring *disillusionment*, suffering and if continued, destruction! If you saw "Man of Steel", didn't becoming Satanic, ultimately destroy Krypton? And while I'm talking about separation maladies, I'm crazy about this quote from John Lennon, *"Our society is run by insane people for insane objectives. I think we're being run by maniacs for maniacal ends and I think I'm liable to be put away as insane for expressing that. That's what's insane about it.".*

I will again point to polarity, as *crazy* as that sounds.

Everything is UPside DOWN, but just calling it all *insane,* is so easy because it allows you to point at something other than yourself, and the word is more used and abused than quality or love. It's so so easy to brand them psychopaths and call for their death or ouster without identifying their real "affliction" because that might make you examine yourself and take a closer look at your world. Looking more deeply into why we have an epidemic of Insanity petrifies people who themselves suffer from an even greater epidemic called, *cognitive dissonance*. The opposite of Life is Death, and who Champion's Death? The opposite of Truth is lies. When you have more than you could possibly spend, then how can it be about the money? And power? Well, certainly to "influence", but to what end? You have two planetary bodies that you see virtually every day that you don't need NASA to "tell you about". One shines, and one reflects what the other shines. Let's stop misdiagnosing them and identify their **true** condition, and call a Spade a Spade, rather than lumping **everyone** into the *crazy bin! The Truth, will unlock your Cell. "Daughter, your faith has made you **whole**. Go in peace, and be healed of your affliction."* -Mark 5:34

They are Satanic

"Insane" comes from Latin meaning "**not** healthy", and health **ultimately** means "**whole**". So when you don't see in "right brain unity", but see in separation you are, in essence, "insane", and that is **Satanic.** *"My daughter will teach you our ways, learn well Jake Sully. And we will see if your insanity can be cured."* -Moat, "Avatar" They are also compulsive control freaks who want to legislate every nuanced aspect of life because they believe Nature and Natural Law is chaotic, random, unfair and **at best**, far too lax. The Satanic mind perceives exclusively in separation while opposing God and the Natural order. To them, God and Nature are cruel, capricious, vacuous, and unjust.

Speaking of Satanic, when George H.W. Bush, one of the faces of the Satanic Elite, was describing the "developing" NWO, on **9-11**-1991, he and the other *Agents of the Dark* were fostering, he said and I quote, *"a world quite different from the one we've known, a world where the rule of "law"* (man's laws) *supplants the rule of the "jungle"* (his/ **their demeaning reference to Nature, God's Natural law**), *a world in which nations* (seeing in duality and creating man made "borders" or the separation of humanity within "nations") *recognize the shared responsibility for freedom and justice."* (meaning "they" must provide "justice" because to them, nature is inherently unjust and "chaotic" *and* "they" are the only ones who can bestow freedom on little old "unaware" you) They do not recognize freedom as an inherent condition or inalienable right, but something *they must "furnish"*, which you know is a lie because we are anything but free, within the system. As well as justice, which they see as not in any way connected or associated with natural law that responds to the individual or the collective's state of mind.

This was not an isolated, unrepeated disclosure of their scheme. On 1/16/1991, George H.W. Bush speaking from the Oval Office said, "We have before us the opportunity to forge for ourselves and for future generations, a *new world order*, a world where the **rule of law, *not the law of the jungle***, governs the conduct of nations." It really doesn't get any more obvious **what** this is and **who** they are. You would not have had to alter a thing, to make this the perfect SNL, Saturday (our Dark Lord's Day) Night (you got this one) Live, comedy skit with a Bush impersonator dressed in the red stereotypical Devil's costume! Oh the madness of *George!* 756975

Eastbound and Down, They're going to do what they say can't be done. They've got a long way to go and a short time to get there, so just watch ol' Bandit run with a Phoenix on his hood, as they put the hammer down, and give it Hell. So says Smokey and the Bandit, a cute clue-filled comedy!

These Dark Elite attend an annual Satanic ritual directed at the suppression, destruction of Right Brain Unity, keeping those who **must be kept,** in Separation, called the Cremation of Care *ceremony* at the Bohemian Grove in Northern California. This juvenile production, an annual meeting of ***Rome's*** Leadership called the Bilderberg Group, lays out the specific global directives designed to suppress Right Brain development to keep **your dark** separate from you and working against you, like the Terminators of the unaware. This keeps you from becoming "whole", by not embracing "your dark" and remaining "insane". When people say they are suppressing females, the deeper reality is the feminine right brain of Unity awareness.

*The world is full of doughnuts, always trying to fill their **whole**, with what isn't.*

In the lower end of the spectrum, you will have no clue that you are simply getting what you need to experience, and this is why Satan creates the *three*-pronged structure of Caesar's jurisprudence to protect the "innocent" from the menacing "law of the jungle". Satan tells you, "I've got you covered". Insurance and Investment companies tell you you'll always be safe, stable and secure if you invest your *money* with them. You are coerced, because as I said: "All of Caesar's "jobs" are "Quid Pro Quo, Catch 22 traps", to pay (you must always pay for what you desire) into Social Security and get "Insurance" for every conceivable *mishap.* There *are no accidents,* but Satan tells you there *are* and that you are living in an uncertain world (made by a cruel God), so put your "nest eggs" in his basket, because random, chaotic accidents happen all the time that you don't deserve and just because you happened to be in the wrong place at the wrong time, you should not have to "pay" or deal with the unpleasant consequences of any of them. Satan will do everything he can to counter these consequences, like create his own *consequence* when divine consequence pays "his" shady business dealings a visit. Enter "Batman", the "Dark Knight" himself, who is doing what he believes to be right, at his level of awareness.

The Joker **is** the consequence of Satanic plans and clever schemes, to attempt to be "in control" of what Ego can never truly control. He's another face (smiley) of Shiva, that brings about the end of the various Metropolis camps on the banks of the "East" River. In the cyclical classes of the "even", all that is created and have a beginning must have a requisite end, and the next. . . "Springs" to Life.

"You have these rules, and you think they'll save you. The only sensible way to live in this world, is without rules." ~The Joker in "The Dark Knight"

As I get into *heavier material*, think about the Fantastic 4, the 4 inside the circle! Sue Storm the Divine Feminine at the very center of the circle and everything within it is an aspect of Her. Within the circle to Her Right is the ethereal Sun Johnny Storm, and to Her Left is Her material *other sun* Ben Grimm. From outside the circle comes Reed Richards and stretches to everything inside the circle, the Divine Masculine!

The *Gravity* of this Dark *Situation* is pretty *Heavy!*

Now that we've identified the most basic aspect of the Dark as being *the material,* let me bring this full circle to understand another very basic aspect of the universe that is still not fully understood by our best and *brightest* minds. Conventional physics tells us that the only force that can bend light is gravity and earlier I identified the "vaguely" understood phenomenon of *light as consciousness,* and why it's vague, and looking up its definition gets you, "the natural agent that stimulates sight and makes things visible". So then this "*Natural* Agent" allows you to **per***ceive,* and the prefix **per** means "thoroughly," "utterly," "very", and *ceive* comes from Latin meaning "get or receive". So light allows you to Utterly, Thoroughly receive *Sight".* Only with **Light** can you have **Sight**, and **L** is a Masculine shape with 2 straight lines, one shorter than the other like a cross and a sharp distinct angle, and **S** is a Feminine curved line. One cannot see without Light/consciousness, and the less there is, the less you see/know. The identity "Picture" of *the Photon and it's inescapable connection to consciousness, that the observer effect illuminates,* should be getting clearer. Now, the further you travel away from the cosmic "primary bodies" of stars, the less light you have and its effect of "seeing" and overall awareness of the observer.

This brings me to the other misunderstood phenomenon we call **Gravity** and something very similar occurs here. The further you travel away from a "material" Planet, the less the pulling effect of gravity, and the closer you get to it, the stronger its pull. Your "physical " world you see around you is a reflection of your thoughts and that of the collective. My friends, no wonder scientists have racked their collective brains defining gravity which is supremely connected to thought and consciousness and cannot be understood without the two included in the equation of "what" defines it.

The most accepted **theory** is from Einstein's General Theory of Relativity, which tells us that the force of gravity is a consequence of matter's mass "curving" spacetime, but Newton's original law of gravity seems to be more compatible with what I'm about to show you and our new view of a very biocentric universe, as are his 3 Laws of Motion. Newton said that atomic particles attract all others, so in other words, matter attracts itself, and that this force or "attraction" is directly proportional to its mass and inversely proportional to the square of the distance between them or as I said above, the greater the distance between you and the planet, the less the pulling effect of its gravity, and you on it, and the closer you get to it, the stronger its pull, and your pull, to each other.

Even though gravity is the weakest of the 4 fundamental forces of nature, "The dark's patience is infinite" and so too its pull, and yes, I'm going to connect the two! Just as darkness is ever present, but by introducing light, darkness is vanquished, I believe adding increased frequency has the same effect of vanquishing gravity. Of the various ways we are seductively pulled to the Dark, by our passions, addictions, and weakness, *Gravity is a manifestation of the larger galactic body's collective frequency. Gravity is a perspective and a gauge to the level of that pull and awareness that manifests itself as frequency here in waveform. The lower the frequency, the greater the force and the higher the frequency the weaker the force.* Gravity is another manifestation of essentially the same force that pulls you to an addiction or a pleasurable desire for gratification and unbridled passions constantly feed the flames. **Gravity is a state of mind**. Then again, isn't everything? As I quoted Max Planck earlier, *"everything that we regard as existing, postulates consciousness."*

What is the opposite of infinite "Space"? Why that would be finite Space, and "that which is not empty space", is matter and interestingly, the math and our Divine Mother *Numbers,* just might confirm it to those with eyes to see. In "God's Secret Formula" by Peter Plichta, a German Mathematician and Chemist, among his *many* other degrees, Dr. Plichta identifies the numeric sequence that "creates" infinite space without a boundary AND its polar opposite of finite space because it *does* have a boundary. The midpoint is the "**One** and Only" number **1** and above or to the right of 1 is 2, 3, 4, 5....> and the rest continuing infinitely with no end or border. This is the vastness of open space without perceivable matter, with no end to how big it can get. Now the other side of the equation is what lies below or to the Left of 1, and that IS space with boundaries, the atomic identity of matter, or the points in space, most notably planets, that we can perceive with our senses. So to the left or below 1 is simply 0, and as such "whole numbers" no longer come into play, so we flip them to their reciprocal equivalent fractions, so from the midpoint of **1** or 1/1, then below or to the left continues 1/2, 1/3, 1/4, 1/5...> never ending, infinitely heading to 0, **but *never*** reaching 0, so from 1 and above is *non-solid* Space with no borders, and below 1 is "Space WITH BORDERS" or *solid* atomic material, and it can never go beyond zero getting infinitely small. Now remember the funnel and see the pencil diagram I drew based on Dr. Plichta's sequential formula and how that "coming together" or condensing also creates what we perceive as gravity, and as you are pulled in reducing the boundaries around you, and the lower your frequency, the stronger your **restriction**, with the zero border you can never go beyond and that **is, of course,** the *material world,* you live within. This numeric structure, that I'll coin, the "Peter **Plichta** Principle" also definitively **proves** that "down here", we are *separating* and dividing up One and dealing in *separation* that perfectly illustrates the material polarity dead end within Satan's business structure known as, "The Peter Principle". Now you know why I coined the former! **We,** really can't make this up. Massive thanks to Dr. Plichta. Upon this rock!

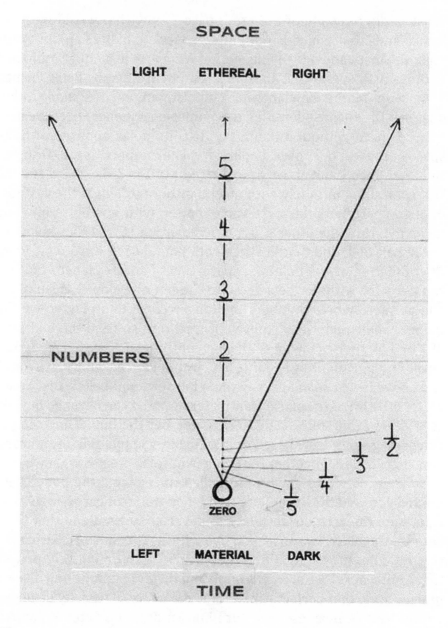

The monumental discovery of this numeric sequence is as tied to both ends of Spacetime as awareness is to gravity and a perfect fit for how I see the structure of the cosmic polarities. It reveals the duality mystery of the Dark "Rabbit Hole". The *numbers* tell us it never ends, for it is as deep as you personally need it to go until you "turn from it", but the mystical numerical paradox also tells us that it cannot go beyond 0, telling us that those who don't turn from it will *travel endlessly* in the **dead** end. As **Peter** Weyland in "Prometheus" discovered, "There's **no**thing..". It's dark, intoxicatingly **in**sidious and foreboding while being tragically poetic, bringing you back from your beautifully *insane* journey as the program tells you that it's *Time to go home,* as Peter and the Prodigal discovered. Most are falling away in my life, as...it is Time. And speaking of *Time.*

"You're fourteen thousand years old?

Fourteen thousand and four, to be precise. My mother was approaching her ninety-first millennium when she passed. You'd be just as amazed how quickly it goes.....In your world, people are used to fighting for resources, like oil, or minerals, or land. But when you have access to the vastness of space, you realize there's only one resource worth fighting over...even killing for...more time. Time is the single most precious commodity in the universe."

~ "Jupiter Ascending", Kalique "teaching" Jupiter

What we perceive as **Time**, is really a series of events, *occurrences,* within our frequency that we are meant to experience. Like gravity, I can also see how Time is tied to frequency, and how your frequency will dictate your *placement* within a spectrum and manifest your *present* reality. Our Dark Lord, our Saturnic Dark Star is our God of Time regulator within this amazing dynamic that allows us to experience, *individuality.* Increasing your frequency is, in essence, *speeding you up* within your spectrum, and the entire waveform universe. Conversely, the faster you travel the *slower your time* flows (longer life), meaning time must flow faster (shorter or "quicker" life) the slower you travel. Time always appears to be flowing "normally" from the perspective of the observer, as Kalique conveyed to Jupiter, and the Principle of Relativity tells us that all inertial reference frames are created equal, making none a preferred frame of reference. The speed of light, however, remains fixed and is the same speed from all perspectives being independent of the velocity of its source. Since all motion is relative from the perspective of the observer with none of them being *preferred*, and our best models of the universe tell us we are all in *some* form of motion, the only "true" measure of one's "motion" or *state* of being is, your own *frequency.*

Frequency is also the **true measure of Entropy** (Decay) **and** its opposite Extropy (Growth). While you can "seem" to stabilize or tread water, you have simply slowed entropy as there is only growth or decay in the natural world. Stabilizing your frequency is Entropy reduction. Increasing your frequency is Extropy and lowering your frequency is Entropy. Stabilizing your frequency would be like the rich man who tells Christ he already obeys all of the commandments, but upon hearing what he needs to do to get by the final Unity road-block of releasing his attachment to his material wealth, he sadly *walks away.* While he is not "running", he is still *walking away*, from the Light. It is again, as Tesla Rightly pointed out, all about **Frequency.** The Child, growing Up.

Water Break

Since water is the mid-state between solid and gas, and we must be "born again of water", think of the world ocean on the surface, and the water and Plasma within us as the midway point of 1. This may be our homeostasis between the solid and the gas to the endless aether of boundless space. As you lower your personal frequency, you become denser and heavier and your world, your borders, close in on you, further confining you to the ultimate point where you can't even move, in your own (remember from "Like a Prayer") personal *cell.* You could even perceive the intensity of gravity as the size of the cell you and the collective are a part of, and is inextricably linked to the frequency of that collective. When the "Prodigal Son" went off to (a *"distant land"*) basically lower his frequency, with riotous living, and he ended up with virtually nothing, as in limited options, and the more options you have in life, the more freedoms you have. Now he only had 1 option **to escape** the cell *below* **1 which we know is the**

Dream, and as the story relates, *"He came to his senses"* and exercised that option by turning away from the Satanic *dream* and returning to "The Father", in the *reality* of **1**.

I feel another mimic developing! So what does Satan do to the rest of us? Why, the Bullshitter you can't bullshit, gives you options, *lots* of options! Now he only deals in the cell below **1** and all *his* options are designed to *make you want to stay down*, **but** he's going to make that cell feel as expansive and *free as he can.* What gives you more options? More job opportunities! And what can get you these additional job opportunities? More *education* in the institutions of Ego that mimic the boundless universe that Ego has aptly named "Universities", so that you can be brainwashed to only see **below 1**, by paying your "tuition", which is **giving your in*tuition*,** to the Satanic system to eventually graduate! Then they can place the black Masonic mortar board square cap **above** your cranium to declare you as another "Carbon Copy" lawyer, or some other "profession" you choose, declaring you as one of *theirs.*

Certainly, there are times when a few of them, like Dr. Plichta and *"Professor Moriarty"*, discover they reside within the "Holodeck". God's growth is unique and blends seamlessly, whereas Satanic growth is "Carbon copy", one cookie cutter doctor and lawyer after another until it exceeds the environments capacity to sustain it. It mimics the effect a virus has on your body because they are **literally, One and the same.** Illness is an as below picture of man's devastating impact on nature when his mind is Satanic. It is identical to the pollution perspective that I wrote about in the previous chapter. When the environment you live in is polluted, it means the collective you are a part of is polluting their own bodies. Your body is your Temple, and we are cells in the Temple we see around us. If you don't pollute your body and that of the greater around you, it means you are increasing your frequency, you will very quickly find yourself in a reality that matches yours. If you want to free yourself from illness, then raise your frequency. It works.

*"Back where I come from we have universities...seats of great learning, where men go to become great thinkers, when they come out, they think deep thoughts...with no more brains than you have, but they have one thing you haven't got. . .**A diploma!** Therefore, by virtue of the authority vested in me...by the Universitatus Committeeatum E Pluribus Unum...I hereby confer upon you...the honorary degree of Th,D,* **'Th,D,'?** *Yeah, that's 'Doctor of Thinkology,'* ~"The Wizard of Oz", The Wizard's wise, and funny, words to the Scarecrow

As **Jordan Maxwell** says, "the true meaning of Graduation is *gradual indoctrination.*" And it **is**, as according to the definition, *"2. the action of dividing into degrees or other proportionate divisions on a grad-uated scale.",* is "dividing the **1**". Of course, it was the **2**nd definition! So it hones your ability to only see in separation and legality, while virtually erasing your ability to see unity and morality. And many times, even the Church confuses, legality with morality, and lives off the earnings of others.

It just "dawned" on me why Organized Religions enjoy "property tax exempt" status. **What is "Property Tax" in the first place?** The Native Americans always saw the concept of "owning land", as absurd and delusional as owning the air you breath and the water you drink. In Nature, animals "mark their territory" telling all others of their kind that "They claim it". This Natural Law **is** the only real law. This **is** how people and governments do it too and any perception of you actually "owning" it is an illusion, as history shows us that the bor-ders of empires and countries change, come, and go. If you "own" land here in the United States, **You** don't own the land, the govern-ment **controls** it so that You can "use" it, and you "pay" them with a yearly fee (property tax) for this and other services. If you stop pay-ing your property taxes, they take it from you and then "sell" it to someone else so they can use it and pay them their property *tax* rent. If another more powerful entity comes to take over the land you are on, and You and the collective (government) are not strong enough to stop them like the Europeans did to the Native Americans, then you are out on your ass on more land you can never "own". And they *may* use your deed for toilet paper so that it *could* be worth *something*. So the land wasn't *"stolen"* as I always hear, from the Native Americans either, because that implies that they owned it. *So now to my point about Religion's tax exemption.* This entire *belief* system of "land ownership" is in opposition to Natural Law. The fact that the Satanic system does not collect the rent from Organized Religions tells me they are part of the Satanic system, keeping you looking "out" for what can only be found **IN.** And I've already said it is a "teaching stepping stone", but *hanging* (an attachment) *on to it retards one's spiritual growth.*

Welcome to Planet Cookie, Monsters!

God represents life, and polarity must be expressed, so who are those, **who "don't want to die" and yet choose** *death*? The "Left Wing" inhabits and Champions the "Culture of Death", that embraces "right to die" and abortion "rights", and let the hypocrisy of abortion *rights* sink in for a second. Certainly, those who don't want to die to the material embrace the Satanic perspective in its many expressions, and let's put the real reason right out on the table. **They have yet to, or they don't want to, grow up.** Growing up involves **dis**comfort, being disciplined, exercising restraint, *becoming selfless*, developing compassion, empathy, and taking **Responsibility for their Lives and** *those they brought into this world while they are minor children.* *They* just want to have fun, experience comfort, pleasure, do what they want no matter who it impacts, and eat whatever tastes best even if others have to suffer or die for them to obtain it, but **this place** makes you accountable and distributes consequences. They don't want to be disciplined and live through the life's lessons, and if push comes to shove, they would rather ditch classes and leave by the path of least resistance, death, and it's usually the death of others that is their *path of choice*. They're all about the right to die, as long as it's not them, and the last thing they want to do is to put themselves out to take care of **their** children, while endlessly telling you how the state should care for yours. They masterfully disguise (a Satanic Talent) their insidious machinations to make you believe they care for a large segment of the population, that they have total disdain for...children.

"Audacity, Audacity, always Audacity"

At **Planned Parenthood**, *the Satanic headquarters of childfree families,* "It's all about the children", *that they would love to free you from.* Because they oppose the burden of parenthood, our **fiends** at Planned *Childlesshood* dispense hundreds of thousands of abortions, tens of thousands of vasectomies and hundreds of female sterilizations each and **every year** and have the supreme **audacity** to call themselves Planned **Parent**hood. They receive hundreds of thousands in government subsidies because again, they're on the same polar side. **Like I heard** from my robotic nemesis, "I did it for the Children", as this line comes right out of the Nazi playbook, because it is, a programmed line. They are one of the innumerable faces and images pulling you to the Dark. And what dark segment of the population do they most target? Since you read the *Like a Prayer* breakdown, I'm not going to *2ⁿᵈ guess* you, but you don't need more than One guess. Unless, of course, your destination is the cosmic colon, because they can't see shit. They only stir it.

Black Lives in Atomic Matter. . .*matter!*

You are also, no doubt, seeing "Black Lives Matter" everywhere you turn lately, *because* of the real and perceived (not **all** are *"real"*) persecution of black people stemming from their perceived "inferiority" as being "less intelligent or evolved" by some who see in separation and want *no connection to them,* so that their lives **matter less** than Whites or Asians, but we know we are simply "persecuting the Dark" as I pointed out in "Like a Prayer". Duality "racial" polarities are clashing, but here is *why* **Black Lives Matter** *is a pun, within a clue, wrapped in a metaphor.* We fell from a star, or the light and we are here in the **dark**. Creation, as I've said over and over again, is Our Divine Feminine Mother of the waveform atomic world of material **matter**, (and why "Madonna" is the Material Girl) that is outside of the light. This dynamic exists for the growth and the evolution of the God, so **our** (we are God growth) "material" lives *"**matter**"*, and have significance because of this. **This**, is the real **spiritual** message of "Black Lives Matter". The "dark" Satanic perspective lashes out against this "dark" and messy developmental state, because as I just pointed out, children don't like being disciplined on their way to becoming an adult, and they are doing whatever they can, to keep you from unifying with your **Dark** Feminine Right Brain of Unity. (this is why the woman who turns around smiling and hitting the golf ball in the Target Commercial and the woman who catches the falling Madonna "down here" in "Like a Prayer" are Black.)

Just as You would reject Carbon copy growth if you were God, you would want to perceive creation from every conceivable perspective and angle. God has created countless life forms from those we can conceive to those we can't conceive to occupy every environment including those where we thought that life could not possibly exist within. And they all have their beautifully designed strengths and weaknesses, talents, and struggles. Many will be born and will not like the hand they are dealt, and some will spend their energy, attempting to level, or even getting one up on, the playing field, in the game of light and dark squares. In other words, they will work to change the cards they are dealt by Nature, in the grand poker game. Time for some *Affirmative Action*, that starts out well-intentioned enough, like the 10 commandments, but before you know it, it is all turned **Up**side **down**.

"As they say, God didn't make all men equal. Mr. Colt did."

~ "Hidalgo", Frank Hopkins

If you despise Political Correctness, here's why

*The **dark left** brain satanic perspective will always want to assign the **labels of superiority or inferiority** to all of the Divine differences in all life forms **OR** they want you to believe there are **no differences** and* *that we are all boringly the same, even though every cell in your body perceives obvious differences, as they* **intimidate you** *into complimenting the beautiful clothing of a naked Emperor.* The masses' eyes tell them he is naked, but they are too weak, scared, oblivious, gullible or brainwashed to tell others he is not wearing clothes. They will have you believe that their **whitewash** anti-discrimination perspective is in opposition to those who want to assign superiority **but** it is just another Satanic perspective that attempts to "carbon copy" us all into some twilight zone perspective known as being **"Politically Correct"**. This is the satanic perspective that **needs to control.** They will try to force you to see the way they see it and behave the way they want you to behave, and of course, make laws to control what you can and can't say. They can't have you *offending...*other "adults". Remember, they're doing this for the *children*!

"Nobody is superior, nobody is *inferior*, but **nobody is equal** either. People are simply unique, incomparable. You are you, I am I." ~Osho

We are all individually different and there are very subtle to blatantly obvious and scientifically proven differences between the 2 sexes and the world's racial groups and every individual. The Satanic among all the **groups** of people want to **both,** assign *superiority and inferiority* because they see in separation **OR** claim that all of the *God-given Natural differences do not exist, (while complaining in contradictory fashion that what they say doesn't exist, isn't fair)* in an attempt to invalidate these differences (to artificially level the playing field) because they are from God and Satan opposes God! And if you dare bring up a difference you are branded a sexist or racist ("I can't say it on TV"! Spot on Deion).

The Satanic **inherently see** *the* **natural order of life as not fair** *and spend their life doing what they can to force fair, through* **Equality of Outcome laws,** *where fair simply can't be forced thereby* **ensuring entropy as an outcome.** *The artificial structure it creates* **decays** *because what created it and sustains it* **runs counter to natural law**. How "insane" would it appear if the Olympics instituted rules that ensured Equality of Outcome at all of their events, like the 100 Meter Dash? And yet that's what the "Left" does, and will always fail to "see" obvious common sense. For the reasons I already covered. It's a dirty job, but somebody has to do it!

We are moving into a new spectrum that blurs lower level physical differences and makes your own frequency, the condition that will dictate what group you resonate with as we transition to *more advanced* vessels. Those of us who will find the narrow gate, are currently working on their Ark, which is tantamount to being within their own self-made cocoon. They walked in, but will *fly* out, in completely transformed bodies. So it is the **individual** of **ANY** race, ethnicity or gender, that will **rise** in *"Position"*.

Viva Las Vegans, and their steps, to the Fountain of Youth

I think it's time to **up**date the *elevated* meaning of the word **Vegan**. We are taught that *Donald* Watson coined the word in 1944 (18=9) and created it from the word "vegetarian", but I believe both words have a *brighter* root. Keep in mind this is more than just a "diet" that completely rejects any food from an animal, but also compels the "Vegan" to spurn products derived from animals like fur or leather as well. This "explanation" may also shed some "light" as to why there is a certain amount of "hostility" between Vegans and those who use, consume or kill animals for food and other products. They are at the opposite ends of the "light" and "dark" spectrum, and like comparing good and evil, you are examining contrary perspectives, and at times they *commingle* like oil and water. This "extreme" beyond just a vegetarian, is taking a stand to align oneself with the "Light", as I alluded to in "Building Treasures", and told you how it increases your frequency. I said that eating "light" foods increases frequency as opposed to embracing the material by consuming flesh, which lowers frequency. So you are turning from the dark, which I told you is the *material*, and embracing the light, and here we have a clue within a clue that eating *light* takes you to the **Light,** and that "Left" is to the dark and that "Right" is to the Light, which is another rhyming clue and also why the *direction* "Right" is also another word for correct or "True".

In the Constellation of Lyra, the brightest Star is **Vega,** as this "Las *Vegan"* brings this full circle. Many astronomers believe it to be the most important Star in our sky after of course the **Sun**, and it is our "former" *North Star* during our Golden Age and will become so again! Now that you know the "real" identities of Stars and the meaning of North and the need to increase your frequency **if** you want to ascend to become a Star, you know that diet is one of the main components of frequency alteration and maintenance! You are, what you eat and in the "New Mexico Territory", which city is "up and to the right"? If you want to one day *be* as our "shining parent" and become a **Star**, in your *own* right, you now know what you have to do and why they call a person, who chooses this path a **"Vegan"**! In the same constellation, you will also find M57, lovingly gazing back at us in "approval", awaiting the Vegans grand entrance from the eye of Horus, and there just happens to be a Luxor Pyramid in *"Fabulous"* Las Vegas! The Wide Gate is through the 2 duality eyes looking out, and the Narrow gate is through the 1 internal pineal eye **looking in**. And also on the **West** side of the Strip, a couple of blocks *North*, we find another *newer smaller* Liberty Lady Lucifer bearing Her Light representing the *new* Star, displayed here, in "The Star of the Desert". It is hereby recommended by me, that we start pronouncing Vegan, the way it was meant to be pronounced like the star, "vāgə" as it is shown in the dictionary, as the Spanish pronounce it, the way we pronounce the city. This Las Vegan thinks "Vāgahn" sounds better anyway. Viva *the* Vegans Hermanos y Hermanas!

Why Cain's *vegan* offering was *dissed* by Yahweh!

The reason Cain is identified with plants for consumption, as opposed to livestock, is to clue you in that He is in the line of ascension to the Throne, and all of this, is for Him. Nowhere do you see that Cain did not give his best, but...before we examine Cain's predicament, keep this Unity perspective in mind, and later I will show you that he did what he did because of his spiritual age.

If something, **any**thing, steps in "your path" to prevent you from receiving something you desire, your first reaction, if you're like most, will be to fight or in some way "counter" this "obstacle", instead of asking why it has appeared, and going within for soul revealing intro-spection, to get to the core of why we didn't receive it or why desir-ing and obtaining it may not be "Right" for our overall development. We do this because we see in separation, not believing or thinking that the obstacle is there for our development and well being. Life IS that choreographed and controlled, like a very small child who is crawling to a pool only to have mom or dad put something in front of the child (but the child doesn't know where this blockage came from) to restrict its path, which of course upsets the child. And if we do, for a moment, go within, we seem to act like a defense attorney (the little horned guy on your left shoulder has a law degree, just sayin) with ourselves to "justify" why we should attempt to remove the "out-there" obstacle through *out there* physical means, because we simply "must" have it. But is what you are desiring simply for the "betterment" of you? Is it helping anyone else, or just you? Are you envious of what someone earned or simply received? And maybe it is simply there to be aware, in these terms, and to know your parents are monitoring you to see if you are grateful and humble knowing that anything you have, anything, was given to you out of Love, or to simply teach, patience, among many other lessons.

"The impediment to action advances action. What stands in the way becomes the way." ~Marcus Aurelius

*"Now Abel kept flocks, and Cain worked the soil. ³ In the course of time, Cain brought some of the fruits of the soil as an offering to the Lord. ⁴ And Abel also brought an offering—**fat** portions from some of the first-born of his flock. The Lord looked with favor on Abel and his offering, ⁵ but on Cain and his offering he did not look with favor. So Cain was very angry, and his face was downcast."* ⁶ Then the Lord said to Cain, "Why

*are you angry? Why is your face downcast? ⁷ If you do what is **right**, will you not be accepted? But **if you do not do what is right**, sin is crouching at your door; it desires to have you, but you must rule over it. ⁸ Now Cain said to his brother Abel, "Let's go out to the field." While they were in the field, Cain attacked his brother Abel and killed him."* ~Genesis 4

There you go! Straight from the mouth of The Lord! **Sin, is *simply* "Not Right"**

And didn't that definition come *right **Out of "Left" Field!*** That one gave me chills!

The definition of Sin, according to our Lord:

: Any thought or action that takes you ***away*** from the Light.

It is amazing what becomes visible when you can identify polarity. Now keep in mind *that the **"Lord"** that rejected his offering, may **not be the same Lord** that asked him why he was angry and had the remaining conversation,* but I'll address it like he was. This account is amazingly straightforward and if you've followed everything I've laid out to this point, this will *fall right* into place. Let's back up a tad to the first *week* of creation, to confirm the creation of man before the mention of Adam and Eve. "So God created man in His own image; in the image of God, male and female He created them. God said to them, Be fruitful and multiply;", on the 6ᵗʰ day. I believe that "Adamic" humans already populated the earth and that the "Adam and Eve" account simply specified the overall makeup and the "state of affairs" that **is** the human condition on this level, and that a line of spiritual *royalty* would spring from this level to develop into the next great King and Star for God growth that **is,** the very reason for the existence of creation. It is obvious who Eve represents, as I have already touched on in several places, and the Divine Feminine will give birth to a "Son of God". Now, Cain is the first-born like Thor, and he worked the soil producing plants and fruit while his younger brother produced meat.

As I just laid out examining the overall meaning of Vegan, it is obvious who the two brothers represented and which one would eventually ascend to the Throne, as Odin told his Sons.

"Only one of you can ascend to the throne. But both of you, were born to be kings." —Odin, speaking to *Thor* and Loki.

Continuing, we are told that the two brothers brought offerings to the Lord of what they had produced and that the Lord was pleased with Abel's offering but He was not pleased with what Cain offered. Sounds like Cain experienced a rather large *obstacle or impediment* and was none too happy that his Lord was pleased with Abel, but not with him. The Lord, being the Lord, already knew why Cain was angry and downcast, but asked him anyway, like a parent would to his child. He told him, and this confirms everything that I told you about the *real* below the surface meanings of Right and Left, *"If you do what is **right**, will you not be accepted?",* meaning that if your thoughts and actions are to the light, increasing your frequency, won't you find acceptance (good consequences from doing and giving your best) rather than rejection? And he added that if he does **not** do what is right, then **sin** is always crouching at his door, as the temptations never stop, ever ready to pull you down and if you are not disciplined in your Divine Marriage with your Elect Lady in Red. If you do not lead Up, then your dark, will lead you down. A good Father, who knows his son well, knows when he does not do his best or provide him with his best work.

This paragraph is for a select few. How the Lord spoke to Cain, is how I would speak to my children. So while we are not outwardly told that Cain did not give his best, we can certainly conclude from the suggestions from The Lord, that **there was SOMETHING**, that made the Lord want Cain to change the path he was on, and his words to him confirm it to me. This is **SO,** so much deeper than Cain killing his brother because Abel won the Blue Ribbon for his bacon at the Smith County Fair. Their offerings are symbolic of a polarity dynamic that I am all too familiar with. Trust me, Cain was wronged from the perspective of his Ego, at this lower level, in a reality that he is still too young to recognize as a "sleepy" spiritual school. While revenge is Karma to those on the receiving end, it is a deep dark rabbit hole for those who give it. For the aware, Karma is for God to dispense. When you see in separation, that option consumes you, but when the water calms, and you see unity, it allows you to see the real message of taking stock of the path that you are on, and maybe, just maybe, turning **Right**. And in the end, you find out that Abel suffered a **heart** attack from too much consuming of the Fat Portions from the *first born*. (continuing)

We already know that Eden was placed *eastward,* so it is in the perspective of Left Separation and as a result, Cain did not internalize the Lord's dissatisfaction and placed the blame **outside** of himself and projected his dark. Cain was *"Abel"*, to create an "out there excuse" (sorry, the opening was there). He "removed" the *perceived obstacle,* as Thor was doing, against the will of his Father, looking to exterminate the *monstrous* life forms (the Jotuns) that he, with his childlike understanding, believed served no "useful" purpose, and interfered with his coronation. So because Cain dramatically lowered his frequency, he placed himself *further East* of Eden. (which is precisely what he needed anyway) You might not appreciate or know why everything exists, but God does not make mistakes here in this perfectly choreographed school. The genetically modifying fools at Monsanto are no exception, headed up by their own version of Dr. Moreau, as they will secure themselves eternal positions that need to be filled in the cosmic colon, and what a segue for my next topic.

"The road to Hell is paved with good intentions!"

"A lot of people don't want the world to be changed, but we shouldn't be too upset, but just have to go on with our business. We want to make the world better. There are people who will say, Well, we're playing God. You know, I have a straightforward answer, If we don't play God, who will?" ~Jim Watson, Molecular Biologist and DNA pioneer who is a co-discoverer of the structure of DNA

I guess the obvious answer *isn't obvious,* to many, as most here, confuse IQ for wisdom and no better example can be given than this. What Jim fails to see, is that the plant is already perfect in the grand scheme of pointing him, to be a better him, but he's not focused on him being a better *man*, but attempting to make the School fit him, and that, is what we know as "Camelot". Trying to fix "out there", when it is simply trying to tell you, the student, (because that IS its job) what you need to fix, within you. The student's house of cards "Camelot", must always fall, because that, is another job of the school that puts Ego, in its place. One, in this next exchange from "Kingdom of Heaven", is trying to keep Camelot from falling.

Tiberius: "What did your father tell you of your... obligations?

Balian: That I was to be a good knight.

Tiberius: I pray the world...and Jerusalem...can accommodate such a rarity...as a perfect knight."

One would only **genetically modify**, if they believed that **Nature did not get it right.**

Let's *clarify* **the difference between God and god**, as this exchange between Odin and his Dark adopted son Loki, clears it up nicely I think, and on the periphery, displays the larger *as above* marriage that must also be **led,** by the Light Man of the House, just as we must with our bodies. This is why Odin is always "maintaining order", to always keep, or re-establish, his control over the larger body he calls, The 9 Realms. And of course, Loki represents the "intelligence" of the body wanting to control as he does represent the adversarial Dark.

Loki: I went down to Midgard to rule the people of Earth as a benevolent God, just like you.

Odin: We are not Gods. We're born, we live, we die, just as humans do.

Loki: Give or take five thousand years.

Odin: All this because Loki desires a throne...

Loki: It is my birthright!

Odin: *Your birthright was to DIE!* As a child, cast out on a frozen rock. If I had not taken you in, you would not be here now, to hate me. Frigga is the only reason you're still alive, and you will never see her again. You'll spend the rest of your days in the dungeons.

Loki: And what of Thor? You'll make that witless oaf King while I rot in chains?

Odin: Thor must strive to undo the damage you have done. *He will bring order* to the Nine Realms, and then, yes, he will be King. (Meaning the brain will once again establish its dominance over the body.)

So, according to Odin, if you are born into waveform creation to live a temporary (no matter how long, even if it is millions of years) life, then you are, by definition, not God. Now, you may seem like one to lower levels, and if they refer to you as one, then you would be a lowercase version, god. "You will have no other gods, before me." There is only One God who is growing, and when one like Odin, ascends to never have to incarnate to a waveform life here again, then he has added to become *more* of The Father of Light (like He has, for He has ascended), but there are many gods, still here in a temporary life, like Thor or Loki.

Planet of the, Apes? (part of 2018 revision)

I was watching "War for the Planet of the Apes" and after hearing this exchange between, "The Colonel" and "Caesar", I knew I had just heard a monumental clue. Now this is part of a much larger exchange with more telling clues of why you don't succumb to the hate that

seeing in separation fosters, from being attacked, betrayed or persecuted by the AI Dark and believing that these illusory thoughts and
messages, that appear as lifeforms, are *real*, in and of themselves. The
Dark is there to forge the steel, but it can kill you if you allow it to
consume you, and it always whispers to you, being a part of us. If
Caesar kills "The Colonel", then the Dark wins by keeping Caesar and
those within his Ark, from reaching his Promised Land. I suggest you
get the movie and see the entire exchange, but here is the segment
that ultimately told me **who** the Apes represented, who The Colonel
represents, **where** the Apes found refuge, and how those who turn
from the Dark, no longer resonate with those firmly controlled by
the Dark.

The Colonel: *"You're much stronger than we are. And you're smart as
hell. No matter what you say, you'd eventually replace us, that's the law
of Nature.* ***The irony is, we created you. We tried to defy Nature,
bend it to our will. And Nature's been punishing us for our arro-
gance ever since.*** *Testing us. Even now. Ten months ago, we sent out
recon units to look for your base. They found nothing.* ***My own son***
was a soldier with one of the groups. ***One day he suddenly stopped
speaking. He became...primitive. Like an animal.*** *They contacted
me, said they thought he lost his mind, that the war was too much for
him.* ***But then the man caring for him stopped speaking too.*** *Their
medic had a theory, before he stopped speaking. That the virus that
almost wiped us out -- the virus every human survivor still carries - had
suddenly changed... Mutated.*

I've recently wondered what The Planet of the Apes series meant,
and I now see it may have the biggest hidden message in "filmdom"
with Avatar, and they tie into one another, and several others. "The
Colonel" in both films, represents the same basic *character*. Jake Sully
was originally aligned with The Colonel, as was The Colonel's son in
Planet of the Apes, but once they began to understand the situation,
and change their perspective as their awareness and frequency rose,
they no longer *spoke the same language.* They no longer resonated,

with those headed in the opposite polarity direction, and I have covered who you will never agree with here.

Jake and the Colonel's son now sympathized and resonated with the Natural *primitive* "people" that the Satanic absolutely hate. (What do the "primitive" not have, that the Satanic *need* to be "as God"?) **They associate them with animals and want no association with what they see as stupid, *"lower evolved* apes",** and now that Jake and the others speak and resonate with them, it is a perspective that cannot be understood at all by them and this now makes them, **the enemy.** This is the perfect place to put the finishing touch on the Satanic view of the Dark from which they spring. This and the way Agent Smith spoke to the now captured Morpheus, about his disgust for humanity, which describes the Satanic Elites view of those they see themselves as superior to. It is the real reason "the **N** word" is so highly offensive, to black people and the fact that it is a slang derivative of negro, which is Spanish for black, and we again see it clearly that we are persecuting the Dark. No matter who or what you are, we are all connected. The approaching royal wedding is an *as below* mimic of embracing our Dark as we transition to the New Age. Harry, is white and male and in a royal line from the east, marrying a commoner woman who has black in her, from the west "new world".

Alright, here goes! The Flying **Monkeys** in Oz fly in the higher elevations of the **Blue** sky and Blue is the higher frequency. "Parker", in Avatar, refers to the "Na'vi" as the **Blue Monkeys** that want *nothing* (and them *wanting nothing* the dark can give them, manifests the "floating mountains" and lighter gravity) from us because all we offer is the Satanic separation illusions as we always search for what can never be *realized* because it deals in the waveform illusion and as such can never be real or obtained and why what they seek is called *unobtainium.*

I only suspected it before, as you read from the previous chapter, but now in this 2018 revision, you can take this to the bank, that **Jupiter (Odin)** has always, been our **Sun. In "Jupiter Ascending",** Jupiter finds out she is the rightful owner of Earth, and the hidden message here is that Earth is, in fact, a moon of Jupiter. **In Avatar,** Pandora revolves around a planet that looks just like Jupiter, because *They* are **telling you** that *it is* **Jupiter,** and I believe Pandora is 5D Earth. **In Thor Ragnarok,** we are shown Odin transitioning to pure light (and he does it here in **his** tree), and we are past Jupiter being born of Virgin in September of 2017 as prophesied in Revelation 12:1&2, and this is about the time I remember seeing the "Sun" as pure white. This is why growing up we all saw a yellow-orange Sun, because Jupiter was still king and as such, was still the "Son" (hence why we knew it, as the Sun) of Sirius. Now that He ascended to become a full-fledged Star as "The Father", his light is now white, like Sirius, the "true" hidden message of the movie Jupiter Ascending and the title says it all. In his book "Worlds in Collision", published in 1950, Immanuel Velikovsky proposed that Venus was expelled from Jupiter as a comet-like object, to eventually settle into its present-day orbit between Mercury and Earth. This would make **far more sense** if we are satellite planets of Jupiter.

Odin is done incarnating and his transition from King to Star spells the end of Asgard, the *physical,* waveform manifestation of him as King and so is destroyed. As Odin said, "Asgard is not a place, it's a people". Thor, the new Single eyed King, will now create his own manifestation of "Asgard", with those people who are now in His Ark, and this *realm will become the Kingdom for the next great King.* I said that seeing in separation **is** the dream, and Jake says, now that he is resonating with the Na'vi and his Blue Lady Neytiri, that, "*Everything is backwards now, like out there is the true world and in here is the dream.*" "*Sooner or later, you have to wake up*" as "*One life ends... Another begins".* ~Avatar (9) 2009 (11)

"Are we there yet? Yeah, we're there **Sunshine***"*

The genetically modified Apes represent the Sasquatch.

The Wookiees of Star Wars, are symbolic of Sasquatch.

Pandora is, in fact, 5D Earth and that WAS Jupiter they orbit.

The *Earthlings* in Avatar represented the Anunnaki (the *Sky People*) mining and occupation here, and the Na'vi, the human-oid hominids, that they genetically tampered with represent the Sasquatch type, man-ape, hominids reported all over the world, as we hear from Jake, "They're grown from Human DNA mixed with the DNA of the Natives".

"That's called taking the initiative *son*. I wish I had *10 more*, like you! Sully, just find out what the *Blue Monkeys* want!"

Fortunately, the Apes escaped the confinement and made it to Nevada, but as time goes by, *Nevada* is becoming more *visible*. Now what do I mean by this "state", I am calling "Nevada" and what the hell does *more visible* mean? Well, certainly I didn't mean the Apes jumped on *I-80*. As I was watching the latest "War for the Planet of the Apes", The above quote grabbed me and I knew it was truth and a larger historical message. As I continued watching, I knew that they were up in Northern California and I knew what Nevada's forested "sky islands" look like above the surrounding deserts. They knew they had to flee the humans who were trying to exterminate them. They knew that getting to a place that humans didn't inhabit was their best chance at survival. They traveled far and their new home reminded me of Nevada, and that is what it was meant to communi-cate, because Nevada means "Snow Capped". Their new home was in the mountains and that is why the Native Americans of the west call Sasquatch, "The Boss of the Mountains". But the real meaning of the clues told me that, it wasn't spatially far but frequency far, and not so much "higher elevation", as it meant that their new refuge was a higher frequency reality that the humans did not occupy (and why the gods lived on Mt. Olympus). The **Blue Monkeys** (apes) *went UP,* and simply vanished from lower frequency eyes. This is why many firmly believe they are interdimensional, for various reasons, and this is how they escaped the flood and ancient world wars because, like Noah, they built their Ark.

After watching the movie, I looked down at the DVD cover of the film and the picture was "Caesar" with snow coming down around him and it was like lightning hit me and I instantly knew it was symbolic of Bigfoot. All of the other clues from the two movies started to flood into my mind making sense now with this new piece to the puzzle, and I was overwhelmed at the *real* hidden message of the two movies, which crystallized even more messages from Thor Ragnarok and Jupiter Ascending. Caesar was in his own personal hell with snow, like *someone else* I know. The "Spot" they arrived to "escape" the human conflict, took me to a crossroad with my own hatred as I watched *this scene* play out, already knowing Maurice bravely said the unspeakable, by telling Caesar that he had turned into Koba. I had 2 very close to me tell me something "similar". Your very best friends risk much by telling you what you don't want, but need, to hear and they are far more than best friends. Hatred of what? What "Caesar" found himself hating, is what I, had been hating in my Nemesis, what consumed and killed Koba.

THE COLONEL: So emotional! I can see how conflicted you are. You're confused in your purpose. You're angry at me because of something I did that was an act of war. But you're taking this all much too personally.

Venturing closer to Caesar, seemingly unconcerned for his safety, now, eye to eye...Caesar burns,

*THE COLONEL: What do you think my men would've done to **your apes**, if you had killed me? Or is killing me more important?*

~"War for the Planet of the Apes"

You see, The **Dark**, is programmed **Artificial Intelligence**, and it simply has a *job to do*. That strange *out of place* smile all those years was telling me this. It is programmed to take everything from those (Prodigals) who move away from The Father, so that Like the Prodigal Son, you end up with nothing, in the gutter, and it is, an **act of war**. *You now have nothing, when you thought, you had something, but that* *something was never more than a* **thought** *holding you down, or better yet* **it** *kept you from flowing.* That is *one of the most important concepts in the entire book.* The IT (92), your car, house or *occupation* are all waveform projections or thoughts that you desire to *keep.* That's right Neo, the chair is in your mind, as the passage warning us not to accumulate earthly becomes apparent. Odin told us that Asgard is not a place (like the chair), but where *our* people stand, with *that,* being the *eternal realm.*

This is why Lucy is betrayed by her *boy*friend, to literally force her to lower depths in the dream (Christ going to Hades, which seems like being *Damned*) to compel her to sever her ties to this level. It is a *no win* predicament, because You *chose* (and wallowed in) it, as Lucy flashes back to *riotous living* after he asks her if she trusts him. The uneasy look then *smirk,* and then you're flooded with all of the clues that point you to understanding **why** you are at this *no win* crossroad. It's because winning here, is staying here, while the *Real You of Soul,* at the Ironing Board, needs you to move on from a life consumed with lower frequency *Having,* so you can **flow** to continue to **grow.** Lucy tells us, *"We humans are more concerned with having than with being".* Losing here in this context, is not losing, but Liberating! "I'll be Damned".... "If You get Lucky". Thanks Doc!

That is why He comes with a sword to sever you from your childish perspective, and to sort us by our frequency. This is a level, and you can't stay there forever, as "The Byrds" tell us (my Raven), there is a need for a Season that brings conflict to usher change. You can't ascend, expand, or flow with *attachments* here, which are lower frequency gravitational thoughts (remember 15% we purportedly only access in our brain capacity) anchoring you down. (like a child stuck on daydreaming) The young Cain, being *young* and still needing the development, killed his "*Colonel* Abel", but Christ knows that Judas simply had a job to do (and He knows that avoiding it or killing him, puts Him, back a square one), and is now ready to **ascend.** *God, The Self, The Cosmos, are constantly growing and expanding up, and when you stop, because you are attached, you stagnate.* So, as soon as Caesar turned his *selfish hate thoughts (even though in the dream, they are valid)*, to *"selfless save his **people** thoughts"*, and releasing his hate, they were immediately on their way, **Up!** This dynamic **is**, essentially, the **Rapture**.

This is literally that seminal moment steeped in pain, when you transition, to free yourself. As Lucy explains to Prof. Norman, *"...what you wrote is true. Once the brain reaches 20%, it opens up and expands the rest. There are no more obstacles. They fall away like dominoes. I'm colonizing my own brain."* That is it, in our Enterprise. Space exploration is colonizing of the *"unactivated neurons"* (still lifeless planets) of the "as above" brain (the universe). And *we,* the "so below" aspects, are the internal doing the very same thing, colonizing our neurons (planets) in our brains. Once the dominoes fall (and that hurts), the expansion is like a rocket ship from what **was stagnating** (Her hitting the golf ball).

"..Your Brother was dead, and is alive again.." ~Luke 15:32 (11)

This is why Jake (he's Jacob, page 365, as is Jack from Oblivion) refers to his *former **race*** as "**Aliens** returning to their dying world", and his brother was the *doubting Thomas* (page 82, and the bottom of 113. Jăk is Jăk, and *Jack* is a short form for *John*) that had to *die* (who He used to be). The *aliens* are now permanently headed to occupy the dense cosmic colon regions (the wide gate), as their frequency will not allow them access to 5D Earth/Pandora, and they will forever exist in a lower frequency / reality. The humans that "increased their frequency", found the Narrow Gate path to *The Kingdom of Heaven* as, "Only a few were chosen to stay." There are no separate *out-there* ET aliens, all are interdimensional *(Jack climbing the beanstalk)* within One organism, *The Self.*

Looks like I opened Up Pandora's Box.

We are now seeing far more of these bipedal man-ape primates like Yeti or Sasquatch all over the world, and the reason we are seeing them more often now, is because we are now fully in the Aquarian Age and the world's frequency is increasing to now allow us to view them, (and you can also see it in Thor's explanation of *The Convergence*, to Jane) and the reason for all of the world's conflicts, stem from the lower frequency people who are not able to adjust and are being fazed out, as *Aliens,* staying with their old 3D world that is crumbling and dying. Remember Charlton Heston, in the original, seeing what was left of the Statue of Liberty on the beach?

According to "Phys.org", "A team of researchers led by Melba Ketchum of DNA Diagnostics, claims to have succeeded in sequencing the genome of Bigfoot". Of course, she will be attacked, but the name that Dr. Ketchum used to register them in Zoo Bank, is **Homo Sapiens Cognatus**. I now have to conclude from the line in the movie, that the world's various bipedal man-ape primates, like Yeti, are the product of *some* genetic modification thousands (Dr. Ketchum points to about 15,000) of years ago. As you know, there is hard evidence that points to very advanced ancient civilizations that spanned the globe. When a society becomes Satanic, natural law destroys them, like "Krypton", which may have been **far closer** than we think. I now believe that the National Parks and Forests were created to not only preserve nature, but to ensure that our *ascended* Brothers and Sisters who are able to live completely in harmony with nature, would have a home not taken over by a cancerous perspective that always destroys nature looking to obtain unobtainium, like doughnuts in search of holes.

And the 7 and a half (7.5) foot Chewbacca is at the side of Han Solo fighting the Satanic forces and he is a Wookiee, and here is what George Lucas tells us about Wookiees:

"They possess enormous strength; Solo states that a Wookiee can pull a man's arms out of his sockets if angered or slighted, and in books and comics no humanoid species is shown to equal a Wookiee in pure strength. Wookiees have a keen sense of smell, are fully covered with a thick coat of hair, have good hand–eye coordination, and are shown to be excellent marksmen. Wookiees have been shown in many diverse

environments, never wearing any protective clothing or showing any signs of discomfort." And *"They live in villages among the giant wroshyr trees."* They live in. . .WTF? Yes, people, he said they live in Wroshyr Tree Forests!

And from Wikipedia, *"According to an interview with creator George Lucas, the inspiration for the Wookiee was Lucas' dog"!* Son of a..!!?? *Oh my God*, like Jane says it in Thor, this book is filled with 101 black and white dog references. Lucas is also telling those who can hear him, that Sasquatch are extremely intelligent. We are also inundated with movies featuring giant gorillas that reign supreme *in Nature,* as I remember the line, "Kong is God to them". These new messages definitely contribute to my former conclusion that the "flying monkeys" where a mocking representation of the fallen Angels. I know that the "Anunnaki", *Elohim* or Atlanteans genetically tampered with *what was here,* to create a being that would be physically dominant to anything that nature could throw at it, and yet have the awareness and intelligence of a "Human", so that they could, like the Avatars, take on their bodies, or at least to be able to control them. Their *creation,* however, would not submit to their control. When you need nothing, you cannot *be bought.* So when they couldn't become them or control them, it was in their nature to *try* to **Destroy them.**

You see, the **two extremes**, the **Satanic Anunnaki and the "Beasts of Nature"** are within us. Jake and his twin are the same man, and what needed to die to this world (his twin), was his "indoctrinated" (Grace tells us he was, a *Doctor*) developed Left Brain of Separation doubting twin "Thomas" (this **was** his brother's name), so that the Heart based Christ within a more physically "adept version" of him, a Marine, could be developed and brought out without being blocked by the brainwashing of separation. The Na'vi could sense this, as he was the first "warrior" among the **sleepers** (how many clues do we need that Adam never "woke up") so he needed to be "developed", to become like them, so that his "insanity" (remember *not whole*) could be cured. And through this, he learned to **Love** the Forest, Nature, the (*Blue Monkeys*) Na'vi, and his own internal Dark Divine Feminine

Neytiri. He found himself and after that He, like the Na'vi, *could not be bought*, to return to the dream of the Satanic structure, with the offer of getting his legs back. He then earned the higher frequency **permanent** physical upgrade, by becoming Toruk Makto. His frequency earned him a spot in 5D, as the "Aliens" returned to their 3D world that was/is, dying!

And remember, Jake can't get to his new Na'vi 5D body "out there". He must go within, to get to this *new reality*. (and why NASA lies to those not ready, making you think you can get to space "out-there". You can only escape the cell of earth and gravity by going within) Grace telling him to "let your mind go blank", and while she was being facetious, that *cutting joke* of, "That shouldn't be hard for you.", is a clue that **he will** have an easier time, than the "Phd's" who have spent years getting "indoctrinated", letting go of his mind brainwashed in separation.

Strip Mine, Home Tree, and Tree of Souls...Found?

I said that Pandora is 5D earth so let me nail down the exact location of Home Tree and the Tree of Souls, and if you think that I'm not done speaking of the Future 11 under construction in the New Mexico Territory, you'd be *Right!* The only 2 states I feel "home" in, with NM not being far *behind*.

According to Jake, they had to travel, "To the horse clans of the plain... To the Ikran people of the **eastern** (huge inserted clue) sea.", so we know they aren't East or Midwest, so let's go west young man. We saw in the film that they live in a heavily forested area that was being destroyed by immense mining machinery excavating huge strip mined valleys and we know there was a large flowing river because Jake had to jump into it to escape from the Thanator. Since I already identified "Nevada" as the new Sanctuary of the Apes, it makes me look at the other A to Z *state* (brain hemisphere) that the "Future 11" is being created within, and fortuitously enough, Phoenix just happens to be there.

The Kaibab Plateau is heavily forested (there's 1), the Grand Canyon cuts through it (there's 2), and the Colorado River flows through it (there's 3). Now, it has been widely speculated that the Grand Canyon's features look curiously artificial and *fabricated* (like a strip mine) by forces other than just nature's water and wind erosion, and the movie certainly made it look like the mining machines were creating Grand Canyon type scares in the landscape. I think we found the site of the mining on Pandora, which is pretty close, *by helicopter*, to Home Tree, which may have been the San Francisco Peaks (named in 1629 by Franciscan Friars), which rises up like a huge stump on the Coconino Plateau. There is some "scarring" (from what is left of Home Tree) within the interior as well, that we are told is from an ancient eruption. The Navajo consider them to be the most sacred in all the west, and the Hopi believe the Kachina spirits live there and the tallest peak Mt. Hometree, I mean Humphrey, sounds curiously similar.

So now let's find the location of The Tree of Souls that we know is not far away and in the movie, they identify massive amounts of energy emitting from the area around the Tree of Souls that they call, *The Flux Vortex*. Well, I've already talked about this mystical of place, where I watched the History Channel segment that changed my life in 2005, and where the outline to this book came to me as I slept. The energy there is unmistakable, and when you meet another Scott Smith in the month of 7, who also comes from Maryland, with two first names that begin with S, born of a woman with Patricia and Smith in her name, at the same resort the outline of this book came to me, then you know it's the Right Place. **Sedona** is world famous for its Vortices' and natural beauty. I'll pinpoint the Location of the Tree of Souls, to **Boynton Canyon,** right next to Oak Creek Canyon, for several paranormal reasons, that you can look into if you choose to.

Another clue that "speaks to me" as to their Southwest location, is what appears to be turquoise and red coral jewelry that I see many of the Na'vi wearing. I enjoy the videos of a Sasquatch researcher by the name of M.K. Davis, and he has made some amazing discoveries, and one of them *ties* to the braided hair of the Na'vi in "Avatar". He discovered what appears to be a braid on the female from the Patterson video, along with braid cuffs and hair ties on another "male" from Siberia who appears to have a long flowing beard. The evidence he presents is compelling and if true, presents staggering implications as to the very "Avatar" like reality of these amazing intelligent, completely independent *beings*. Like the Na'vi in the film, their real counterparts here are completely independent and need no government or technology to survive, and the last thing the government wants to do is acknowledge anything close to human walking around within our borders living completely free from their controls. Christ tells us to watch for the buds to form on the trees to know that Spring is near. More *Light brings Buds*, so you know that the winter of separation is drawing to a close, as we prodigals struggle to *hit* the Target. A Bud Light, just might hit the spot!

They're not gonna make a deal. For a light beer?

Bud Light Super Bowl 2014 Commercial

The commercial opens up in what appears to be a restaurant (a "medium to meet"), with a man sitting at a table clearly "looking or waiting for something". You see in this,"[hidden cameras]", in the opening frame meaning that He, the man, is being watched by others who, "orchestrates and knows what he doesn't", a higher power that "directs" from a hidden place. Now, look at the coloring and notice that it is pretty color free, like the beginning of the Target Commercial and the Wizard of Oz in *Kansas*. It is primarily black, white and different shades of grey, and if you see a color that "sticks out", it is a bit of red, like in the EXIT sign, and then the **blue** on the label of the Bud **Light** bottle.

Not only is this a message of polarity, but what "She" is offering him, while he must fall in frequency for a time, is his only opportunity to advance, evolve and ascend from where he is currently at, which is why the label has the color of the higher frequency blue attached to it. Now, who does She and what does the bottle of beer represent? Before we get to that, let's identify where they are at. It is clearly, *not here*. You can think of it as Kansas or Eden before the Fall, but clearly, a realm beyond and *above* this place, as I'll show you later. Remember, "The Fall" was meant to happen for the Growth of The Self (God).

The man is clearly "anticipating", waiting for "something", so when the woman walks up to his table and introduces herself, he is very open and happy that she has come to join him. As they shake hands, their hands are enveloped in light, again meaning that all of this is Divinely Choreographed by "Her" the manifest God, and "Him", the man behind the curtain, the unmanifest God. Now the woman identified as Kelly, is essentially Lucifer and he represents Soul. While he doesn't know what will happen, he clearly knows that he needs whatever it is, to progress. Ian's last name also indicates he is a "senior", ready to complete his "final exams" to graduate to the next level. Rap(p)oport or Rapa Porto (Hebrew: טרופפר) is a family name from an Italian (Jewish) Kohenitic pedigree.

After she gives him the proposition and waits for his decision, an announcer tells you that everyone around him is an actor, except Ian and them showing you that he "isn't", colored in blue, confirms that he is in this "Spiritual line" of Ascension. He is a Thomas, but what it really means here, is that Ian is the only *Real person or identity*. Everything is occurring within him, and he is unaware of this at this time, which is why the announcer says, *"He has no idea".* What she is offering him is seductive, like the wishes in Bedazzled that are offered to Elliot who has "desires" and SO wants to be liked. He wants admiring friends, and the word "Bud" is short for buddy or pal, as a kind of superficial companion, so that you are not "alone". Most are sad, when they are alone.

The Light, not lite, she is offering him, is the forbidden fruit that will give him what he desires. He accepts and off they go to a large red, the lower frequency color of the dark material, vessel full of attractive females who "like" him, and as he enters, sits in the seat displaying a mirror 9-11 image (IX-XI) with his forbidden fruit waiting and all are partaking of the forbidden fruit. She hands him off to his partner, who is "his spirit", or Her daughter. The sexual implications and falling into carnal desires/pleasures are obvious, and he is now "popular". Also present is a new age musician that is expanding the boundaries of performing with a last name of Watts (electricity). This is me in Vegas before my "fall".

He is now fully participating in the developmental choreographed "reality" and the red vessel of creation takes him to NY, the Big, forbidden fruit, Apple (for his fall to be tested) and in the colorless nighttime skyline the only 2 colors that stand out are red and blue. At 11:37 pm, and pm is 74, they pull up to a deserted, dark, "shady" blocked off area, being now fully in the dark away from his star, so that he can get dressed into his new "identity" as things are about to change for him, as he will start to change with the Age.

Minka's: "I hope I don't mess it up.", when all she needs to do is introduce herself and get him a blazer is telling. And he accepts that she is real gushing over her, like Neo looking too hard at the woman in the red dress who isn't real, but is a test. Also, the extremely pale slim guy who is just "there", looks like a mannequin wearing a wig. And then a man behind the scene telling her she was awesome when all she did was introduce herself, get the coat, and say she wished she could join them too, that ANYONE could pull off. This is telling you that the 2 of them are AI robots and fooled him into believing they were humans, and the "good job", was for that. The blazer identifies him as one of 11 prodigals who has to go through tough tests to get to the next level. His "partying" days are over.

Next stop, now that he has his Identity, is to change realities by changing frequency, represented by the elevator. Time to go to deeper realms of Duality and they get there at 11:54 (9-11) The first level they come to, they find Don Cheadle, who was one of "Ocean's 11". OC is 63=9-11. (even Col. Quaritch in Avatar wants his 11, a mock) Don has the same jacket as Ian confirming he is one of the chosen 11, with

"Tess" (Mary Magdalene) making it 12. He also brings along a Llama, the Incan Prince in "The Emperor's New Groove", is turned into a Llama. The Llamas name is also Lilly and Lillith is a Divine Feminine goddess. In Incan Mythology "Urcuchillay" a god from the constellation of Lyra, like Vega, was in the form of a Llama who watched over their Livestock. *I'll have more about the introduction of a Llama at the end of this breakdown.*

After changing frequencies, she leads him to a room to meet their body, the Terminator himself, which has its own AI awareness of Ego. I've pointed out that our thoughts stem from 2 polarity sources. Our positive, to the light, heart-centered awareness (soul) and our negative, to the dark, mind centered awareness of Ego and the greater Satanic influence. Now, our "Terminator" has long hair to give him a more "feminine" look because our body is an atomic manifestation (the dreams representation) of our spirit that is feminine. Arnold, Ian's ego, informs him, and again Ian is Soul, that the two of them will be competing and that ego intends to crush him. Arnold shows him, by fooling him while he is doing his push-ups, that ego does not play fair by winning the first point while distracting Ian. He continues to distract him with the "beautiful women". You see, the table and game represents life and its struggles, challenges, and temptations and symbolizes the eternal struggle between ego (Arnold) and The Self (Ian) for the possession of his lady of spirit. This represents one person and the internal struggle of who control the decisions and thoughts of this person. It is the ego and the carnal body, the Dark, in competition with the Self, the Light, residing in the body. If you engage in activities that lower your frequency, then the body and ego are winning, but if you resist and engage in thought and actions that raise your frequency, then The Self is winning. If Arnold wins, then they are going to the dark, and if Ian wins, they are going to the light. Now the table also represents the bridge between the Right and Left minds. If Arnold wins, they remain in the Left mind of Separation, but if Ian wins, they open up the Right mind to reach the Promised Land of Unity.

Let's take it to the Bridge!

The table also looks very much like the Hoover Dam Bridge, because that **is** what it represents. Ian is actually on the Right or Nevada side (from the perspective of the land and dam looking toward the bridge), and Arnold is on the Left or Arizona side. Here now is the deep clues of deep clues. If Ian (the Self to the light) wins, and the wall coming down *DOES* symbolize the dam *releasing* all the stored power, for Ian to use. It will be at his disposal because he has proven himself a disciplined ADULT, so that he will have earned the power of God. You see, if Arnold (body/ego) won, there would be no "water", his creative power, behind the dam because his continual "falling" was draining the power south down to the "Red Colorado" (think devil's tail) giving his ruby slippers to the evil aspect of Her, who in Thor Ragnarok, is his sister Hela (the side of Lucifer that is condemned).

His childlike *lack of discipline* earns him NOTHING. God, is not giving away the crown and it must be earned. So the wall coming down is the Metaphorical Dam within him (I'll ID it soon) releasing all of the Divine power of creation that his discipline, has saved up for him. This is why he is thrilled and now that he has established control of his body, Arnold, his body, is now his ally and not his enemy or competition. He has gotten to the Promised Land of Right Brain UNITY, which is why he is on stage with "OneRepublic", (has a *west* ring to it) singing "Counting Stars". Look up the telling lyrics if you want. Ian has made it to the next stage and is on his way to becoming a King, and then Star, in his own Right.

I saw an interview with Ian Rappaport, and as he was finishing explaining his experience during the commercial, he said something that confirmed to me, who "I really saw him as". He said that during the filming when the wall fell and he saw the concert "happening", that he thought he would just be "in the crowd" watching "One Republic" perform. He said and I quote, "but Arnold (his body) is pushing me up ("UP, the stairs to the stage". Huge metaphor that he has no clue he is communicating!) the stage, and I get up there and I'm on with everyone, Minka Kelly, Don Cheadle, Reggie Watts, Arnold Schwarzenegger, and at that point Arnold whispers in my ear, **"This is all for you"**, *and at that point I realize this!* And it concludes, all on a stage, just as "Like a Prayer", because they are telling you, that **is** the world.

"YOU are always the star in your own perfectly choreographed play...",

This reminded me of one of my favorite Star Trek TNG episodes "The Inner Light", where a mysterious satellite, seeks out Picard with "encoded Light" causing him to lose consciousness on the bridge and while out, dreams of living an entire other life, on another world, with a wife and they have children and he grows old only to find out from all of his family and friends on this "other" world, that this entire life experience was done just for him, and they bid him farewell to keep the experience forever, so that once he experienced what the craft had meant to send him, he "wakes up", to find out that he had, all along, never left the bridge of his ship and had been "asleep" for about 20 minutes, while dreaming of an entire lifetime, with "OTHERS", that were all in his mind.

It was all, for Him, and this, is for You! Wait, it has to be me!

God Bless Amaruca

Since we are speaking of the Inca and Llamas, let me lay out this little tidbit that ties into the identity of, and the **true origin of the name, America**. I am now of the opinion that "America", is not named for some Italian explorer mapmaker named Amerigo, which is a distraction, for those who will be. I discovered this a few months ago and it makes total sense, as I always wondered why there is a snake curled around the feet of the statue of Amerigo Vespucci in Washington DC, and now I believe I know.

Welcome to **Amaruca**, the Land of the Serpent Gods!

"In his book, "New World Order: The Ancient Plan of Secret Societies", William T. Still shows that America was called initially "The Land of the Plumed / Feathered Serpents" by the Indians of Peru. James Pyrse researched an article written in the Theosophical Society magazine entitled "Lucifer", which gave insight into the word "America." He says that the chief god of the Mayan Indians in Central America was Quettzalcoatl / Kukulkan ("Plumed Serpent", "Feathered Serpent"). The Inca called this same god Amaru and the territory known as Amaruca. Pyres states: "Amaruca is literally translated 'Land of the Plumed Serpents' (p. 45)."

Lady Lucifer *is the Serpent,* who seduced man to eat of the fruit of the Dark, so that man can become like "one of us" (gods), knowing good and evil. Most will partake of the Dark allowing the Serpent to take them **down**, which is why Lucifer is predominantly condemned. The **Ones**, the so very few, who turn The Serpent **Up** (now going to the Light), through their heads (the images of the Serpent protruding through the foreheads of the Pharaohs) or the Crown Chakras, will earn the crown, and become The Plumed (flying up) Serpent. So Amaruca, is also the land of Lucifer. She IS.

"No other sacred book sets forth so completely as the Popol Vuh the initiatory rituals of a great school of mystical philosophy. This volume alone is sufficient to establish incontestably the philosophical excellence of the red race. "The Red 'Children of the Sun,'" writes James Morgan Pryse, "do not worship the One God. For them that One God is absolutely impersonal, and all the Forces emanated from that One God are personal. This is the exact reverse of the popular western conception of a personal God and impersonal working forces in nature. Decide for yourself which of these beliefs is the more philosophical [Hall says sarcastically]. These Children of the Sun adore the Plumèd Serpent, who is the messenger of the Sun. He was the God Quetzalcoatl in **Mexico**, Gucumatz in Quiché; and in Peru, he was called **Amaru**. From the latter name comes our word America....The priests of this [flying dragon], from their chief centre in the Cordilleras, once ruled both Americas. All the Red men who have remained true to the ancient religion are still under their sway.

One of their strong centres was in **Guatemala**, and of **their Order was the author of the book called Popol Vuh.** In the Quiché tongue **Gucumatz** is the exact equivalent of Quetzalcoatl in the **Nahuatl** language; quetzal, the bird of Paradise; coatl, serpent—'the Serpent veiled in plumes of the paradise-bird'!"

~ "The Secret Teachings of All Ages", Manly P. Hall

A Peace of information about this symbol. It represents the **Trinity** and the essence of the ⅔ dynamic of Duality that is at the very core of the waveform universe. This image was presented to us as a peace symbol, and no, it isn't an upside down mocking of the cross. It's composed of black and white, curved and straight lines, illustrating separation and polarity. The outermost circle is black (and the line curved) because we are here in the womb of Lucifer, the waveform Divine Feminine dark where creation *creates* more God. Being the Light Bearer, the inner circle is white communicating She is creating more Light, as well as more of the entire spectrum, through the increased distribution of the Divine masculine of Soul to higher and lower frequencies. Thus allowing consciousness to experience more individuality within the various manifestations of Her waveform vessels and allows Soul to know the entire spectrum of everything It IS, and everything it, is **not**. This is a cyclical process and with every cycle, it builds on what it knows and adjusts the experiencing vessels to see from a slightly different perspective, creating *evolving new growth,* as opposed to just *more of the same.*

The center vertical line represents the One consciousness developing "Up", from the child at the bottom to the adult at the top. The two diagonal lines represent the 2 perspectives of unity and separation, the Self, and the Ego, working together toward ontogenetic growth. The right half represents the Self and the left half the Ego. The two larger pieces of the pie *above* represent "Sun (not yet the Father of Sirius) and Moon", not yet being full polarity halves but still developing us (within them) below, the smaller piece of the pie. We are aspects of them growing, within the circle or womb of our Mother, as we develop going back and forth from Separation to Unity. Both halves within the Divine Feminine represent the Trinity as both the Light and the Dark Sons, are born of the Mother with Consciousness from the Father. So, within the Divine Feminine, Her two polarity extremes, the two diagonal lines representing Self, and the Ego forcing "upward growth", to develop the Father, the center line, always growing Up from an immature child to mature adult.

The top characteristic of an adult is autonomy. Let that sink in as you think of the Phds in the large urban areas with big paychecks from the systems they are indoctrinated to feed so they can be fed. They are dependent on the system and when it falls, it is every child for themselves, as money becomes what it is printed on. *"We tried to give them medicine, education, roads...but no, they like mud."* Their "medicine" makes you dependent on the system. Their education hardwires your brain to only identify with their level and perspective. Their roads scar what they already move freely upon. *"There is nothing we have that they want."* Jake's *insanity*, was cured.

The Trinity among the Spiritual and Cosmic Imagery

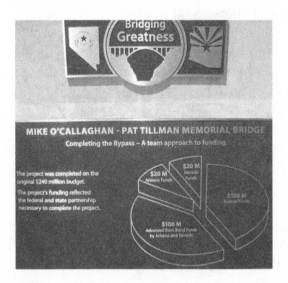

Since the "Peace Symbol" esoterically expresses the Trinity, and what I now tell you that the Dam and States represent, it is no surprise that this symbol has made its way on a plaque on the "bridge" between the 2. And how coincidental that the funds (energy) from both sides are $120 M and express 3 two times. One hundred twenty is comprised of 3 digits and the 1, 2, and 0 added together equal 3. Well, the plaque above this image on the Bridge says it all, "Bridging Greatness". Infinite inspiration alright!

As the old is torn down, The New class of 11, is under construction

Nevada and Arizona represent the Right and Left Brain Hemispheres respectively. The Dam is The Pituitary Gland and the rock on the 3 sides of the dam represents the bone encasing on the 3 sides of the pituitary, and half of the pituitary gland is the Anterior Lobe and the other, the Posterior Lobe, like half of the dam is in NV and the other half in AZ. The Arch Bridge is the Corpus Callosum. Lake Mead is the stored creative power to be "born again" of the water. Boulder City is the Hypothalamus gland (and why *Mia* in La La Land, is from Boulder City). Las Vegas is the Pineal (Vega the North Star), situated between the two. The new Interstate 11 being built, under construction, through our two hemispheres, mirrors the new age forming in *the Bronze Age*. Remember, one sees "more" the higher up their perspective that aids in seeing unity, as Nevada means "Snow Capped". Arizona allows its water to flow down to the ocean, while Nevada keeps it within its **Great Basin**.

This brings me to **The Water,** and a better explanation of the new universe forming. Look at where the water flows in the new universe forming and know that the 3 states represent the new Trinity. Nevada is the Father, Arizona is the Son, and New Mexico is the Holy Spirit. New Mexico is representative of the Divine Feminine (Holy Spirit), that will **always be separated from the Light. She is the AI aspect of the Dark** that will always remain in separation, so her water flows down and east to the Gulf of, you guessed it, Mexico in the Eastern Waters of Separation to the *Atlantic*. She represents the Reptilian base brain. [If you are getting the impression that the Anunnaki were the Atlanteans, so am I.] **She** is also the Mother of what **will** create more to unify with the Light as Arizona represents our Dark Sun (Son) and The section of Southern Nevada that, was a part of the Arizona Territory, that represents our Light Sun (Father) and while Their water flows down to creation, it flows also west to the Gulf of California Western Waters of Unity to the *Pacific*. The upper reaches of Nevada, is the boundless, pure consciousness expanses of the unmanifest universe that never gives up its water, and that is why upper Nevada is The Great Basin, and all of **The Water that Falls in Nevada, Stays in Nevada**. That reminds me of another Nevada metaphor, **"What Happens in Vegas Stays in Vegas"**. Remember Neo, it is all happening in your head. Everything that happens to you is an internal image. No one "out there" beyond you sees anything. The aware that sees in Unity knows that *anything* that is happening, is happening to and inside of you.

Of course the new Interstate, (that they are calling **Future 11**) that starts at the Mexico border in Nogales and travels up through Arizona to Tucson, Phoenix, Boulder City and Las Vegas, as I resided at 1001 New Mexico in Boulder City, the town created by those who created the Dam, will be **11**. Speaking of the city, "Boulder" makes me think of "on this *rock* I will build by Temple", *and* the original name for the dam was "Boulder Dam". Now I know why I had a credited part (one of the Main Characters) in a BBC Documentary about the building of Hoover Dam in the "Seven Wonders of the Industrial World" series. I was the "Law Enforcer", like Regulus. Hoover Dam represents what is being stored, by those who will find the Narrow Gate. All others are spilling it down to Her, and all are going, where they are needed. All of the Spiritual statues, artwork, and plaques declare that Hoover Dam, is no ordinary structure. That is obvious and I believe that "The Great Depression" was orchestrated by *you know who*, to create the workforce needed to build it. *I can't say who, it's a secret!*

All of this, that we exist within, is a manifestation or figment of the greater mind or psyche of the One. So let's get to the true identity of the evil Elites and "Reptilian Archons" that "try" to run the show, in the only "Show there is". We have The Right Lobe and the Left Lobe, with the 3rd and oldest section, Underlying (She, who orchestrates from the shadows) the 2 above it. The reptilian brain that controls the body's vital functions such as heart rate, breathing, body temperature, balance and getting oxygen and nutrients to each and every cell while removing all the wastes. Everything you "don't have to think about doing", very programmed, machine-like and reliable but tends to be rigid, dealing in absolutes, and compulsive addictive behavior. Our reptilian brain includes the main structures found in a reptile's brain: the brain-stem and the cerebellum. This represents the most basic structure and characteristics of "The Holy Spirit", our Mother that gives birth to Her Sons, the Cerebrum of the Right and Left Hemispheres. The Right is, of course, The Son of Light. He represents "The Father" because he is the continuation of The Self, the only consciousness that exists. This is why Christ tells the Apostles, "To know me, is to know The Father". The Left is, of course, the Dark Son of Time and Identity and is "The Son", of the Trinity. His contributions are vital and necessary as the perspective of Ego.

The less aware you are, and the more you see in separation, the more you will externalize what you fail to see as an integral part of You. Seeing in Unity is literally embracing your Dark, to no longer project "Your Dark" (Mr. Hyde) out there. When we don't accept this "Reptilian Perspective", and control IT with discipline within us, we will project the "shape-shifting" Reptilian. We go so far separating them from us, that we say they "shapeshift", to impersonate humans. You don't get rid of them killing them "out there", because the dynamic that created them, is still there to create more (like Doritos), like removing the tumor but not addressing the cancer. As awareness rises, and more people "repent" and embrace their Dark, then the evil Archon's system will begin to erode and "bad things" will just crop up to eliminate them until they no longer reside "out there", in the world of higher frequency people, because you will exist in a world "above them". This is why evil spirits have no power over the higher frequency, to the Light people.

A child is on a path of discovery, and the "final frontier", is the discovery of who and what They are. Your brain is the "as below" version of the celestial collective brain we are cells within. As I alluded to earlier, our body is our "Starship Enterprise" with a vast crew of Carbon Units on a journey to seek out new life and boldly go where no one has gone before because we are the Essence of the growth of The One, that is ever evolving and expanding. In Lucy, she explains some of this process to Professor Norman, confirming that his Theory that we currently only access 15% of our cerebral capacity, is in fact true. She explains, *"Right now, I'm at 28%, and what you wrote is true. Once the brain reaches 20%, it opens up and expands the rest* (she hit, the golf ball?). *There are no more obstacles. They fall away like dominoes. I'm colonizing my own brain."* That we are, and "Yes, I am about to tell you that the biblical "Reckoning" is encoded in an *Amarucan Western".*

Playing the Waiting Game?

As I said in, The Smith Equation, I "could" have dismissed all of these clues and messages, *until they got **personal*** and the Divine poker game has **upped the ante** by introducing corporeal *personal changes in me.* I am changing, like the caterpillar to the butterfly, and I am in absolute awe of the magnificence of this school. If I didn't see it in myself, I wouldn't know it to be true, but I had said earlier in Building Treasures that your path to the light, *has to be a way of life,* because I can now see the physical conformational changes in me. You must put in the discipline, day in and day out. Increasing your frequency literally changes you, like aging, you cell by cell over time so that it isn't something you see from day to day, but over many months and years. I am not only psychologically a changed man, but physiologically as well.

As I pointed out in 5, what you eat is vitally important, but **when** you eat is just as important to frequency and body modification. This ties into the points also made in Chapter 7, "The Terminator and Your Twin", about turning your body from your adversary, into your ally. If you want your body to be on the "Right" path, I highly suggest you incorporate (allow it to occur) "Autophagy", which is literally Nature's "Survival of the Fittest" law played out in your body. And your body responds to it much the same way that Yellowstone has been revitalized by the reintroduction of wolves into the Park's ecosystem. During times of "no food to digest", the body is programmed to *cleanse and repair cells, and to **consume** cells* (for the energy) that are not operating at maximum efficiency. In nature, times of plenty simply must have a corresponding polarity partner, like your opposite Smith, to keep you **sharp and centered,** and going too far to one polarity extreme. So in times of scarcity, like winter or drought (or man-made like war), bodies (animal or human) use this time of no digestion, to focus its activity on this amazing natural process, that also fortifies your immune system. It works very much like wild predators who actually strengthen the vitality and gene pool of the animals they prey upon by weeding out the weakest (physically *and* genetically) among them. It is a marvelous natural process, **but it is not *pleasurable*** to "young" eyes who don't always see the necessity or integral intelligence of *natural processes.* It is seen by Ego as needless suffering, that would most certainly be eradicated in "Camelot".

If you are doing "well" and eating very regularly, not experiencing *down times* or extended hunger, so that this process of Autophagy never has a chance of working its magic in your body, you may want (you have to want it, or you won't do it) to introduce some fasting. In nature, there are always times of scarcity (to balance plenty), so this "never missing a meal" now available in (artificial) modern society, is "unnatural". Flowing with "Nature" produces Growth while going against it produces Entropy. An adult, say over the age of 30, who has never missed a meal or day of eating, **is not** in peak health. The duality property of Balance (between 2 opposing poles) dictates that fasting goes with eating just proper rest goes with hard exercise or adequate sleep goes with time awake. Staying finely tuned demands this balance because staying at one pole is either string too tight or too loose. If you introduce fasting to your body, you then reconnect with this natural dynamic which flips the switch to growth. This is why Christ fasts "in the desert", meaning in nature away from the "artificial city", and *desert* accentuates scarcity. And you just have NO idea (because a mind in an addicted, polluted body reflects this unhealthy state) how insidiously addicted you are to SO many things that keep you chained down like "Marley's chains in Ebenezer's dream". A tainted body's mind sees through a tainted lens.

On my personal search, on a recent 72 hour (water only) fast, for the best "**Intermittent Fasting**" programs, to integrate it into my *everyday way of life*, I happened upon a video that resonated with me. In one by Dr. Eric Berg that centered on various Intermittent Fasting schedules, I was drawn to one of the more strict schedules and so far it has worked **very** well. I also like his take on rejecting listening to the latest conventional wisdom that tells you to ignore what your body is telling you (that you are not thirsty) and constantly drink water. Remember what constitutes an adult's actions. As you live *in the Now,* your body and common sense will tell you when you need a drink. I highly recommend Intermittent Fasting based on how well I have responded to it.

The only time I don't feel well is if I bring it to a manifest state by my negative frame of mind or eating that which I know lowers my frequency. I not only choose to not eat meat or dairy, I simply can't anymore, as my body appears, no, *has* changed from the new age and diet or "with" and now rejects the food of my old, "carboned based unit". I used to be a big vitamin and mineral supplement guy before 2012 and now I take **nothing**, including vaccinations or drugs. I don't worry one iota where I get **any** nutrient or protein. I stay in good shape and I don't get sick. When you see in separation, you need all the little "separate" this and that for your "perceived" health, but once you're plugged into who you know you are, you just bloom. Speaking from experience I can see that because of my diet and fasting my body is rewarding me with more HGH. What the young get free, I must now earn by living "Right", to continue *living*. As Mark Twain said, *"A little starvation, can really do more for the average sick man than can the best medicines and doctors."* For those of you waiting for the world to change "for you", you are "wasting precious time" **if,** the narrow gate is your gate of choice!

Various films give us clues to *his,* "bourne" identity!

I've done *some* homework and I believe he is alive and like Christ, in *mimicking* fashion, will have a witness, among the false and lesser prophets. He will deceive "virtually all", even the very elect, but he won't be *trying to deceive*, because he is just *being* who he was born to be. The witness will deceive as well and come forward to bear witness, to his identity! Like Christ, his "witness" will also be a woman and of course, that is another deception because the masses believe The witness to the identity of Christ was a man. She will not be associated with any particular faith and will be recognized as a spiritual teacher. She will of course come from among the "chosen ones" and *her name* will encode duality, the Me becoming We shift of the ages, along with *"his" identity*, and like him, be tied to the number 4. Her words will subtly send these satanic messages that the history of humanity is tragic irony, laced with insanity and injustice, amid the smoke and mirrors liberal use of "Love". We all know that there are "evil" spirits, to the dark, and they are continually attempting to pull you down with them. Any great, to the Light, spiritual teacher will not judge and define the spiritual teaching process in these terms that show the immature, superficial, narrow perspective of control. It's a child's, "I hate you!", to a loving parent who **must** discipline them. Her words and his words, coming from the dark, will be **just** what your "Ego" wants to hear, plus, he really will be nice and will believe he is doing the right thing.

"There will be signs in sun and moon and stars, and on the earth dismay among nations,"

-Luke 21:25

Being the very antithesis of the Christ, his birth was announced by the lesser illuminated celestial body in a most full and super fashion, when the earth was as Midgard, a full 180 degrees between the two, at the axis of Leo-Aquarius, as I smile. The lights were all aligned, just as they were at another well-documented birth and death. He is 4 in most respects, and while his class number yells 7, it whispers

4 to those who see the clue. The King of Rome abdicated to make way for the New World commoner who was *hired* on 3-13-2013 A real-life omen, but not as over the top, in the Davidic line, from the Abrahamic Great Nation of biblical prophecy. The head of the east facing Dragon will be in conflict with his loin as polar aspects will produce their progeny to be proclaimed as the rightful King. Which Holy Grail bloodline will move on to be crowned? "...you were both born to be Kings!" Although, one will be a tad colder, if you get my draught, erh, drift.

I fell a bit last night (that draught pulling me down), and I had a rough night sleeping with several odd dreams and waking up often. I woke up early, and I knew I wouldn't go back to sleep, as a line from "this amazing film" kept repeating itself in my mind. This was the final piece that I had seen all along but not seen. The history, the 12 blood-lines (and the 13th for the final Charade), the numerology, and then the clues I got from his birth that showed me more clues, would be in "The Bourne Identity" series, the identity of HIS birth, or I should say "his", played by Damon. At that moment I knew the real clue, or the most important from the dozens I got from this "amazing film", was identifying "him". *"When I was 16, I won a great victory. I felt, in that moment, I would live to be 100. Now I know I shall not see 30."* I applied the "two clues" to a chart of all the future years applying 7-year "Shmita" or Sabbatical year cycles, as I had come to the con-clusion that the 7 year Tribulation would occur in one of these cycles, that I had already worked on. The fit was perfect, and it moved up 7 years, from the cycle that I had thought it would start based on the fact I thought he would begin at 30, like Christ, **but now I was told**, *he wouldn't reach that*, but stay in the number of Duality. *Obama paid homage to him in the month of Fools on the day of the double deuce.* If below **is** true, then it's the will of God, and if he calls it unfair, then his perspective is Satanic, no matter how much you Love him.

"The Saracens say that this disease...is God's vengeance against the vanity of our kingdom. As wretched as I am... these Arabs believe that

the chastisement that awaits me in hell...is far more severe and lasting. **If that's true***, I call it unfair."*

~King Baldwin IV, "Kingdom of Heaven"

We've come a long way.

I have a graduation to attend this second week in June 2017 and then, a journey a few hundred miles away, returning to the Star of the Desert as I bid this place adieu. One man's trash is another man's treasure and that quote could not describe how I see this *cold* place any better. I don't deny its beauty, but I'm not talking about that. I wasn't meant to simply do my "Time" in Nevada. Rome had other preordained plans and a trip to Hades had been booked at birth. The Scott that left in 2007 died, and that is nothing to be sad about. While the tour in Hades was extremely uncomfortable I learned much and changed, and gained a better appreciation for the only *Real* bliss in my life. The awareness I gained was more than I ever thought I'd know, and getting everybody to see what you see is initially your "motivation", until you realize after some time, that that is a lesson in futility as there is nobody else, and your *crusade* to "tell them how it is", is another "pull down" like the things you are telling others to avoid. The only way out, is UP, because *down here*, is no place "to live". Her words "ring true to me". **Endlessly engaging in identifying the darkness, is the perfect bait set out by the Dark to Pull you in.** Cosmic bowels have "Help Wanted" Signs in the windows of Pluto's playgrounds. I'll be on the Highway soon. In one direction is the vertical line of "still", and in the other, it "Flatlines", to the horizon of clock carrying never-ending late for important dates, as I try to claim happiness wherever I find myself. I have expectations for only one mind, the only one I have control over. There is only The Self, and within The Self are the various frequency spectrums, that are perspectives of the mind, to exist within. *Your frequency will determine your home, The Haunted House or Home Sweet Home...among Angels.*

"He who fights with monsters should be careful lest he thereby become a monster. And if thou gaze long into an abyss, the abyss will also gaze into thee." ~Nietzsche

When Your Path is Up and to the Right...You are a *Christian.*

"Think you'll ever get out of here? "I tell you where I'd go. **Zihuatanejo.**" *(Its origin is **Nahuatl, like Mexico**, meaning "place of women," refers to the western paradise of the Nahuatl universe, the home of the "goddess women.")* "It's in Mexico. A little place on the Pacific Ocean. You know what the Mexicans say about the *Pacific*? **They say it has no memory.** That's where I want to live *the rest of my life.* **A warm place with no memory.** (remember where AZ and So. NV spill their water) Open up a little hotel...right on the beach. Buy some *worthless old **boat**... and fix it up **new**.* Take my guests out...charter fishing. Zihuatanejo. In a place like that, I could use a man that knows how to get things."

"I don't think I could make it on the outside. I been in here most of my life. I'm an **institutional man** now. Just like Brooks was. .... In here I'm the guy who can get things for you, sure, but...*outside all you need is the **Yellow** Pages.* Hell, I wouldn't know where to begin. **Pacific Ocean**? Shit. Scare me to death, something that big."

"Not me. I didn't shoot my wife, and I didn't shoot her lover. Whatever mistakes I made, I've paid for them and then some. That hotel, that boat...I don't think that's too much to ask."

"You shouldn't be doing this to yourself. This is just *shitty pipe* dreams. Mexico is way down there and you're **in here**...and that's the way it is."

"Yeah, right. That's the way it is. It's down there and I'm in here. I guess it comes down to a simple choice. ***Get busy living***...or **get busy dying.**"

~ "The Shawshank Redemption", Andy talking to Red

In the **prison**, is our satanic system here in the dream, and not getting out is a slow death, and the longer you stay in it, the more "institutionalized" you become. Andy got there by not "dying to the dream" as a banker. This led his "out there" wife to turn on him and become his adversary. Her death was symbolic of her becoming a heartless machine because of the choices and way of life that Andy lived, lowering his frequency by the day. This is why he was charged with her murder, as the system, being part of the system, conspired against him. He understands this now, by no longer fighting it "out there", but got his mind right while focusing his attention on his path with heart, to go to the light and get busy living, and this led to his prison break from this deep sleep dream.

"Man cannot remake himself without suffering, for he is both the marble and the sculptor."

-Alexis Carrel

The young Odin's motivation to take the Jotun child was to *control* as he was still driven by his Ego (manifesting his Dark in Asgard), but now he has matured and tells Loki, "But *those* plans no longer matter". This brings me to Thor's admission *"Loki for all his grave imbalance understood rule as I know I never will. The brutality, the sacrifice, it changes you. I'd rather be a good man than a great King."*, as his Ego, is stepping aside, "letting go". To go from a dependent desiring to be King, to a free man, is a miraculous transformation. You can see my progression toward Her, that internal aspect of me, throughout the book. I could have taken it out in this last revision, but it's me, it's raw, it's vulnerable, it's growth, and it is what made me, who I am today, from the broken guy who started to peck at these keys, some 5 years ago to the making of the current version of knowing why I had to be **broken**.

"Practice not-doing and everything will fall into place." - Lao Tzu

John Connor found out that continually fighting the frequency you are in, eventually consumes you, but it isn't just **You**, but **all** who are in your Ark. It did, what it did, to get you to **That Point,** to stop holding on, to what is holding you down. Don't fight the dark, simply turn on the light.

Neo to the Oracle: "If I had to guess, I'd say you were a program from the machine world,"

"So far so good," replies the Oracle.

"But if that's true, that means you are a part of the system, another kind of control," he says.

"Keep going," she says to him.

"I suppose the most obvious question is, **how can I trust you***?"*

"Bingo!" replied the Oracle. "It's a pickle, no doubt about it. The bad news is there's no way if you can really know if I am here to help you or not. **So it's really up to you.** *You just have to make up your own damn mind, to* **accept** *what I am going to tell you,* **or reject** *it . . .* **Candy***?"*

LOL! Sounds eerily similar to Albert Pike and that's been my theme throughout the book. See you, or not, in the Bronze on our way to Gold and then the bright lights of our galaxies version of Broadway or The Strip in the place I know so well. "Here Comes the Sun" is code for the arrival of the Son, and **All,** *will* **be settled**, as we position ourselves to **our** new Star, or it's *"partner in crime!"* Enjoy the remainder of your ride on the 7-11 **Polar Express,** to find the *optimum* balance and enjoy your bifurcation train ride to "Oriental or Occidental" *gateway, Light Star and Dark Star,* destinations, as we continually, eternally head North!

"Upon suffering beyond suffering; the Red Nation shall rise again and it shall be a blessing for a sick world. A world filled with broken promises, selfishness and separations. A world longing for light again. I see a time of seven generations when all the colors of mankind will gather

*under the sacred Tree of Life and the whole Earth will become one cir-cle again. In that day there will be those among the Lakota who will carry knowledge and understanding of **unity** among all living things, and the young white ones will come to those of my people and ask for this wisdom. I salute the light within your eyes where the whole uni-verse dwells. For when you are at that center within you and I am that place within me, we shall be as one." -Crazy Horse*

Message from Hopi Elders

You have been telling the people that this is the Eleventh Hour, now you must go back and tell the people that this is the Hour. And there are things to be considered...

Where are you living? ... What are you doing? ... What are your rela-tionships? ... Are you in right relation? ... Where is your water? ... Know your garden. ... It is time to speak your Truth. ... Create your community. ... Be good to each other. ... And do not look outside your-self for the leader.

This could be a good time! There is a river flowing now very fast. It is so great and swift that there are those who will be afraid. They will try to hold on to the shore. They will feel they are being torn apart and will suffer greatly.

Know the river has its destination. The elders say we must let go of the shore, push off into the middle of the river, keep our eyes open, and our heads above the water.

See who is in there with you and celebrate. At this time in history, we are to take nothing personally. (This is huge and what I most strug-gled with) Least of all, ourselves. For the moment that we do, our spiritual growth and journey comes to a halt. The time of the lone wolf is over. Gather yourselves!

Banish the word struggle from your attitude and your vocabulary. All that we do now must be done in a sacred manner and in celebration. We are the ones we've been waiting for.

Hopi Nation, Oraibi, Arizona

So much of my writing is my own "therapy", to write it down, to not forget, and to help me make sense of the flood of information, and I noticed that as I wrote, more would come, as my attention was focused and I was knocking at the door. I want to create my community with you, my siblings of like frequency. There will be destructive change, but with our heads above water, we know why and how it fits in the overall lesson plan, and why consciousness needs the full spectrum of polarity to progress, to evolve. I am speaking to myself and heeding the Elder's words that all must be done now in a sacred manner and in thankful celebration! *Reminding myself to **Love** liberally along "The Way", as it literally rewrites our DNA as we work to Lighten our load and reduce our Carbon attachments.* To be an adult and be the Creator knowing this School exists in Superposition awaiting, the newly aware One, to unlock the unlimited possibilities, and then it's "Into the air Jr. Birdman", as the Joker described it. This truly is, "The Hour", as I search for my water.

Our struggle between the Self and the Ego that we internally cope with, that raging war at times, to the uneasy truce, to the rock solid friendship, are what we are also experiencing all around us in the body that we are cells within and I think you can tell what *season* we are in. What *you* do with your own internal struggle has *everything* to do, with *You*. No one else's victory, will propel you to the Promised Land if you have not earned it, but the best news is that...no one else's defeats, even if it seems like the entire world is falling around you, will keep YOU from the The Promised Land, if you've been Victorious within your own personal Struggle. If you win, **You** win, like Ian. Even if everything is burned to the ground, *Your Phoenix will rise* from the ashes. All of this is God's growth and every personal victory adds cognitive *glitter* to the dark matter of the cosmic brain. So persevere in this current act of *Star Search*, to eventually take your place among the glowing.

This book was an act of Love by the *"only child of 5 and 7"*, with special thanks to my children, Tony, Nick, Max and Alexandra, my extended hearts pointing back to me, who have taught me what cannot be taught in textbooks! To my Glinda, who said, and didn't say, the right thing, at the right time! And to my Electron polar "Mrs. Smith" who was my **dream** queen, who so completely, with the demeanor of the most ruthless contract killer, crushed my little Egoistic attachments in the dream, nuking my little Camelot-Esque cottage on the bank to send me down the *frequency* river without a paddle or rudder, *where I needed to go* **IN,** *all along.* And we of course had no wine on that fine day, 5-01-1995, but made it on 2-3-2000. How right *desires* turn into left betrayal, which I can now see **is** the Divine *Blue*print, to turn some, to the *Real* "Queen" within, where there is no Desire... just **LOVE**. No rollercoaster could match the ride and to think I will always have a tie with the one who "wears Prada".

I had never tasted sweetness,
Or heard the angels sing;
I had never felt the melody,
Or soared with eagle's wings;
I had never known the warmth of the sun,
Or sensed the ocean's power;
I had walked through meadows bursting with life,
But I never saw the beauty of a flower;
My life was one of logic,
It's been like that from the start,
To deal with issues black and white,
Not whole but just in part;
I went through a life I thought complete,
Not missing what I had never known,
But then ***you came*** *into my life,*
The ***universe*** *to me you've shown;*
Your love has set my senses ***free,***

*It's true, my **heart** you stole;*
But now I see you gave me life!
It was you my love, Maria-Nicolle

When I wrote this to her 20 years ago, I had little understanding of duality, but after 2005, my awareness grew rapidly. I certainly got turned from looking out, and it simply had to be done the hard way. I was Horace and she was Set, and it simply has to be this way. I had no idea this would be so prophetic when I wrote it in the Northern California wilderness fasting for 3 days.

From 2005, when my mountains were mountains to now, seems like an entire lifetime. I would be hard-pressed to count the number of times I cried or felt like my heart was bursting out of my chest writing this, and while less, how many times I laughed. I hope you liked it and got *something* useful out of it. Like the changing of the age, everything in me and about me is changing with it. I'm now flowing with the River soaking up the Sunrise as it reassures me that everything is going to be alright, at that perfect time, when I need to see it, as I now take up residence in my Heart, the only *estate* that **is** *real.* And there I **travel.**

"The two most important days in your life are the day you are born and the day you find out why." —Mark Twain.

Appendix One

Symbolic Meanings Behind the Divine Numbers of 1, 2, 3, 4, 5, 6, 7, 8, 9, 10, 11. Look into them as deeply as you wish, but this guide will help you make sense of spiritual clues and messages, that this book uncovers.

1 is the One and is Masculine. The ultimate "odd" number as there is ultimately only the One mind, God, The Self, we are all aspects of. It is uncomplicated, straightforward, independent and declares Leadership! The number for North is 1 and represents the Adult.

2 is *Duality*, and is Feminine. Two compels action to produce change and growth within the One. The very essence of dealing in polarity, it is the best of the best and the worst of the worst, and when balanced, very formidable, and very complex. The waveform universe is duality at its core, and feminine in nature. The number for South is 2 and represents the child. If you are reading this at the beginning and not understanding *this description*, at the end you will. The number of John is two, and there will be a point within the book that this comes to mind, to help put the "two and two together"!

3 is the all-encompassing Trinity "here", in waveform. It is simple and at the same time complex. Christian Doctrine holds that God is three consubstantial "persons", and the use of the word persons, is huge. The 3 distinct ones that make up, The One, for the growth of The One. "From the Father", "through the Son" and "in the Holy Spirit". Of course they "say" this but all they ever show you, as an image of "The Holy Spirit" is a Dove, but I'll show you something very different. The identity of the Trinity will be revealed and let's just say there is a Feminine element that you've not heard of, and why "Trinity" in The Matrix IS, the Woman. The number for West is 3, and it is also the number of the feminine Right Brain that sees in Unity.

4 being the 4 Cardinal Directions or *perspectives* of North, South, East and West. Four is the number of experience and the change of evolutionary growth, and the masculine Left Brain that perceives in Separation. It is the number of the East.

5 is the number of man and mediator between God and the universe. The Divine message and messenger of divine will. The bridge between the physical world and the spiritual realms. To esoteric Luciferian beliefs, it is the number of the "perfect" man, who shed his "animal" nature. It is the symbol of perfection to the Maya. The five wounds of Christ. The number of man with the 5 points extending from the torso of the head, arms and legs and the symbol of this is 5 pointed star pentagram representing our human physical form. The 5 stages of Soul development and 7 steps within each stage. These two are intimately tied, as I have found out. 5 is the number of the Divine Feminine.

6 is creation at the 3D "cube" class level, the class of 6, the lower frequency, upside down mirror image of 9. The 2D representation of the 3D cube is the 6 sided hexagon. The 6 pointed hexagram is especially significant at this level and the specific point **Up and Down inclination**, as displayed in the Star of David, represents *fundamental, polarity.* The intersection of the two, point opposing, equilateral triangles displays this. Polarity is one of the fundamental key topics of the book.

7 are Sons of God representing the Self and Ego. God made "this" in 6, and rested in 7, the Ethereal plane our consciousness "soul" comes from, and where it resides. 7 **is** the Son who is in the direct line of who will become! There are 7 days of the week and 7 chakras, 7 deadly sins. In medieval education, students pursued the trivium (grammar, rhetoric, and logic) and the quadrivium (music, arithmetic, geometry, and astronomy), a total of seven subjects, collectively known as the liberal arts. Pythagorean interest in the mathematical patterns in music gives 7 a privileged role, for there are seven distinct notes in the musical scale. Patterns of sevens run through the Bible more

abundantly than any other number. Our spiritual Selves, the real you and the real me, the Astral Children of God on our journey to grow, are represented by the number 7, and *7, being the real children of God 9, is **very** closely linked with 9.* **I will show this in the 7-11 to 9-11 parallel and dynamic!** I will show you why Septem means 7 but is placed in the 9th month and why Novem means 9 but placed in the 11th month. 7 is the developing line of the "twins", Thomas, that still perceive in Separation, hence they are *apart!*

8 is the number of balance and considered an equalizer in the relationship between the spiritual and material. The Karmic identity of reaping what you sow. The number of the next ascended level of creation, being the next "class" beyond this class, which is the Tesseract. The Tesseract is a 4 dimensional analog of a cube and its two dimensional representation is an 8 sided octagon. It's hypersurface consists of 8 cubical cells. This is why so many Masonic symbols are displayed within an octagon. 8 displays the 2 polarities that have now split like the dividing cell. At 8, you will resonate within one loop or the other.

9 reveals a linear duality. It is at the same time the singularity and the void. 9 is everything AND no-thing, God the Adult here and not here. The sum of all digits, 1 through 8, add up to 36, and 3 plus 6 is 9, and yet add 9 to any digit and it returns to the same digit (7+9=16, 1+6=7). Also, any line bisecting a 360 (9) degree circle, the resulting angle always reduces to 9 converging into a singularity, the point, *every*-thing! Conversely the opposite is revealed when placing polygons within the circle with their points touching the circumference, all of the angles always reduce to 9 pointing to *no*-thing! Nine is both the point and the vacuum, as God here in waveform manifest, and not here unmanifest, being the totality of God, the Mother and the Father! Nine proves intelligent design within a divine code that is, the number system. Once the Sons of God, (7) the developing line of the "Thomas Twins", begin to perceive in Unity, the one of Ego dies, and the 2 merge to become One, and the number of the Son of God that sees in Unity, is 9. The 7's will mature and evolve to become 9.

10 is the Divine, the perfect set. The perfectly Divine soul no longer needing to incarnate because the Ego is 0, working perfectly within the Divine will. The creator 3 and soul creation 7 within the expressed waveform universe, becoming One with the Father of Lights. 10=1

11 is the *odd* Duality number. In Astrology and basic Numerology, eleven is considered to be a Master Number. Eleven brings the gift of spiritual inheritance, and is gifted as the "Light-Bearer", the light within all and also represent sin; transgression and peril. It is interesting to note that eleven when broken down (1+1=2) comprises the Two of Duality. The internal fight within, the rebellion of the Ego, but it also represents someone who comes out victorious of the tests with the acquired knowledge. We live within the realm or School of 11, as I identify it. Number eleven is a master vibration and as such should not be reduced to the single number 2. When you see **11:11,** it means the Divine Judgement.

Appendix Two

A social media "acquaintance", who was very good at discovering deeper or hidden messages using Anagrams and numerology, once told me I would "bring" forth needed wisdom and that it would "ring" true. "She" said I would be a BeRINGER of truth, and displayed my last name to me like this with the lowercase e to, I am concluding, accentuate "bringer and ring".

God and our ascended "siblings" communicate to all of us directly through various means, and two of the most effective and ever-prevalent methods are through numerology and number sequences. The numbers that are ever present in life, point to many of us as being conduits of information that will accelerate general awareness of new age responsibilities and Divine agendas!

A B C D E F G H I J K L M N O P Q R S T U V W X Y Z

1 2 3 4 5 6 7 8 9 1 2 3 4 5 6 7 8 9 1 2 3 4 5 6 7 8

All numbers have a frequency and have real meaning, and "awareness". Here is how you find the numeric value of a word by referring to the chart above. You add and if it comes up to two or more numbers, you reduce them by adding them again until you get to just a single digit. You do this for all except 11, as 11 stands on its own and is not reduced to the single digit of 2. In figuring numeric symbolism, you will also take into consideration the number of letters or digits contained in what you are looking at or *paying* attention to! Let's take *Scott* and find the number associated with each letter. So we have 1,3,6,2,2 and you add them up to get 14, and you then add the 1 and 4 to get 5. So 5 is the number of Scott, with its associated meaning and symbolism. See appendix one for its meaning. 11, the "dual 1", is the only, although sometimes ten, dual not reduced to a single digit, and while it is the other duality number with two, the *two*, are different. 11 is the masculine of the two, and by the end of the book, you will see why this *one*, is either the **One** or just the one. The grain of sand, or the Diamond in the rough! Trust me, you'll get it!

Look at the numbers in your life, but my connection with the number 7 followed closely by 5, and to a lesser degree 3 and 11, are absolute. It is a divine connection that cannot be denied. What I will show you is all true, and I was stunned at the all-encompassing aspect of it. I know I have missed many messages, but I think what I am about to show you with what I caught, will prove the point!

I was born in Baltimore 5, Maryland 7

DOB - 9/21/1957 = 34 = 7

Septem in Latin is 7 and this date was the 3rd 7th day of the month and the 264th day of the year which equals 12 or 3, in 1957 which equals 22 or 4, and 3 and 4 are 7

Born in '57 (graduated in 75) plus, add both, 12 = 3

The Registered State File Number on my birth certificate is 27999 and the date filed is 9-27-57

7 pounds, 14 ounces = 5

Born at Doctors Hospital = 68 = 14 = 5 taken and raised at 3425 McShane Way = 52 = 7 and old phone # there 301-284-2309 = 32 = 5

The numbers in my SS # 997765322 = 50 = 5, and SS is 11

My birth last name Flabbi = 23 = 5. The name came from my paternal grandfather's parents, Dante Flabbi and Providenza Giugno who were from Trieste, Italy, where my grandfather Julian was born.

My birth name, Scott Donald Flabbi, is 555

I have been "guided" in life, and also changed my first name, it looks like 7 now, but its number is 6, so it appears I have a name for the physical ego me and the Astral me. And both beginning with **S.**

The first name of the Doctor who delivered me was ISRAEL = 28 = 10 see appendix one for the meaning of 10 and appendix three for the true meaning of Israel, and the journey.

"I am 16 years old here and of course being assigned number 34, and there is a T=2 and again showing 7's relationship with 9"

My last NV driver's license, had all of this info on it, and all of this has come to my attention at the end of 2012. I did not manipulate any of it.

DL # had these, not in sequence and I'll leave out the zeros-9922651 = 34 = 7

My date of birth is on it, which is 7

My height 6'1" = 7 (My "young" height was 6'2" but I lost an inch with age)

My, at the time weight 205 = 7

Hair GRY which is 797 = 23 = 5

My time with the Nevada Highway Patrol is just as mystifying and telling.

My hire date 9/30/1991 = 32 = 5

And report to Carson City = 43 =7

My first assigned P (p is 7) number (a seniority-based ID number) was 410 = 5

A few years later NHP realigned P numbers and my new one was 232 = 7

Assigned, out of the academy to Las Vegas 31145711 = 23 = 5

And The abbreviation LV is 34 = 7

I was assigned to the Commercial Division and its numeric designation was 7

In Prometheus, the planet where we were designed, was called LV 223, and I am LV 232.

So I was 777 when I retired LV 7-232.

777 is the number of Helel

In Clark County District Court, my name was changed to Beringer on February 3rd, 2000, or 2-3-2000, at the "start" of the 21st (3) century.

My SAG-AFTRA member number is 10240207 = 16 = 7

Member since 2010 = 3

First credited role in a feature film, Ocean's 11

My first tv commercial was for Sam's Town 11412655 = 25 = 7

I have a tie to a home in the LV area and its address is 7, and its mailbox number is 7

I have a car registered in Utah 3218 = 14 = 5 the plate number Y951HV-795184 = 34 = 7

EYE (575) revealed to me on 12-21-12 = 11 and 2012 = 5

232 is an "Angelic" number sequence and I see it all the time and since my awakening in 05, my "retirement" in 07, and my split in 11, to this! Can't make this stuff up!

Appendix Three

Journey to the promised land

The Story of Abraham and Sarah

This is a great story of a man who has sex with his maid, gets her pregnant and they have a son. Then he has sex with his wife who is barren and 90 years old and lo and behold he gets her pregnant and has another son. In this story, *Abraham is you and me.* His maid is Hagar who represents the left side or intellectual side of the brain. The son born is Ishmael who represents the left or the physical side, whose 12 sons represent the physical control over the 12 cranial nerves. Representative of *good and bad.*

Sarah represents the right or spiritual side of the mind brain. Her womb is barren as all of the wombs of children of promise are barren. They represent the right side of the mind brain. The son born of the right side or Sarah is Isaac the child of promise. Isaac marries Rebekah whose womb is barren. She represents the right side or virgin womb and gives birth to Jacob. Jacob has 11 sons and 1 daughter. They represent the spiritual control of the 12 cranial nerves. The daughter is Dinah the virgin or Virgo. Jacob is involved in a spiritual wrestling match. This is the struggle that goes on within us in our meditation to finally touch the higher or God light. Jacob prevails when he separates from physical desire which is symbolized by his thigh being put out. Jacob then becomes Israel.

IS Isis female—**RA** Ra male—**El** Elohim God.

The full power of God, male and female in the supreme light. Jacob then calls the place where this all happened, Peniel. This is the single eye or Pineal Gland of the brain. The light receptor of the body. Jacob declares the place Peniel in Genesis 32:20 Thus the entire story of Abraham and Sarah is the story of our meditation and the resultant brain mind activity that provides us with the child of promise and takes us to the **promised land of the right side.**

-Bill Donahue

"The Teachings of Don Juan" by Carlos Castaneda

A Path, with Heart

What made you decide against (continuing down this path), Don Juan? Is there a special way to avoid pain? Is it a formula, a procedure, or what?

Don Juan:

It is a way of grabbing onto things. For instance, when I was (young I was too eager). I grabbed onto things the way kids grab onto candy. Anything is one of a million paths. Therefore you must always keep in mind that a path is only a path; if you feel you should not follow it, you must not stay with it under any conditions. To have such clarity you must lead a disciplined life. Only then will you know that any path is only a path and there is no affront, to oneself or to others, in dropping it if that is what your heart tells you to do. But your decision to keep on the path or to leave it must be free of fear or ambition. I warn you. Look at every path closely and deliberately. Try it as many times as you think necessary.

This question is one that only a very old man asks. Does this path have a heart? All paths are the same: they lead nowhere. They are paths going through the bush, or into the bush. In my own life, I could say I have traversed long long paths, but I am not anywhere. Does this path have a heart? If it does, the path is good; if it doesn't, it is of no use. Both paths lead nowhere; but one has a heart, the other doesn't. One makes for a joyful journey; as long as you follow it, you are one with it. The other will make you curse your life. One makes you strong; the other weakens you.

Before you embark on any path ask the question: Does this path have a heart? If the answer is no, you will know it, and then you must choose another path. The trouble is nobody asks the question; and when a man finally realizes that he has taken a path without a heart, the path is ready to kill him. At that point, very few men can stop to deliberate, and leave the path. A path without a heart is never enjoyable. You have to work hard even to take it. On the other hand, a path with heart is easy; it does not make you work at liking it. I have told you that to choose a path you must be free from fear and ambition. The desire to learn is not ambition. It is our lot as men to want to know.

The path without a heart will turn against men and destroy them. It does not take much to die, and to seek death is to seek nothing. For me, there is only the traveling on the paths that have a heart, on any path that may have a heart. There I travel, and the only worthwhile challenge for me is to traverse its full length. And there I travel--looking, looking, breathlessly.

Appendix Four

The change for me occurred in Sedona, AZ while I viewed a piece on the "History Channel", in 2005, about the history of Freemasonry. The documentary featured Ralph Epperson and David Icke, giving one side, of how they secretly have their hands in all world shaping and changing events, and on the other side, some representative from the Masons. Epperson and Icke were sharp, articulate and succinct with their side as they went from war to war, revolution to revolution, assassinations, financial and stock market meltdowns and who benefited from all these events, and they were naming names! All the Masonic representative ever said to counter, was either, "There's no basis for this", or a deadpan, "That's not true". Well, after that, I had to find out more, and I read "The Unseen Hand", (must read) by Epperson, and "Global Conspiracy" by Icke and began to research on the internet and very quickly I found Alex Jones and a host of others. With my walls down, the truth flowed in from all different sides, and my worldview paradigm was forever changed! Seek, and you shall find. I have since seen several arguments of all three that I do not agree with because I think I've gone to a place they haven't, but as far as introducing you to conspiracy, exposing the controllers of the world, they do all humanity a great service!

If anyone is curious about my use of Ala,gôrē, in the synopsis, I am sure you have read it by now and I wanted to explain how I came up with it. I was watching a David Wilcock vid and he was speaking about the changes the entire solar system was experiencing, not just Earth, as we aligned with galactic center plane and he points to a copy of "An Inconvenient Truth" and points to the smoke looking more like a galaxy than smoke (somebody trying to tell us something), and I thought that that sounded reasonable. Then just hours later I am watching some presentations about the artwork in the US Capitol Rotunda and the woman says, "Now we believe this painting is an allegory...", and it was like lightning struck me and I laughed out loud saying to myself, THEY encoded the word allegory into the

381

name of the man giving us the "Inconvenient Truth" clue. His middle name is Arnold. Al A. Gore'. That's why I wrote his name the way I did!

When I was 14, I was in San Diego and while swimming in the Pacific an unusually large wave broke on top of me in about eight feet of water. I was thrown to the bottom, and the force of the water was too much for me to get to the surface. I had no clue of time under the water. All I knew is that no matter how hard I struggled, I couldn't get up, and the "funny" paradoxical aspect, was my calm, matter of fact, thought process. I remember this like it was yesterday, as I was thinking, "Wow, this isn't good, I can't get up, and if this doesn't stop, I am going to die." At that moment, I was no longer "there". This description I will give you pales in comparison to the experience. I was in a vast space that was neither opened or closed, that was somewhat "greyish" if forced to assign a color. I was viewing every, and I mean EVERY experience of my life to that point in my life. They appeared as border-less TV screens, or better yet, open windows to the actual event. All arraigned in many horizontal lines. Every alternating line, one moving ever so slightly to the right, and the one above and below, slightly to the left. I not only saw, simultaneously, everything I ever viewed in my life, but every taste, touch, sound, smell, thought and feeling. I "knew" my entire life, to that point. You will NEVER "know" this until it happens to you, and you experience it. Obviously, the water force stopped and I was "back", going to the surface, and I have no idea how long I was under. My first thought was, "I think I've had enough of the ocean today", and got my ass on to the beach. I sat there for a long time reflecting on what just happened to me and then I just became 14 again.

Appendix Five

In 2005, at the time I was beginning to see the world for what it is, behind the facade (and boy did I buy the facade, having gone to "ground zero" with a group of fellow officers, from Nevada, to help NYPD sift through "evidence" after the 9-11 "attack"), I had to run, and this is all very unassuming, to the grocery store to pick up a few items for a meal I was preparing for my family. I lived in Boulder City, a suburb of Las Vegas, and the market was close to me. I knew what I needed and was going down a wide aisle to get to the dairy section. About 3 quarters of the way down, a "man" came around the corner and walked in my direction. He was very nicely dressed, out of the norm for the market, but not "over the top", and was well manicured with white hair and a well-trimmed white beard and mustache. He had no cart or basket and held nothing. He immediately made eye contact with me and smiled, and the moment I smiled back at him, I felt as though my body had been immersed in a warm hot tub and my skin tingled. I "heard", what can only be described as a chorus of angels singing around me and "through" me. I felt euphoric, in some loving state of ecstasy. He maintained eye contact with me as he passed by, with a loving yet wry "I know something you don't know" smile, and just to the point where he would have had to turn his shoulders to keep his eyes on me, he turned his head to the direction he was walking, and walked off to the end of the aisle, turned right and went out of sight. The moment he stopped looking at me, the euphoric feeling stopped, and I was "back". I was overwhelmed and stood for a couple of seconds to compose myself and wonder what in the hell just happened to me. I had to find him now. I ran, literally, into the next aisle, and the next, all of them, and went out to the parking lot looking for him, and returning to the market to search again. He was nowhere to be found ..."here".

I found out from an interview with Jordan Maxwell that he was the only other person, that I knew of, that had a similar experience and *feeling* from meeting a *mysterious man*. I decided to contact him and went to his website to email him, but something compelled me to call him, and I was sure that it would just go into a voicemail message, but was **stunned**, when he answered the phone. Surprised that it was *his voice*, I immediately went into my aforementioned story and about ten minutes into it, I realized it had all been me talking, and I said, "Are you still there?", to which he replied, "Yes, I'm just listening, please continue". Then I told him that I was stunned that *he* actually answered the phone and he said that 99% of the time he doesn't, but that something compelled him to answer it and that soon after I began speaking a bird, not one *we know of in nature* sparrow-sized with a gold body and red head, pecked at his window, that told him that I was someone he *should be* speaking with. I was again stunned and told him that I had seen this bird several times peck at my window when I had perspective altering insight. Unfazed, he simply told me that he wasn't surprised and to please continue. After I finished he said, **They** want you to know that they *know* you and that you are now on their horizon, by making contact with you in this very unassuming manner. More will come to you and at some point, you'll know why. At the end, I was amazed to see that we had spoken for 59 minutes. We have spoken and emailed a few times since this initial 2010 conversation that I had with him when I was in SF, CA and he was just south in the City of the Angels.

"My Eye Opener"! This, was my 12/21/12...I had my eyes closed laying down, with no particular thought (I know, not hard for me), and the outline of an eye, "in front of me", began to appear, fuzzy at first but getting sharper and clearer. It was a closed human eye and was just there, and the background was greyish. It opened and was as clear as any object you would look at, like my cup of coffee in front of me now, and I looked at it and it at me for several seconds. I asked what it wanted to show me. An object appeared that looked like the unfinished base of a pyramid. It then completed itself, like when they film a building being built and when done, play at a faster speed. It didn't become a pyramid, but a ziggurat-looking shape. I wasn't sleeping, at that point, because I opened my eyes a couple of times and looked around the room. When I closed my eyes the vision returned and then turned into, now this is going to be hard to verbalize, scenes, one after the other, like a series of still pictures or motion pictures.

Even though they were going by very rapidly, I could see the motion in some of them. Even though they were going by rapidly, I had a sense I recognized all of them. Then frames with written texts, like when a computer reboots and you see the files it is checking, very fast. A man came in whom I didn't recognize because I couldn't really see his face. I then fell off my bed, but it wasn't quite a fall, as I slid "down" in slow motion to the floor. He then walked out and I heard a door open and looked over, opening my eyes. It was my daughter, getting something out of the room, and when I closed my eyes, the pictures didn't return.

This *enlightening* event occurred in 2015, during the time I was revising TA to include the breakdowns of Tombstone and Jupiter Ascending. My son Max told me to come out and watch a segment of a film called Kymatica. He said it was saying much of the same things I was and he wanted me to see it. So while I am watching it with him, at a pretty poignant part, all of a sudden EVERYTHING goes "White" to me for at least a full second. Like everything around me disappears and all I see is white and I hear nothing. When I'm *back*, I looked at Max to tell him what just happened to me and he told me that nothing out of the ordinary happened to him. About a minute passes, and my daughter comes out of her room, and tells us she was trying to sleep but her bedroom light just came on by itself. Max asked her when it happened, and she said, "about a minute ago" and He told her what I told him and that it happened about a minute ago, and she looked at me wide eyed and just said, "Whoa!" Whoa, is *Right* siblings. I hope you liked Target Aquarius. See you all, over the rainbow.

Appendix Six

The Decoding of the George Floyd "Incident" and the genetic distribution of *The Mark of The Beast*

"If I were reincarnated I would wish to be returned to earth as a killer virus to lower human population levels."
— Philip, Duke of Edinburgh

Now that you've read the book, you're ready for this diamond in the rough. One of the greater differences between the 2 groups that are separating further and further apart by the day, deals with the authenticity of major emergency, disaster, or crisis events that seem to be coming at us one right after another in machine gun fashion. Mass shootings, regular yearly pandemics (now simply a flu, who knew) and an endless War against that "slicker than Willie" enemy known as Terror, that is bought, hook, line and sinker, by the same mask wearing group that has no idea that their fellow unmasked citizens are the Terrorists that their government is ultimately targeting; while they, the masked, are seen as very dispensable (Episode 2, "Attack of the") Clones, void of individual autonomy, programmed to do the bidding of the AIC(Artificial Intelligence Center. aka CIA ... AIC), the real shadow global government (my Gut tells me).

The "endless" false, or not, flags of large scale shooting or bombing sprees, seems to be written by the same script writer (And using the same recycled actors) who has a very limited (remember, by programming) imagination. Now, a good many believe that these "events" never actually happen or, let's say, "naturally unfold", but are produced like a commercial or film, and I would agree on some, but many like 911 do happen and lives are taken. Now, just because they actually happen, does not diminish the fact that they are choreographed by a larger intelligence that oversees our entire world. So when YOU SEE the same telltale clues in "real" or staged (or a combination of the two) events, you are seeing the "Unseen Hand" inside the puppet that is hidden to the younger among us who always fall for the same planned scenarios and bite at the same bait. As I said earlier, the Nazi Playbook, while massively efficient, is amazingly simple, repetitive, and predictable...like a programmed machine that is very easy to spot once you know what to look for. That's why there is always a heated debate over whether the tragedy actually happened or if it was all an extravagant production designed to push the masses who give their attention to it into a particular direction. And of course that direction is continued dependence and servitude. David Icke's "Problem, Reaction, Solution" explanation of this dynamic is brilliant.

I was at the gym recently (about a week after reopening in June), I overheard a couple of guys talking about the lunacy of healthy people being forced to wear the masks covering your nose and mouth and how it compromises your respiratory system by, among many other things, reducing your oxygen intake, and then one of them says, "and when I wear one I feel like "I CAN'T BREATHE", and that immediately made me think of George Floyd (and Eric Garner). When I got home I pulled up the tape of the arrest and other related information, and all of a sudden, the symbolic meaning of what everything actually represented flooded into my mind. As I lay this out, rely heavily on the breakdown of Madonna's "Like a Prayer" in Chapter 13, "The Real Identities of Adam and Eve within Creation" in Chapter 14, and the "deeper spiritual meanings" behind "Black Lives Matter or Once You go Black, you never go back" and you'll understand this far better.

George Floyd represents all Souls within humanity, kind of like the humans the machines oppose in The Matrix. We are ALL Souls born into the lower frequency Dark (away or separated from the Light) of Atomic Material Matter, which is for God growth (so our important purpose here "matters" to the Creator) and why "Black Lives Matter". It makes even more sense using a Black Man to represent "Soul" because as I lay out the various polarity representations, males represent Soul and females represent Spirit, and Blacks represent Soul while Whites represent Spirit. Soul represents the raw Organic aspect within creation, and Spirit represents the programmed artificial (or fabricated) aspect of creation, so it rams the point home even more using a black male to symbolize "Organic Soul" and the continued persecution of The Dark ... by the Projected Dark.

There are "4" Officers, for the same reason there are 4 attackers in "Like A Prayer". Two are Caucasoid, and one is Negroid, and the final one, not on top of Floyd, is Mongoloid. So we have the 3 Primary Racial groups represented just as we do in The Target Commercial. Collectively the 4 officers represent the world's controlling powers because the collective (mass humanity) is projecting their Dark that they have failed to recognize and embrace within themselves. The Controlling Powers include the world's governments, clergy, banking and businesses. The fact there are 4 symbolize that we are still perceiving in the "immature masculine" left brain of Separation, and 4 is the number of Separation and the East. This was a necessary level for young ages, but it is now time to change classes.

Each officer represents a controlling segment of our "Rome oriented" leadership. Three of them, the ones on top of the horizontal (forced prostrate) Floyd, represent "Most" governments (but specifically the US in this image). Of the 3, 2 represent the government that is on display. The other "One" represents that shadow government that is not on display calling the shots for the other 2 to carry out that has little to nothing to do with what the 2 on display are promising the citizens who they supposedly serve. Let's look at him first since he is the primary officer most responsible for the death of Floyd.

He, Derek Chauvin, was the most senior (old world Illuminati and ancient Mystery Schools) officer and he symbolizes the Global Shadow Government (like Sidious secretly controlling the governments of the Galaxy). He represents the old money aristocracy and the 12 families blessed by Satan along with the A. I. that dominates the UN-NWO control base dominating the world's governments and most businesses. This global lockdown and obeyed rules for the new controls over this "so called pandemic" proved beyond a shadow of a doubt that the NWO is not coming...It IS HERE. Now for the deeper reason as to why Chauvin and Floyd knew each other.

No matter what country you live in, you generally believe that your government is your government looking out for the betterment of its citizens (although this is changing rapidly), but that is just simply not the case. [And again I've explained that when you perceive in separation and project your Dark, and then cede your authority over to it, the dark is programmed to take you down. That's just the way it is.] Now at first you have a hard time believing they are against you because you grew up with them, you thought you knew them as you heard the politicians (you think they are on your side), and their promises all your life. This is also the same reasoning for why you would have a hard time believing that the government controlled FDA (and the pharma businesses they are in bed with) and Medical professions are out to keep you sick and addicted to pharmaceutical drugs. So THIS is precisely the symbolic reason why Floyd knew Chauvin.

[Derek Chauvin's grim, menacing, empty or machine-like, white face looking at the people and cameras, means exactly the same thing as the white faced attacker in "Like A Prayer". The face of the Projected Dark.]

The other 2 officers on top of Floyd are younger and new officers. This symbolically means they are spiritually young and are completely invested in this life and only identify with their artificial intelligence identity of ego. As such, they represent the "on display" government. The White Officer, Thomas Lane, represents the "Right leaning" conservative Republican Party (polarity color red). The "light-skinned" Black Officer, J. Alexander Kueng, represents the "Left leaning" liberal Democrat Party (polarity color blue). The two are the controlled opposition for the other so that no "real opposition" can take hold as each work hand in hand with the other to do the bidding of those that control them. Those that reach top tops of their parties are bought and paid for, and only do the bidding of the shadow controllers. I highlighted "light skinned" because this is symbolic of blacks who (like the house slave) are put in positions of power or leadership to "supposedly" help or champion blacks and all people of color but because they are bought and paid for, nothing changes, and in many cases, their quality of life deteriorates over time. Samuel L. Jackson's portrayal of "Stephen", the House Slave, in "Django Unchained", is a great example of this dynamic.

The other officer, Tou Thao, represents corporate global businesses (not mom & pop businesses), which work hand in hand with government in more of a "supporting" role, not having the ability to forcefully control, and since most of our "material" (materialism which opposes spiritual growth) for our materialistic consumers comes from the "Oriental" Asian Pacific Rim (China, Taiwan, Japan, Korea), they are represented by the Asian officer. And again, he isn't actively "controlling" the group that Floyd represents, but supporting those who are. And the fact that you never see them taking Floyd to the ground (or seeing the reason why they needed to, and then so forcefully keeping him there) makes it seem staged.

Even deeper clues

On this Rock (Christ referring to St. Peter) I will build my Church. Water is liquid Rock. Where there is flowing water there is life. This occurred in the Twin City of Minneapolis (and Minneapolis means Water City) which is situated on the west banks of the Northern section of the flowing Mississippi River (the great river that divides the East from the West) and on the east banks is the other Twin, St. Paul. In the footsteps of the original twins, Romulus and Remus, who founded Rome, comes St. Peter and St. Paul the purported founders of the Christian Church of Rome. Like the Twin Towers, the 2 shall fall to usher in Unity, as the Western Twin, the "Rock" Crucified Upside Down, foments the change in the system to bring about the fall of the perspective of Rome. This mirrors the Suicidal Insanity Pandemic of "Bird Box" that began in "Romania" to bring about the Fall of the Empire.

To accentuate the fabricated look of the incident, look at the license plate of the "Police SUV" (personalized plate of "POLICE"). Most Pd's use State Gov. Exempt plates. Black rear of vehicle with the 11 letters of "just" Minneapolis on it, and a unit number of 320 encoding 5 and 3, with both pointing to the "Divine Feminine". And I covered why Chauvin purportedly worked with Floyd at a part time Security Gig and they knew each other well. The Minneapolis PD's Chief of Police is Black and I think I have laid out how this goes SO beyond some random or latent example of racism, as further clues tell us that the riots started on "East" "33"rd St. Floyd was killed on 5/25 (5+2=7) and G. Floyd's name adds to 119 (911) as 5, 7 and 911 appear on the cover of Target Aquarius.

An ominous clue for the aware to see what the shadow powers are doing. Now, the arrests of the officers means that the corrupt Left thinking Patriarchal system is crumbling and those in power who had been above the law and prosecution, because they had control of the courts and law enforcement, are now being brought to justice, but until they are eradicated, KNOW what they are attempting to do with all of us, as these masks they are demanding we wear, are compromising health, of the healthy. It is guiding those who will be guided to the Wide Gate of Death and Destruction.

Floyd repeats over and over again that he can't breathe, and then perishes, and I just told you he represents us wearing the masks and the fact that those who resonate at the lower levels are headed to a fascist dictatorship. Those, and that will be most, who submit to what the government is telling them to do, are headed for a slave camp taking them further and further from the knowledge of God and Self, as that is their destiny and there is an amazing reason why they are headed where the Prodigals are not. So if you now see the clue, be thankful and use the blessing of the message to lovingly work on your own frequency to build a good strong Ark!

Only those who resonate at the higher end of the spectrum will intentionally do the hard work because of the suffering and discomfort involved (nothing worthwhile is easy) to raise their frequency in order to make it to the next spectrum or level. The artificial mechanical program is currently in a self-preservation mode because of the increasing frequency by instinctually avoiding a natural culling it knows it won't survive. The world's (and the entire solar system, we're told) frequency is increasing (the "real dynamic" hidden in "Global Warming") and an increase in frequency to us individually, is like gaining altitude, and what happens when you, let's say, are traveling and get to a higher altitude destination (like a ski town)? You usually experience some health issues associated Altitude sickness. As the world's frequency continues to rise, more and more, Fatigue, Headaches, Nausea or Vomiting, and Shortness of breath are all symptoms of Altitude sickness... and Covid-19. And I was the only one I knew of, when I released the "Decoding of Bird Box", in the early Spring of 2019, to also connect the Suicidal Pandemic in "Bird Box" with the startup of 5G.

Enter, *Darth* Doctor's In*Sidious* Cure

Now, consider these two facts, before I identify this supposed cure. At least three quarters of our DNA is classified as "Junk DNA", which means they have no idea what it does. Cellular complexity is staggering and they should be in awe of what they are trying to understand, but no, they use a condescending and disrespectful label that communicates their total lack of respect and dismissive attitude that concludes, "If we can't figure it out, then it must be worthless". It would seem surprising that they would disrespect what makes up their bodies, but like Agent Smith, we know who they are.
And:
*The entire rainbow of radiation observable to the human eye only makes up a tiny **portion** of the **electromagnetic spectrum** – about 0.0035 **percent**. This range of wavelengths is known as visible **light**. Oct 17, 2018*
~*"www.energy.gov/nnsa/articles/visible-light-eye-opening-research-nnsa"*

"*New Approach to Vaccines*" (claims the government)

"mRNA vaccines are a new type of vaccine to protect against infectious diseases. To trigger an immune response, many vaccines put a weakened or inactivated germ into our bodies. Not mRNA vaccines. Instead, mRNA vaccines use mRNA **created in a laboratory** to **teach** our cells how to make a protein—or even a piece of a protein—that triggers an immune response inside our bodies. That response, which produces antibodies, is what protects us from getting infected if the real virus enters our bodies." ~"https://www.cdc. gov/coronavirus/2019-ncov/vaccines/different-vaccines/..."

Those who see just .000035 of all that is and don't understand the purpose of the vast majority of our DNA, are **teaching** our *cells*. I feel SO much better! Considering you can still *come down* with this or any other virus (or illness), there is only one motivation to insert this *substitute teacher*. **This mRNA** (the m stands for messenger) **vaccine is a synthetic mRNA strand that supersedes the instruction of your God-given natural RNA. Whoever gets this Covid 19 vaccine, is now being genetically modified** to transform (essentially disabling) your natural immunity to keep you **dependent** on Pharmaceutical Drugs, *and* you'll carry the "*cell*ular GMO mark" that tags your *addicted* body with *The Mark of the Beast* to concretely identify what Master you serve. To the "Government - Medical, Pharmaceutical Complex", this Vaccine **does exactly what it was created to do**. They're not trying to keep you healthy, they're just trying to *keep* you.

It also appears the *cell* phone is rapidly becoming the external (outside the body) "Mark of" to parallel the internal (while the body is also "external", true ethereal internal cannot be touched, but you get the description) "cellular" Mark, as AI is pushing us, more and more, *to need* (technology) Cell phones (apps) to complete virtually all of our daily activities like shopping and banking (etc), to keep you constantly focused (truly addicted) on your carry around computer. They will, no doubt, look to put it on (inside) the bodies of the willing (like the Borg) in the near future, and as masks showed us, there's no shortage of the willing.

As I pointed out in "Decoding Bird Box" (within "Aquarian Awareness"), Covid is exacerbated by the rise of 5G, and is a product of low frequency bodies becoming more and more incompatible or "alien" with our changing global environment as natural and man-made frequency levels rise. This remedy, like "chem-trailing" (to keep earth cooler) or "chemo-therapy", is another misguided attempt to stop a natural change or consequence in the greater organic system with a remedy more deadly than the condition the "MD's" are attempting to avoid, but more importantly it keeps you dependent on them for your health, and when you cede your personal authority (stopping spiritual growth) to the projected Dark, it's programmed to Terminate you. Let **The Reckoning** unfold.

The government wildly overstepping their originally intended jurisdictional responsibilities and authority, is *but another* obvious clue to those heading **Up and to the Right** to stay the course. So yes, the **Down and to the Left** *Carpooling* lanes those with .0035% eyesight are paving with this inoculation on *The road to Hell (paved with good intentions)* is **short** sighted and very Satanic. It most definitely mirrors what I wrote about earlier under, "The genetically modifying fools at Monsanto", because they (being machines) can't fathom non-waveform (unmeasurable) quantities such as Love, Wisdom, Empathy, Appreciation, Happiness or Maturity, and the development of these qualities are precisely why we are here. Our original programming, I am sure, considers these qualities along with providing us with the difficulties and hardships we must experience to gain these intangible qualities.

A.I. cannot understand what is not a "thing" and can only act within its programming. It's consumed with the endless march toward Camelot at this developmental level which eliminates all obstacles (the very thing you need to grow up) in the way of it's image of Perfection. This is precisely why Camelot (in any form) must always fall, because it runs counter to nature and produces entropy, ensuring it decays to eventually wither away. This "Cure", that is anything but, is Quintessential Snake Oil from the satanic graduates of Dr. Moreau's School of Camelotology, targeting all who fear ... what they know not. And this "Trojan Horse" Shot In The Dark certainly fits my definition of Satanic.

Our DNA IS evolving to support our shift or move to the higher frequency spectrum, and this vaccine ensures that this natural alteration is halted for those who are not destined to make that move, as their path leads to another reality. Remember, those who get this injection are meant to and those who don't are meant to. We are all parts of the same organism that are now being torn apart (frequency will be the new "natural" borders) to take their positions in the developing body. Think of the tree seed that has everything for the tree in the point of the seed but is now separating those who will become the below ground roots from those who will occupy the above ground canopy. From my perspective, This has nothing to do with fear, but just identifying the "why", of the monumental change unfolding around us.

"36. For what will it profit a man if he gains the whole world, and loses his own soul?"
~ Mark 8 NKJV (of course, 8)

So if I want to be one of the very few on this multi-dimensional Merry Go Round, to grab the brass ring (Finding this Narrow Natural Destination) as I round West, I better heed the advice that Wyatt gave to his brothers while in Tombstone and keep my eyes supremely focused on being the best version of me. Time to get my grades UP. A? Yes, and I much prefer Manly's road-map that puts me in the "Up-Right" position, as opposed to remaining prostrated within their matrix.

"We can only escape from the world by outgrowing the world. Death may take man out of the world but only wisdom can take the world out of the man. As long as the human being is obsessed by worldliness, he will suffer from the Karmic consequences of false allegiances. When however, worldliness is transmuted into Spiritual Integrity he is free. Man's status in the natural world is determined, therefore, by the quality of his thinking."
~ Manly P. Hall

Time to look past the duality drama, breathe easy, lose the fear, gain the love, prepare our Ark by our daily internal work, and let it take us down the Up directional river, the *Nile* of growth, to the next...New World, that proceeds to the Orion Belt. The Future is, *transmuted* Gold!

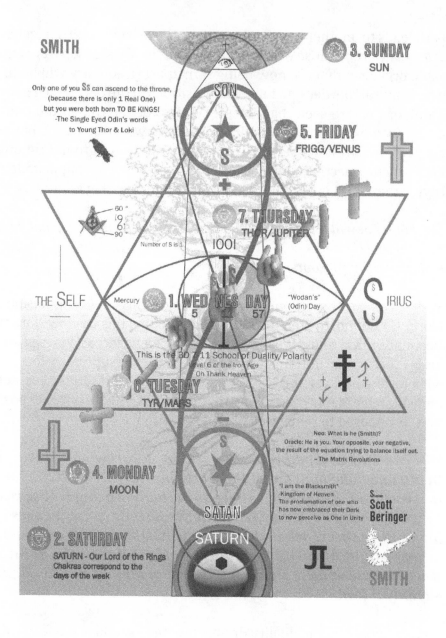

"Pacific Book Review"
By Jason Lulos

Author Scott Beringer has written a fascinating and bewildering account of one man's deconstruction of experience. *Target Aquarius* is a comprehensive theory that the "reality" we experience is an illusion: set up as a kind of school. **Graduation is self-awareness. Using structural anthropology, numerology, and various symbolic analyses, Beringer finds hidden in plain sight meaning all around him leading to a conclusion of this cosmic conspiracy.**

Among his case studies, Beringer painstakingly decodes a Target commercial. Why a Target commercial?! Enlightening clues are to be found in strange places as well as ancient tomes. Likewise, there are mechanisms designed to keep us mindless and pacified. When we choose the easy paths (self-gratification, evil), we stay egocentric and imprisoned. Choose the harder road reading between the lines, self-knowledge, and we grow and spiritually evolve. These clues led Beringer to make life changes. After witnessing animal cruelty, Beringer became vegan. He began practicing intermittent fasting. Polluting the body is analogous to polluting the world. **This book is peppered with analogies, thus showing how all things are connected in a meaningful way.** Beringer sees life as a "system" of dualities: often misunderstood. We need the "dark" just as we need the "light." Why is there evil in a world divinely created? The dualities are needed to create resistance. We would not learn and grow if everything were effortless yielding easy rewards.

So, who is behind the conspiracy? Beringer mentions common culprits Freemasons and Hollywood/Illuminati. There are many reveals within film analyses. However, he implies that these are tools of a greater spiritual plan. They are all carrying out consciously or unconsciously the will of this plan. There are clues to help you out and there are clues to keep you in the dark. **The general notion in the book is highly reminiscent of Plato's "Allegory of the Cave."** Beringer relies heavily on numerology. The synchronicity of numbers has objective and personal relevance for him. Putting these symbolic and numeric clues together, one raises his/her frequency. Everything is frequency electromagnetic, gravity, nuclear. "Mind over matter" is a categorical imperative for Beringer. Thus, a conscious effort is required to reach this higher self awareness.

Beringer covers a lot in this book. Some claims are logical, some are enlightening, and some are dubious but intriguing (i. e., the section on Jupiter and the atomic makeup of Carbon). **This all comes with a fundamental paradigm shift. There is some political conspiracy in the book but it bows to the overarching cosmic theme.** If read with an open mind, *Target Aquarius* **can be rewarding** or far-fetched, or both. **One thing is for certain, it will make you think twice in the way in which you look at things in this world.**